Dog Training

5th Edition

by Mary Ann Rombold Zeigenfuse, LVT, with Wendy Volhard

A Wiley Brand

Dog Training For Dummies®, 5th Edition

Published by: **John Wiley & Sons, Inc.,** 111 River Street, Hoboken, NJ 07030-5774, www.wiley.com

For general information on our other products and services, please contact our Customer Care Department within the U.S. at 877-762-2974, outside the U.S. at 317-572-3993, or fax 317-572-4002. For technical support, please visit https://hub.wiley.com/community/support/dummies.

Wiley publishes in a variety of print and electronic formats and by print-on-demand. Some material included with standard print versions of this book may not be included in e-books or in print-on-demand. If this book refers to media that is not included in the version you purchased, you may download this material at http://booksupport.wiley.com. For more information about Wiley products, visit www.wiley.com.

Library of Congress Control Number: 2025947881

ISBN 978-1-394-35630-0 (pbk); ISBN 978-1-394-35631-7 (ebk); ISBN 978-1-394-35632-4 (ebk)

Printed and bound by CPI Group (UK) Ltd, Croydon, CR0 4YY

C9781394356300_0910205

The manufacturer's authorized representative according to the EU General Product Safety Regulation is Wiley-VCH GmbH, Boschstr. 12, 69469 Weinheim, Germany, e-mail: Product_Safety@wiley.com.

Contents at a Glance

Table of Contents

Introduction

Both of us have had dogs of one kind or another since childhood.

I, Mary Ann, have trained dogs ever since my early 20s and every day since. I have had mentors, read books, gone to seminars, and trained with more experienced people than myself at the time. I studied and earned a Veterinary Technology degree. I took what I learned from everyone, blending it, until I found Wendy Volhard. After Wendy showed me the complete package, the Drives Theory, I adopted it all and have helped grow it to what it is today. This book is based on exactly that: how dogs think and understand us through body language and communication.

Through all these years, we're still sharing what we have learned along the way. Every one of our dogs has been more of a teacher than a pupil, and we've discovered much more from our dogs than we could ever have hoped to teach them. This book is our attempt to pass on to you what our dogs have taught us.

Without help, few people can become proficient, much less an expert, in a given field. We certainly have had plenty of help. A well-trained dog is the result of education, more yours than your dog's. You need to know what makes a dog a dog, how they think, how they react, how they grow, how they express themselves, what their needs are, and most importantly, why they do what they do. When you understand your dog fully, you can achieve a mutually rewarding relationship. A dog isn't a homogenous commodity. Each one is a unique individual, and in their differences lies the challenge.

Every dog teaches you something. Most dog trainers you meet also show you something even if it's only how they communicate with the dogs with which they work. Communication is the key to all dog training. Without communication no training can take place. Dogs need to understand what you want, they need to know when you're pleased, and they need to know when you're finished and moving on. Play is a big part of training a dog. After all, training can be viewed as play as well as work, enjoyable either way.

Our goal in writing this book is to show how communication works and how you must communicate with your dog so that both of you can learn the game of dog training. Enjoy as you read and put into practice all the information and advice in this book.

About This Book

We truly want this book to be a useful tool for you. And we don't want dog training to feel like a chore that you have to slog through every day. We've structured this book in such a way that you can jump in and out of the text as it interests you and applies to your situation. For instance, is your dog partially trained but needs to learn a few things? If so, consult the table of contents or index and go directly to the chapters you need.

Nor do we expect you to internalize every bit of information in this book. Throughout the text, we include reminders of key points and cross-references to more information about the topic at hand. Remember, dog training is fun! It isn't a series of tests that you have to pass — unless, of course, you and your dog enter the world of competitive events. Competing is when it truly becomes a hobby, spending time with your dog on the road and going to shows and events.

Because training starts the moment you bring your little bundle of fur home, we tell you about behavioral development and what to expect during the first few weeks and months. We guide you with tips on training, tell you about up-to-date training equipment, and help you establish a daily schedule. We devote a whole chapter to housetraining and crate training.

This fifth edition of *Dog Training For Dummies* is full of new and revised exercises for you. In addition to a wide array of new photos, we've also

>> Reorganized many of the training exercises to make them more accessible and easier to follow.

>> Updated exercises to reflect current training trends.

>> Added exercises to make living with your dog easier and more fun from the start.

>> Updated and revised Wendy's nutrition chapter with the most current information available.

We consider our older dogs our friends as well and have included in this edition a chapter on keeping your old dog young. We offer exercises that you can use to limber up the old joints, tips on feeding, information on the latest supplements, and much more.

All in all, this is a practical book that we hope will make your relationship with your dog the very best it can be.

Foolish Assumptions

In writing this book, we assume a few things about you:

>> You have a dog or plan to get one.

>> You want your dog to be well behaved — for their sake as well as yours.

>> You're self-motivated and ready to make training a priority.

>> You're looking for an inexpensive guide that gives you the freedom to train your dog in what you want them to do and when you want them to do it.

>> You want to know more about training and communicating with your dog.

No matter the amount of training experience you have, you can find this book helpful. Through our many years of working with a wide variety of dog breeds and personalities, we've picked up many tricks that are sure to prove useful, even to experienced dog trainers.

Icons Used in This Book

To help you navigate your way through the text, we have included some highlights of important material, some hints, some cautions, and some true stories of success. This key information is marked with little pictures (or icons) in the margins. Here's what the icons tell you:

TIP

This icon draws your attention to ways to save time, money, energy, and your sanity.

WARNING

This icon raises a red flag; your safety or your dog's may be at risk. It also tells you about the don'ts of dog training. Proceed at your own risk!

REMEMBER

This icon directs you to information that's important to remember — key points that you want to focus on.

TECHNICAL STUFF

This icon highlights in-depth information that isn't critical for you to know but can enhance your knowledge of dog training and make you a better teacher.

Where to Go from Here

The important thing about dog training is to get started *today.* The sooner you train your dog to behave the way you want them to, the sooner the two of you can live in peace together, and the more problems you can prevent down the road. So turn the page (or use the table of contents or index to get to the information you need the most) and get going! Your dog will thank you for it. You can also visit www.dummies.com and search for the Dog Training For Dummies Cheat Sheet for access to information you may need on a regular basis. You can also find an online bonus chapter on getting expert dog training help here: www.dummies.com/go/dogtrainingfd5e.

1

Setting the Stage for Successful Training

You get the dog you train, so train for the dog you want.

Become aware of what your dog is learning from you. Whether you know it or not, you're sometimes teaching your dog something and other times stopping them from doing something unwanted. Pick the six most important commands you want to teach your dog as the foundation of their training.

Look into your dog's personality and see how you affect everything they do. Discover how your body language is one of the main ways you communicate with your dog.

Find out what it takes to be the best dog trainer for your dog. Be aware of the other factors that surround your dog, such as their environment, as well as those things born within your dog, such as how they perceive the world.

Read about how your dog's nutrition and health affects their learning and retention of the training.

Know which training aids you should buy to help you train your dog. A wide selection is available. Different things work better for different dogs.

Start on the right foot as you bring your new dog or puppy home, what to plan, and what to do first. Training doesn't end with Sit and Down; it also includes brushing fur and teeth and saving your house from destruction.

See what it takes to raise the best dog in the world, from birth to adolescence. All the critical periods of development can change your puppy for life, so learn what they're all about and what you need to do during each of those critical periods.

Chapter **1**

Dog Training: The Key to Your Dog's Safety and Your Sanity

So, you have a dog? You are so lucky. You want to train your dog, right? Lucky dog. There is nothing you can do to build a bond more quickly between you and your dog than training together, working as a team, and spending time productively. Lucky team.

You want your dog to want to be with you, work for you, and then do it all again — for a treat, for praise, for play, because it's worth your dog's while. This chapter serves as a jumping-off point as you begin to develop your relationship with your dog. Training can be fun for you and for your dog. The results are what make all the time you put into training your dog worthwhile, but the journey of training is what can be so much fun — spending time with the dog who will become your best friend.

Someone once wrote: "All owners think they have the best dog in the world, and luckily they are all right." Hence, the role of the dog will be played by your dog, and we refer to them in this book as Buddy, your buddy. Please insert your dog partner's name where necessary. We want your relationship with your dog to be a joy. No Dog; No Joy! Know Dog; Know Joy!

Understanding Why You're Training Buddy: To Do Something or Not to Do Something

Your dog is learning from the moment you meet each other, so you want to make sure that you know what they're learning from you. Are you a pushover, a litter-mate, or the leader of the pack? You want your dog to see you as the pack leader, the coach. That means you set the rules, what games to play, when to eat, when to sleep, when to exercise, and when to train. Dogs don't know you're training them. All they know is you are spending time together, which is magical.

The important question when training your dog is this: Are you training your dog to *do* something or to *not do* something? The answer really can be both. You're teaching Buddy to be a good dog, to do this instead of doing that. To do something would be to sit here while you come in the door and greet your dog. To not do something would be not to jump up as you come in the door. Teaching your dog to sit while greeting you is so much more fun than teaching your dog not to jump up on you. As often as possible, you're going to teach Buddy what you *want* them to do rather than what you don't want them to do.

Identifying a Well-Trained Dog

A well-trained dog is a joy to have around. They're welcome almost anywhere because they behave around people and other dogs. They know how to stay and come when called. They are a pleasure to take for a walk because they don't pull and can be let loose for a romp in the park. They can be taken on trips and family outings. They're a member of the family in every sense of the word. This is your goal for Buddy, to be a well-trained dog!

REMEMBER

The most important benefit of training your dog is safety: for you, for others, and for your dog's own safety. A dog that listens and does what they're told rarely gets into trouble. A trained dog is a free dog — they can be trusted to stay when told, not to jump on people, to come when called, and to walk nicely with you.

For decades, I (Mary Ann) have taught dog-training classes, private lessons, seminars, and weeklong training camps. Working closely with veterinarians allows me to spend a lot of time doing behavior counseling with their clients. I ask people to tell me what a well-trained dog should look like and what they want to successfully train their dogs to do. They want a dog to be housetrained (Chapter 8 can help you with that task). Sadly, more dogs are given up to shelters for failure to become house-trained than any other issue. After that, in order of importance, a well-trained dog is one who

>> Doesn't jump on people

>> Doesn't pull on the leash

>> Does come when called

>> Doesn't beg at the table

>> Doesn't bother guests

Note that these requirements, with one exception, are expressed in the negative — that is, "Dog, don't do that." For purposes of training, we express these requirements in the positive — teach your dog exactly what you expect from them. Here's what the new list of requirements for a well-trained dog looks like:

>> Sit when I tell you. (Chapter 11 gives you the how-to.)

>> Walk on a loose leash. (Chapter 12 is your go-to.)

>> Come when called. (Chapter 10 explains how to teach the Come command.)

>> Go somewhere and chill out. (Head to Chapter 13 for more information.)

>> Lie down when I tell you and stay there. (Chapter 11 can help.)

The Sit and Down-Stay commands (see Figure 1-1) are the building blocks for a well-trained dog; if Buddy knows these commands and nothing else, you can still live with them. Of course, your Buddy may have some additional issues that need ironing out, some of which are more matters of management than training. (Chapter 11 discusses these essential commands in greater detail.)

FIGURE 1-1:
Well-trained dogs.

For instance, a favorite pastime of some dogs is raiding the garbage. Prevention is the cure here: Put the garbage where your dog can't get to it. By moving the trashcan to a secured location, you're managing the environment that fixes the problem. By purchasing a trash container that can't be raided, again you're managing the environment and fixing Buddy's bad behavior. Management is much easier and more quickly successful than having to train an unwanted behavior out of your dog. Of course, teaching the Leave It command and giving Buddy other things to occupy his attention is also great training. Management and training work hand in hand and together result in the best possible dog you can live with and be most proud of.

WHAT IS AN UNTRAINED DOG?

The untrained dog has few privileges. When guests come to visit, they're locked away because they're too unruly. When the family sits down to eat, they're locked up or put outside because they beg at the table. They're never allowed off leash because they run away and stay out for hours at a time. Nobody wants to take them for a walk because they pull, and they never get to go on family outings because they're a nuisance.

Dogs are social animals, and one of the cruelest forms of punishment is to deprive them of the opportunity to interact with family members on a regular basis. Isolating a dog from contact with humans is inhumane. Spending quality time with your dog by training them will make them the beloved pet they deserve to be.

Selecting a Training Model

You have many ways to train a dog, ranging from rather primitive to fairly sophisticated. Even technology has had its impact on dog training. For example, rather than fenced yards, people often now have invisible fences, which contain dogs within their confines by means of an electrical shock or tone.

Our approach to training is for people who like their dogs and have them first and foremost as pets and companions or for people who want to like their dogs. Either way, we like your dog and want them to be the best possible dog and you to be the best possible trainer for your dog.

The training involves three phases:

>> **The teaching phase:** In the *teaching phase,* the dog is taught specific commands in an area free of distractions so they can focus on you and be successful.

>> **The practicing phase:** When the dog reliably responds to the commands they have learned, distractions are introduced (we explain distractions in more detail in Chapter 10). As the dog progresses in this practice phase, the distractions become increasingly more difficult to simulate real-life situations.

>> **The testing phase:** In the *testing phase,* the dog is expected to demonstrate that they're a well-mannered pet around other dogs and people.

REMEMBER

The ultimate object of any training is to have your dog respond reliably to your commands. Ideally, they respond to your first command. Telling your dog to do something only to have them ignore you is frustrating. Think of Buddy's response in terms of choices. Do you want to teach Buddy to think they have a choice of responding to you? You want a dog that understands — after you have taught them — that they must do what you tell them, no matter what is happening around them. A truly trained dog listens for your voice above all distractions.

Distractions do cause Buddy to struggle to hear your voice above other things, as does the genetic influence of those things that Buddy was bred to do instinctively, that which is in harmony with Buddy's basic nature. Are all dogs the same to train or does the breed or mixture of breeds make a difference? Like people, dogs are individuals and have individual needs. Understanding breed characteristics and different teaching models helps to make the job of training that much easier.

First things first: Considering your dog's breed

Before you embark on your training program, consider what you want your dog to master, and then compare your answer to the task for which the breed was originally bred. Many people typically select their dogs based on appearance and without regard to breed-specific functions and behaviors. Whatever trait is in harmony with the breed of your dog is easier to teach or harder to break. For example, a Beagle uses their nose everywhere they go. Teaching a Beagle to track or follow a scent is much easier than teaching a Greyhound to track. Greyhounds are bred to visualize movement rather than to sniff out prey.

Although most dogs can be trained to obey basic obedience commands, breed-specific traits determine the ease or difficulty with which they can be trained and lived with. You also need to consider other traits, such as energy levels and grooming needs. High-energy dogs must have outlets for all that energy. Chapter 20 discusses problems that occur if your dog doesn't get the exercise they need. After all, a tired dog is a happy dog, and a tired dog has a happy owner. Grooming, brushing, bathing, and clipping of hair coats is time consuming and expensive if you hire a professional. For a dog to be healthy, the coat and skin need to be cared for regularly. Chapter 6 discusses grooming.

REMEMBER

Do some research: How much exercise and type of yard does Buddy need? Does this fit your lifestyle? How much grooming is needed, and will this fit your budget? Is this breed a good fit with kids if you have a family? Doing the research before you get your dog can save you heartache and headache later.

Training a dog or untraining them: What are you really doing?

When training a dog, you're either teaching them to do something (build a behavior) or not to do something (abstain from a behavior). For example, consider the Stay command. Are you teaching your dog to remain where they are or not to move from where they are? You can look at any command and ask this question. When training a dog, you're usually building a behavior. Look at Figure 1-2 to help understand.

In the figure, the first column lists how to build a behavior. The second column lists how to abstain from a behavior. When talking about behavior in proper training terminology, *positive* means adding something, indicated with the plus sign (+), and *negative* means removing something, indicated with the minus sign (−). These two terms don't mean good and bad, which is so often associated with positive and negative.

	Action	Abstention
	Build behavior	Eliminate behavior
+	Pos. reinforcement (add good)	Pos. punishment (add bad)
−	Neg. reinforcement (avoid bad)	Neg. punishment (remove good)

© John Wiley & Sons, Inc.

FIGURE 1-2: The difference between training to do something and training to stop an unwanted behavior.

We need to define two other words in terms of behavior:

» *Reinforcement* is used in the building of a behavior.

» *Punishment* is used in the abstaining of a behavior.

An easy way to remember this distinction is that reinforcement of something makes it stronger or builds it, and punishment tends to stop something or abstains from something. These two sections examine reinforcement and punishment in more detail.

Reinforcement: Building a behavior

When training a dog, you want the dog to do something new and different. To do that, you need to motivate them by either giving them something they want for doing the new task or getting them to avoid something they don't want for not doing it. Consider the following:

» *Positive reinforcement* (+) is adding something the dog wants to encourage them to do something they wouldn't do on their own. For example, you want the dog to go upstairs, so you put a tiny treat on each step to induce the dog to go upstairs.

» *Negative reinforcement* (−) is eliciting a behavior the dog wouldn't do on their own by making them avoid discomfort. The dog does what is wanted because they want to avoid the reinforcement from happening to him. For example, you want the dog to go upstairs, so someone gooses the dog's behind to get them to go upstairs to avoid the discomfort of the pinch. At the top of the stairs, you praise them because they went upstairs.

Which approach works best? It may depend on how hungry the dog is, how much they like the treat being used, and whether something more interesting isn't going on around the corner, such as a cookout. In the negative reinforcement approach, it may depend on how hard of a pinch you use and if they don't mind the pinch versus the effort it takes to climb the stairs.

Training comes with so many variables. The cookout is a distraction, which is why it's best to do early training when no distractions are around. The ability to climb the stairs or the difficulty of the task you're teaching plays a big part on how willing your dog is. Buddy may suffer the consequences instead of climbing the stairs or jumping into a pool if water is too scary or if Buddy really likes people and wants to join in the party next door. Make sure you break the task you're teaching into small parts to make it more easily understood and achievable.

Later, you can add distractions to the training after Buddy has learned the command. Distractions make the task more difficult for Buddy. When working with distractions, your dog needs to choose doing the task over being distracted. The objective of distraction training is to train until your dog does the task no matter what is going on around them simply because you asked them to do so.

Punishment: Eliminating an unwanted behavior

When training a dog to stop doing an unwanted behavior, there should be a consequence. The consequence can be either adding something the dog doesn't want or removing something they do want. Consider the following:

>> **Positive punishment:** *Positive punishment* adds an unwanted consequence (+) at the start of the bad behavior just as it begins. For example, as soon as a counter-surfing dog sniffs the edge of the counter, you can shake a bottle half-filled with pennies at the dog as an unpleasant consequence. (***Oops:*** If the dog is already on the counter or eating off the counter, using the bottle with pennies is too late. The dog has been rewarded by getting the food off the counter. Because the Oops happened, the dog has learned to counter-surf, which is why it's an Oops.) To eliminate the bad behavior, you must add something that the dog doesn't want so they avoid the counter because of the penny shaker. When the bad behavior stops, you don't offer praise; you never want them to counter-surf, so don't praise them for wishing they could still get up on the counter to eat.

>> **Negative punishment:** *Negative punishment* removes something (–) that the dog wanted because the dog behaved badly. For example, if a dog is jumping up on you when you come into the house, turn your back to the dog for a split second, removing your attention that was wanted because they jumped up. Turn back toward them once more, and if they jump again, turn back around so that they no longer have your attention and can't see your expression. Then, praise them for being *off* you and having four feet on the ground. Remember, they get praised for being off, which is the behavior you want.

HOW TO MAKE YOUR DOG RING-WISE BY ACCIDENT!

The term *ring-wise* refers to a dog who won't perform in a show ring or in front of an audience or for friends. The dog becomes ring-wise because when a dog is performing in an obedience ring, the owner isn't permitted to use food to aid the dog to perform. Therefore, the dog won't perform in a ring after they have learned something because doing so isn't worth their while. Ring-wise is an unwanted label because dogs should perform whether there is food present or not.

Adding rewards or removing rewards, praising or not praising, adding an unpleasant consequence, or stopping an unwanted consequence all make the difference in the dog's learning. Let me explain:

When you use food all the time while training or practicing a behavior you're building, you're using positive reinforcements; that is, adding something the dog wants. When you stop using the food you normally use all the time, you're using negative punishment because you're taking away what the dog wants. The dog unlearns the trick or stops giving you the behavior under these conditions in front of an audience. In other words, they'll become ring-wise.

To avoid this problem, randomly use food. As they learn a behavior, you need to diminish their reliance on food. Instead of giving a treat every time, give it only every other or third time; skip a time occasionally and make it random. Buddy learns to try harder to get the treat; they try to do the best for you and remain focused on you as you continue to work. They learn that food comes if they keep trying. Keep it fun by praising and smiling, and Buddy will work always, even in front of an audience.

Identifying Six Basic Commands Every Dog Needs to Know

Every dog needs to know six basic commands: Sit, Down, Stay, Come, Heel, and Leave It. You can look at these as safety and sanity commands — your dog's safety and your sanity. Here's a look at each of these commands:

>> **The Sit command:** You use the Sit command (see Chapter 11) anytime you need your dog to control themselves. You can use the command to teach your dog to do the following:

- Sit politely for petting instead of jumping on people
- Sit politely to allow the collar and leash to be put on your dog

- Sit at the door instead of barging ahead of you

- Sit when you put his food dish on the floor instead of trying to grab it out of your hand

>> **The Down command:** You use the Down command (check out Chapter 11) when you want your dog to stay in one place for prolonged periods, such as when you're eating dinner or at the vet's office.

>> **The Come command:** You need to teach your dog the Come command (flip to Chapter 10) so you can call them when you take them for a hike, when they'd rather chase a squirrel, or when it's time to come inside.

>> **The Stay command:** When you want to teach your dog to remain in place without moving, you teach them the Stay command (see Chapter 11).

>> **The Heel command:** Also known as the Let's Go command, depending on what you want, the Heel command is when you want your dog to walk politely and not pull you on the leash (see Chapter 12).

>> **The Leave It command:** You teach your dog the Leave It command (head to Chapter 9), so they leave stuff alone when you don't want them to have it or grab it or chase it.

Recognizing Factors That Influence Success

Of the many factors that influence success, you are the most important one. You're the one who decides how to approach training and what you want your dog to learn. Your dog is your responsibility and whatever your dog does — good or bad — is under your control. Remember, you get the dog you train, so train for the dog you want.

Having a good relationship with your dog

The goal of training is to create a mutually rewarding relationship — you're happy and your dog is happy. To foster such a relationship, become aware of how many times you use your dog's name to change or control his behavior. Your dog's name isn't a command and certainly isn't a reprimand. Their name is used to get their attention and is then followed by a command. See Chapter 9 for how to train Buddy to recognize their name.

Stop nagging and learn to communicate with your dog through training. Focus on teaching Buddy what you want them to do rather than on what you don't want them to do. Above all, limit negative verbal communications, such as "No," to emergencies. Repeatedly yelling "No" isn't the way to foster a good relationship. Instead of using "No," use a command that you've taught and means something. Too many people use "No" for everything and therefore it means nothing. Use Come or Leave It instead.

A good relationship also requires spending quality time together. You can spend time with your dog by training, going for walks, playing ball, doing tricks, and so on. Chapter 17 provides some great ideas for things you can do with Buddy.

Owning a healthy dog

Your dog's health has an enormous influence on their training success. A dog who doesn't feel well won't learn well either. First and foremost, their health depends on what you feed them. You need to feed them a high-quality food that provides the nutrients they need (see Chapter 4).

Your dog also needs an annual checkup by your veterinarian, preferably with bloodwork. Regular bathing and grooming are similarly important. If you live in an area where there are ticks, check their skin regularly. Deer ticks spread Lyme disease, which can have debilitating effects on your dog. Ticks, heartworms, and internal and external parasites need to be diagnosed and treated by your veterinarian.

Making training time a priority

One of the most common complaints for not training is: "I just don't have the time to train my dog!" First, look at training as a fun game — something you and your dog enjoy doing together. It shouldn't be a chore. Then identify the times during the day when you interact most with your dog.

Here are some times when you can take advantage of training opportunities:

>> **Feeding time:** If your dog is still a puppy, you feed them four, three, and eventually two times a day. Each meal is a training opportunity — teach them to Sit and Stay before you put the dish down. Make them wait for a second or two and then let them eat. You'll be surprised how quickly they catch on to this routine. You also can put the dish down first and follow the same procedure.

>> **When exiting and entering buildings:** If you have more than one dog, door manners are an absolute must. They're equally important for the single-dog household. It usually takes about 30 seconds for the dog to catch on that they're supposed to wait before you tell them it's okay to exit (or enter). It's a matter of consistency on your part until the behavior becomes automatic. Chapter 14 discusses door manners.

>> **While relaxing with your pooch:** You can teach the Leave It command while you're watching TV. Take a few treats to your favorite chair and have fun teaching the progressions to the exercise (see Chapter 9).

>> **During walks:** Every time you take your dog for a walk is a training opportunity to teach them to sit at the curb, to heel when passing other dogs, and to walk on a loose leash when walking beside you as you say, "Let's go" and "Heel" (head to Chapter 12.)

All of these commands teach your dog to focus on you and look to you for direction — and they all happen as a part of your daily routine.

Oh, the Places You and Your Pooch Can Go: Beyond the Basics

Performance events: The purpose of obedience trials, as stated in the American Kennel Club (AKC) Obedience Regulations, is to "demonstrate the dog's ability to follow specified routines in the obedience ring and emphasize the usefulness of the purebred dog as a companion of man." Now, AKC allows mixed-breed dogs in all of their performance events; having a purebred isn't required to compete in AKC events. Following are some of the options you can explore if you want to take training to the next level. For all the following, visit www.akc.org.

The Canine Good Citizen Certificate

In 1989, the AKC developed the popular Canine Good Citizen (CGC) test, a program for both purebred dogs and mixed breeds. The CGC test uses a series of exercises that demonstrate the dog's ability to behave in an acceptable manner in public. Its purpose is to show that the dog, as a companion for all people, can be a respected member of the community and can be trained and conditioned to always behave in the home, in public places, and in the presence of other dogs in a manner that reflects credit on the dog.

Now AKC has expanded the CGC to include the Urban and Farm and Advanced CGC tests. Your dog also can earn a Temperament Testing. AKC is just one of the national dog clubs, though it is the largest and most well-known.

TIP

In many areas, you can find classes to help you train your dog and prepare the two of you for the CGC.

AKC S.T.A.R. Puppy program

The goal of the AKC S.T.A.R. Puppy program is similar to the Canine Good Citizen program, except that it's aimed at puppies. Just like the CGC program, the AKC S.T.A.R. Puppy program includes a Responsible Dog Owner Pledge as well as a basic training program in which puppies up to 1 year of age are eligible to participate. After you attend a basic training class locally, your puppy must take a test. Look online for information on dog training in your area. When the puppy passes the test, they receive a certificate and a medal.

AKC tricks titles

AKC offers multiple titles for your dog as they learn and perform different levels of tricks — from Novice to Performer and Elite Performer and several in between. There is no limit to getting your dog to become a star and earn a title to prove it.

More than training: Understanding how dogs help people

People and dogs have been together for a long time. It didn't take people long to recognize the dog's potential as a valuable helper. Originally, the dog's main jobs were guarding, hauling, herding, and hunting. Over time, more jobs were added to the canine's resume; now dogs perform an amazing variety of tasks. These tasks fall into four broad categories: service dogs, detection dogs, assistance dogs, and companion dogs.

For more information, visit the websites for these organizations: Canine Companions (canine.org), **Canine Assistants** (www.canineassistants.org), **Dogs for Better Lives** (dogsforbetterlives.org), Assistance Dogs International (assistancedogsinternational.org), and Guiding Eyes for the Blind (www.guidingeyes.org).

An Exercise to Get You and Your Pooch Started

Eager to get started with some training? We hope so! We begin with an exercise that shows you how to train your dog while you're feeding them. We chose this exercise because you're going to feed your dog two times a day (and even more frequently if they're a puppy), and each time you do it is a training opportunity. It's also a good exercise because the dog quickly figures out what is to their advantage — namely, they stay, and they get to eat. They also learn leadership while you work this exercise. Leadership means that you own the food, and you give it to them, but only when you release them to the bowl. Leadership means you're the leader of the pack, the coach of the team, and your dog is the player.

TIP

If your dog is enthusiastic and bouncy, you'll have more success with this exercise when they're leashed rather than loose.

Follow these steps to successfully train your pooch to Sit and Stay before eating:

1. **Prepare the meal as you normally do.**

2. **While your dog is wearing the leash and collar, pick up the leash with your left hand and hold it as close to the collar as is comfortable for you, but without any tension on your dog's collar.**

3. **Pick up the dish with your right hand, say, "Stay," and then put the dish on the floor.**

   When they make a dive for the bowl, pull up and back on the leash and pick up the dish. They don't have to sit; they just aren't allowed to dive for the dish.

4. **Repeat Step 3 until they hold their position when you put the dish on the floor; see Figure 1-3.**

5. **After they're successful at maintaining their position, say, "Okay," and let them eat in peace.**

   Okay is a release term to tell the dog they're now free to move. If you don't like *Okay*, you can choose a term of your own liking, such as "You're free."

FIGURE 1-3: Teaching your dog the Stay command as a part of feeding them.

REMEMBER

As a general rule, it takes about three to five repetitions on the first try for the dog to get the message. *Avoid* the temptation to use negative communications, such as "No" or "Ah-Ah." Instead, use the leash to gently yet authoritatively control your dog. After several sessions, they'll more than likely sit on their own in anticipation of getting their meal.

IN THIS CHAPTER

» Reading your dog's mind

» Looking at your dog's behavior through drives

» Examining your dog's Personality Profile

» Working with drives

» Making sure that your dog isn't training you

Chapter **2**

Getting to Know Your Dog and How They Perceive the World

I n this chapter, we discuss how your dog thinks. Discovering how your dog thinks isn't as complicated as it sounds. Knowing how to read your dog and how you affect their thoughts is what communication is all about. Not only do you want to know how your dog perceives the world, but you also want to see if you can change any misconceptions they may have. Most importantly, you need to know what your body language says to your dog. Body language includes tone of voice, body movements, and signals. Are you saying what you mean to say, and is your body language congruent with your meaning?

Each dog is an individual, and your training efforts need to take their personality into account to succeed with their training.

Determining What Motivates You and Your Dog

Motivation is defined as the reason one has for acting or behaving in a particular way. To help you understand motivation, look at Table 2-1 to see that humans and dogs have very similar motivations.

TABLE 2-1   **Comparing Motivation of People and Dogs**

People	Dogs
Money and what it buys	Toys/food
Love	Companionship
Success	Status
Competition	Territory

Dogs protect what they have and want what they need — food and shelter — just as people do. Dogs need companionship and seek it out, just as people do. Dogs live under a hierarchy and communicate their known position in the group or pack, the same as people do. And when it comes to self-preservation, dogs exhibit fight-or-flight behaviors, similar to how people do as well.

Dogs live by one basic rule: What's in it for me? If they think they'll benefit from something, they'll do it. If not, they won't. Chapter 1 examines positive and negative reinforcements. For example, a dog thinks: "Give me a reason for doing this, something I want, food" (obvious motivation) or "I'll do this to avoid something I don't like from happening" (motivating as an avoidance). Positive reinforcement and negative reinforcement are based on the question, "What's in it for me?" That is, food or reward (positive reinforcement) versus removal of something uncomfortable (negative reinforcement). Dogs reason this out and learn from it.

Being Aware of Your Dog's Body Language

Dogs communicate between themselves and between people. Although dogs have verbal communication, such as barks, whines, growls, and so on, they use body language all of the time, such as facial expressions, which includes the set of the eyes, the position of the whiskers, how the ears are set, tail wags, the elevation of the tail, and head postures, just to name a few. Dogs also communicate through scent. For example, urine-marking behaviors and scent glands (anal glands) alert other dogs to dangers. Dogs also use pheromones to communicate, which we can't even begin to understand yet.

People also use verbal and nonverbal communication. For dogs, body language is powerful; however, for people, voice plays a bigger role than body language. When training, you need to learn what your body says. Body language is the main way you and your dog communicate.

Recognizing Your Dog's Instinctive Behaviors

Your dog — and every other dog — is an individual animal that comes into the world with a specific grouping of genetically inherited, predetermined behaviors. How those behaviors are arranged, their intensity, and how many components of each are at work determine the dog's temperament, personality, and suitability for a task. Those behaviors also determine how the dog perceives the world.

Researchers have studied dog behavior and have made a list or catalog of all the different forms of behaviors that dogs display. Researchers have divided those behaviors into four groups that benefit dog training and how humans communicate with their dogs. To give you a better understanding of your dog, we group instinctive behaviors into four drives:

>> Prey

>> Pack

>> Defense fight

>> Defense flight

   Defense drive is divided into fight and flight because they're stimulated by the same factors yet are exhibited completely differently, one with fight behaviors and the other with flight behaviors.

These drives reflect instinctive behaviors that your dog has inherited and that are useful to you in teaching them what you want them to learn. Each one of these drives is governed by a basic trait. Not all dogs inherit all of these behaviors, but you can see many parts of each of these drives in your dog.

The following sections break down these four drives in greater detail.

Prey drive

Prey drive includes those inherited behaviors associated with hunting, killing prey, and eating. The prey drive is activated by motion, sound, and smell. Behaviors associated with prey drive (see Figure 2-1) include the following:

>> Air scenting and tracking

>> Biting and killing

>> Carrying

>> Digging and burying

>> Eating

>> High-pitched barking

>> Jumping up and pulling down

>> Pouncing

>> Seeing, hearing, and smelling

>> Shaking an object

>> Stalking and chasing

>> Tearing and ripping apart

FIGURE 2-1:
Dogs showing the chase, a typical prey-drive behavior.

© John Wiley & Sons, Inc.

CAN DOGS REASON?

As much as you want your dog to be able to reason, dogs can't reason in the sense that humans can. Dogs can, however, solve simple problems. By observing your dog, you learn their problem-solving techniques. Just watch them try to open the cupboard where the dog biscuits are kept. Or see how they work at trying to retrieve their favorite toy from under the couch. During your training, you also have the opportunity to see Buddy trying to work out what you're teaching them.

REMEMBER

Typically, chasing is the most common part of prey behaviors. It's triggered when Buddy chases a moving object, such as a toy, cyclist, jogger, or car. Buddy also may shake and rip up soft toys or bury bones in the couch. Failure to recognize the strength of prey behaviors in dogs is the most common reason for so-called behavior problems. For managing prey-drive behaviors, see Chapter 18.

Pack drive

Pack drive consists of behaviors associated with reproduction, being part of a group or pack, and being able to live by the rules. Dogs, like their distant relatives wolves, are social animals. To hunt prey that's mostly larger than themselves, wolves live in a pack. To ensure order, they adhere to a social hierarchy governed by strict rules of behavior. In dogs, this translates into an ability to be part of a group that includes humans in their pack and means a willingness to work with people as part of a team.

Pack drive is stimulated by rank order in the social hierarchy. Behaviors associated with this drive include the following:

>> Being able to breed and to be a good parent

>> Demonstrating behaviors associated with social interaction with people and other dogs, such as reading body language

>> Demonstrating reproductive behaviors, such as licking, mounting, washing ears, and all courting gestures

>> Exhibiting physical contact with people or other dogs

>> Playing with people or other dogs

A dog with many of these behaviors follows you around the house, is happiest when with you, loves to be petted and groomed, and likes to work with you. (Check out Figure 2-2.) A dog with these behaviors may be unhappy when left alone too long, which is a feeling that can express itself in separation anxiety.

FIGURE 2-2:
A dog enjoying physical contact with a person, a typical pack-drive behavior.

© John Wiley & Sons, Inc.

Defense drive — fight and flight

Defense drive is governed by survival and self-preservation and consists of both fight and flight behaviors. Defense drive is complex because the same stimulus that can make a dog appear aggressive (fight) can elicit avoidance (flight) behaviors, especially in a young dog.

Defense drive — fight

Fight behaviors aren't fully developed until the dog is sexually mature or about two years old. You may notice tendencies toward these behaviors at an earlier age, and life experiences determine their intensity. Behaviors associated with fight drive include the following:

>> Exhibiting hair (hackles) standing up from the shoulder forward

>> Growling at people or dogs when they feel their space is being violated (see Figure 2-3)

>> Guarding food, toys, or territory against people and dogs

>> Lying in front of doorways or cupboards and refusing to move

- » Putting their head over another dog's shoulder

- » Showing aversion to being petted or groomed

- » Standing tall, weight forward on front legs, tail high, and staring at other dogs

- » Standing their ground and not moving

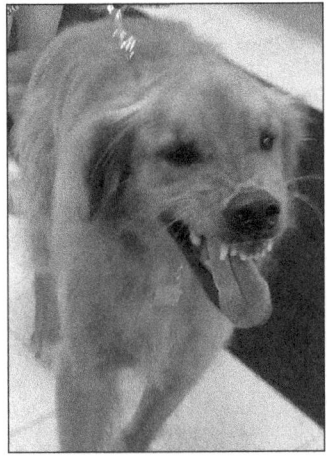

FIGURE 2-3:
A dog growling, a typical fight behavior.

© John Wiley & Sons, Inc.

WHOA! BUDDY'S GOT THEIR HACKLES UP

Hackles refer to the fur along the dog's spine from the neck to the tip of the tail. When a dog is frightened or unsure and in defense flight, the fur literally stands up and away from their spine. In a young dog, it may happen frequently because the dog's life experiences are minimal. When they meet a new dog, for example, they may be unsure of whether that dog is friendly, so their hackles go up all along their back. A dog's whiskers also are a good indication of their insecurity; in a frightened dog, they're pulled back, flat along their face. Their ears also are pulled back, their tail is tucked, and they cringe, lowering their body posture and averting their eyes. All in all, they'd rather be somewhere else, which is the defense flight.

On the flip side, when the hackles go up only from the neck to the shoulders, the dog is sure of themselves. They're the boss, and they're ready to take on all comers. Their ears are erect, their whiskers are forward, all their weight is on their front legs, the tail is held high, and they stand tall and make direct eye contact. They're ready to rumble, which is defense fight.

Defense drive — flight

Flight behaviors demonstrate that the dog is unsure. Young dogs tend to exhibit more flight behaviors than older dogs. The following behaviors are associated with flight drive:

>> Demonstrating a general lack of confidence

>> Disliking being touched by strangers

>> Exhibiting hair (hackles) that stands up the full length of the body, not just at the neck

>> Flattening the body, with the tail tucked, when greeted by people or other dogs

>> Hiding or running away from a new situation

>> Urinating when being greeted by a stranger or the owner (submissive urinating)

Understanding how the drives affect training

Because dogs were originally bred for a particular function and not solely for appearance, you generally can predict the strength or weakness of the individual drives in the different breeds. For example, the northern breeds, such as Alaskan Malamutes and Siberian Huskies, were bred to pull sleds. They tend to be low in pack drive, and training them not to pull on the leash can be a bit of a chore. Herding dogs, such as Border Collies and Australian Shepherds, were bred to herd livestock under the direction of their master. Although high in prey drive, they also tend to be high in pack drive, and it should be relatively easy to train them not to pull on the leash. The guarding breeds, such as the German Shepherd, Doberman, and Rottweiler, were bred to work closely with man, so they tend to be high in fight drive with a desire to protect family and property. They easily can be taught to walk on a leash. The Retrievers, which were bred to hunt with humans and retrieve the birds shot in the hunt, tend to be high in both prey and pack drive and generally love to retrieve. They, too, easily learn to walk on a leash.

Many of the behaviors for which dogs were bred, such as herding and hunting, are the very ones that get them into trouble today. These behaviors involve prey drive and result in chasing anything that moves. A guard dog may guard your home against intruders and protect your children, but those "intruders" may include the children's friends.

Clearly, these are generalizations that don't apply to every dog of a particular breed. Today, many dogs of different breeds were bred solely for appearance and without regard to function, so their original traits have become diluted.

Determining Your Dog's Personality Profile

To train Buddy, you need some insight into what's happening in their brain at any given moment. Here, your powers of observation can help you. In many instances, Buddy's behavior is quite predictable based on what they have done in similar situations. You may be surprised at what you already know. You can almost see the wheels turning when they're about to chase a car, bicycle, or jogger. If you're observant, Buddy will give you just enough time to stop them.

However, you don't need to rely on observation alone. To help you understand how Buddy's mind works and, in turn, understand how to approach your dog's training, you can take the Volhard Canine Personality Profile later in this section. The profile catalogs ten behaviors in each drive that influence a dog's responses that are useful in training. The ten behaviors chosen are ones that most closely represent the dog's strengths in each of the drives. The profile doesn't pretend to include all behaviors seen in a dog nor does it interpret the complexity of their interaction. For example, what drive is Buddy in when sleeping? For purposes of training, it's not important. Although this Personality Profile is an admittedly crude tool for predicting Buddy's behavior, you'll find it surprisingly accurate.

The results of the profile can give you a better understanding of why Buddy is the way they are and the most successful way to train them. You can then make use of their strengths, avoid needless confusion, and greatly reduce training time.

The profile or test is answered in a scale of 0 to 10, with 0 being never and 10 being always, and every option in between. When completing the profile, keep in mind that it was devised for a house dog or pet with an enriched environment and perhaps even a little training, not a dog tied out in the yard or kept solely in a kennel — such dogs have fewer opportunities to express as many behaviors as a house dog does. Answers should indicate behaviors Buddy would exhibit if they haven't already been trained to do otherwise. For example, before they were trained properly, did they jump on people to greet them or jump on the counter to steal food? Answer as they were before you trained them, so always or 10. Don't let your ego say otherwise. You want to know Buddy's true personality profile, their natural drive numbers. If you answer that they would never jump on someone because you worked hard teaching them not to, you aren't going to get accurate results in this test, so in this example you would choose 10 for always.

The possible answers and their corresponding point values are as follows:

» Almost always — 10

» Sometimes — 5 to 9

» Hardly ever — 0 to 4

For example, if Buddy is a Beagle, the answer to the question "When presented with the opportunity, does your dog sniff the ground or air?" is probably "Almost always," giving them a score of 10.

You're now ready to find out who Buddy really is. You may not have had the chance to observe all these behaviors, in which case you leave the answer blank.

You're now ready to find out who Buddy really is by completing the Volhard Canine Personality Profile. When presented with the opportunity, does your dog

1. Sniff the ground or air? _____

2. Get along with other dogs? _____

3. Stand their ground or show curiosity in strange objects or sounds? _____

4. Run away from new situations? _____

5. Get excited by moving objects, such as bikes or squirrels? _____

6. Get along with people? _____

7. Like to play tug-of-war games to win? _____

8. Hide behind you when they feel they can't cope? _____

9. Stalk cats, other dogs, or things in the grass? _____

10. Bark when left alone? _____

11. Bark or growl in a deep tone of voice? _____

12. Act fearfully in unfamiliar situations? _____

13. Bark in a high-pitched voice when excited? _____

14. Solicit petting or like to snuggle with you? _____

15. Guard their territory? _____

16. Tremble or whine when unsure? _____

17. Pounce on their toys? _____

18. Like to be groomed?   _____

19. Guard their food or toys?   _____

20. Cower or turn upside down when reprimanded?   _____

21. Shake and "kill" their toys?   _____

22. Seek eye contact with you?   _____

23. Dislike being petted?   _____

24. Act reluctant to come close to you when called?   _____

25. Steal food or garbage?   _____

26. Follow you around like a shadow?   _____

27. Guard their owner(s)?   _____

28. Have difficulty standing still when groomed?   _____

29. Like to carry things in their mouth?   _____

30. Play a lot with other dogs?   _____

31. Dislike being groomed or petted?   _____

32. Cower or cringe when a stranger bends over them?   _____

33. Wolf down their food?   _____

34. Jump up to greet people?   _____

35. Like to fight other dogs?   _____

36. Urinate during greeting behavior?   _____

37. Like to dig or bury things?   _____

38. Show reproductive behaviors, such as mounting other dogs?   _____

39. Get picked on by older dogs as a young dog?   _____

40. Tend to bite when cornered?   _____

Score your answers by using Table 2-2.

After you've obtained the totals, enter them in the appropriate column of the "Profile at a Glance" shown in Figure 2-4. Simply shade in the columns to see your dog's profile at a glance.

TABLE 2-2

Scoring the Profile

Prey	Pack	Fight	Flight
1.	2.	3.	4.
5.	6.	7.	8.
9.	10.	11.	12.
13.	14.	15.	16.
17.	18.	19.	20.
21.	22.	23.	24.
25.	26.	27.	28.
29.	30.	31.	32.
33.	34.	35.	36.
37.	38.	39.	40.
Total Prey	**Total Pack**	**Total Fight**	**Total Flight**

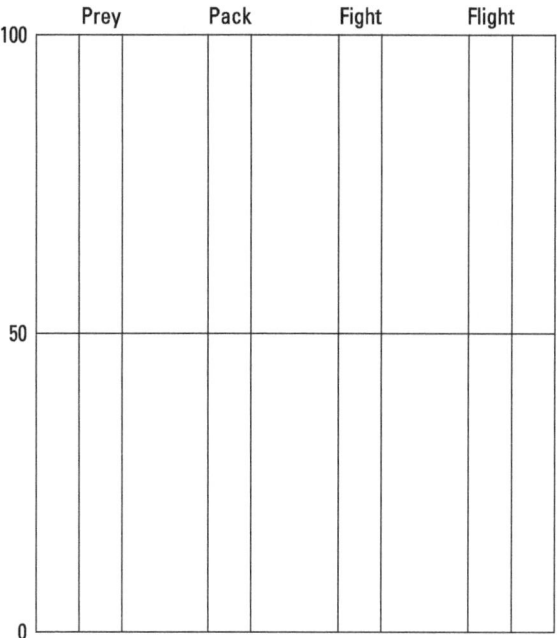

FIGURE 2-4: Your dog's Profile at a Glance.

© John Wiley & Sons, Inc.

REMEMBER

To make best use of the concept of drives in your training, you need to know what you want Buddy to do or stop doing. Usually, you want them to be in pack drive, and they want to be in prey. When you've mastered how to get Buddy out of prey and into pack, you have a well-trained dog. We discuss switching between drives later in the "Switching drives" section.

Deciding How You Want Buddy to Act

Before you can use the results of the profile in the preceding section, you need to look at what you want Buddy to do or — and this is often more important — stop doing. For example, when you walk Buddy on leash and want them to pay attention to you, they must be in pack drive. If Buddy, on the other hand, wants to sniff, maybe follow a trail, or chase the neighbor's cat, they're in prey drive.

For most of what you want Buddy to do, such as the following, they need to be in pack drive:

>> Come

>> Down

>> Sit

>> Stay

>> Walk on a loose leash

For most of what Buddy wants to do, such as the following, they're going to be in prey drive:

>> Chase a cat

>> Dig

>> Follow the trail of a rabbit

>> Retrieve a ball or stick

>> Sniff the grass

You can readily see that when you want Buddy to behave you must convince them to forget about being in prey drive. Dogs high in prey drive usually require quite a bit of training. Dogs with high pack and low prey drive rarely need extensive training. Such dogs don't do the following:

>> Chase bicycles, cars, children, or joggers

>> Chase cats or other animals

>> Chew your possessions

>> Pull on the leash

>> Roam from home

>> Steal food

In other words, they are perfect pets.

Theoretically, Buddy doesn't need defense drive (fight) behaviors for what you want them to learn, but the absence of these behaviors has important ramifications. A very low defense-fight drive determines how Buddy has to be trained. For example, a Labrador, Bean, was low in defense drive. If anyone would lean over him, he would collapse on the floor and act as though he had been beaten. Katharina, a German Shepherd, on the other hand, who was high in fight-drive, would just look at you if you leaned over her, as though to say, "I'm good. What do you want?"

Training each dog required a different approach. With Bean, a check on his leash (a *check* is a quick tug on the leash that is like a snap back, quick and short) caused him literally to collapse — he didn't have enough fight behaviors to cope with the check. A slight tug on the leash or a quietly spoken command was sufficient to get him to ignore chasing a rabbit, switching him out of prey drive. Katharina, high in both prey drive and fight drive, required a firm check to convince her to override the prey drive and forget about the rabbit. The only difference between the two dogs was their score in fight drive on their Personality Profile. The high fight drive allows the dog to recover from the needed check that gets the dog out of prey drive and back into the desired pack drive. See the following sections for the different profiles and how to deal with them.

REMEMBER

The beauty of the drives theory is that, if used correctly, it gives you the necessary insight to overcome times when you and your dog are at odds with each other over appropriate behavior. A soft command may be enough for one dog to change the undesired behavior, whereas a firm check is required for another.

Bringing out drives

When you grill hamburgers on the grill, the aroma stimulates your appetite as well as everyone else's in the neighborhood. In effect, it brings out your prey drive. The smell becomes a cue. Incidentally, the smell also brings out Buddy's prey drive.

The following is a short list of cues that bring out each of the dog's major drives:

>> Prey drive is elicited by the use of motion (hand signals, running, swinging arms), a high-pitched tone of voice, the movement of an object of attraction (stick, ball, or food), smells, and the act of chasing or being chased.

>> Pack drive is elicited by calmly and quietly touching, praising and smiling, grooming, and playing and training while you stand up straight with an erect body posture.

>> Defense drive is elicited by your threatening body posture, such as leaning or hovering over the dog from either the front or the side, staring at the dog with direct eye contact (this is how people get bitten), leaning over and wagging a finger in the dog's face while chastising them, and checking the leash on the dog or using a harsh tone of voice.

Switching drives

Buddy can instantaneously switch from one drive to another. Picture this scene. Buddy is lying in front of the fireplace:

They're playing with their favorite toy. (They're in prey drive.)

The doorbell rings; they drop the toy, start to bark, and go to the door. (They're in defense-fight drive.)

You open the door; it's a neighbor, and Buddy goes to greet them. (They're in pack drive.)

They return to play with their toy. (They're in prey drive.)

Buddy has switched drives from prey into defense, into pack, and back into prey. Dogs can switch from drive to drive willingly and freely. There are no limitations; they can go from drive to drive as they feel the need. Figure 2-5 shows how the dog goes back and forth between all the drives.

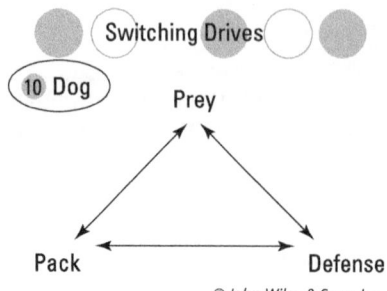

FIGURE 2-5:
How a dog can go between any drive as they choose.

© John Wiley & Sons, Inc.

During training, your task is to keep Buddy in the right drive and, if necessary, switch them from one drive to another. For example, say you're teaching Buddy to walk on a loose leash in the yard when a rabbit pops out of the hedge. They immediately spot it and run to the end of the leash, straining and barking excitedly in a high-pitched voice. They're clearly in full-blown prey drive.

Now you need to get them back into pack drive where they need to be to walk at your side. The only way you can do that is by going through defense drive. You can't, for example, show them a cookie in an effort to divert their attention from the rabbit. The rabbit is going to win out, unless you have a bigger rabbit. Look at Figure 2-6 to see how you must first take Buddy through the defense drive when switching Buddy from the prey drive into the pack drive.

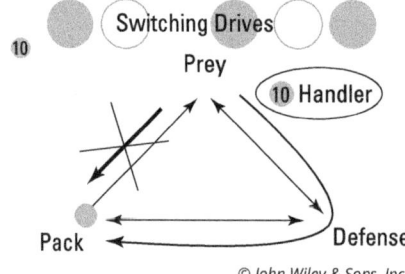

FIGURE 2-6:
Switching from defense drive into pack drive.

© John Wiley & Sons, Inc.

TIP

The precise manner in which you get Buddy back into pack drive depends on the strength of their defense drive. If they have a large number of defense (fight) behaviors, you can give them a firm check on the leash, which switches them out of prey drive into defense drive. Now you want them in pack drive, so touch them gently on the top of their head (don't pat), smile, and tell them how clever they are. Then continue to work on walking on a loose leash. If they're low in defense (fight) behaviors, a check may overpower them, and a voice communication such as "Let's Go" will be sufficient to get them out of prey drive into defense drive, after which you put them back into pack drive with praise and a smile.

If your dog has few fight behaviors and a large number of flight behaviors, a check on the leash often is counterproductive. Body postures, such as bending over the dog or even using a deep tone of voice, usually are enough to elicit defense drive. By their response to your training — cowering, rolling upside down, not wanting to come to you for the training session — your dog will show you when you overpower them, thereby making their learning difficult, if not impossible. Use only enough defense-drive actions or communications as necessary to elicit defense drive in your dog. Every dog will be different depending on their Personality Profile and the amount of each drive they have

Here are the basic rules for switching from one drive to another:

>> **From prey into pack:** You must go through defense drive by applying a defense-drive action, such as using a firm voice or giving a check on the leash.

>> **From defense into pack:** Gently touch or smile at your dog, which is a pack-drive action. Stay still when you do it.

>> **From pack into prey:** Use an object (such as food) or motion, which is a prey-drive action.

Understanding which drive Buddy needs to be in speeds up your training process. As you become aware of the impact your body stance and motions have on the drive that Buddy is in, you can deliver clear messages to them. Your body language becomes congruent with what you're trying to teach. Because Buddy is an astute observer of body motions, which is how dogs communicate with each other, they'll understand exactly what you want.

Applying drives to your training

After looking at your dog's Personality Profile (see the questionnaire earlier in the "Determining Your Dog's Personality Profile" section), you know the training techniques that work best and that are in harmony with your dog's drives. You now have the tools to tailor your training program to your dog. Here are the different drive categories your dog may be in:

>> **Defense-fight drive — more than 60:** A firm hand doesn't bother your dog much. Correct body posture isn't critical because your dog's high defense-fight drive numbers are very forgiving. Your tone of voice can be firm, but it should always be pleasant and nonthreatening.

>> **Defense-flight drive — more than 60:** Your dog won't respond to strong corrections. Correct body posture and a quiet, pleasant tone of voice are

critical. Avoid using a harsh tone of voice or hovering — leaning over or toward your dog. Focus on still body postures and standing up straight with gentle handling.

- » **Prey drive — more than 60:** Your dog will respond well to a treat or toy during the teaching phase because of their high prey drive. A firm hand may be necessary, depending on the strength of their defense-fight drive, to suppress the prey drive when necessary, such as when chasing a cat or spotting a squirrel. A dog high in prey drive is easily motivated but is also easily distracted by motion or moving objects. Moving hand signals mean more to this dog than commands. Focus on leaning backward with your body posture, using hand signals, and keeping your leash from dangling and swinging, so as not to confuse the dog. Any motion will put this dog into prey drive.

- » **Prey drive — less than 40:** A dog low in prey drive probably isn't easily motivated by food or other objects but also isn't easily distracted by or interested in chasing moving objects. Use every prey drive your dog has and feed them before you need them in prey drive, such as when you want them to retrieve so they are in prey drive from the morsel of food. Use quiet verbal praise; you don't want a loud voice to flip them out of prey drive and into defense drive.

- » **Pack drive — more than 60:** This dog responds readily to praise and physical affection. A dog high in pack drive likes to be with you and will respond with little guidance. The act of being together, training or playing together, will make this dog happy.

- » **Pack drive — less than 40:** A dog low in pack drive probably doesn't care whether they spend much time with you. They like to do their own thing and aren't easily motivated through pack-drive activities. Your best plan is to rely on prey drive in training. Low pack drive is usually breed-specific for dogs bred to work independently of man.

Consider the following important hints to keep in mind when planning your training strategy:

- » Dogs with a low defense-fight drive of less than 60 rarely get into trouble; in fact, they avoid it. Many young dogs without life experience fall into this category, and although their numbers may be quite low as pups, they may vary slightly with age. With a low fight-drive dog, a straight body posture is more important. Don't bend over; rather you need to squat down — as opposed to bending at the waist — to the dog's level especially when greeting them.

>> Dogs who are high in prey or pack drive also are easily trained. Pay attention to the strengths of each drive. Dogs are happiest in the drive that they have the most of. Training should come more easily to them because most training needs both prey and pack drive. Review the switching behaviors you need to communicate with your dog in those two drives.

>> If your dog is high in defense-fight drive, you need to work diligently on your leadership and control exercises and review them frequently. You want to be the pack leader with this dog. Bonding is great with a high defense-fight drive dog after they see you as the coach of the team.

>> If your dog is high in prey drive, you also need to work on the leadership exercises to control them around doorways, objects, and similar distractions. A dog who is high in prey drive is distracted by everything — noise, motion, smells, and things near and far away. Life is distracting. Training is the key to all things.

>> If your dog is high in both prey and defense-fight drives, you have a dog that is alert and demanding, but with the defense-fight drive you have a dog with enough personality to work though the prey drive and distractions of life. This dog may be the dog you dreamed of, and they may want to do it all. Work on your leadership and training and how to switch between the drives.

The following are the nicknames for a few of the profiles. See if you can recognize your dog:

>> **The Couch Potato or some may say "The born perfect dog"— low prey, low pack, low defense fight:** This dog is difficult to motivate and probably doesn't need extensive training. They need extra patience if training is attempted because they have few behaviors to work with. On the plus side, this dog is unlikely to get into trouble, doesn't disturb anyone, makes a good family pet, and doesn't mind being left alone for considerable periods of time.

>> **The Hunter — high prey, low pack, low defense flight:** This dog gives the appearance of having an extremely short attention span but is perfectly able to concentrate on what they find interesting. Training requires channeling their energy to get them to do what you want. You need patience because you need to teach the dog through prey drive.

>> **The Gas Station Dog or Sentry Guard Dog — high prey, low pack, high defense fight:** This dog is independent and not easy to live with as a pet. Highly excited by movement, they may attack anything that comes within range. They don't care much about people or dogs and work well as a guard dog. Pack exercises, such as walking on a leash without pulling, need to be built up through their prey drive. Every dog is perfect for the task for which they were born. A sentry dog may not make a good family pet, but a good

family pet wouldn't make a good sentry dog. Be practical when setting the goals that you have for the dog you have.

>> **The Runner — high prey, low pack, high defense-flight:** Easily startled and/or frightened, this dog needs quiet and reassuring handling. A dog with this profile isn't a good choice for children. Knowing what drives your dog and what personality they have before you get them would be ideal. A dog with high defense flight can feel cornered easily. Always give this dog space and train with a calm, reassuring tone. Know what your plan is and don't get discouraged.

>> **The Shadow — low prey, high pack, and low defense fight:** This dog follows you around all day and is unlikely to get into trouble. They like to be with you and aren't interested in chasing much of anything.

>> **Teacher's Pet — medium prey, pack, and defense fight:** This dog is easy to train and motivate, and mistakes on your part aren't critical. Teacher's Pet has a nice balance of drives. Figure 2-7 shows the graph for Teacher's Pet. Having medium drive in all the drives except defense-flight which is low, does give a personality that should be playful with people and other dogs. They should be able to handle most households and goals you may have for training a dog.

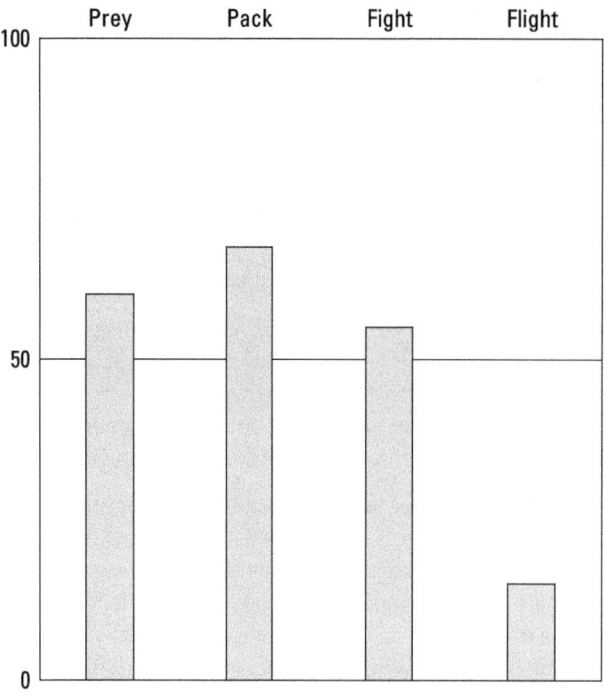

FIGURE 2-7: A typical Teacher's Pet profile.

© John Wiley & Sons, Inc.

REMEMBER

The easiest dogs are balanced among all drives. No matter what you do, the dog seems to be able to figure out what you want. As we mention, dogs are happiest in the drives in which they're highest. There are no bad dogs; there are only dogs best suited for one thing over another. By applying the principles of drives, you can turn your dog into a well-trained pet.

People frequently ask us, "Can you change a dog's drives — either reduce or enhance a particular drive?" In a few instances you can enhance a drive through training. For example, after you've taught a dog with few prey behaviors to retrieve, they'll be more inclined to participate in fetch games. As a general rule, however, you can't change a dog's drives. Your dog's personality is like the computer program you bought. Its personality is programed a certain way. Nature versus nurture does give you some room to build on your dog's drives. Through training and learning about drives you can communicate with your dog and training becomes more successful. By controlling your body language and keeping Buddy in the proper drive, you'll have more fun training them, and therefore you'll get the dog you want.

As we always say, "You get the dog you train, so train for the dog you want."

Each drive has joy associated with it. Prey drive has retrieving and jumping, pack drive has companionship and play, defense-fight drive has confidence and the ability for great bonding, and defense-flight drive has quiet and peace and security. Find the joy for your dog together and build on it.

IN THIS CHAPTER

» Considering your dog's internal influences

» Understanding stress and its effect on training

» Taking your dog's environment into account

» Seeing how you affect your dog's training: Are you prepared as the trainer?

Chapter **3**

Developing Training Savvy

Your dog's ability to learn and retain information — just like yours — is directly related to what goes on around them and how they feel. A noisy and distraction-filled environment makes it difficult for Buddy to concentrate on learning new commands. Strife in the household may cause Buddy to become frightened, irritable, and even aggressive, which can impede the learning process. Even what you feed your dog affects their ability to learn.

How Buddy feels, both mentally and physically, influences their ability to learn. If they feel anxious, depressed, or stressed, learning and retention decrease in direct proportion to the degree of the dog's distress. If they're physically ill or in pain, they can't learn what you're trying to teach. These observations are stating the obvious — just think how you'd react under similar circumstances. Yet, we must point this out because some dog owners often seem to be oblivious to their effect on the dog's ability to learn.

As Buddy's teacher, you play a key role in their learning process — and not just because you're giving them physical instruction. You also should create a positive training atmosphere that maximizes their chances for success by easing any stress that can get in the way. Some of that stress comes from within Buddy, and you can alleviate that part by tending to their unique emotional and physical needs. The rest comes from you, so be aware of what you bring to the table as a trainer. Setting realistic expectations, having a plan, setting up for each sequence, and being prepared to give each command all go a long way toward creating a pleasant experience for both you and Buddy.

Managing the Dog Within

Even though some principal influences on your dog's ability to learn are under your control, some influences come from within your dog:

>> Breed-specific behaviors

>> Temperament

>> Mental sensitivity

>> Responses to visual stimuli

>> Sound sensitivity

>> Touch sensitivity

All these influences affect how the dog learns, what they find difficult, and what comes almost naturally. For more information, head to Chapter 2 and take the Personality Profile of your dog. This profile examines all these elements in great detail.

Breed-specific behaviors

Whether you have a designer dog, a dog of mixed origin, or a purebred, they come with some specific behaviors, such as hunting or herding, among others. By studying the task or tasks for which a particular dog was bred, you can get a pretty good idea of what's going to be easy and difficult for your dog to learn. Most terriers, for example, are lively little dogs because they were bred to go after little furry things that live in holes in the ground. Shetland Sheepdogs like to round up kids, because they were bred to herd. Retrievers bring the game back (see Figure 3-1), and Spaniels flush it out of the weeds. Each one has its own special talents.

© John Wiley & Sons, Inc.

FIGURE 3-1:
A Labrador Retriever bred to bring a bird to hand seen here working with a retrieving dummy.

REMEMBER

Because most dogs were bred to work with or under the direction of people, these talents help with your training efforts. But sometimes the dog's instinct to do what they were bred for gets them into trouble. You may not want them hunting or herding or whatever, so you need to spend some of your training efforts redirecting these behaviors. Whenever you run into a roadblock in your training, ask yourself, "Is that what this dog was bred to do?" If so, it will take them more time to change that particular behavior, and you'll need to be patient.

Temperament

Most people readily agree that good temperament is the most important quality for pets. Unfortunately, the explanation of exactly what a good temperament is often gets vague and elusive and sometimes contradictory. The official breed standard of most breeds makes a statement to the effect that the dog you're considering may be loyal, loving, intelligent, good with children, and easy to train. We hope that is true!

Simply defined, *temperament* is made up of the personality traits suitable for the job you want the dog to do. If you want your dog to be good with children and your dog has that personality trait, then they have a good temperament. They may not do so well in other areas, such as guarding or herding, but that may not be what you wanted.

Similarly vague and elusive have been attempts to define the dog's intelligence. Again, it goes back to function. We define a dog's *intelligence* as the ease with which they can be trained for the function the dog was bred.

You can better understand your dog's temperament if you have a sense of their drives (prey, pack, flight, and fight). The Personality Profile (see Chapter 2) can help you discover your dog's strengths and limitations. You'll find which drive molds Buddy's behaviors.

REMEMBER

You need to recognize your dog's strengths and limitations because they have a profound influence on the ease or difficulty of teaching your dog a particular task. Circus trainers have an old saying: "Get the dog for the trick and not the trick for the dog." Exploit your dog's strengths.

Mental sensitivity

Dogs, like people, vary in their ability to deal with negative emotions. No matter how they cope, most dogs are keenly aware of your emotions. Moreover, the more you work with Buddy, the greater bond you'll develop. It may seem as though they can read your mind. Okay, they may not be able to read your mind, but they certainly sense your emotions. If you're feeling frustration, disappointment, or anger, Buddy can sense it.

REMEMBER

Because dogs are ill-equipped to deal with these emotions, they tend to become anxious and confused, which then slows or even prevents the learning process. Your job in training Buddy is to maintain an upbeat and patient attitude. As your dog's teacher, you must teach them what you want and don't want them to do. Without your guidance, your dog simply does what comes naturally to them — they're a dog! Blaming Buddy for what you perceive to be a shortcoming on their part doesn't help and undermines the very relationship you're trying to build.

Responses to visual stimuli

Saying that a dog responds to *visual stimuli* is a fancy way of saying that a dog responds to moving objects. For purposes of training, it relates to the dog's distractibility when faced with something that moves. This, too, varies from breed to breed and depends on the nature of the moving object. Consider a few examples:

>> Terriers are notoriously distractible. For example, a Yorkshire Terrier, although technically a member of the Toy Group, is convinced that they must investigate every moving leaf or blade of grass. Although this behavior makes perfect sense to them because they are so low to the ground, it makes training them to pay attention a real challenge.

>> In the Hound Group, some breeds, such as the Basset Hound, Beagle, and Bloodhound, are more stimulated by scents on the ground or in the air than by moving objects. Training a Beagle to walk on a loose leash while paying attention to you and not sniffing the ground can be a Herculean task.

>> The guarding breeds, such as the German Shepherd, Doberman Pinscher, and Rottweiler, were bred to survey their surroundings — to keep everything in sight, as it were. They, too, find it difficult and stressful to focus exclusively on you in the presence of distractions. Remember, their job is to be alert to what's going on around them.

>> The Newfoundland, an ordinarily sedate companion (see Figure 3-2), becomes a raving maniac near water with their instinctive desire to rescue any and all swimmers, totally disregarding the fact that the swimmer may not want or need to be rescued.

FIGURE 3-2: The Newfoundland, a large breed, is a laid-back dog except around water.

© John Wiley & Sons, Inc.

Sound sensitivity

Some dogs have a keener sense of hearing than others, to the point that loud noises literally hurt their ears. For example, Dachshund puppies can get quite upset when the vacuum cleaner is turned on. They're not afraid of the machine itself; they're just upset by the noise. They find it difficult to focus on lessons if a machine is running at the same time. Fear of thunder also can be the result of sound sensitivity.

REMEMBER

Under ordinary circumstances, sound sensitivity isn't a problem, but it can affect the dog's ability to concentrate in the presence of moderate to loud noises. A car backfiring can cause one dog to jump out of their skin, whereas it may only elicit a curious expression from another dog.

Touch sensitivity — the adrenaline effect

A dog's threshold of discomfort depends on two things:

>> Their touch sensitivity

>> What they're doing at that particular time

For purposes of training and for knowing what equipment to use, you need to know Buddy's touch sensitivity. For example, when a dog doesn't readily respond to the training collar, they're all too quickly labeled as stubborn or stupid. But nothing can be further from the truth. The trainer must select the right training equipment.

Discomfort thresholds tend to be breed specific. For example, a Labrador Retriever, that's supposed to be able to cover all manner of terrain as well as retrieve in ice-cold water, more than likely will have a high discomfort threshold. Shetland Sheepdogs tend to be quite touch sensitive and respond promptly to a training collar. What one dog hardly notices makes another one change their behavior. And therein lies the secret of which piece of training equipment to use.

Touch sensitivity isn't size related. Small dogs can have just as high a discomfort threshold as large dogs. Nor is touch sensitivity age related. A puppy doesn't start out as touch sensitive and become touch insensitive as they grow older. Some increase in insensitivity may arise, but it's insignificant. A dog's touch sensitivity, however, is affected by what they're doing. In hot pursuit of a rabbit, their discomfort threshold goes up, as it would during a fight. This phenomenon is referred to as the *adrenaline factor*. For example, consider if you're at a rock concert with loud music and dancing, a person may bump into you, and you barely notice. Conversely if you're reading in a library and someone taps you on the shoulder, you might jump out of your skin. You're neither touch sensitive nor insensitive; your reaction is the adrenalin factor response.

REMEMBER

When you have an idea of Buddy's discomfort threshold, you'll know how to handle them and the type of training equipment you'll need. See Chapter 5 for more on training gear.

Stressing the Effects of Stress

Stress is a byproduct of daily life and can result from many factors — health, family, your job, the state of the economy, the state of the country, or even the state of the world. Even pleasurable experiences, such as taking a vacation, can be a source of stress.

Stress is a physiological, genetically predetermined reaction over which the individual, be it a dog or person, has no control. Stress is a natural part of everyone's daily lives and affects each person in different ways. Dogs are no different. Just like people, they experience stress. As your dog's teacher, you must recognize the circumstances that produce stress and its manifestations and know how to manage it.

REMEMBER

Your personal experiences with stress help you relate to what your dog is experiencing. Knowing how to identify the signs and symptoms isn't difficult when you know what you're looking for.

Understanding stress

In both dogs and people, stress is the body's response to any physical or mental demand put upon it. That response prepares the body to either fight or flee. Stress increases blood pressure, heart rate, breathing, and metabolism, and it triggers a marked increase in the blood supply to the arms and legs.

Stress takes its toll on the body, be it a person's or a dog's. When stressed, the body becomes chemically imbalanced. To deal with this imbalance, the body releases chemicals into the bloodstream in an attempt to rebalance itself. The reserve of these chemicals is limited; you can dip into it only so many times before it runs dry and the body loses its ability to rebalance. Prolonged periods of imbalance then result in neurotic behavior and the inability to function. When the body's ability to counteract stress has been maxed out, stress will then be expressed in more than just physical ways: It will manifest into behavior problems, possibly bizarre behaviors often referred to as mental problems. This is as true for your dog as it is for you.

Mental or behavioral and physical stress ranges from tolerable all the way to intolerable — that is, the inability to function. Your interest here lies with your dog's stress experienced during training or going to a class, whether you're teaching a new exercise, practicing a familiar one, or administering a test, like the Canine Good Citizen test (see Chapter 1 or go to www.akc.org.) You need to be able to recognize the signs of stress and manage the stress your dog may experience.

REMEMBER

Stress is characterized as both positive and negative. When stress is *positive*, it manifests itself in increased activity; when it's *negative*, it results in decreased activity. The following list explains both:

>> Help, I'm hyperactive! So-called positive stress results in hyperactivity. Your dog may run around, not be able to stay still or slow down, not pay attention, bounce up and down, jump on you, whine, bark, mouth, get in front of you, anticipate commands, or not be able to learn. You may think your dog is just being silly and having fun, but they aren't. They're actually exhibiting coping behaviors for positive stress.

>> Why am I so depressed? So-called negative stress causes lethargy, with related behaviors such as lacking energy, being afraid, freezing, slinking behind you, running away, responding slowly to commands, showing little interest in exercise or training, or displaying an inability to learn. In new situations, Buddy gets behind you, seems tired and wants to lie down, or seems sluggish and disinterested. These aren't signs of relaxation; they're the coping behaviors for negative stress.

Recognizing the symptoms of stress

In dogs, signs of either form of stress — positive or negative — are muscle tremors; excessive panting and drooling; sweaty feet that leave tracks on dry, hard surfaces; dilated pupils; and, in extreme cases, urination, defecation (usually in the form of diarrhea), self-mutilation, and anxiety.

Anxiety is a state of apprehension and uneasiness. When anxiety is prolonged, two problems arise:

>> The dog's ability to learn and think is diminished and ultimately stops. It also can cause a panic attack.

>> Anxiety depresses the immune system, thereby increasing the dog's chances of becoming physically ill. The weakest link in the chain is attacked first. If the dog has digestive upsets, you can see GI problems, such as diarrhea or salivation.

REMEMBER

In and of itself, stress isn't bad or undesirable. A certain level of stress is vital for the development and healthy functioning of the body and its immune system. Only when stress has no behavioral outlet — when the dog is put in a no-win situation — is the burden of coping borne by the body. The immune system then starts to break down.

Origins of stress — internal or external

Internal sources of stress are inherited and come from within the dog. They include structure and health. Dogs vary in coping abilities and stress thresholds. Realistically, you can't do much to change your dog — for example, you can't train them to deal better with stress. But you can use stress-management techniques to mitigate its impact.

External sources of stress come from outside the dog and are introduced externally. They range from the diet you feed your dog to the relationship you have with them. Extrinsic sources include the following:

>> Frustration and indecision on your part

>> Lack of adequate socialization

>> The dog's perception of their environment

>> Training location

>> Use of an appropriate training method

Fortunately, all these sources of stress are under your control (see the later section "Managing Your Dog's Environment").

Relating stress to learning

When you train Buddy, you can't prevent them from experiencing some stress, but you can keep the stress to a level at which they can still learn. If you find that your dog is overly stressed during a training session, stop the session. (One indicator of when Buddy has had enough is that they no longer take a treat.) At that point, your dog's ability to learn is diminished, and neither of you will benefit from continuing.

What should you do? Don't think of training as a win-lose contest between you and your dog, such as: "If I stop, Buddy will think they has won, and they'll never do it for me." This line of thinking presumes that you and Buddy are adversaries, in some kind of a contest, or "You'll do it no matter what." Not exactly a teacher-student relationship!

Training Buddy has nothing to do with winning or losing, but with teaching. You can walk away from a training session at any time, whether or not you think you've been successful. When you see that no further learning is taking place, stop. If you don't and you insist on forcing the issue, you'll undermine both your dog's trust in you and the relationship you're trying to build.

TIP

Let Buddy rest for a few hours and try again. You'll find that the light bulb suddenly seems to turn on. By having taken a break at that point, you get *latent learning* — the process of giving the point a chance to work. Our advice is to quit training when you find yourself becoming irritable or when Buddy starts to show signs of stress.

Stress and distraction training

Prepare to be patient when you first introduce your dog to training with distractions. Naturally, Buddy is going to be distracted (that's the point!), but over time, they'll learn to respond correctly and ignore distractions. If you feel yourself becoming upset, it's time to take five.

REMEMBER

Try to make every new exercise or distraction a positive experience for your dog. A favorable introduction will have a positive long-term impact. The first impression leaves the most lasting impact. Whenever you introduce your dog to a new exercise or distraction, make it as pleasant and as stress free as possible so that it leaves a neutral, if not favorable, impression.

Managing stress

Become aware of how Buddy reacts to stress, positively or negatively, and the circumstances under which they experience stress. Something you're doing, or even a location, may cause them stress.

Understand that Buddy has no control over their response to stress — they inherited this behavior — and that it's your job to manage it as best as you can. Through proper management, Buddy will become accustomed, with every successful repetition, to coping with new situations like a pro.

Managing Your Dog's Environment

Your dog has a keen perception of their environment. Continuous or frequent strife or friction in your household can have a negative impact on your dog's ability to learn. Many dogs also are adversely affected by excessive noise and activity and may develop behavior problems.

Look for the following signs that your dog has a negative perception of their environment:

» Aggression

» Aloofness

» Hyperactivity

» Irritability

» Lethargy

Under these circumstances, learning is reduced — if it takes place at all — and your dog won't retain the lesson. However, if you have a keen perception of how your dog responds to their environment, you'll more easily attain your training goals. This section provides some tips on creating the best possible environment for learning.

Starting on the right foot

You've heard the saying, "You don't get a second chance to make a first impression." You also know that the first impression leaves the most lasting impact. The stronger that impression, the longer it lasts.

TIP

Introductions to a dog's new experiences need to be as pleasant as possible. For example, Buddy's first visit to the vet needs to be a pleasant experience, or they'll have an unpleasant association with going to the vet. Ask the doctor to give them a dog treat before their examination and another treat at the end of the visit.

The importance of making a good first impression applies to your dog's training as well. A particularly traumatic or unpleasant first experience can literally ruin a dog for life. The object is to make your dog's first impression of training as pleasant as you can.

Recognizing your dog's social needs

Dogs are social animals that don't do well when isolated. For example, if you work outside the home, you may need to leave your dog alone at home. Then when you get home, your dog is terribly excited and wants to play and be with you. But you also may need to go out in the evening, leaving your dog alone again.

If you simply don't have the time to give your dog the attention they crave, consider a doggie daycare. Your dog will spend their day playing and interacting with other dogs and having a good time using their excess energy needs. A tired dog is a happy dog and has a happy owner. In addition to keeping Buddy entertained and amused, many doggie daycare facilities provide other services, such as bathing and grooming. Also consider whether the daycare facility offers nap times. Playing all day for hours with no rest can backfire into neurotic behaviors or redirected aggression.

A potential downside of doggie daycare is that Buddy may think it's playtime whenever they meet another dog, making them difficult to control around other dogs. Other potential downsides are possible exposure to disease and parasites, trauma due to inexperienced handling by daycare personnel, and personal liability for Buddy's actions. If you're considering a doggie daycare, do your research first and visit the doggie daycare before you select one. Ask if the dogs get rest periods during the day. Also see how well the staff monitors the play time.

REMEMBER

As with any behavior, when it comes to exercise, your dog has a certain amount of energy. After Buddy has expended that energy, they're tired. If that energy isn't expended, it may redirect itself into barking, chewing, digging, house soiling, self-mutilation, and similar behaviors — clearly not what you have in mind for the well-trained pet. If your schedule doesn't allow for enough exercise for Buddy, investigate doggie daycare or dog walkers in your area to help you.

Feeding your dog's nutritional needs

The most important influence on your dog's ability to learn, and the one under your most immediate control, is what you feed them. Because feeding is so important, we devote Chapter 4 to this topic. Nutrition is the fuel that runs Buddy's engine. Poor fuel provides a poor performance, so understanding how to feed Buddy correctly avoids stressing their system by providing enough nutrients for it to work properly.

So many dog foods are on the market today that making the best choice for Buddy can be a bewildering task. Just as you do when buying food for yourself or your family, you need to look at the ingredients. Dogs are carnivores and need animal protein. Select a food that lists animal proteins, such as chicken, beef, or lamb, in the first three ingredients. Avoid foods containing a lot of grains. When it seems that more comes out of your dog's rear end than went into the front end, you can safely bet that the food contains more filler than protein.

Understanding the "You" Factor

Several factors influence how successful you'll be in turning your pet into a well-mannered companion. Some of these are under your direct control, and others come with your dog or come from their surrounding environment. We discuss the factors that are out of your control in the earlier sections in this chapter. Here in this section, we examine the factors that are under your direct control. A direct relationship exists between your awareness and understanding of the following factors and your success as your dog's teacher.

Knowing your expectations

Most people's expectations of their dogs vary. Some of these expectations are realistic; others aren't. You've heard people say, "My dog understands every word I say," and perhaps you think yours does as well. If it were as easy as that, you wouldn't need dog trainers or training books. Your words coupled with your body language aid your dog to be able to understand your words.

Sometimes your dog may seem to really understand what you say. Enough truth does exist to perpetuate this myth. Although dogs don't understand the words you use, they do understand tone of voice — and sometimes even your intent. Scientists have found that words used in the same tone of voice and inflection and with the same body motions allow a well-trained dog to learn to the capacity of a 2-year-old child.

Ask yourself these questions for a clearer picture of your expectations:

Are your expectations realistic?

Do you believe your dog obeys commands because they

>> Love you?

>> Want to please you?

>> Are grateful?

>> Have a sense of duty?

>> Feel a moral obligation?

We suspect that you answered yes to the first and second questions, became unsure at the third question, and then realized that we were leading you down a primrose path.

WARNING

If your approach to training is based on moral ideas regarding punishment, reward, obedience, duty, and the like, you're bound to handle the dog in the wrong way. No doubt your dog loves you, but they won't obey commands for that reason. Do they want to please you? Not exactly, but it sometimes seems like they do. What they're really doing is pleasing themselves.

REMEMBER

Buddy is usually interested in only one thing: What's in it for me right now? Buddy certainly has no sense of duty or feeling of moral obligation. The sooner you discard beliefs like that, the quicker you'll come to terms with how to approach their education.

Are your expectations too low?

Do you believe your dog doesn't obey commands because they are:

>> Stubborn?

>> Hardheaded?

>> Stupid?

>> Lying awake at night thinking of ways to aggravate you?

If you answered yes to any of these, you're guilty of *anthropomorphizing,* or attributing human characteristics and attributes to an animal. It's easy to do, but it doesn't help in your training.

Dogs aren't stubborn or hardheaded. To the contrary, they're quite smart when it comes to figuring out how to get their way. And they don't lie awake at night thinking of ways to aggravate you — they sleep, just like everybody else.

What should your expectations be?

So why does your dog obey your command? Usually for one of three reasons:

>> They want something.

>> They think it's fun, like retrieving a ball.

>> They have been taught specific behaviors.

When they respond to a command for either the first or the second reason, they do it for themselves; when they respond for the third reason, they do it for you. This distinction is important because it deals with reliability and safety. Ask yourself this question: If Buddy responds only because they want something or because it's fun, will they respond when they don't want something or when it's no longer fun? The answer is obvious.

REMEMBER

The well-trained dog responds because they have been taught. This doesn't mean you and they can't have fun in the process; just make sure the result is clearly understood. When you say, "Come," there are no options, especially when their safety or the safety of others is involved.

Knowing your attitude

Look at the following situation: Buddy has taken themselves for an unauthorized walk through the neighborhood. You're late for an appointment but don't want to leave Buddy out on the streets. You frantically call and call. Finally, Buddy makes an appearance, happily sauntering up to you. You, on the other hand, are fit to be tied, and you let them know your displeasure in no uncertain terms by giving them a thorough scolding. Ask yourself, "Is this the kind of greeting that will make Buddy want to come to me?" If the answer is no, then stop doing it, no matter what. This is unintentionally training Buddy to *not* come to you after a long outing. Always, always praise Buddy for allowing you to touch and catch them no matter how frustrated you are or how long it took.

REMEMBER

Don't train your dog when you're irritable or tired. You want training to be a positive experience for your dog. If you ever get frustrated during training, stop and come back to it at another time. When you're frustrated, your communications may consist of "No!" or "Bad dog!" or "How could you do this?" or "Get out and stay out!" You're unhappy, and Buddy is unhappy because you're unhappy. An unfriendly or hostile approach doesn't gain you their cooperation; it needlessly prolongs the teaching process. When you become frustrated or angry, Buddy becomes anxious and nervous and has difficulty learning. A better approach is to train Buddy when you're in a better frame of mind. You want training to be a positive experience for both of you.

One of the commands you want Buddy to master is to come when called. To be successful, remember this principle: Whenever your dog comes to you, be nice to them. Don't do anything the *dog* perceives as unpleasant. No matter what they may have done, be pleasant and greet them with a kind word, a pat on the head, and a smile. Teach your dog to trust you by being a safe place for them. When they are with you, follow you, or come to you, make them feel wanted. That is the definition of Come — pleasant and rewarding to be together. Watch out for unintentional training, as we mention above.

Being consistent with commands and tone of voice

If any magic is involved in training your dog, it's consistency. Your dog can't understand "sometimes," "maybe," "perhaps," or "only on Sundays." They can and do understand "yes" and "no." For example, you confuse your dog when you encourage them to jump up on you while you're wearing old clothes but then get angry with them when they joyfully plant muddy paws on your best clothes.

REMEMBER

Consistency in training means handling your dog in a predictable and uniform manner. If more than one person is in the household, everyone needs to handle the dog in the same way. Otherwise, the dog becomes confused and unreliable in their responses.

TIP

Most dogs eventually ignore commands that don't lead to tangible consequences. When Buddy responds to a command, praise them. When they choose not to respond to a command they have been taught, show them what you expected from them. Reinforce your command; don't repeat it over and over again.

So, does this mean that you can never permit your puppy to jump up on you? Not at all. But you must teach them that they may do so only when you tell them it's okay. But beware that training a dog to make this distinction is more difficult than teaching them not to jump up at all. The more black-and-white you can make it, the easier it will be for Buddy to understand what you want.

Outlasting your dog — be persistent

Training your dog is a question of who is more persistent — you or your dog. Some things they can master quickly; others will take more time. If several tries don't bring success, be patient, remain calm, and try again.

How quickly your dog will learn a particular command depends on the extent to which the behavior you're trying to teach them is in harmony with the function for which they were bred.

For example, a Labrador Retriever, bred to retrieve game birds on land and in the water, will readily learn how to fetch a stick or a ball on command. A Shetland Sheepdog, bred to herd and guard livestock, will learn to walk on a loose leash more quickly than a Beagle, which is bred to hunt rabbits.

Knowing to avoid "no"

As of right now, eliminate the word "no" from your training vocabulary. All too often, *no* is the only command a dog hears, and they're expected to figure out what it means. No exercise or command in training is called "no."

You need to avoid negative communications like "no" with your dog because negative communications undermine the relationship you're trying to build. Also, don't use your dog's name as a reprimand. If you find yourself in a situation where it's imperative to interrupt Buddy's behavior, use the word "stop" instead.

REMEMBER

Begin to focus on the way in which you communicate with Buddy. Do they perceive the interaction as positive or negative, pleasant or unpleasant, friendly or unfriendly? How many times do you use the word *no*, and how many times do you say "Good dog" when interacting with them? If everything the dog does brings forth a stern "Don't do this," "Don't do that," or "No, bad dog," this negative communication will have a negative effect on your dog's motivation to work for you.

In dealing with your dog, ask yourself, "What exactly do I want Buddy to do?" Use a *do* command whenever possible so that you can praise your dog instead of reprimanding them. You'll notice a direct relationship between your dog's willingness to cooperate and your attitude. Get out of the blaming habit of assuming that Buddy's failure to respond is their fault. After all, *you* are the teacher! Your dog's conduct is a direct reflection of your teaching.

Does this mean you can never use the word *no*? Not exactly. In an emergency, or when Buddy commits a felony, you do what you must, but only when the need is dire. By the way, a training issue is not a felony. Growling at you or leadership issues are defined as felonies, not simple errors during training.

Repeating commands

In training, use your dog's name once *before* a command to get their attention, as in "Buddy, Come." The quickest way to teach your dog to ignore you is to use their name repeatedly — and raising your voice doesn't help, either. When trying to communicate with someone who doesn't understand English, shouting doesn't improve their understanding.

TIP

Get into the habit of giving a command once and in a normal tone of voice — a dog's hearing is 80 times better than yours. By repeating commands, you systematically teach your dog to ignore you, and changes in inflections from please to threats don't help. Most people are unaware of how many times they repeat a command. Give the command, and if your dog doesn't respond, show them exactly what you want them to do.

Giving a dog a short name or even changing their name can change their behavior, as strange as that sounds. A student came to class once who had a rescue dog named Trouble. She worked with Trouble for a long time and made a very good show dog out of him. Her complaint was that he always looked downtrodden and unhappy. We suggested that she rename him — at first just when she worked him — and then gradually in his daily life. His name was changed to Puppy; he responded happily to his new name and perked right up. Hard to believe, but true. Saying your dog's name should elicit a tail wag and happy look from your dog (see Chapter 9 for the Name Recognition game). The power of words and how you feel when you say them comes through. If you use a negative name, you say it with a negative tone. A dog can react to that subtle tone. By changing the name Trouble to something more positive such as Puppy can change not only how you think about your dog but also how you react when you say it, which bleeds onto the dog as well. Words are powerful. Be as positive as you can be as often as you can be.

REMEMBER

When training your dog, think of teacher and student — with you being the teacher. As every teacher knows, learning is a process of successive approximation. Children aren't born knowing how to read and write; they learn these skills in small increments. Similarly, a dog learns commands in small increments, one step at a time. Repetition enforces that incremental learning.

Chapter **4**

Understanding the Vital Role That Nutrition and Health Play in Training

Your dog's behavior, training, happiness, health, longevity, and overall well-being are inextricably intertwined with what you feed them. Dogs, just like humans and all other animals, have specific nutritional requirements that need to be met. What your dog eats has a tremendous impact on their health and trainability. Dogs' lifespans in the last few years have decreased and what Buddy is fed has so much to do with this.

In this chapter, we help you figure out what food is right for Buddy, including the different kinds of dog food on the market and our suggestions, common health issues and our solutions for dealing with them, your vet's role in your dog's health, when vaccines are necessary, and the expanding role of veterinary medicine into acupuncture, homeopathy, and chiropractic. We also explain when complementary medicine may be helpful for your dog, especially during the years when they're growing and being trained, and as they age. Training a dog that isn't feeling well is frustrating for both you and your dog.

These last years have seen an explosion not only in the amount of dog foods on the market, but also in canine nutritional research. Did you know that one in two dogs now die of cancer worldwide? Many dogs also are dying from heart problems. What these two facts have in common is that both diseases are directly related to certain kinds of dog food.

We aren't trying to turn you into an expert on canine nutrition, but having a basic knowledge is important. What we are going to do is to tell you from our experience the best ways to feed your dog so that they enjoy good health, longevity, and as few visits to the veterinarian as possible. If you do want to become an expert on feeding your dog, see *The Holistic Guide for a Healthy Dog,* 2nd Edition, by Wendy Volhard and Kerry Brown, DVM (Howell Book House). For additional information about any of the information in this chapter, go to www.volharddognutrition. com/. (All the dogs photographed in this *For Dummies* book were and are fed from the food options mentioned in this chapter.)

REMEMBER

When a dog's body is under stress — from poor health, vaccines, or poor nutrition — their brain doesn't have the ability to retain the information you're teaching. This explains why some dogs get stuck in their training and don't seem to progress.

Finding the Right Food for Buddy

Not all dog foods are alike; enormous quality differences exist between the different types. Since the massive recall in 2008 of dog foods containing contaminated ingredients from China (which killed thousands of cats and dogs), the market has exploded with different types of food. Dry, freeze-dried, frozen, raw, dehydrated, canned, semi-moist, and grain-free foods are available in a bewildering variety. With so many choices, trying to make an informed decision can become an overwhelming task. Here are the main choices:

>> **Kibble:** This type is the most popular one to feed your dog, but it has its disadvantages. Most kibble diets contain a lot of grains, but research has shown an increase in cancer in dogs with a large amount of grains in their diet. Grains are starch, which breaks down into sugar which in turn feeds cancer. Grain-free kibble diets are available on the market, but they too have their problems because they've been associated with heart disease in dogs.

Even if the package says "complete and balanced," if kibble is your choice, then you must add a complete food supplement to the bowl of kibble to return all the nutrients that are cooked out during the heating process. Also adding some vegetables and raw meat can offset the lack of nutrients in these foods.

>> **Raw diet:** A totally *raw diet* is probably the best way to feed a dog. However, getting that diet properly balanced is difficult, which is why so many people shy away from it. You can buy raw diets that are balanced at some pet stores, but they're inclined to be rather expensive. Some of them say they're balanced but they aren't, so carefully read the labels.

>> **Dehydrated whole food base:** Our choice over the last 35 years has been to feed a *dehydrated whole food base* mix, which contains all the vitamins, fat, and minerals a dog needs. It's made from human-grade, nongenetically modified ingredients that are sourced in the United States. Each ingredient has been tested for molds and bacteria before it's mixed, during the mixing process, and before it's put into bags. To our knowledge, no other food produced has these built-in safeguards. We simply add a fresh, raw protein to it and some water to rehydrate the base mix, and it's done. And even better, the dogs love it. It's great for dogs at all life stages: puppies, pregnant females, old dogs, and dogs in performance events.

Frozen, freeze dried, canned, dehydrated, and semimoist are other choices you can make. The same rules apply: Read the labels to make sure that you're feeding a balanced product. If the food is processed (cooked) in any way, you must add a whole food supplement to achieve balance. We recommend adding a supplement like Endurance.

Good health starts in the gut, which contains different kinds of bacteria. The simple fact is that if bacteria is kept in balance, your dog will live a long and healthy life. Bad health, even small issues like reoccurring ear problems, dirty teeth, and bad breath, can be directly attributed to poor gut balance. To get Buddy's diet just right, you need to know the most common and most visible symptoms of nutritional deficiencies. Recognizing these deficiencies saves you a great deal of money in veterinary bills because you can make the necessary adjustments to their diet. The closer you are to a raw diet, the longer your dog will live.

If you want a really healthy dog like CJ (see Figure 4-1), we show you how to do it in the following sections.

FIGURE 4-1:
A very
healthy dog.

Deciphering dog food labels

On the back of every dog food package is information that helps you decide which food is right for your dog. The information lists the ingredients in order of weight, in descending order. The package contains the guaranteed analysis for crude protein, fat, fiber, and moisture, and often calcium, phosphorus, and magnesium ratios. The label also may state that the food is nutritionally complete or provides 100 percent nutrition for the dog. To make this claim, the food must meet the nutrient requirements of the Association of American Feed Control Officers (AAFCO) — a guarantee that some form of testing, anywhere from two to six weeks, has been done on the product.

By law, the heaviest and largest amount of whichever ingredient contained in the food must be listed first. By looking at the list of ingredients, you can easily discover the protein's origin. For example, if the first five ingredients listed come from four grains, the majority of the protein in that food comes from grains. The more grains in a dog food, the cheaper it is to produce. We wonder what Buddy — the carnivore — thinks of such a food.

Make sure that you carefully read the labels of the dog food and do some research. Don't allow the visual on the package or the perception of certain ingredients determine your overall purchasing decision.

Look for a food that has two or three animal proteins in the first five ingredients — or better yet, one that lists animal protein as its first two or three ingredients. Check out foods that are listed for all growth stages or that are specifically designed for puppies. For more information on which are the best foods for each growth stage, go to www.dogfoodadvisor.com. This site, run by a well-respected nonprofit, keeps a list of current recalls from manufacturers not only for dog food but for dog treats as well.

Different types of meat have different levels of protein, with beef being low and chicken and fish being high in protein. Lamb is in the middle. Venison has the highest protein content and should be fed sparingly. Feeding Buddy a food too high in protein is as dangerous as feeding a diet too low in protein. Long-term use of a high-protein food can damage the kidneys. We recommend beef-based foods for most dogs as a maintenance diet, chicken-based food for dogs that have had surgery or are healing from some disease, and lamb-based food if your dog doesn't like beef. Fish-based foods are too high in protein for regular use and make the kidneys work too hard.

Most pet foods use similar formulas and are allowed to have no more than 1 percent salt in their formulas, which makes salt a convenient marker of quantity. Read the list of ingredients on the bag you're choosing and find salt. Anything that follows salt is basically found in minuscule amounts in the product. Those beautiful pictures on the bag of expensive ingredients, organic ingredients, and GMO-free ingredients actually fall almost 5 to 25 ingredients past the salt divider. The promise of cranberries, along with images of blueberries, apples, and duck, which took up more than half the front of the bag, was deliberately misleading. The reality was that the amount of those four ingredients together most likely equals the size of a single blueberry. If you want to give your pet cranberries, then go buy some that are fresh and locally grown and add them to your dog's food occasionally.

A dog food company also must list its name and address and give its telephone number, plus provide the date of manufacture, the weight of the product in the package, and the life stage for which the food is intended. The *life stage* can be puppy, maintenance, adult, performance, old age, or lite food for overweight dogs. Some breed-specific foods are now popular, including Labrador food, Dachshund food, and so on. Some foods are designed specifically for those dogs with health-related issues, such as hip dysplasia. Organic and natural kibbles also are available.

Evaluating Buddy's current food

The following is a quick checklist to help you determine whether Buddy is getting what they need from the current food you're feeding. Note that for each item Buddy is the source of your information:

>> They don't want to eat the food.

>> They have large, voluminous stools that smell awful.

>> They have gas.

>> Their teeth get dirty and brown.

>> Their breath smells.

>> They burp a lot.

>> They constantly shed.

>> They have a dull coat.

>> They smell like a dog.

>> They have frequent diarrhea or vomiting.

>> They are prone to ear and skin infections.

>> They have no energy or are hyperactive.

>> They easily pick up fleas and ticks.

>> They must be wormed frequently.

REMEMBER

All these conditions happen occasionally with any dog — but only occasionally. When several of the items on the list occur frequently or continuously, you need to find out why.

Understanding the Nutrients Your Dog Needs

Since the 2008 pet food recall, pet owners have become more concerned about the ingredients in their pets' food, and their demands for greater quality have been answered in the marketplace. The cliché "garbage in, garbage out" applies with terrifying validity.

Like yours, your dog's body consists of cells — a lot of them. Each cell needs 45 nutrients to function properly. The cells need the following nutrients:

>> Protein

>> Carbohydrates

>> Fat

>> Vitamins

>> Minerals

>> Water

All these nutrients need to be in the correct proportion for the necessary chemical reactions of digestion, absorption, transportation, and elimination to occur. If the cells are going to be able to continue to live, the exact composition of the body fluids that bathe the outside of the cells needs to be controlled from moment to moment, day by day, with no more than a few percentage points variation. So, feeding a balanced diet daily is critical for Buddy's overall health. To find out whether the diet you're feeding is balanced, consider visiting your veterinarian for a blood test (chem screen and complete blood count). This blood test will reveal whether Buddy is in balance.

These preceding nutrients are the fuel that's converted into energy. Energy produces heat, and the amount of heat your dog produces determines their ability to control their body temperature. Everything your dog does, from running and playing to working and living a long and healthy life, is determined by the fuel you provide and the energy it produces.

The term *calorie* is used to measure energy in food. Optimally, every dog will eat the quantity of food they need to meet their caloric needs. The food you feed must provide the appropriate number of calories so that your dog's body can

>> Produce energy to grow correctly

>> Maintain health during adulthood

>> Reproduce

>> Grow into a quality old age

In the following sections, we start off by discussing a puppy's special nutritional needs, and then we move on to the nutritional needs of all dogs during their adult life. For information on older dogs (8 years old and older), see Chapter 20.

Meeting a puppy's nutritional needs

In contrast to humans, dogs grow *fast.* During the first 7 months of Buddy's life, their birth weight increases anywhere from 15 to 40 times, depending on the breed. By 1 year of age, their birth weight increases 60 times, and their skeletal development is almost complete. For strength and proper growth to occur, they need the right food. They also need twice the amount of food as an adult does while they're growing, especially during growth spurts. Nutritional deficiencies at an early age, even for short periods, can cause problems later. Some of the larger breeds continue to grow until they're 4 years of age.

The most critical period for a puppy is between 2 and 7 months, which is the time of maximum growth. Their little body is being severely stressed as their puppy teeth drop out and their adult teeth come in. Their adult coat also comes in at this time. They're growing like a weed, and at the same time their body is being assaulted with vaccines. During this time of growth, Buddy needs the right food so that their immune system can cope with all these demands and onslaughts.

Puppy foods contain more protein than adult or maintenance foods. Manufacturers know that puppies need more protein for growth. Nonetheless, you still need to know the source of the protein — that is, animal or plant. These foods also must be carefully balanced with calcium, phosphorus, and magnesium. If you choose carefully, you can select a food that's suitable for a growing puppy (see Figure 4-2) as well as for an adult dog.

FIGURE 4-2:
Choose a food that can be fed in all life stages.

REMEMBER

If you're raising a giant-breed puppy (one that will mature to weigh more than 75 pounds), your choices are limited because the dog food companies have conducted little to no research on how to successfully raise these larger dogs. The research that has been done was on dogs weighing 25 to 75 pounds at maturity. In many dog foods, the ratio of calcium, phosphorus, and magnesium is insufficient in relationship to the protein content. So, you'll often hear breeders of these large dogs tell their puppy owners to buy adult foods for their pups to make them grow more slowly. But this is a double-edged sword. Pups of these breeds don't get the amount of protein they need to develop correctly, and this malnutrition often leads to structural problems early in life. Adding some fresh raw meat such as a quarter-cup of ground beef and some broccoli twice a day for a 50-pound dog is a great way to improve kibble and prevent cancer.

After you've selected a food for young Buddy on the basis of its protein percentage, your job isn't quite done yet. You also must check the items we discuss in the following sections, which apply to both puppies and adults.

Keeping your dog's diet rich in protein

Your dog is scientifically categorized as a carnivore by the shape of their teeth. They aren't vegetarian. They need meat to be healthy and to maintain their proper protein levels. Their teeth are quite different from yours — they're made for ripping and tearing meat. Also, digestion starts in the stomach, not in the mouth as does a human. All the enzymes in their system are geared toward breaking down meat and raw foods.

The dog food packages tell you how much protein is in a specific food. The amount of protein is important, but the source of that protein is even more important. The manufacturer has choices as to what kind of protein to put into the food. The percentage of protein on the package generally is a combination of proteins found in plants or grains, such as corn, wheat, soy, and rice, plus an animal protein, such as chicken, beef, or lamb.

REMEMBER

The activity level of your dog is likely to correspond with the amount of animal protein they need in their diet. The majority of the Working breeds, Sporting breeds, Toys, and Terriers need a higher level of animal protein in their diets. For instance, the busy little Jack Russell is apt to need more animal protein than a pooch that spends their time lying around the house.

TECHNICAL STUFF

Amino acid is the name given to the building blocks of protein. When amino acids are heated, they're partially destroyed. All dry and canned commercial dog food is heated in the manufacturing process. So, commercial food contains protein that's chemically changed by heat and therefore deficient in amino acids. We show you how to compensate for that in the "Making Choices about How to Feed Buddy" section later in this chapter. The freeze-dried, frozen, and dehydrated diets provide protein that's in a more natural form.

Going easy on the carbohydrates

Your dog needs the carbohydrates found in grains and most root vegetables for proper digestion. The digestive process first breaks down carbohydrates into starch and then into simple sugars and glucose, which are necessary for energy and proper functioning of the brain. Buddy also needs carbohydrates for stool formation and correct functioning of the thyroid gland.

ANIMAL PROTEIN: GETTING TO KNOW THE SIGNS OF DEFICIENCY AND EXCESS

The signs of a deficiency and an excess of protein (or any nutrient for that matter) are almost identical. In other words, both too much and too little protein have the same symptoms. When Buddy doesn't get enough protein or eats a food that's too high in animal protein, one or more of the following may occur:

- Aggression
- Chronic skin and/or ear infections
- Compromised reproductive system, heart, kidney, liver, bladder, and thyroid and adrenal glands
- Excessive shedding and poor, dull coat quality
- Gastrointestinal upsets, vomiting, or diarrhea
- Impaired ability to heal from wounds or surgery, such as spaying and neutering
- Kidney problems
- Lack of pigmentation
- Poor appetite
- Some kind of epilepsy or cancers
- Spinning or tail chasing
- Timidity
- Weakened immune system that can't properly tolerate vaccines

This is only a short list of the more common symptoms associated with animal protein deficiencies or excesses. That's why we suggest getting bloodwork done to make sure that Buddy is in balance before changing their diet or adding supplements.

Dogs don't need many carbohydrates to be healthy, however. A diet low in carbohydrates and high in protein is ideal. Oats, barley, wheat, and brown rice are carbohydrates that contain a lot of vitamins and minerals. They also contain protein and fat. Corn is a popular ingredient because of its low cost, but avoid foods that contain corn because those foods are lower quality. Many grain-free foods are on the market, and it's difficult to know whether they're in fact good for your dog. If you want to feed Buddy a grain-free food, make sure that the protein is balanced out with enough root vegetables. Grain-free food has been associated with heart problems in dogs, so be careful and ask your vet to run bloodwork.

Soy is another carbohydrate found in some of the cheaper foods. Soy is high in protein, but it binds other nutrients and makes them unavailable for absorption. We recommend that you stay away from dog foods containing soy.

Carbohydrates must be broken down for the dog to be able to digest them. Dog food companies use a heat process to break them down, and therein lies a problem. The heat process destroys many of the vitamins and minerals contained in the carbohydrates. The question that immediately comes to mind is, "Where do dogs in the wild get the grains and vegetables they need?" The answer is from the intestines of their prey, all neatly predigested.

If you feed raw vegetables to a dog that has only been fed dry kibble, chances are they won't be able to break them down and you'll see them in their stool. Their stomach acid and digestive juices are too weak to digest them. If you want to introduce your dog to a healthier diet by adding fresh vegetables and meat, our suggestion is to first lightly cook them, and then over a week, cook them less and less until the fresh foods are eaten raw. If you still see vegetables in the stool, consider keeping Buddy on lightly cooked vegetables. Doing so allows their stomach acid to come back to the proper pH for digestion.

Knowing the value of fats — in moderation

Fat is either *saturated* or *polyunsaturated,* and your dog needs both. Saturated fat (omega-3) comes from animal sources, and polyunsaturated fat (omega-6) comes from vegetable sources. Together they supply the essential fatty acids (EFA) necessary to maintain good health. Look for a dog food that contains both animal and vegetable oils.

REMEMBER

In the manufacturing of the majority of kibbled dog foods, fat is sprayed on as the last ingredient. Fat makes the dog food palatable, like potato chips and French fries. This fat often is used by fast-food restaurants first and collected by the dog food manufacturer to spray onto dog food to make even poor-quality food taste good. Fat goes rancid quickly, which causes all sorts of health problems. Buy in small quantities and keep what you aren't using in the refrigerator. Don't leave opened kibble at room temperature. After it's exposed to air, kibble loses what little nutrients are left after cooking.

Saturated fat is used for energy. So, for dogs who get a great deal of exercise or participate in competitive events, the food they eat needs to contain 20 percent animal fat.

Not enough animal fat in your dog's diet can create

>> Cell damage

>> Dry skin

>> Growth deficits

>> Heart problems

>> Lack of energy

On the other hand, too much animal fat in the diet creates

>> Cancer of the colon and rectum

>> Mammary gland tumors

>> Obesity

Polyunsaturated fat is found in vegetable sources such as flaxseed oil, safflower oil, sunflower oil, wheat germ oil, olive oil, and corn oil. Your dog needs polyunsaturated fat for a healthy coat and skin. Lack of polyunsaturated fat in your dog's diet can cause

>> Coarse, dry coat

>> Extreme itching and scratching

>> Horny skin growths

>> Improper growth

>> Poor blood clotting

>> Skin lesions on the belly, on the inside of the back legs, and between the shoulder blades

>> Skin ulcerations and infections

>> Thickened areas of skin

REMEMBER

Linoleic acid is one of the three essential fatty acids that have to be provided daily in your dog's food. Safflower, sunflower, and flaxseed oil provide the best source of this acid and are the least allergenic. Flaxseed oil is fragile and can become rancid quickly if not stored correctly, however. These oils are better than corn oil or olive oil that contain only a tiny amount of linoleic acid. We advise refrigeration after the oil has been opened.

Ensuring that your dog's diet is fortified with vitamins and minerals

Your dog needs vitamins and minerals in their food to release the nutrients and enzymes from the ingested food so that their body can break down food and absorb its nutrients.

We called dog food manufacturers that produce kibble to ask them about their source of vitamins and minerals and how they protected them against destruction from the heat process. We were astonished by their responses. They acknowledged awareness of the problem and said that to overcome it, they added more vitamins to the food to make up the difference. Of course, doing so is nonsense. If vitamins are destroyed by heat, it doesn't make any difference how much you put in the food. They'll still be destroyed.

We also discovered that most of the finished products weren't tested as to their vitamin and mineral content after being made. This lack of testing also applies to many of the raw and frozen diets in the marketplace. In other words, vitamins and minerals go into the food, but what actually reaches your dog seems as much a mystery to some of the manufacturers as it is to us.

REMEMBER

Two types of vitamins exist:

>> **Water-soluble:** Vitamins B and C, which are water-soluble, are necessary for the breakdown of protein and many other chemical processes in the body. Any excess is filtered through the kidneys and urinated out between four to eight hours after ingestion. For this reason, these vitamins must be present in each meal.

>> **Fat-soluble:** Vitamins A, D, E, and K are fat-soluble and stored in the fatty tissues of the body and the liver.

Your dog needs both types of vitamins. Your dog's overall health is dependent on the availability of both vitamins and minerals in a usable form. So, you need to add these to any kind of commercial kibble, to canned food, and to some of the frozen and raw diets.

Minerals make up less than 2 percent of any formulated diet, and yet they're the most critical of nutrients. The minerals are needed to

>> Correctly compose body fluids

>> Form blood and bones

>> Promote a healthy nervous system

>> Function as coenzymes together with vitamins

Although your dog can manufacture some vitamins on their own, they aren't able to make minerals. As a result, you need to add them to their diet with a product like the balanced, all-in-one supplement, Endurance. Trying to supplement your dog's food by using individual vitamins and minerals isn't a good idea. To do supplement properly, you would need to have a lot of experience in clinical nutrition.

Vitamins and minerals begin to break down when you open a bag of dog food and expose the food to the elements. So, make sure you close the food tightly and keep it away from light. Doing so helps to retain the quality of the contents. (Vitamins B and C are particularly sensitive to exposure.)

Don't forget to quench their thirst: Keeping fresh water around

Water is the most necessary ingredient for dogs. They need it on a daily basis. If a dog has adequate water, they can live for three weeks without food, but they can live only a few days without water. Your dog uses water for the digestive processes, for breaking down and absorbing nutrients, and for maintaining their body temperature. Water helps to transport toxic substances out of the body through the eliminative organs. Water also keeps the acid levels of the blood constant.

Make sure that your dog has access to fresh water in a clean bowl at all times. The exception is when the puppy is being housetrained. During that time, you need to limit access to water after 8 p.m. so that the puppy can last through the night without having to go out. Use a heavy grade stainless steel or glass bowl — they keep the water fresh. Some ceramic bowls can leach lead out into the water.

Do you know that the dog's drinking bowl is the third most germ-laden place in the house after the toilet bowl and the kitchen sink? Merely topping up the water level does nothing to control harmful bacteria or even toxins that can be lurking in the water. Not only are these bugs unpleasant, but they also can cause illness in people, especially those with weak immune systems. Wash your dog's bowl every day. Rinse them under running water and either hand-wash in hot soapy water or put them on the top rack of the dishwasher. Use a stainless steel or glass bowl for food and drink and stay away from plastics and ceramics.

The kind of food you feed Buddy determines how much water they need. For example, kibble contains about 10 percent moisture, so your dog needs about a quart of water for every pound of food they eat. A dog fed only canned food, which is around 78 percent moisture, needs considerably less water. If fed raw foods, a dog may drink less than a cup of water a day because the food contains sufficient water.

If you store your dog's food in a container different from the original bag, wash the container when it empties and before you add a new bag of food to replace what was eaten.

Paying close attention to preservatives

Dog food manufacturers have choices on how to preserve the fat in food to prevent it from becoming rancid. They can use the chemicals BHA, BHT, ethoxyquin, or propyl gallate. If a fat is preserved with these chemicals, it has a long shelf life and isn't significantly affected by heat and light. Even so, many dog owners prefer not to feed these chemicals to their dogs, especially ethoxyquin, which has been associated with chronic degenerative diseases, allergies, arthritis, and shortened life spans to name a few.

A manufacturer also can use natural preservatives, such as vitamins C and E and rosemary extract. Vitamin E is listed on packages as *tocopherol.* Most of the newer foods use these natural preservatives. The downside to natural preservatives is a shorter shelf life — no more than three to four months (provided that the food is stored in a cool, dark place around 40 degrees, refrigerated or frozen).

Making Choices about How to Feed Buddy

You have several options for feeding Buddy — from using commercial dry food (or beefing up a commercial kibble diet) to using the natural and raw diets to making your own. All the options have their pros and cons, so only you can decide which options are best for your lifestyle and comfort level. The following sections explain each option.

Feeding a dog twice a day is the most efficient way to feed them. And always be sure to have fresh water available. We suggest feeding at 7 a.m. and 6 to 7 p.m. We suggest feeding breakfast at 7 a.m. and dinner between 6 and 7 p.m. Feeding dinner earlier in the day may result in too much time between meals. As a result, some dogs vomit yellow bile first thing in the morning. If you have to feed earlier, give Buddy some small biscuits before bedtime.

Feeding Buddy commercial dry food

Your first option is, of course, feeding Buddy a commercial dry kibble diet that you buy at the pet store or grocery store. Dry kibble has been the staple of the dog food market, and now many of the natural or organic foods on the market are challenging it. You have a huge variety from which to choose, but be aware that the latest findings on feeding only kibble to your dogs. Research has shown a 50 percent rate of cancer in all dogs worldwide who eat dry kibble only. The carbohydrates in dry kibble break down in the body to sugar, which fuels cancer. Most dry and almost all prescription diets have more than 50 percent carbohydrates and therefore more than 50 percent sugar. Look for a food that has around 15 percent carbohydrates, which is ideal.

REMEMBER

If Buddy doesn't eat the amount recommended on the package for their weight, they're not getting the minimum daily requirement of known nutrients that are necessary on a daily basis for good health. If Buddy is turning up their nose at their food, we recommend that you change their food to something they're more tempted to eat. If you can't find a dry kibble that works for them, try one of the other options in this chapter.

The most important information to know is that you must choose a kibble that lists two to three meat-based ingredients (animal proteins) in the first five ingredients on the label (see the earlier section, "Deciphering dog food labels" for the basics of reading a label). This is true for dogs in all life stages, including overweight and less active dogs. You'll find foods that advertise "grain free," which isn't necessarily a good thing (see the earlier section "Going easy on the carbohydrates"). Select a food that contains some grain (preferably oats, barley, wheat, or brown rice or one that has a large number of root vegetables), up to 25 percent of the total ingredients.

REMEMBER

You want to choose a kibble that has 26 to 34 percent protein in it. When reading labels, you'll see that the levels of protein for dry kibble vary from 16 to 47 percent. Some of the newer brands of kibble have far too much protein in them, and dog owners are now seeing the result of long-term feeding of this food in the form of kidney problems because the kidneys get overworked trying to break down the protein. Kibbles that are too low in protein, often advertised for senior or overweight dogs, cause your dog to get fat, don't provide enough protein to rebuild cells and maintain health, supply too many grains, and often contain soy, which isn't digestible by dogs.

WARNING

Stay away from foods that contain corn, rye, soy, spinach, bell peppers, tomatoes, trans fats, soy oil, artificial coloring and preservatives, or genetically altered grains. These are cheap ingredients with little, if any, nutritional value. Some actually stop the digestive tract from working properly. Most of these items can't be digested and make Buddy's digestive tract work too hard for no benefit.

Offering beefed-up commercial dry food

If you want to continue feeding your dog a commercial dry kibble diet or one of the grain-free kibbles but you're concerned about the nutrients that they're getting, you can beef up that diet to give them what they need. You can upgrade the diet in one of two ways: with an all-in-one supplement that contains all the food groups of protein, carbohydrates, vitamins, minerals, and oils or with a supplement, plus fresh foods. We explain both options in the following sections.

Enhancing dry kibble with an all-in-one supplement

Feeding commercial kibble enhanced by an all-in-one supplement is the simplest method of adding the nutrients lost in the manufacturing of commercial cooked kibble. To apply this diet, choose a kibble according to our guidelines in the preceding section "Feeding Buddy commercial dry food" and then add a complete supplement to it. Follow the directions on the product as to how much to add.

TIP

The supplement we suggest is called Endurance. It has been clinically proven over many years and is dehydrated. It contains a small amount of liver, natural vitamins, minerals, herbs, dried fruit, fish oil, and ginger. It aids digestion by settling the stomach, reduces shedding, and increases vitality and longevity. Many police forces and professional trainers use it to keep their working dogs in good health.

Adding a supplement plus fresh foods to dry kibble

With this option, you add a supplement such as Endurance plus fresh meats and vegetables to commercial kibble. The quantities of the respective ingredients listed in this section are for a 50-pound dog. You can adjust this recipe according to your dog's weight. This option offers digestive enzymes contained in the raw foods, which aids digestion and cuts down the time the food is in the stomach. The University of Helsinki in Finland recently ran a study on the feeding of both raw food and kibble to see their effect on health, particularly cancer. The study showed that adding fresh food to a dry kibble reduced the chance of cancer by 40 percent. Dogs fed only kibble showed cancer markers in their blood within four months of feeding.

REMEMBER

When calculating the amount for the weight of your dog, err on the side of too little rather than too much. Some dogs eat more than their weight indicates, and some dogs eat less. Your dog's metabolism and the amount of daily exercise they gets determine the amount of food they need. Use common sense and keep all ingredients in proportion.

For this diet, mix the following ingredients and give them to your dog twice a day:

High-quality dry kibble (follow the directions on the package as to how much to feed).

¼ teaspoon Endurance plus 2 tablespoons of water to rehydrate the supplement.

¼ cup of ground beef (80 percent meat to 20 percent fat) lightly cooked for the first week, then cooked less and less over time until it's raw; rotate once a week with canned mackerel or cottage cheese; if your dog prefers chicken, serve it lightly cooked. However, chicken, because of the way the chickens are fed, is one of the most allergenic meats in the marketplace. Try to use organic chicken if you can.

2 tablespoons fresh vegetables (lightly cooked the first week, and then cooked less and less over time until they're raw).

For vegetables, use carrots, parsnips, beets, sweet potatoes, broccoli, leeks, zucchini, squash, kale, cabbage, or any vegetable your dog likes. Chop the vegetables in a food processor or parboil them so that it's easier for your dog to digest the cellulose. Whenever you can, use vegetables that are in season, because they have more nutrients. Vegetables that are shipped long distances contain fewer nutrients. For treats, try chopped carrots, broccoli, parsnips, rutabaga, lettuce, bananas, prunes, cucumbers, or any in-season fruit or vegetable that your dog likes.

WARNING

Stay away from those fruits and vegetables that are commonly sprayed many times with pesticides before they reach the marketplace — for example, apples, bell peppers, carrots, celery, cherries, grapes, kale, lettuce, nectarines, peaches, pears, or strawberries. If you can find organic versions, they should be safe. However, grapes and onions have been associated with gastric problems and even death in dogs that already have underlying disease states. As always, a small amount isn't harmful, but too much can make Buddy feel sick.

REMEMBER

Making major changes in Buddy's diet without keeping track of how these changes affect them isn't a wise idea. They may be out of balance nutritionally, which will have short- and long-term effects on their health. We recommend that you have a blood test done before making a dietary change and again six months later.

Trying a raw food or frozen diet

Our more than 40 years living with dogs have made it abundantly clear that feeding a balanced raw diet — which emulates what Buddy would eat in the wild — is the best and most efficient way to feed a dog. A correctly formulated raw diet provides all the known nutrients in a form the dog can quickly digest and turn into energy. Dogs fed this way tend to live longer and healthier lives than their counterparts who are fed commercial dry foods.

One-third of all dog food sold now in pet stores and in some supermarkets is in the form of natural or raw diets, which include kibble with organic ingredients, frozen food, and dehydrated foods. Some of these foods are complete in themselves, but others suggest adding raw ingredients.

We have always felt that many disease states — including musculoskeletal disorders like hip dysplasia, skin diseases, and gastric upsets — certainly are exacerbated (if not actually caused by) poor nutrition. For more information on feeding raw diets, visit rawfed.com/myths/research.html.

Many natural and raw diets are available for you to choose from, but making the correct choice is even more difficult than comparing commercial dry foods. We apply the same criteria to the examination of natural and raw food diets as we do to commercial dry foods: Both need to be clinically tested and provide a balanced diet for a dog. Diets, especially homemade ones (raw or cooked), that don't meet these criteria can do more damage to your dog than dry dog food.

WARNING

Many of the new raw and frozen diets aren't balanced and haven't had any long-term clinical testing. Some even use ingredients that are known to be canine allergens. Some use indigestible vegetables, and some lack fiber and the correct ratio of nutrients. Other diets suggest feeding raw chicken wings or backs; that sounds easy enough, but it's hardly a balanced diet. Just because a food's ingredients are advertised as human grade, organic, or whatever doesn't mean they're good for your dog. So, clearly you must be cautious when choosing your dog's raw or frozen diet. Write to the manufacturer and ask how many years of clinical testing have been done on a particular diet. You'll be surprised by the answers. Generally testing is done over a six-week period with dogs in a laboratory. One raw food we like is Dr. B's Longevity food, which is available at www.drbslongevity.com/. Formulated by an integrative veterinarian, it has medicinal mushrooms, vegetables, and raw meat. If dogs have difficulty eating after surgery, they usually like this food.

So, are any of the available raw or frozen diets balanced? Of course. Just be vigilant in choosing the correct one for your dog. Read the label to make sure that the diet is completely balanced. If they aren't, read the guidelines as to what you should add to make them complete. Long-term feeding of an unbalanced diet can create a battery of new health problems not seen before in dogs.

TIP

Before changing Buddy's diet, we recommend that you take them to the vet for a baseline blood test. After Buddy has been on their new diet program for six months, have the vet perform another blood test and compare it to the previous one. The follow-up blood test will tell you whether their new diet is an improvement and whether they're in nutritional balance.

A dog's digestive system isn't the same as a human's — it's much shorter and food is processed more quickly. The dog's stomach acid is extremely strong, and in a healthy dog, this acid kills any bacteria that enters the dog's stomach. A sick dog, or a dog switching over to a raw diet from a kibble diet, needs a transition diet to rebuild that stomach acid to the point where it can deal with either E. coli or salmonella.

REMEMBER

Feeding raw meat or raw chicken to a dog can cause digestive upsets if the meat contains high levels of bacteria in the form of E. coli or salmonella. Although a dog that has been fed raw foods for a long time can easily deal with both of these bacteria, a sick dog or a dog that has just been transferred over to a raw diet may experience digestive problems. We suggest that you buy your meat or chicken from a reliable supermarket where the products are for human consumption.

After you follow the transition diet (see the later section "Transferring Buddy to a new diet"), you need to use a simple method of killing bacteria the first time uncooked meat is used. To do so, put the meat or chicken into a sieve in the sink, pour boiling water over it, and cool it before feeding. Doing so kills the bacteria. After taking this step for a couple of weeks, the dog's stomach acid will be strong enough to deal with the bacteria without problems, and you can introduce the raw meat.

Making your own food: Wendy's Natural Diet

Making one's own dog food is hardly a new idea. Every dog alive today can trace its ancestry back to dogs that were raised on homemade diets. The dog food industry, in comparison to dogs themselves, is young — maybe 70 to 80 years old — although canned meat for dogs was sold at the turn of the 20th century. Originally, the commercial foods were made to supplement a homemade diet.

REMEMBER

A homemade diet allows you to tailor make it for your dog's nutritional needs, and it's ideal for all dogs. The drawback to this type of feeding is that you have to gather all the ingredients and make the food.

Many, but not all, present-day dogs are the beneficiaries of poor breeding practices, a lack of understanding of genetics on the part of many breeders, and 30 years of overvaccination and poor nutrition. Because of poor genetics (whether pure bred or a mixed breed), many can't thrive on commercially prepared rations. They exhibit disease states, which often are mistaken for allergies. These disease states can be deficiency diseases caused by feeding cereal-based foods or foods where the fat has turned rancid. Making the food from scratch or taking advantage of the new clinically tested food called Rescue, which is formulated for these dogs, is a viable, available option. Check out www.volharddognutrition. com for more information.

Wendy started making her own dog food almost 40 years ago. Based on the pioneering work of Juliette de Bairacli Levy and the National Science Foundation's guidelines for dog food, her homemade diet was a 12-year labor of love to get the balance required. The results were amazing, as seen by Pavi, a Newfoundland who competed in both agility and obedience competitions until he was almost 12 years old. He garnered more than 20 titles. You can see Pavi in competition in Figure 4-3. The diet increases health and longevity, contains a lot of moisture in the natural ingredients, and produces more manageable stools. Plus, dogs love to eat it. Wendy is still seeing great results today with the newer dehydrated versions of the food. See the next section for more information.

For more information on raising your dog holistically, transferring to a purely Natural Diet, making the diet and storing it, as well as a list of suppliers for ingredients, go to www.volharddognutrition.com. You also can look to the *Holistic Guide for a Healthy Dog*, 2nd Edition, by Wendy Volhard and Kerry Brown, DVM (Howell Book House).

TIP

The easiest way to travel with homemade or NDF2 diets is to make the required number of meals and freeze them in portion-control plastic bags. Keep the bags in a cooler, adding ice every day. You can travel safely up to ten days using this method of packing the food.

FIGURE 4-3:
Pavi, an 11-year-old Newfoundland, in Agility competition.

© *John Wiley & Sons, Inc.*

Using the Natural Diet Foundation (NDF2)

The Natural Diet Foundation, or NDF2, is a dehydrated version of the original homemade Natural Diet. It came about because so many professional dog people asked me to come up with a diet to which they only needed to add one ingredient. These are busy people who train dogs for a living and travel a lot, so they don't have time to shop around for fresh ingredients for their dog food. They all wanted the benefits of feeding naturally but didn't have the time to do it. They also wanted to stay with this diet that had been clinically proven over so many years rather than experimenting with many of the new diets on the market.

So, 20 years ago Wendy worked out the NDF2 diet, which is essentially the same as the original diet but in a dehydrated form. The only ingredients you must add are meat and water. It has been an amazing success story, and she's now seeing 16-year-old dogs, raised from puppies on this food, who are in incredible health and whose structure is outstanding — a necessary trait for dogs being worked or shown.

NDF2 contains all the non-meat ingredients your dog needs for a healthy, vigorous, and long life. It's made every two weeks in small batches with whole human-grade foods and herbs that come from the United States. Overall, this recipe has been clinically tested for more than 40 years. It's a food for all life-stages, from puppies to older dogs. It's also hypoallergenic and contains no genetically modified products.

Transferring Buddy to a new diet

When changing from dry kibbled foods to a higher-grade kibble and supplemented diet as those suggested earlier in the chapter, you must give your dog's system time to get used to the new ingredients. Your dog's intestinal tract needs about 6 to 11 days to be fully able to break down and digest a new diet.

When switching Buddy to a diet that is supplemented with raw foods, use the following transition diet. The transition diet allows time for the internal bacteria to adjust to a change in diet. (Transitioning your dog to a completely raw diet requires a different process. See the earlier section, "Trying a raw food or frozen diet" for more information.)

Here's how to transition your dog to a supplemented dog food diet:

Day 1: Add a small amount of your new food to each of Buddy's meals.

Day 2: Double the amount you fed on Day 1 of the new food and decrease Buddy's old diet by the same amount.

Days 3 through 6: Gradually increase the new diet and decrease the old diet until you have changed them over completely.

REMEMBER

If at any time Buddy has loose stools, their digestive system needs more time to adjust to their new food.

After your dog has been introduced to the new additions in their diet for a couple of weeks, it's time to introduce bones. Once or twice a week, give your dog a bone as a special treat. They love beef (soup) bones, raw chicken necks, chicken feet, and the tips off of chicken wings. If you're not sure about how long these items have been in the supermarket case, douse them with boiling water to kill any bacteria before feeding. One of the benefits of feeding bones is that your dog will have beautiful, pearly white teeth.

When you give your dog a bone, leave them alone (but not unattended) — dogs can get possessive about their bones. It's a special treat, and they want to be in a place to relax and enjoy it. Their crate is the perfect place. It also keeps contained any soggy mess associated with gnawing on their bone. Give Buddy an hour or so to enjoy their bone and then pick it up, refrigerate it, and give it to them the next day. Too much marrow in the bone's center may be a little rich for some dogs to digest all at once.

WARNING

Feeding Buddy too many bones can give them constipation and hard, chalky stools. Only give your dog bones that can't splinter. We recommend you feed bones no more than twice a week.

WHAT ABOUT TABLE SCRAPS?

There's nothing wrong with adding table scraps to Buddy's food, provided they don't exceed 10 percent of their total diet. Many dogs love leftover salad, meat scraps, and veggies. However, you do need to avoid certain foods, particularly those with a high sugar count, such as chocolate (which can be poisonous) and highly salted foods. Also avoid giving raw spinach, an ingredient that is found in so many of the newer raw food diets. It contains oxalic acid that binds calcium and some minerals from being absorbed by the body. Avoid peppers, which are part of the deadly nightshade family, and can be allergenic. Processed human foods also aren't recommended for dogs.

Sizing up supplements

The reality is that if you're feeding correctly, you rarely need supplements of any kind. The nutrients should be in the food; they shouldn't have to be added as extras at high prices. The number of supplements available tells you a lot about the quality of the food on the market. If you're adding a lot of supplements to Buddy's food, it's time to think of changing to a balanced food that contains these ingredients.

REMEMBER

You occasionally do need supplements. We've sorted through the thousands of products on the shelves and can recommend some that are known to work (we've used them ourselves, and our students have had good results as well). We mention a few supplements in the following health section, and we go into more detail regarding the supplements that we recommend in Chapter 20, which focuses on older dogs. As dogs get older, they need supplementation.

Exploring Common Health Issues That Affect Behavior and Training

A dog that's fed correctly and given enough exercise and mental stimulation rarely exhibits behavior problems. They deal well with stress, hardly ever get sick, and keep they youthful characteristics into their teens. Also, a dog that's fed properly and is in good health, ages well and has few to no gray hairs. In fact, it's often difficult to tell this dog's age.

When your dog doesn't feel quite right, they won't act quite right. When they don't feel well, they don't have the ability to learn or retain information. Training them can be perplexing because you've properly taught a sequence of an exercise and yet they show no knowledge of what you've taught. Not feeling well can manifest itself in many ways, but you as their owner know that they aren't acting as they did before. In the following sections we provide information on some common health issues that affect behavior and training. We also discuss some supplements that may help Buddy feel better. Checking with their veterinarian is also a wise decision if you notice something unusual.

REMEMBER

Prevention is the best policy when it comes to your dog's health. Here are some things you can do to prevent health problems later on and have a long and happy training career with Buddy:

>> **Visit your veterinarian annually.** When you take Buddy to the vet, choose to have titers done (rather than vaccinations) to see Buddy's level of protection

against parvovirus, distemper, and Lyme disease. (We explain what titers are in the later section "Looking at the problems with overvaccinating.") At the same time, ask your vet to perform blood work (a chem scan, a complete blood count, and a thyroid [T4]) to see whether Buddy is in nutritional balance and whether all of their organ systems are working properly. Signs of problems can show up on bloodwork long before physical manifestations appear.

REMEMBER

Take Buddy on their birthday the first thing in the morning for their blood test. For accurate results Buddy needs to have fasted overnight on a 12-hour fast. Subsequent testing over the next years, always taken at the same time of day, allows you to see how Buddy's body is aging. Take in a fecal sample at least twice a year.

>> **Provide an arthritis formula if necessary.** If your puppy's structure isn't perfect or if they're in performance events of any kind, consider using an arthritis formula as a preventative. In the past, these products have been used after the dog was diagnosed with arthritis. Since then, however, research has shown that when structural problems become obvious in the young dog, the use of these products can be helpful in preventing arthritis later in life.

The product we have recommended for years is called Myristin. We have used Myristin successfully with clients' dogs who were experiencing cruciate ligament problems as well as loose shoulders, loose hock joints, poor hips, and so on. This product works for 90 percent of dogs. The other 10 percent require a different form of supplement. We recommend System Saver, which is an anti-inflammatory and works to build up the immune system. See www.volharddognutrition.com for more information on these products.

>> **Keep their teeth healthy.** Dirty teeth can cause harmful bacteria buildup resulting in gingivitis, loose teeth, and bacterial infection of the gums. The bacteria drain into the system via the stomach and can, over a period of time, cause heart ailments. Clean teeth also prevent doggy breath. To keep teeth clean, feed the correct diet with bones a couple of days a week. Or you can clean Buddy's teeth with a toothbrush and dog toothpaste or cleaning gel. We recommend Petzlife products, available through www.petzlife.com.

>> **Choose an appropriate food for your dog.** Feeding the correct food helps to prevent internal and external parasites. External parasites, like fleas and ticks, are less likely to be attracted to a dog that's fed correctly, because their skin has a correct pH that deters external parasites. The acid/alkaline balance of their digestive tract makes a poor environment for internal worms to survive. Check out the earlier section "Making Choices about How to Feed Buddy" for more information.

Here comes that needle again: Examining vaccination issues

Giving vaccines is a necessary part of owning a dog. What part of the United States or Canada you live in can play a role in which vaccines your vet suggests. Here are some of the more common vaccines:

>> **Bordetella:** Also known as *kennel cough,* many boarding kennels require this vaccine before they'll accept a dog, although the vaccine is a regional thing.

>> **Distemper:** This is a core vaccine.

>> **Hepatitis:** This is also a core vaccine.

>> **Leptospirosis:** This one isn't advised unless there is a local outbreak.

>> **Lyme disease:** We don't advise this vaccine because it has too many side effects.

>> **Parvovirus:** This is a core vaccine.

>> **Rabies:** Every county in the United States has a rabies vaccine requirement. The rabies vaccine is the only mandatory one.

Except for rabies these vaccines are voluntary. Just make sure that your veterinarian doesn't give multiple vaccines at the same time. Whether you vaccinate your dog is your choice. If you choose to, you can refuse them and/or ask for titers instead. This way you can make an informed decision.

Vaccines can disrupt a training program for your dog by making them feel unwell for a few days after they have been given. Sometimes vaccines interrupt the ability of the dog to do scent work like tracking or scent articles in obedience competition. The effects can last from three weeks to nine months. Some breeds of dogs have adverse reactions to vaccines and can experience swollen joints (as Great Danes can do with the rabies vaccine), some temporary paralysis (such as German Shepherds and Rottweilers from the parvovirus vaccine), seizures (such as Labradors from the rabies vaccine), and so on. Make a wise decision for you and your dog after you have researched all the facts.

To help you decide what is correct for your dog, check out *What Vets Don't Tell You About Vaccines* by Catherine O'Driscoll (Abbeywood Publishing). She did a worldwide study of vaccines and reports of the long-term effects of overvaccinating. She charts diseases associated with overvaccinating and quotes the noted authorities in the United States, including Jean Dodds, DVM, and

Ronald Schultz, MD, DVM, of the University of Wisconsin, on the current vaccine protocols recommended. For more information on O'Driscoll and her research, visit www.canine-health-concern.org.uk.

Looking at the problems with overvaccinating

During the past 30 years, dog owners have seen a steady increase in the number of vaccinations that dogs receive each year. Sadly, instead of improving the dogs' health and longevity, the practice has frequently had the opposite effect.

Overvaccinating has created unintended and undesirable reactions to vaccinations, which result in *vaccinosis,* the term used to describe those undesirable reactions. The reactions can range from none to constant ear infections, licking feet, skin problems, paralysis, and even death. And they may occur as a result of one vaccine, several vaccines given at the same time, or repeated vaccinations given in a relatively short time frame.

WARNING

Too many vaccinations too close together can cause a puppy's immune system to break down and can result in serious health problems. We aren't against vaccinations, but we're against random, repetitive, routine, and completely unnecessary vaccinations. Thank goodness, in the last few years vaccine protocols have changed and most up-to-date veterinarians are using vaccines more sparingly.

For instance, one of our students who had a young 16-week-old Newfoundland puppy took her dog to the veterinarian for booster vaccinations. The puppy received eight vaccinations all at the same time including rabies. By the time she got home her dog was completely paralyzed, and after four months of treatment ranging from acupuncture, homeopathy, and ozone, the paralysis, although improved, had not enabled her to walk and they had to be put down. Veterinary medicine had nothing to offer. Some breeds of dogs are prone to vaccine reactions. If this happens to your dog, ask your veterinarian for a certificate that exempts that dog from further shots.

Search online for your breed of dog and find out if your dog is prone to vaccination reactions.

Where do annual booster shots fit into this picture? Actually, they don't. According to Kirk's *Current Veterinary Therapy* XI-205 (W.B. Saunders Co.) — the textbook used for many years by veterinary schools — no scientific basis or immunological reason necessitates annual revaccinations. Immunity to viruses can last for many years — even for a dog's lifetime.

REMEMBER

When your dog already carries the antibodies against a particular virus, a revaccination can wreak havoc with their immune system. The many adverse reactions to unnecessary vaccinations have caused breeders, dog owners, and vets to begin questioning the need for boosters and to become more cautious in the way vaccines are administered. By law, your dog only needs a rabies vaccination and the rabies booster only every three years. Don't ever give your dog a rabies shot before they're 6 months of age.

Some breeds of dogs have extreme — even fatal — reactions to vaccines. Others develop odd behaviors and reactions such as the following:

>> Aggression

>> Anaphylactic shock

>> Anxiety or fear

>> Epilepsy and other seizure disorders

>> Excessive licking

>> Insomnia

>> Separation anxiety

>> Snapping at imaginary flies

>> Swelling of the whole body, cutting off air supply

WARNING

A rabies vaccine given in conjunction with other vaccines can be responsible for aggression, epilepsy, and other seizure disorders. Labradors seems to be especially vulnerable.

How do you know if your dog will have a reaction to a vaccine? You don't, and that's the problem. Fortunately, you don't have to take the chance. The dog should get a titer test, a blood test that tells you whether Buddy has *antibodies* (or resistance) to the diseases for which they're already been vaccinated. If they have a high *titer*, or level of antibodies, to the disease, you don't need to have them revaccinated. Titering is becoming a more acceptable alternative to revaccinations. (See the next section for information on whether businesses accept titering in place of revaccination.) Titer your dog in late spring or early summer when the viruses are active. Titering in the winter doesn't give you the correct information.

Whether you're rescuing a dog from the local humane society, adopting an "off-the-track" Greyhound, or buying a puppy from a pet store, be aware that the dog will probably have been vaccinated before you get them. Humane societies usually give you the dates when your rescue dog was vaccinated. Taking them to your veterinarian for a once-over health check is a good idea, but don't vaccinate again. Either titer the dog in the next six months or wait another year and titer before vaccinating, if necessary. However, remember that if your dog has reacted in the past to vaccination, the next time they're vaccinated, the reaction will be worse. So be careful! See how to deal with adverse reactions in the later section "Quelling fear, anxiety, and other conditions with homeopathy."

Vaccinating for boarding or schooling

Sometimes you must vaccinate your dog. Many boarding kennels, obedience schools, and dog parks, for example, require proof of vaccination. However, titers are becoming more acceptable with these businesses and schools. The Pet Care Services Association (formerly known as the American Boarding Kennel Association) considers titers acceptable. Before you board your dog at a member kennel, ask about titers.

TIP

Before you vaccinate, call any facilities to which you may take your dog. If you do need to vaccinate, remember that it takes your dog three weeks to build immunity.

Because not everything's cut and dried in this world, suppose that Buddy is one of those dogs who have adverse side effects from vaccinations, and as a result, you adamantly refuse to vaccinate them. But now you can't find a boarding kennel that will honor your wishes. What then? Well, you're going to have to find someone to come in and dog sit for you while you're away. If you can't find a reliable local pet sitter, try Pet Sitters International (www.petsit.com), which is an international organization that has trained pet sitters in most areas of the United States and Canada. The local obedience organization also may be able to help you.

WARNING

Vaccinating a healthy dog stresses their immune system, whether you see a reaction or not. Boarding a dog also is stressful — even at the nicest boarding kennels. Under stress, Buddy is vulnerable to picking up disease. It can affect their training and their ability to handle stress, especially at dog shows. If you must vaccinate, do it at least three weeks before kenneling.

Using flea and tick medications

Flea and tick medications can affect Buddy's health and behavior in numerous ways. After using them, Buddy can become lethargic or limp or they can vomit or have loose stools, seizures, and reoccurring skin problems.

In fact, any time you use chemicals with Buddy, you're running the risk of side effects. Your goal is to raise them without using anything but natural products. Some medications can affect the balance of bacteria in the gut. It takes about three weeks after finishing the medication for the gut flora to be re-established. To fasten the process, you can use a tablespoon of fermented veggies (such as sauerkraut) in their food twice a day for a 50-pound dog. For a toy breed, use just a teaspoon.

Ask yourself if you need to use flea and tick medications at all. If you live in the southern part of the United States, you probably need to use some form of prevention. Here are three lines of defense other than the traditional flea and tick medications:

>> **Make sure your dog eats a proper diet.** A proper diet is a deterrent because the skin's pH isn't attractive to parasites.

>> **Use an herbal spray that doesn't have unwanted side effects.** We recommend Wondercide, which is available online. This product is all natural and protects your pet from mosquitoes, which in turn protects them from heartworm.

>> **Make your own natural solution.** Mix a solution of apple cider vinegar and water (half and half), put it into a spray bottle, and spray Buddy before they go for walks or to the dog park. This deterrent is effective, and you get used to the side effect of having Buddy smell like salad dressing.

Uncovering the rise in doggy hypothyroidism

Providing poor nutrition, overvaccinating, and neutering or spaying a puppy too early can cause a disease called hypothyroidism or suppression of the thyroid gland. *Hypothyroidism* refers to an underactive thyroid, which causes physical as well as behavioral abnormalities. Successfully training a dog who has hypothyroidism is difficult. When a dog has hypothyroidism, their ability to learn and retain information is severely curtailed. This lack of learning ability is frustrating for both dog and handler. Very few veterinarians have that much knowledge about this disease, which is perhaps the most common disease in dogs.

Rarely seen until the 1970s, this condition has become more prevalent because the way of managing dogs has changed in the last 50 years. Fewer homemade or raw diets and overvaccination are mainly the cause. More than 50 percent of young dogs today show some signs of hypothyroidism. As the dog ages, the percentage increases. When you take Buddy for their yearly checkup, have your veterinarian add a thyroid test to their blood draw.

The thyroid gland is part of the endocrine gland system. This system controls not only many of the hormones in the body, but it also controls the brain's ability to deal with stress. It certainly affects their behavior. In a study done at the University of Southampton in England, it was found that more than 50 percent of dogs turned over to a humane society because of aggression problems were suffering from hypothyroidism.

The physical manifestations of hypothyroidism can show from as young as 5 months of age onward. This disease is most commonly diagnosed at around 4 years of age, but dogs 8 years and older also have hypothyroidism, which correlates to the aging process. Dogs with this disease may show the following signs:

>> Heart disorders

>> Lack of control over body temperature — the dog is either too cold or too hot under otherwise normal conditions

>> Oily, smelly, scaly skin and blackened skin on the belly and under the arms

>> Some kinds of paralysis

>> Seizures

>> Thinning of the hair on each side of the body, usually around the rib cage and shoulders, on the tail and inside the back legs (see Figure 4-4)

>> Unexplained weight gain (see Figure 4-5)

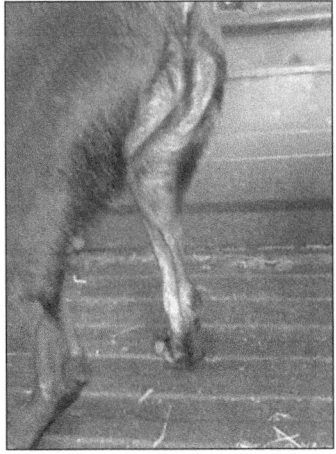

FIGURE 4-4:
Thinning hair due to hypothyroidism.

© John Wiley & Sons, Inc.

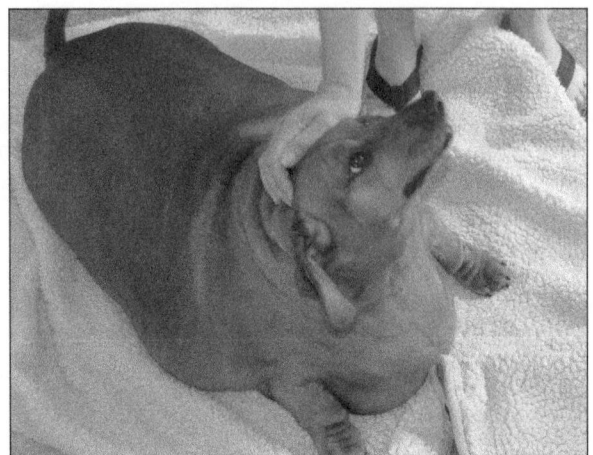

FIGURE 4-5:
Obesity due to
hypothyroidism.

© John Wiley & Sons, Inc.

Behavioral manifestations of hypothyroidism may include

>> Unexplained aggression toward people or other dogs

>> Being picked on by other dogs

>> Difficulty learning

>> Fear and anxiety, including separation anxiety and fear of thunderstorms

>> *Lick granulomas,* where the dog licks constantly at one spot, usually on a leg, and goes down to the bone

>> Obsessive-compulsive behavior, such as spinning and extreme hyperactivity

>> Overreaction to stressful situations

>> Self-mutilation

TIP

How can you tell if Buddy has a thyroid-related problem? If they're exhibiting any of the physical signs or behaviors listed in this section, make an appointment with your vet as soon as possible. This condition often is overlooked by veterinarians as was the case shown in Figure 4-4. If you want to reassure yourself that Buddy doesn't have hypothyroidism, ask your vet to do a blood test and ask for a complete thyroid panel. The results can tell you whether Buddy needs medication. All laboratory reports indicate a low and high normal reading for each test done. High readings are uncommon in adult dogs. Low normal readings need to be supplemented with a low dose of thyroid medication.

The bone crusher: "Oh, my aching back"

Performance events, especially agility, are athletic activities for a dog. So you really shouldn't be surprised that various parts of performing dogs' bodies may go out of whack. After all, human athletes have troubles all the time. Because the dogs' performances are affected, many competitors routinely take their dogs in for chiropractic adjustments. Agility competitors have found that it can shave seconds off a dogs' performance if they are in perfect alignment. It makes sense — if the spine is straight, the dog can move more quickly and easily. Even if your dog isn't a performing dog, remember that simply playing ball or Frisbee with Buddy can have the same effect as performance events.

TIP

To keep your dog in tip-top shape, have a chiropractor examine them. Buddy may need an alignment. To find an animal chiropractor in your area, visit the American Holistic Veterinary Medical Associations website at www.ahvma.org.

Quelling fear, anxiety, and other conditions with homeopathy

Many dogs experience fear or anxiety under different conditions. For example, anxiety can occur when Buddy

>> Encounters situations that they perceive as stressful

>> Goes on a trip away from home

>> Has a reaction to a vaccine

>> Senses and experiences thunderstorms

>> Visits the vet

We've been quite successful in dealing with this sort of anxiety with homeopathic remedies. We even carry a small homeopathic emergency kit with us wherever we go, just in case. (We also provide information on anxiety and handling other special situations in Chapter 19.)

Homeopathy relies on the energy of natural substances, that come from plants or minerals. Homeopathic remedies come in pellet, granular, or liquid form. Popular until the discovery of antibiotics in 1928 but used almost exclusively after 1942, homeopathy fell out of favor during the middle of the 20th century. Today, it's enjoying resurgence all over the world, and many vets in Europe are trained both in traditional medicine and homeopathy.

REMEMBER

Because the homeopathic remedies are so diluted, they're safe to use and don't cause side effects. You can find many of these remedies in large supermarkets and health food stores. We suggest the potency of 30c. These remedies most often come in pellet form, and one dose is three pellets fed 15 minutes before or after food.

The following list includes a few common homeopathic remedies and the problems they treat. We find the following remedies helpful and use them frequently:

- » **Aconite:** Fright, anxiety, and fear of thunderstorms
- » **Apis:** Bee stings and any shiny swellings
- » **Arnica:** Bruising from falls and dog bites and recuperation from any operation
- » **Belladonna:** Heat stroke, hot, red ears, and hot spots
- » **Carbo Veg:** Bloating or gas (settles the stomach if used 15 minutes before eating)
- » **Chamomilla:** Vomiting of yellow bile and teething problems
- » **Ferrum Phos:** Stops bleeding
- » **Hydrophobinum (or Lyssin):** Reactions to rabies vaccine
- » **Hypericum:** Stops pain to nerve endings after injury or operations
- » **Ignatia:** Grief, insecurity, stress, or sadness
- » **Ledum:** Tick, insect, or spider bites
- » **Nux Vomica:** Any kind of poisoning; recuperation after anesthesia
- » **Phosphorus:** Sound sensitivity
- » **Rescue Remedy:** Use for stress or trauma. (We always carry it when we travel with our dogs.) Bach Flower Remedy comes in liquid form.
- » **Rhus Tox (poison ivy):** Rheumatism and itchy, oozing rashes
- » **Sulphur:** Skin conditions and mange
- » **Thuja:** Reactions to core vaccines (distemper, parvovirus, and so on)

TIP

Many holistic veterinarians are trained in homeopathy, and you probably can find one in your area without difficulty. To find a holistic vet, go to the American Holistic Veterinary Medical Association's website at `www.ahvma.org/find-a-holistic-veterinarian`.

Treating chronic conditions with acupuncture

Many vets today use acupuncture for a variety of chronic conditions. Acupuncture specializes in putting the body back into balance. Among its many applications, acupuncture is particularly effective with allergies, skin disorders, ear problems, incontinence in old dogs, and the aches and pains that come with age. It also can be effective for structural problems and chronic diseases of major organs, such as the heart, kidneys, liver, lungs, and stomach.

TIP

We advise seeking the help of an acupuncture veterinarian for dogs who are in performance events and for those who are middle-aged or older. Treatments can make an older dog feel like a puppy again. To find a veterinarian in your area who's trained in acupuncture, contact the American Holistic Veterinary Medical Association's website at www.ahvma.org.

IF YOUR DOG GETS POISONED

Here's one resource that you need to have on your fridge door just in case Buddy gets into something they shouldn't have: the Animal Poison Control center. You can call the center for 24-hour emergency information. The center has 20 full-time veterinary toxicologists on-call to work with you on an emergency with your dog. The number is 855-764-7661. For more information, you also can check out www.petpoisonhelpline.com.

Chapter **5**

Gearing Up for Training Success

og training is no different than any other activity — you need the right equipment for the job. Many choices are available to you, and in this chapter, we address the factors that determine what training equipment to use under which circumstances.

As a general rule, undesired behaviors need to be corrected, usually with a collar and leash, to deal with the dog when they do something undesirable on their own, such as chasing a cat. Treats and positive rewards are used to teach desired behaviors that the dog wouldn't do on their own, such as sitting on command. In this chapter we focus on just what you need to help you prepare for training so that you and Buddy are successful.

Just because you have a collar and leash doesn't mean you can use them to train your dog. In Chapter 7 we discuss how a mother dog teaches her puppies to stop doing something she doesn't want them to do. She uses a *correction,* something the puppies perceive as unpleasant, to get them to stop. This unpleasant experience teaches the puppies responsibility for their own behavior. Puppies say to themselves, "If I use my teeth on Mommy, I'll get nailed. If I don't, mommy will lick my face." So, puppies choose not to use their teeth on Mommy. That, at any rate, is the gist of the puppy's thought process.

Teaching your dog responsibility for their own behavior is the key to training. Therefore, the dog must perceive the correction as unpleasant so they can avoid it. If they don't perceive the correction as unpleasant, they have nothing to avoid, and the objectionable behavior continues. Therein lies the importance of the correct training equipment. The degree of correction is the secret sauce. You must use the least amount of "pressure" on the leash and collar to achieve an interruption of the undesirable behavior.

Choosing the Right Training Leash and Collar

The type of training collar and leash you need depends on a number of factors, including the following:

>> Your dog's Personality Profile (see Chapter 2)

>> Your dog's touch sensitivity or threshold of discomfort

>> Your dog's size and weight in relation to your size and weight

>> The equipment's effectiveness to get your dog's attention

>> Your dog's safety

>> Your aptitude for training your dog

REMEMBER

Training isn't a matter of strength but of finesse. For you, Buddy's teacher, it doesn't have to be a heavy aerobic workout. Also, in selecting training equipment, keep in mind the circumstances. A dog's *touch sensitivity,* or threshold of discomfort, increases proportionally with the interest the dog has in what appeals to them (see Chapter 2 for more information about understanding your dog's mind). For example, when you train Buddy in your backyard where there are fewer distractions, a buckle collar may be sufficient to get them to respond. When they're out in the real world and want to chase a squirrel or another dog, you may need to use a training collar to get them to listen to the command given.

We provide info to help you choose the best leash and collar in the following sections.

Deciding on a leash

Leashes come in an assortment of styles, materials, widths, and lengths. The following are the most common materials:

>> **Cotton web:** Cotton web leashes are readily available in pet stores and through catalogs and websites, and they come in a variety of colors and lengths (see Figure 5-1).

>> A good training leash is a 6-foot cotton web leash — it's easy on the hands, easily manipulated, and just the right length. It's also the most economical. For the average-size or larger dog, such as a Labrador, a cotton web leash that's ⅝-inch wide is ideal. For toy dogs, such as a Yorkshire Terrier, a leash that's ¼-inch wide is a good choice.

>> **Nylon:** A nylon leash is another good one for training. Looking a lot like the cotton web leash, the nylon type also is economical and can be easily manipulated, which is an important factor for the training method in this book. However, nylon isn't as easy on your hands as cotton web, especially with larger dogs.

>> **Leather:** Leather leashes also are quite popular, although they're more expensive than cotton web and nylon leashes. They're usually bulkier than cotton web or nylon but don't fold up as nicely in your hand.

>> **Chain:** Chain leashes are cheap but are noisy and awkward. Chain leashes often are used with large dogs, but they're heavy, unwieldy, and hard on the hands. For example, if you wanted to fold the leash neatly into one hand or the other, as required by the training techniques in this book, you wouldn't be able to do so without considerable discomfort. It's definitely not a leash you should use for training Buddy.

>> **Flexi leashes:** They aren't good training leashes because the purpose of the flexi is to allow the dog to pull the leash out of the apparatus that you hold. The flexi is also clumsy to hold, and because the length of the leash varies as you use it, the dog isn't taught to stay with you at a consistent distance as you walk. A flexi leash is usually good for a potty walk at a motel or at night but not for much more.

FIGURE 5-1:
Cotton web leash.

© John Wiley & Sons, Inc.

Selecting a collar

Collars come in a dazzling assortment of styles, colors, and materials. When training your dog, you need two types of collars:

>> **A training collar:** The purpose of a training collar is for you to be able to guide your dog when they're on leash and, if necessary, to check your dog. (A *check* is a quick, crisp tug on the leash, followed by an immediate release of tension, like a check mark, short and done.) A check is used mainly for *abstention training,* which is when you want your dog to stop doing something that they want to do, such as chasing a cat or a jogger. The check creates an unpleasant experience for the dog, which they can avoid by stopping the unwanted behavior (similar to a mother dog snapping at a puppy). Several different types of training collars are available, which we discuss later in this section.

>> **A buckle collar:** When you're not training, your dog should wear a buckle collar with identification attached. The collar can be leather, nylon, or cotton web. Buckle collars come in an assortment of colors and styles and are made of fabric or leather. If your dog weighs more than 50 pounds and hasn't yet been trained, you're better off using a leather collar with a metal clasp — a plastic clasp may break when your dog lunges after a moving object.

Buckle collars aren't meant to be used for training or walking because they don't allow for communication between you and your dog. Your dog can really pull and lean into a buckle collar, which can pull you off your feet. Train your dog first before leashing them to a buckle collar. Buckle collars are ideal for holding your dog's identification.

REMEMBER

You must use these two types of collars correctly. Remove the training collar when you aren't training your dog or when you can't supervise them. And don't try to use a buckle collar to train. For the untrained dog, buckle collars are virtually useless. Picture yourself trying to hang on as a fully-grown Rottweiler decides to take off after a cat. Trying to control that dog with a buckle collar would definitely be a heavy aerobic workout.

We discuss the advantages and disadvantages of different training collars in the following sections.

Nylon snap-around collars

The *snap-around collar* (see Figure 5-2 for an example) is the first-choice collar because of its effectiveness and versatility. It works well with dogs of all sizes with an average discomfort threshold. For dogs with high discomfort thresholds, consider the pinch collar (see the next section). Getting the attention of the dog is the only reason to use any collar and leash while training. The best way to get your dog's attention is by a quick check or tug on the leash and collar, just enough for your dog to look at you to see what you want or need. The nylon snap-around collar has a metal clasp that enables you to fasten the collar around the dog's neck. That way, you can fit the collar high on your dog's neck where you have the most control.

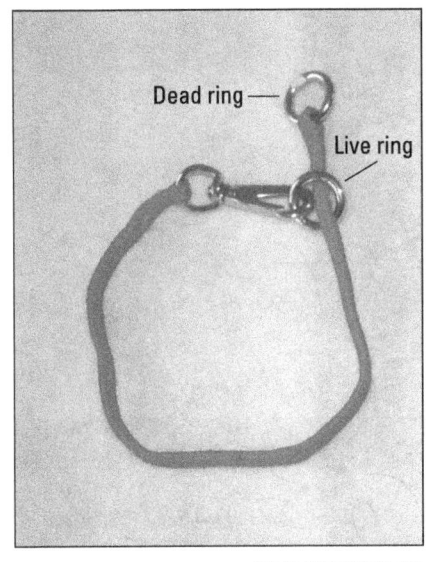

FIGURE 5-2: The floating ring is the live ring and the stationary ring is the dead ring.

TIP

A snap-around collar should fit high on your dog's neck just below the ears, as snug as a turtleneck sweater or necktie, for maximum control (see Figure 5-3). To get a good fit, measure the circumference of your dog's neck directly behind the ears with a tape measure or a piece of string that you can then measure with a ruler.

The placement of the snap-around collar is the secret to its success. It works similarly to a slip collar that we discuss in the later section "Slip-on collars, chain or nylon," but because those fall to the shoulders, they aren't an effective means to communicate with your dog. The snap-around collar lays at the top of the neck, above the trachea or throat, so they're safe to use and move the focus of your dog to you when you give a quick check on the collar. It's amazing how well these collars work to get your dog's attention when fitted properly. Your dog's attention is what you need more than anything. Your dog's joy to work with you is what you want, which you can get with the correct equipment and the success they provide.

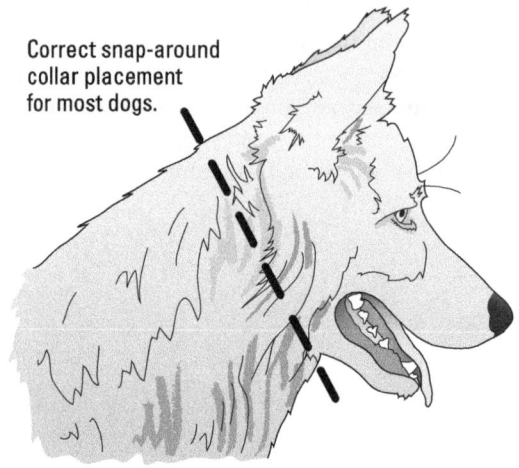

Correct snap-around collar placement for most dogs.

FIGURE 5-3: Correct snap-around collar placement.

Table 5-1 presents some advantages and disadvantages of a snap-around collar.

TABLE 5-1   ## Pros and Cons of Nylon Snap-Around Collars

Advantages	Disadvantages
Fairly inexpensive.	A puppy will grow out of it quickly, and you may need to purchase others.
Can be fitted exactly to your dog's neck.	Not as easy to put on as a slip-on collar.
Very effective.	
Quite safe.	
When fitted to right behind the ears, there is no pressure on the trachea because the collar rests above where a buckle collar would rest.	

Some dogs don't respond to a check on a snap-around collar — that is, the check doesn't create an unpleasant experience for the dog and doesn't change their behavior. The dog may be touch-insensitive and have a high discomfort threshold. Or the dog's size and weight in relation to your size and weight may be such that they don't feel your check. The dog also may be so light or small and have such a high prey drive that they can't recognize the collar check when they're in full prey-drive mode. (See Chapter 2 for more about drives.) When your dog is in full prey drive, you may need to consider a pinch collar.

REMEMBER

Take the training collar off your dog when they aren't being trained and whenever they aren't under your direct supervision so that they don't accidentally get it caught on something that can choke them. Also, don't attach any tags to the training collar. When you're not training your dog, use a buckle collar to which you've attached tags.

The best source for snap-around collars is Handcraft Collars (`www.handcraft collars.com`) because of the quality and durability. The collars from Handcraft come in half-inch increments.

Pinch or prong collars

The names *pinch collar* and *prong collar* describe the same piece of equipment. *Pinch* refers to the effect it has on the dog, and *prong* refers to its appearance. For old-time trainers, the pinch collar was the only collar to use for training. A pinch collar certainly is an effective and efficient training tool (see Figure 5-4). The pinch collar is also wonderful when you can't or don't want to apply too much pressure to the collar. A slight check with a pinch collar is enough to get your dog's attention. Those who use one for the first time often refer to it as power steering. We jokingly call it the *religious collar* because it makes an instant convert out of the dog.

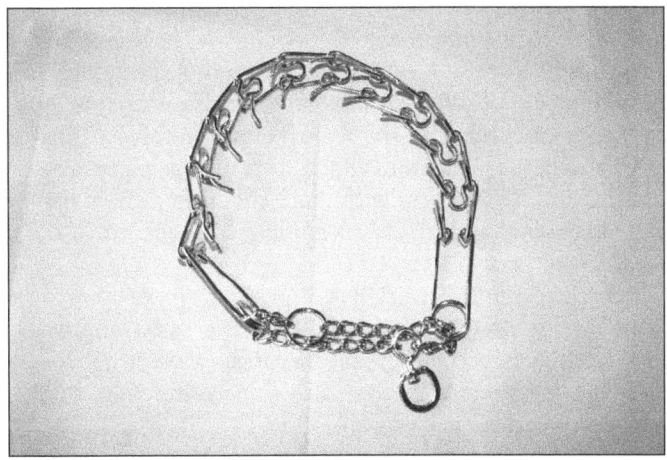

FIGURE 5-4:
A pinch collar.

© John Wiley & Sons, Inc.

According to many certified animal chiropractors, the pinch collar is generally the safest training collar because it doesn't require much force or pressure on your dog's neck or trachea. Therefore, the pinch collar doesn't cause vertebrae or neck injury. The pinch collar is also an effective training collar for strong, rambunctious dogs with a high prey drive. Table 5-2 offers some of the highlights and lowlights of using the pinch collar.

TABLE 5-2   **Pros and Cons of Pinch Collars**

Advantages	Disadvantages
Readily available in pet stores and through catalogs.	Looks like a medieval instrument of torture.
Very effective.	Twice as expensive as a snap-around collar.
Can be fit to the exact size of the dog's neck.	
Very safe — it's self-limiting in that it constricts very little, and it doesn't put pressure on the trachea. Therefore, it's perfect for snub nose dogs or Brachiocephalic dogs, such as Pugs and Bulldogs.	

Pinch collars come in four sizes: large, medium, small, and micro. We never use or recommended the large size, because it appears to have been made for elephants. For a large, strong, and rambunctious dog, the medium size is more than adequate. For Golden Retriever–sized or smaller dogs, the small size is sufficient. For toy dogs, use the micro version, which are harder to find in a local pet store. You can find them on Amazon.

REMEMBER

Any collar or piece of training equipment can be misused or abused. The intent of the user is the key to achieving a harmonious relationship through training. The pinch collar rubs some people the wrong way, because it looks like a medieval instrument of torture. People's perception of a given piece of equipment, however, is immaterial. What counts is the dog's perception, and your dog will tell you. Does your check have the desired effect on the dog's behavior? Are you putting your dog in a position in which you can sincerely praise them for the correct response, or are you angry with them and calling them names? Using the collar that enables you to praise your dog often is the best collar out there.

TIP

When using a training collar, put it on your dog about one to two hours before training and leave it on them for about two hours afterwards. If you put it on immediately before training and then take it off immediately after you finish, they'll quickly become "collar wise," meaning that they'll only respond to commands when the collar is on.

For many dogs, the pinch collar is the most humane training collar, especially if it saves them from a one-way trip to a shelter. The pinch collar isn't the right solution for every training problem or for every dog, but it's the right solution under certain circumstances and is often referred to as a lifesaver.

If you decide to use a pinch collar, it should sit right behind the ears, just like a snap-around collar does. Simply expand or contract the collar by adding or removing links.

Slip-on collars, chain or nylon

A *slip-on collar*, also called a *choke* or *choker collar*, usually made of chain or fabric, is one that slips over the dog's head. Because such a collar needs to fit over the dog's head, it has the tendency to slide down the dog's neck when on the dog. The strongest part of a dog's body is where the neck joins the shoulder blades. The farther the collar slides down the neck, the more difficult controlling the dog becomes and the less effective the collar is as a training tool.

WARNING

Slip-on collars, when improperly used, pose a danger to your dog's trachea and spine. Avoid them! Animal chiropractors have made observations of spinal misalignment caused by this collar. Because slip-on collars aren't effective and have a poor safety record, we recommend that you save your money and get something that works, such as the nylon snap-around collar or the pinch collar.

CLARA'S STORY

When we met Clara, she was in her mid-60s. She lived in a large house outside of town, fairly isolated, although she could see some of her neighbors. We discovered that Clara had had a number of dogs during her life, and after her last dog died, she had acquired a German Shepherd puppy. Clara felt that she needed a dog that would protect her. She named the puppy Ursa. Whenever we talked, Clara would expound on Ursa's virtues — how sweet she was, how easy she was to train, how well she played with the grandchildren, and how many tricks she'd learned.

As time went by, we found out more about Clara. She'd had back surgery with steel rods implanted, and she frequently had to wear a neck brace. She then told us that she had put Ursa on a pinch collar to walk her. Clara said, "She just got too strong for me. Every time we went for a walk, she would sniff the ground where the deer had been and she would pull so hard that I didn't think I could hold her. So, I put her on a pinch collar to control her and now, after two weeks, I can walk her on her regular collar and she no longer pulls me off my feet. Without the pinch collar to help me, who knows what I would have done. I even thought that I might have to give her up, a thought I couldn't bear. Who knows what would have happened to her?"

Now when we meet Clara, she often has Ursa with her, and according to Clara, the dog is a saint. She said, "Instead of being frustrated and angry with her, I tell her what a good girl she is. I'm happy, and she is happy."

Readying a Reward: Treats Are Your Training Buddies

In addition to your ingenuity and intellect (and the proper equipment), treats are another powerful training tool you can use. Treats are most effective when Buddy is hungry rather than after they have just eaten a meal. Fortunately, most dogs are food motivated.

You can use treats in one of two ways:

>> **As a reward for a desired response:** When you use a treat as a reward, you keep the treat hidden from the dog, so they don't know whether they're going to get it. For example, you say, "Down," and Buddy lies down. They may get a treat, or they may not.

When conditioning your dog to a particular command, the treat needs to *immediately* follow the desired behavior so that the dog understands that they're being rewarded for that particular response. Don't fumble around for a treat and give it to them when they're offering a different behavior. If you're teaching Buddy to sit on command and they get up just as you give them the treat, you're rewarding Buddy for getting up, not a result you wanted at all.

>> **As a lure or inducement to obtain a desired response:** When you use a treat as a lure, the treat is in the open. You can use it to entice the dog to obey a particular command, such as lie down, and when they do, they get the treat. When a treat is used in this way, it's within the dog's control whether they get the treat or not.

REMEMBER

Because you're going to use treats both as a reward and as an inducement, you need to decide where to carry them. Some people use fanny packs, some a trouser pocket, and still others a shirt pocket. All these options are fine so long as you can reach them quickly to reward the desired response. Having a few in the palm of your hand when working on a particular exercise isn't a bad idea. The key is to use the treat *before* the dog does something else you don't intend to reward. If you can't get to the treat quickly, Buddy may do something you don't want to reward — and you'll have lost the moment to reinforce the appropriate behavior. A good habit is having some treats with you at all times.

In the following sections, we discuss the ideal treats best for training as well as what to do when your dog isn't excited about food treats.

Picking the ideal tasty treat

A great treat is a dry treat that you can keep in a pocket for easy reach. When you use something moist or soggy that needs to be carried in a plastic bag, by the time you fish it out to give to your dog they have forgotten what it's for. Many dry and semi-dry treats are available. To maintain your dog's health, avoid treats high in salt or sugar. Experiment to find out what your dog likes and responds to. Trying to train dogs with treats they don't like is pointless.

TIP

The ideal treat is dry and no bigger than ¼ inch (even smaller for toy dogs). The bigger the treat, the longer it takes Buddy to consume it, which will break their concentration from what you're teaching.

Dogs also like carrots, broccoli, almost any kind of fruit, and cheese (low-sodium string cheese). For a selection of dog treats, check out a pet store. Make sure that you choose a treat with very few ingredients and preservatives and one that provides good nutrition for your dog.

WARNING

Not all human food is safe for dogs. For example, the chemical agents found in chocolate that make it good and tasty to people are harmful for dogs. So keep chocolate away from Buddy. Also avoid macadamia nuts and onions, which can cause abdominal pain and nausea. Grapes, raisins, and candy that contains xylitol as a sugar substitute can cause liver failure and seizures; xylitol is deadly to dogs. Always check the ingredient list of your sugar-free candies, gums, and even peanut butter before bringing them into your home or car where your dog can get access to them.

Opting for toys when food treats don't work

Some dogs don't respond as well to treats as they do to other objects, such as balls, Frisbees, or sticks. In that case, use whatever turns your dog on — as long as it doesn't become a hindrance in your training. Buddy also may respond to verbal praise or petting as a motivator. Carrying a stick or toy in your back pocket to engage your dog after each exercise can be more valuable to your dog than a treat.

Considering Other Equipment You Can Use

A variety of options are available to control dogs. More than likely you're familiar with some of them; others may be new to you. Some are training tools and others are management tools. The difference between the two is that a training tool teaches the dog to assume the responsibility for their behavior, whereas a management tool doesn't; it simply manages the dog's behavior. For example, a crate is a management tool — it controls the dog's movements.

We mention these tools to familiarize you with them. Some dog owners have successfully used them in special circumstances. We list them here solely to provide you with information about the options available to you.

Using head halters

The *head halter* (see Figure 5-5), such as the popular Gentle Leader, is an adaptation of the head halters used for horses. It works on the premise that where the dog's head goes, eventually the rest of the body will automatically follow.

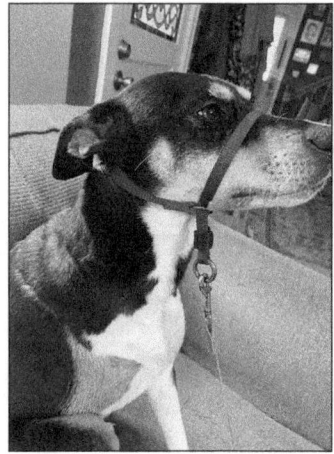

FIGURE 5-5:
A head halter.

© John Wiley & Sons, Inc.

Whereas the pinch collar looks downright menacing, the head halter looks quite inviting and user-friendly. Interestingly, your dog's reaction (and they're the one that counts) is likely to be quite the opposite. They'll readily accept a pinch collar, but many vigorously and vociferously object to the head halter, at least initially. Many dogs don't like anything on their face, and such a dog will most likely try to rub it off and even look like a fish on a line, trying to get it off. You can use food to distract them if your dog starts such behavior, and you should be ready for this reaction. Play, feed, walk, distract your dog until they don't mind the head halter.

The following list describes the principal advantages of the head halter after your dog has learned to accept the effect it has on them:

>> **It's calming and tranquilizing.** This collar is helpful with nervous, timid, shy, or hyperactive dogs.

>> **It's equalizing.** A head halter helps smaller handlers with larger dogs, senior citizens, and handicapped handlers control their dogs.

>> **It's helpful with nuzzling.** This collar helps with inappropriate sniffing behavior, whining or barking, some forms of aggression, and play biting or nibbling by turning first the nose and then the head

>> **It's readily available at pet stores.** You also can find these halters on the internet by searching for them with your favorite browser.

Table 5-3 provides some additional advantages of the head halter as well as some disadvantages.

TABLE 5-3   **Pros and Cons of the Head Halter**

Advantages	Disadvantages
Readily available in pet stores and online.	Greatest potential for serious damage to your dog's neck if you yank on the leash while they are wearing a head halter.
Not very expensive.	Transition tool only.
Minimum strength required to use it.	The dog doesn't learn to accept responsibility for their behavior. When the halter is removed, the dog often reverts to previous behavior.

WARNING

Because this halter controls the head, a strong pull by the dog or the owner can do serious damage to the dog's neck. In this regard, it isn't quite the same principle as the head halter for horses. Because most people are smaller than horses, the halter is used to control the horse's head from below. In contrast, most people are taller than their dogs, and any pull or tug is going to be upward and, at times, simultaneously to the side. Tugging the dog's neck in this way creates great potential for injury. In relation to a person's, a horse's neck also is correspond-ingly stronger than a dog's. The halter can and often does have a depressing effect on the dog. The irony here is that this highly marketable tool has great potential for damage, but the torturous-looking pinch collar is the safest.

Going for a body harness

Body harnesses, which are attached around the chest and back of a dog, are perfectly fine for dogs who don't pull or for small dogs whose pulling isn't terribly objectionable. But for a medium-sized or large dog that pulls, harnesses aren't a good idea because you give up the control you're trying to achieve. The dog literally leans into the harness and happily drags you wherever they want to go. Harnesses are effective if your dog has a neck injury. Veterinary technicians and veterinarians often say a dog who arrives at a veterinary clinic for veterinary care wearing a harness will need a muzzle because a dog who pulls on a harness hasn't had the leadership lessons learned, where the owner is the leader and the dog is not. Harnesses allow the dog to think that they are setting all the rules by pulling their owner.

REMEMBER

Another option for a dog that pulls is a harness often referred to as a *nonpulling harness* or a harness for easy walking (see Figure 5-6). These harnesses are specifically designed to control pulling by applying pressure to calming points under the armpits when the dog pulls. Nonpulling harnesses are a management tool (not a training tool) for dogs with delicate necks, such as sight hounds, and for dogs that have experienced a neck injury. You can order one online or buy one at your local pet store and see if it works for you and your dog.

FIGURE 5-6:
A dog in a nonpulling harness.

© John Wiley & Sons, Inc.

Exploring electronic and other training and management equipment

Electricity has long been used to contain livestock (mainly cattle) as well as horses. Its application to dogs as a training tool and for containment purposes is of more recent origin. Electronic devices became popular with the training of sporting dogs to retrieve birds their owners had shot. The owners needed to be able to control their dogs over distances up to half a mile. Since that time, the concept of controlling the dog through the use of electricity has spawned the many devices that we describe in this section. These training collars are referred to as remote collars because you control the dog from a distance.

REMEMBER

Today's electronic devices don't pose much of a risk for the dog, and we aren't aware of any instances when a device's failure has injured a dog. The main risk to the dog is an owner's lack of knowledge of how to use a particular device properly.

A trainer is an individual who has knowledge of all these training devices and knows when and how to use them when the situation arises. For the beginner or impatient owner without education in a device's proper application, it's far too easy to use the device incorrectly as a means of punishment rather than as a teaching tool to put pressure on a dog to change their behavior.

Electric fences

Many housing developments have covenants against fences. That's a problem when you have a dog you want to keep confined. Tying a dog out on a line, except for brief periods, isn't a humane option.

Never fear, technology is here, and the *electric fence* (or *invisible fence*) can be the answer. The most common system works when a wire is buried around the boundary of the area in which the dog is to be contained. Other systems use radio waves to set boundaries digitally. Initially, the area is marked with little flags to provide the dog with a clear visual stimulus. The dog wears a collar that's designed to vibrate or beep when the dog approaches the boundary. When the dog gets too close, they receive a shock. The intensity of the shock can be adjusted. After the dog has learned to respect the location of the boundary, the flags are gradually removed.

Electric fences are best for neighborhoods that don't allow fences and in farm communities where the dog needs to be prevented from visiting neighbors, who are worried about the dog bothering their livestock.

WARNING

All in all, the system works well for the majority of dogs, but it isn't foolproof. Here are a few of the problems you may encounter:

>> It doesn't keep other dogs, animals, or people out of the fenced area because they aren't connected to the system. If you have a female dog that isn't spayed, you can run into a problem when she's in season and an unaltered male comes to visit with breeding on his mind. It can't keep children out of your yard either.

- Some dogs, in a state of high excitement, will "burn" through the fence. Then they find themselves on the outside of the fence and are afraid to come back in — or they may simply run off.

- Some dogs quickly become "collar wise" and disregard the fence when not wearing the collar. Should that happen, they need to wear the collar every time you let them out.

- Costs of the systems vary and depend on the size of the enclosure. The least expensive systems are found in pet stores, but in this situation, the owner must learn how to use and install them. A more expensive option is to use a company that installs the fence and sends a trainer who does the initial training of the dog and instructs the owner on how to continue to use it.

As a result of these problems, you need to keep an eye on Buddy when they're out in the yard. Don't leave them for prolonged periods without supervision.

Shock collars or remote training collars

A *shock collar* is a buckle collar with a small box attached. The side of the collar that faces the dog has two small prongs that fit snugly against the dog's neck. The handler has a hand-held controller with settings that go from low to high electrical stimulation. Therefore, it's considered a *remote collar* because you have a device to activate the collar when the dog is away from you. The euphemisms for this type of collar are the *e-collar* and the *remote trainer.* The word "shock" is often replaced with "stimulation." In simple terms, the electrical stimulation replaces the check on the collar with a leash. Remote trainers are most successful for controlling dogs at a distance.

REMEMBER

We don't recommend that beginners use these collars without training on the use of the collar first. Remote collar use requires knowledge of training and dogs. When used incorrectly or as punishment, these collars can severely traumatize a dog. Seek a professional trainer if you're considering such a collar. If you insist on using any kind of electronic collar, try it out on your hand first so that you know what it feels like to your dog. Whatever you do, don't point the controller at your dog or wave it at them in a threatening motion — they'll associate the stimulation with you, and that's not what you want. Keep the controller out of your dog's sight.

TECHNICAL STUFF

This collar's origins date back to the 1960s, when they were primarily used for gun dogs. They gave the trainer the ability to communicate with the dog over long distances. The main problems with the early collars were their unreliability and their limitations in terms of controlling the amount of stimulation — even at the lowest setting, the shock administered was needlessly intense.

Enormous quality differences exist within the different makes of remote trainers — essentially, you get what you pay for. The three features influencing the price of a remote-trainer are use of rechargeable versus replaceable batteries, range, and flexibility. The more sophisticated collars provide the most flexibility in adjusting the intensity of the stimulation, its length, and its range (up to 1 mile). Of course, these high-end collars are the most expensive, ranging from $200 to $500. They may include a tone feature, to which some dogs respond without the need for stimulation.

Generally, such collars aren't carried in retail stores and are only available online. The following are some of the manufacturers of these collars: Dogtra, Innotek, PetSafe, and Tri-Tronics. You can purchase the products at the manufacturers' websites or at www.gundogsonline.com or www.amazon.com.

Vibration collars

The *vibration collar* works much the same as a remote trainer or shock collar (see the preceding section), but it relies mainly on vibration (rather than electric stimulation) at different levels of intensity to communicate with the dog. The vibration is more annoying than unpleasant, but for many dogs it's just as effective as a remote trainer.

The vibration collar works well with deaf dogs. Cost varies from $30 to $150. They're available from www.amazon.com. One drawback is that some dogs find vibration more intense than the low-level shock.

Bark collars

To deal with excessive barking, you have several different *bark collars* to choose from. Your options are a mild shock, a mechanism that sprays a liquid (usually citronella), vibration, or ultrasound (a loud noise only the dog can hear). The collars use either a microphone or vibration to set the collar off. The more sophisticated ones use both to prevent loud noises or the barking of another dog from setting off the collar. They range in price from $50 to $100 and are available from the manufacturers listed in the preceding section. There are also features that increase in intensity if the dog continues to bark but reset back to the lowest level if the dog is quiet for a period. With more features, the cost does increase. These can be very effective tools, but they should be introduced to your dog while you're home so that you can help the dog to be quiet, which will stop the stimulation of the collar. Your dog needs to learn how to shut off the stimulation — that is, to stop barking. If the collar were to surprise the dog for the first time and the dog hasn't learned how to turn off the stimulation, they could continue to vocalize unknowingly, and you'd have lost the opportunity for initial training.

LOCATING YOUR RUNAWAY WITH A GPS COLLAR

The latest entries into the e-collar arsenal are GPS tracking and locator collars. You use these collars to locate your pet if they have run away or been stolen. You can even look at a map online that shows you the exact location of your pet. They're fun if you have a lot of property to see where your dog has gone during their romp on your land. Although such collars can locate your pet, training is another option to teach your dog to come when called. GPS is a tool, but it shouldn't become a daily need. These collars are getting more affordable all the time.

TIP

If Buddy is an uncontrollable barker, you may want to consider a bark collar — it's a lot cheaper than being evicted.

Citronella collars

Citronella collars are used as bark collars (as noted in the preceding section), but they're also used to deter chasing. When activated by the owner, the collar emits a puff of citronella in the direction of the dog's nose. For example, if a dog chases a car, just before they get to the car, the owner presses the button, and the dog gets a whiff of citronella. The expectation is that the dog considers the puff of citronella unpleasant enough to stop chasing things. Although not an electronic device, it works on the same principle. Because electric collars aren't allowed in England, citronella collars are the collar of choice there instead of the electric collars.

TECHNICAL STUFF

In a 1996 study at the Animal Behavior Clinic of Cornell University Veterinary School, the citronella collar was found to be more effective to control nuisance barking than the electric bark collar. Now, you can also find *air collars,* which are unscented. The puff of unscented air is the deterrent. Price is around $100, and you can find them on www.amazon.com.

Scat-mats

Don't want your dog taking their daily nap on your favorite armchair or couch while you're at work? The *scat-mat,* with which you cover that coveted piece of furniture, may be your answer. When Buddy jumps on it, the scat-mat gives them a slightly unpleasant shock, which will stop them from jumping on the furniture. The mat also can be used to prevent Buddy from entering another room in the house. No special collar is required.

The customary sizes of scat-mats are 30 inches long by 16 inches wide or 48 inches long by 20 inches wide. They can be extended by plugging two together. They're either battery powered or can be plugged into a wall outlet. You can find scat-mats at most of the larger pet stores for under $75, depending on the size.

Indoor containment systems

Do you want to stop Buddy from counter surfing or jumping on the kitchen table? If so, consider buying an indoor containment system. It consists of a 6-inch disc and a collar for your dog. You place the disc in the center of the countertop or table, and then you adjust the setting for intensity and the distance you want Buddy to stay away. When Buddy gets too close, they receive a mild shock.

The system is battery operated and prevents a dog from jumping on counters or coffee tables. It works on the same principle as the invisible fence (see the earlier section "Electric fences"). These systems are carried by most pet store chains, and they generally cost under $100.

For instance, dear friends of ours acquired an English Staffordshire Bullterrier. Meigs is the most adorable butterball on four legs — one solid muscle with incredible leaping ability. He's affectionately referred to as "a sack of cement on four pogo sticks." Even as a puppy he exhibited aspirations of ascending the coffee table. As early as 9 months of age, he was able to jump on the kitchen table from a dead standstill. Very cute, but hardly acceptable. The indoor containment system took care of it. You can teach Leave It, but of course you need to be present to reinforce that command. With indoor containment systems and scat-mats, you don't need to be present for them to work.

The Pet Convincer

The Pet Convincer is a powerful substitute to yelling or screaming at your dog to control unwanted behaviors. Although the Pet Convincer is a shortcut to patient training, it's nevertheless an effective deterrent to those behaviors dog owners find most annoying and most difficult to deal with; for example, when Buddy goes ballistic when someone comes to the door, when they can't be dissuaded from jumping on people, when they bark incessantly, and so on. It also can be used when taking your dog for a walk. It can protect your dog from being bothered by another dog. It also works well for joggers and cyclists to ward off potentially unfriendly dogs.

This hand-held device, powered by a replaceable CO^2 cartridge, releases a blast of air. The blast of air, whose intensity is controlled with a trigger, is intended to stop the undesirable behavior. The noise of the blast acts as a deterrent. No doubt it will work better than screaming at the dog. It also provides a good chance that the "correction" will carry over to the next time the dog encounters the problematic situation, such as someone coming to the door. You can purchase this product at www.petconvincer.com for $50.

This training tool should never be used in an enclosed space such as a car. When triggered, make sure that it's directed away from the dog's face.

Ultrasonic hand-held devices

Many types of hand-held remotes emit an ultrasonic tone to the dog, and they're viewed as deterrents to the dog's behavior. Some of them work on some issues with some dogs. These devices are relatively inexpensive, but they aren't always effective. There are many claims about them and some do work. They work similarly to the previously described Pet Convincer, but instead of a blast of air, they emit an ultrasonic tone that's unpleasant to the dog's ears. Mainly the device is a distracter to the dog and can help redirect your dog's behavior if you're there to help work on the desired alternate behavior. Training specific alternative behaviors is the most effective tool, always, either with a remote device or not.

New toys and tools are developed every year. Some have great uses and others aren't effective training tools. Use your common sense and read about them before spending your money on them. If you choose to use them, enjoy your dog and the new technology.

2

Performing Puppy Preliminaries

Familiarize yourself with the few simple steps to potty training your dog. The most important part is the role you play in the process. Discover how to successfully housetrain your puppy or new dog; a few weeks of being inconvenienced gives you a dog trained for a lifetime, plus a clean and soil-free home.

Be as prepared as you can be when you bring your puppy home, including having the necessary supplies, such as a crate, food, collar and leash, and toys.

Get your puppy used to using a collar and leash so you can be successful in starting your training plan.

Comprehend more about your puppy's developmental periods to help you understand their physical, behavioral, and emotional needs. You'll be amazed at how quickly they learn.

IN THIS CHAPTER

» **Gathering supplies for your new arrival**

» **Introducing your puppy to your home**

» **Laying the groundwork for training**

» **Training for grooming**

» **Looking at health issues that interfere with training**

Chapter **6**

Starting on the Right Foot with your New Puppy or Dog — Planning and Preparing

You're getting a new dog! Congratulations! How long have you been dreaming of this day? Everyone you know is going to be jealous. Excitement abounds. While anticipating your new arrival, you've probably thought about the day-to-day care that this new family member will need. You even may have made a list of necessities to purchase: food and water bowls, a leash, grooming aids, and so on. But the necessities don't stop there. You also need to think about laying the groundwork for training. Everything you do from now on teaches your dog to be the perfect pet you have always wanted.

Training is about more than getting a response to a command; it's also about raising a dog you can live with and take anywhere and who can be a joy as a companion for many years. This chapter guides you through the first weeks and shows how your training relationship starts on day one.

Preparing for Puppy's Arrival

A little advance preparation for the exciting day makes your puppy's homecoming go smoothly. Before Buddy comes home, you need to gather the following (see Figure 6-1):

>> A crate and crate pad

>> The food you intend to feed and the dishes you're going to use

>> A collar and leash

>> Toys

© John Wiley & Sons, Inc.

FIGURE 6-1:
Items you need before your puppy comes home.

You can get almost everything you need at a pet supply store, whether in person or online. Ordering online makes for convenient shopping, but you may prefer to check out your options at a local pet store.

In the following sections, we provide info on each of the items you need to gather before welcoming puppy into your home.

Puppy's home at home: Readying a crate

The idea of putting your dog in a crate may seem like a form of punishment. Humans often see confinement as punishment, but dogs see crates as their bedroom inside of your home. A crate serves as a den and a place of comfort, safety, security, and warmth. Puppies, as well as many adult dogs, sleep and hang out in a crate most of the day, and many prefer the comfort of their den. For your peace of mind, as well as your puppy's, get a crate — your dog's home within a home. We show you why having a crate is important and how to use one and set it up in the following sections.

Understanding the advantages of a crate

Consider a few of the many advantages to crate training your dog:

>> **A crate is a babysitter.** When you're busy and can't keep an eye on Buddy but want to make sure they don't get into trouble, you can put them in their crate. You can relax, and so can your dog. In other words, it's similar to a playpen for a toddler.

>> **A crate helps Buddy begin housetraining.** Using a crate is ideal for getting Buddy on a schedule for housetraining (see Chapter 8). Dogs don't want to soil their bed, so a proper-sized crate teaches them to hold their elimination.

>> **A crate prepares them for being crated at the vet's office.** Few dogs are fortunate enough to go through life without ever having to be hospitalized. Buddy's first experience with a crate shouldn't be in a cage or crate at the veterinary hospital — the added stress from being crated for the first time can slow their recovery. This stress isn't necessary if you train your dog to be comfortable in a crate at home. Veterinary technicians and staff are so grateful when a dog happily goes into a cage or kennel at the vet hospital, showing that the dog will be comfortable there while hospitalized.

>> **A crate helps with bed rest.** Crate training pays off when you need to keep your dog quiet and calm, such as after being altered or after an injury. Remember that the crate is their secure place inside your home.

>> **A crate makes driving safer.** Driving any distance, even around the block, with your dog loose in the car is tempting fate. An emergency stop can fling your pet around the car like a pinball. Having Buddy in a crate protects you and them. Slamming on the brakes going 35 miles an hour causes a loose dog to move as a 400-pound projectile possibly causing fatal damage to the dog and/or others.

>> **A crate relaxes Buddy while on vacation.** Taking your well-trained dog with you on vacation is fun. The crate is their home away from home, and you can safely leave them in a hotel room knowing that they won't be unhappy or stressed — and that they won't tear up the room. Also, a surprise visit from housekeeping won't allow Buddy to sneak out the door because they'll be safely crated.

>> **A crate gives Buddy their own special place.** It's a place where they can get away from the hustle and bustle of family life and hide out when kids (or other pets) become too much.

Selecting the best crate for your puppy

Get a crate that's big enough to accommodate your puppy when they become an adult dog. Select one that's large enough for your dog to turn around, stand up, or lie down in comfortably, as shown in Figure 6-2.

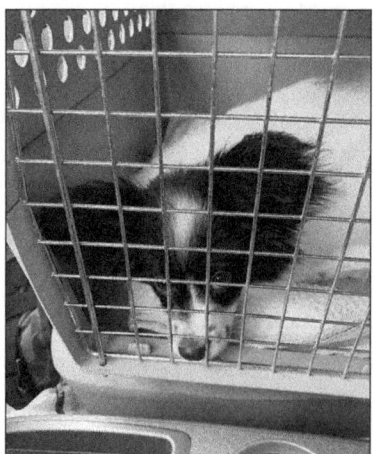

FIGURE 6-2:
A crate is a comfy den for your dog.

© John Wiley & Sons, Inc.

TIP

If you expect that your puppy will become a much bigger adult dog, buy a crate that comes with a divider that enables you to increase the size of the crate as they grow. The most versatile crates have two doors, one on the side and one at the end. You'll appreciate this flexibility, especially when you need to move the crate from room to room.

If you plan to travel with your dog, get a crate that collapses easily and is portable so you can take it with you. Or consider investing in a second crate for the car. Lugging a crate from the house to the car and back again quickly gets old.

The three main types of crates are as follows:

>> **Solid-sided crates:** Often referred to as an *airline crate,* this type (see Figure 6-3) is the most comfortable for your dog. Your dog prefers a solid-sided crate because it gives them the security they want and need. The crate is confining and offers security, like a den, and remember that dogs are den animals.

FIGURE 6-3:
A solid-sided crate.

© *John Wiley & Sons, Inc.*

>> **Wire crates**: Wire crates are collapsible and easy to transport, but they don't provide the security that solid crates do. The wire crate in Figure 6-4 shows the dog in the crate for purposes of our discussion so you can see inside the crate. The wired crate forces the dog out in the open and can make the pup feel exposed. People aren't den animals, so we often think wire crates are better due to the openness, but it's actually the opposite — the solid crate offers much more calmness and security. Dogs often try to get out of wire crates.

FIGURE 6-4:
A wire crate
forces a dog to
be exposed.

>> **Soft-sided canvas crates:** This type (see Figure 6-5) is the most portable type
of crate — it's light and usually folds up for storage and travel. It's not safe to
use in a moving car but can be great in hotels or at dog shows. Soft crates
have canvas sides that dogs can chew to get out, so they are not a good
choice as a first crate.

FIGURE 6-5:
A soft canvas
crate for travel.

All crates need a crate pad — you don't want your growing puppy or adult dog to
constantly be on a hard surface because it's tough on joints. Get a crate pad with
a removable cover that you can clean in the washing machine. Toss a blanket into
the crate to keep Buddy warm.

REMEMBER

Make sure the size of the crate fits the size of your dog. The crate should only be large enough for Buddy to stand up, turn around, and lie down. The crate is a bed to sleep in, not exercise in.

Positioning the crate in your home

Establish an area where your puppy will spend the majority of their time — a place where they won't feel isolated from the family. The kitchen, family room, or whatever room is most used in the house (but still contains a quiet area) is an ideal place where Buddy can eat and take frequent naps.

Another option for a crate location is in your bedroom. When a new puppy is crated in your room, they're aware of your scent and hear your breathing. You set a good example for sleep, and nighttime counts as quality bonding time for you and your puppy. Dogs are pack animals and want to be with their pack. Sleeping together, dog in their crate, you in your bed, counts as social time. Later, you may not need the crate at night, but for a puppy's chewing stages and the housetraining period, a crate is an essential tool.

The first few nights after a puppy leaves their mother and litter can be traumatic. Having the crate in your bedroom will help the transition because they won't be alone; your presence is obvious. You can also reach out and offer a soothing word.

REMEMBER

Make sure Buddy's crate is available and open when they want to nap or take a timeout. Depending on where it is, your dog will choose to spend much of their sleeping time in their crate.

WARNING

Never use your dog's crate as a form of punishment. If you do, they'll begin to dislike the crate, and it will lose its usefulness to you. You don't want Buddy to develop negative feelings about their crate. You want them to like their private den.

Puppy's menu: Selecting a proper diet and set of dishes

Choosing food for your growing puppy isn't easy — a lot of choices are available. Read Chapter 4 and visit www.volharddognutrition.com for more information. What you feed your puppy will determine the ease or difficulty you'll have in training Buddy. The better the diet, the easier it is to train your dog.

ALTERNATIVES TO TRAVEL CRATES

The safest way to transport your dog in a vehicle is in a crate. A loose dog in a car is a danger to you and your dog — keeping Buddy in a crate protects both of you. For some vehicles, such as sedans, crates are too large or cumbersome. Station wagons and SUVs have cargo areas that can be separated from the main cabin. Barriers can be fitted in either type of vehicle. Talk to your car dealer about this option.

REMEMBER

After you settle on a diet for Buddy, be sure to pick out a set of dishes — one for food and one for water. Try to avoid brightly painted or cute ceramic dog dishes. Many companies use lead in the manufacturing process of these dishes; over time the lead can leach into the food in the dish. Stick with stainless-steel dishes instead. They come in various sizes and are easy to keep clean. These dishes will last your puppy a lifetime. Plastic bowls can also lighten your dog's nose from black to brown in some cases. To be safe, stick with stainless steel.

Puppy's everyday collar, ID, and leash: Preparing Buddy to go outside

When you're getting ready to bring home Buddy, you need the following items to keep them safe and speak for you if they get away, such as identification:

>> **Everyday collar:** For your puppy's everyday collar, you need a flat, fabric, adjustable buckle collar that can be made bigger as they grow. This collar holds your dog's identification tags.

>> **ID tags:** Tags should have a good contact number for you, phone number, and address. If you find a dog from around the corner, a quick walk can return them to the rightful owner. Tags should be strong enough to hold up to wear and small enough not to catch on furniture or fencing.

>> **Leash:** Get a 6-foot-long soft fabric leash for training and walking.

Puppy's toys: Playing with Buddy

Toys are a wonderful way to amuse Buddy for hours at a time and keep them from chewing your possessions. Toys also can be used in training for dogs that aren't that interested in food. You need a variety of toys, including the following:

>> **Several large plush toys:** Puppies love to play with soft toys and carry them around. However, avoid stuffed animal toys if you have a puppy who likes to rip and tear them apart. They often contain stuffing and squeakers that puppies consider edible. Also beware of the following:

- Toys with hard eyes or studs that your puppy will pull off — and can swallow.

- Toys that resemble shoes or your clothes. It's difficult for a puppy to understand the difference between toys and your stuff.

>> **Interactive toys:** Interactive toys are great for puppies because they teach as they amuse. The puppy will need to figure out how to get the treat, and it gives them something to work on that provides a reward at the end. Such toys are especially important when a puppy is teething. Here are just a few options:

- **Hard rubber toys:** The Kong Company specializes in hard rubber toys that can be filled with treats or frozen yogurt to keep dogs occupied. Kong toys come in different sizes, colors, and strengths. The colors identify the strength of the toy; black is virtually indestructible and is the favorite retrieving toy of most retrievers who love to hold things in their mouths at all times.

- **Softer treat holders:** Some interactive toys come in different shapes and sizes and can be stuffed with treats. Some puppies prefer them to the harder toys because they're made of softer materials and have Velcro to hold the treats inside.

  - **The Buster Cube:** This toy can be the all-time favorite of many dogs who love to dig and root. You put some treats inside the cube and watch your dog go at it. Dogs learn how to roll the cube so treats randomly fall out.

» **Chew bones:** Gumma bones or natural bones from the butcher can be fabulous chewing toys for your puppy. When picking out real bones, the long bones are much better than the knuckles, which can break off and be swallowed. Purchase bones where the joints have been cut off.

Never give a cooked bone to a dog because it can splinter and cause problems. Stay away from steak bones or bones that are cut into a circle, such as a ham bone, because they're easily caught in Buddy's lower jaw.

» **Unstuffed toys:** Dog toys that have no stuffing are now an option for your dog and available at your pet stores and online. This type of toy still gives your dog the opportunity to shake and carry soft toys around but without the risk of ingesting the stuffing or turning your house into a stuffing snowstorm.

Bringing Puppy Home — Now What?

Adding a puppy or living with a dog is life changing. Living with a dog is time consuming and can be expensive, but it's worth every penny you spend. Living with and loving a dog adds so much to your life, fun, exercise, and companionship. When you bring them home, help them get used to their new surroundings and new life. These sections address which areas to focus on.

Getting your puppy used to their collar and leash

Prior to starting your training, Buddy will need to get used to wearing a buckle collar. Put this collar on Buddy after a nap, take them outside to relieve themselves, and let them eat with the collar on. At first, they may scratch at it, because they aren't used to having something around their neck. As they get used to wearing a collar, the scratching will stop.

After they're comfortable with the collar, introduce Buddy to the leash. Attach the leash to their collar and let them drag it around the room. You need to keep an eye on them so that the leash doesn't get entangled. Don't pick up the leash just yet.

REMEMBER

When they're comfortable with the leash tagging along behind them, your next step is to get Buddy used to walking on the leash while you're holding it. If you try to get your young dog to walk with you right away, they may resist. Instead, pick up the leash and follow them. Watch that your body language is showing your back side, ask them to *follow* you now. Do *not* tug them toward the front of you; tug a little as you show them your back side only, walking away from them, and don't even look back at them. The power of your body language is really strong. They won't close the gap between you if you are looking at them. Occasionally, give them a treat. Remember to make it fun and keep moving.

When you're ready to start doing some training with your dog, you have to put the snap-around collar on them. We use the collars and leashes from www.handcraft collars.com, a site that offers high-quality products that last a long time. A snap-around collar is measured to fit high on your dog's neck, away from any pressure on the trachea. To put the collar on, start with your dog facing you.

1. **Attach your leash to the stationary ring before you get started.**

   Check out Figure 6-6d to see where to attach your leash. It's helpful to attach the leash before you put the collar on. Therefore, the floating ring is left for the hook on the collar in Step 4.

2. **Take the two rings in your right hand with the sewn-on ring and the floating ring together in your right hand, facing your dog.** (All the "Rs" together — ring, ring, and right hand.)

   See Figure 6-6a.

3. **Place the collar under your dog's neck and bring the ends up to the top of the neck, directly behind the ears.**

REMEMBER

   Figure 6-6b shows the proper placement of the collar in this step. When you begin to put on the collar, the dog flexes the neck muscles, expanding the circumference of the neck by as much as a half-inch, creating the impression that the collar is much tighter than it actually is (similar to the effect produced by a horse taking in air as it's being saddled).

4. **Attach the clasp to the floating ring.**

   The smooth side of the clasp needs to be next to the dog's skin. See Figure 6-6c to see what this step should look like.

   You're good to go! Make sure the collar is right behind your dog's ears and high on the neck. This is where it's most effective.

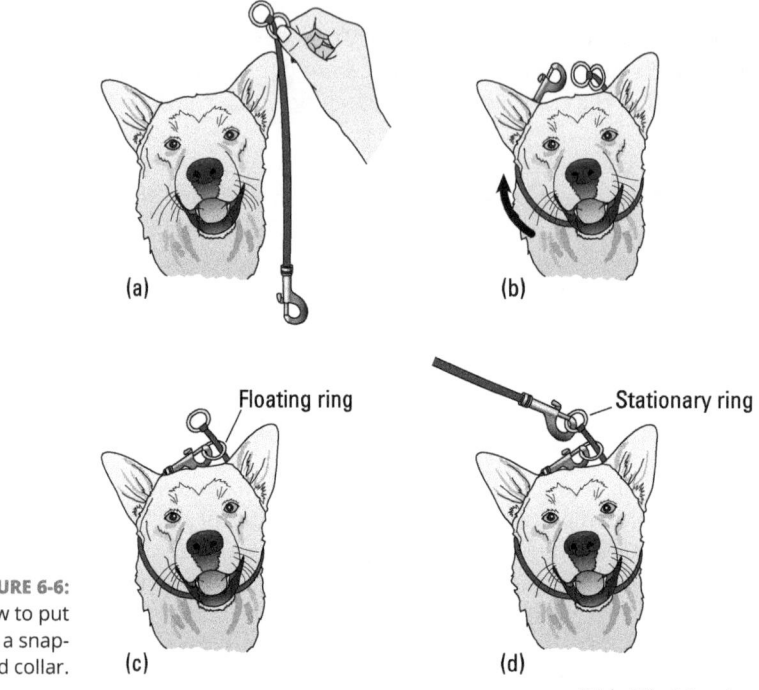

FIGURE 6-6:
How to put
on a snap-
around collar.

(a) (b)

Floating ring | Stationary ring

(c) (d)

© John Wiley & Sons, Inc.

TIP

After you get the collar on your dog, you may get the impression that it's much too tight and that you can barely get it around Buddy's neck. We suggest that after the first time you put the collar on, you wait for five minutes. After the dog has relaxed, you then can test for correct snugness. You need to be able to slip two fingers between the collar and your dog's neck (one finger if you have a toy dog). If your fingers won't fit, the collar is too tight; if you can get three or more fingers through, the collar is too loose.

REMEMBER

Before reaching 16 weeks of age, you puppy will follow you wherever you go. This tendency provides you with endless training opportunities. Start by teaching the Touch command (see Chapter 9), which is an effective foundation for future training and the start of the Come command and signal.

Getting Buddy situated in their new home

Puppies love to explore new areas, but giving Buddy the run of the house, especially right away, can be overwhelming and can lead to trouble. Instead, prepare a specific room or area where they can get their bearings. Placing a baby gate across the entrance to that area can help keep them confined. Carry them into the house and place them in this safe area. In most households, the kitchen is a good area because it usually has an easy-to-clean floor, which is helpful when puppy has an accident. Let them sniff around and get used to their new home. Scatter plenty of safe toys around to play with.

Umbilical cord training: Keeping your puppy on leash and collar while attached to you helps your puppy stay with you and learn to follow you while always being within arm's reach. This way you can see what they're doing at all times. This teaches your puppy that you're their human and they should be with you as leader of the team. Keep a chew toy in your pocket or nearby to occupy Buddy. Remember to take them out to potty on a regular schedule and be sure to give them attention as you work and train them. Keep Buddy attached to you only for short periods of time — 10 to 30 minutes — because puppies need lots of sleep, and being awake too long can overstimulate young puppies and create behavior problems, like jumping up and chewing the leash. After your 10 to 30 minutes of training, potty puppy and let them sleep. Chapter 8 gives you the information you need to potty train your puppy.

You puppy will explore their new world with their mouth, so you need to be nearby to give them appropriate things to chew on. Trade an appropriate toy for what they're chewing on that belongs to you. What you don't want is to look down and find that your puppy has wandered away and gotten into trouble. Use the leash and baby gates to keep them in the same room as you. These steps can be inconvenient, but you only need to do them for a short time. They'll lead to a trustworthy dog in the house for a lifetime.

REMEMBER

The more activity the puppy has, the more they'll need to relieve themselves. Confining them to an area at first will greatly aid in successful housetraining. Being attentive to your dog's potty habits must always be foremost in your mind. (See more about potty training in Chapter 8.)

The first time you feed your puppy, place their food in the crate to introduce them to their den and establish the idea that the crate is where good things happen (see the earlier section "Puppy's home at home: Readying a crate"). Leave the door open when you feed them initially until they learn that the crate or den is theirs. Later you may not need to feed them in a crate, but when you bring them home, using the crate to feed them adds one more reason for them to love being in their crate.

Introducing puppies and kids

Teaching dogs and children to coexist can go well or badly depending on the boundaries you set. Although small children generally can get along well with dogs — especially if their parents are comfortable around dogs — parents do need to make the effort to teach their children how to interact correctly with the puppy. Remember the following:

>> Parents must be watchful that children don't pinch, pull fur, twist ears, fall on, or chase the puppy.

>> Parents need to monitor interactions between the children and the puppy. Children tend to run, squeal, and wear loose clothing, all of which incite the puppy's prey drive and encourage nipping. It's a parent's responsibility to keep children from overstimulating the new puppy.

>> Parents should teach the children to be calm around the puppy and to pet Buddy gently.

>> Parents must stop young children from carrying the puppy, because they may drop them. Until children are completely stable and steady while walking, they shouldn't carry a puppy.

>> Parents must be responsible for training the puppy and then include the kids after the puppy has learned a lesson; the responsibility of training must fall on an adult or teenager, not young children. While training a dog, children are seen as littermates rather than authority figures. Usually 11-year-old kids can handle training a dog that isn't challenging the child's authority.

Tolerance for playing with children varies within and among breeds. Early exposure also is a factor. Dogs between the ages of 7 and 12 weeks that are exposed to well-behaved children generally get along well with kids. The most important thing a parent can teach the child is to respect the puppy, thereby fostering a harmonious relationship.

TIP

Parents do both the child and the dog a favor if they insist that children keep their hands at their sides or cross them across their chest when around puppies or dogs they don't know. Children are inclined to lift up their arms when greeting a puppy, which encourages the puppy to jump. Of course, children also must be taught that they should *never* go up to a strange dog and try to pet them. Only after permission is sought from the owner is approaching and petting a dog acceptable. Figure 6-7 shows how a dog and child can be great friends.

REMEMBER

A safe place where the dog can retreat and not be bothered by a child is essential. When Buddy has had enough play and tries to hide under the bed, don't try and pull them out. The dog is looking for a safe place to rest away from the kids. Listen to your dog and give them a break from all activity.

FIGURE 6-7:
A harmonious
relationship, a
boy and his dog.

Meeting resident pets

When you already have a dog and Buddy is a new addition to your household, you need to stage the introduction. You can't assume that the resident dog will automatically accept Buddy.

REMEMBER

Introduce a new family member to an older dog by first placing them both on leash. The best approach is to take the older dog outside to the front of the house, which is neutral territory. Then carry the puppy from the car to the front and let the two of them meet on leash. Let your older dog sniff the puppy from head to toe but only after the initial introductions and a short walk. Puppies at this age often turn upside down and pee. In dog language this is a sign of great respect. A short walk on leash is always a good idea after a quick sniff when introducing your new dog to an existing pet. The walk distracts everyone and gives the dogs something to do instead of waiting for a possible altercation.

When the older dog has satisfied their curiosity, let the older dog go in the house first. You need to keep an eye on the interaction between the two. Above all, make as much fuss over the older dog as you do over the puppy. You don't want to create the impression that the older dog is being replaced. If the introduction goes badly, alternate between crating the resident dog and the puppy until they get used to each other.

Introducing a new dog to an existing cat in the household requires a small crate for the cat. After all, your new dog may not know what a cat is, so you need to allow the dog and cat to sniff each other and to keep the cat from running off. Running away triggers the chase instinct in the dog, which is never a good idea. By giving them a couple evenings of hanging out together, cat in crate, dog not in crate, you allow them to get used to each other. You can also help redirect the dog away from the crate if they get too curious.

Tending to all potty needs

Housetraining your puppy can be a challenge, but it needn't be a nightmare. We devote Chapter 8 to the topic, so flip ahead for expert advice on establishing a schedule.

REMEMBER

Here's what you need to keep in mind when you bring your puppy home:

>> Establish a toilet area in your yard and take Buddy there after they wake up, shortly after they eat or drink, and after they have played or chewed.

>> When you see Buddy sniffing and circling, take note! They're letting you know that they're looking for a place to go. When you see this behavior, take them out to the toilet area so they don't have an accident in the house.

>> After 8 p.m., remove the water dish so they have a better chance of lasting through the night without needing to potty.

Deciding where your puppy should sleep

We can't stress enough how important sleep is for your growing puppy. After all, they're a baby and need lots of sleep to grow properly, digest their food, and stay calm. Puppies that don't get enough sleep often get overstimulated and bite at hands, have more accidents, and get whiny. Establish a schedule in which your puppy is crated in a quiet place for a couple of hours after morning playtime and again after subsequent play periods during the day.

TIP

If they get whiny when you crate them, put a few small treats into one of the Kong toys. Playing with these toys will use up the excess energy and help them fall asleep quickly.

At night, you have some choices for where your puppy will spend their sleep time. Puppies hate to be alone, so if you isolate the puppy away from you, the first week or so they will scream louder and louder until you can't stand it any longer. They are preprogrammed to do so; they're telling their mother that they're lost and to come find them. We suggest you set the crate in your bedroom and close to you when you first get them.

The best idea is to have a crate by the side of your bed, using it as a bedside table. Put the puppy in the crate when you go to bed, and they'll be happy to snuggle down knowing you're close by. If they get anxious, you can put your fingers through the crate to reassure them that you're there and they aren't alone. Having a soft, stuffed toy in the crate also helps.

If your puppy is part of a multi-dog household, you can leave all the animals together in the same sleeping area so that the puppy has company. Make sure the crate has a soft blanket and large soft toy in it so that the puppy stays warm.

Starting Buddy's Education

Puppies love to learn, and they'll learn with or without you. Naturally, you want to teach Buddy what you want them to learn. Puppies will retain for a lifetime the lessons they learn between 7 and 12 weeks of age. At this age, Buddy is still easy to physically control. The older they get and the larger they grow, the more difficult the task becomes — and the more unpleasant it gets for your dog. The best time to start is now. In the following sections, we show you the most important exercises to start with when educating your puppy.

REMEMBER

Name Recognition is a great first lesson. Chapter 9 gives you instructions on how to teach this fabulous game. As obvious as it seems, an amazing number of dogs don't respond to their names. Training by giving a command to your dog who doesn't respond to their name has little chance for success.

REMEMBER

Furthermore, having a veterinary chiropractor look at your puppy during their first year of life to make sure that everything is in order is a good idea. Vigorous play, especially with other dogs, can cause all manner of misalignments, which can then interfere with proper growth. To find one near you, go to www.ahvma. org/find-a-holistic-veterinarian where chiropractic veterinarians are listed by state.

Training for grooming

You can do much of the routine care a dog needs yourself without having to lay out a small fortune for someone else to do it for you. Examples are brushing, bathing, trimming nails, cleaning ears, and brushing teeth. If you start the grooming training when Buddy first comes home, they'll accept it, and you'll have a puppy that you can groom for the rest of their life. Start now while Buddy is small; this way you can manage to pick them up and put them on a table. The most successful time to introduce grooming is after your puppy has had a playtime or has exercised.

The equipment you need for grooming depends on the kind of dog you have, because the type of dog you have dictates generally how much grooming they need. Even shorthaired dogs require some brushing. Regular grooming saves on vacuuming and keeps their coat and skin healthy.

TIP

For more information on how to make your puppy look their best, see *Dog Grooming For Dummies* by Margaret H. Bonham (Wiley).

Brushing your puppy

Instead of trying to groom Buddy with both of you struggling on the floor, start by putting them on a table. Grooming on a table is comfortable for you and has a calming effect on your dog. If you have a longhaired breed, they'll need to get used to spending a lot of time on a table. If you have a large-breed dog, you may need the assistance of a family member to get them on the table. Outside tables such as picnic tables work well too, so find the perfect spot to use as your grooming area.

Any solid table will do, but you need to place a towel on it to prevent the puppy from slipping. Lift Buddy onto the table and give them a treat. Gently stroke them all over their body. When they relax on the table, bring out your soft-bristle brush and let them smell it. Put a treat on the table, and when they're occupied with it, gently brush the body, mimicking what you did when you stroked them. (Figure 6-8 shows how to groom a puppy.) Give a treat each time you brush another body part. Doing so will keep them occupied, so they won't try to play with the brush. If you follow this routine daily, Buddy will look forward to their grooming sessions.

FIGURE 6-8:
Grooming a puppy on a table.

© John Wiley & Sons, Inc.

Even if your puppy is shorthaired, you need to brush them at least once a week, if not more. Brushing is essential in stimulating the skin; it keeps the skin healthy by bringing blood to the surface. Short hair is more difficult to vacuum up than long hair.

When a pup reaches three to five months, they'll start to lose the puppy coat. The puppy coat usually starts to fall out on the tail, up the spine, and then each side of the body. Before it sheds, the coat gets dull; the fur is dead and is making room for the adult coat to come in. Keeping puppy brushed helps keep dog fur off the floor and your clothes.

Bathing your puppy

Even in the best of households, puppies get into things that smell. Dogs love to investigate new smells by rolling in them. No one wants to spend time with a smelly puppy, so Buddy needs to learn to be bathed.

REMEMBER

Various opinions exist concerning how often a dog should be bathed. The simple answer is that you should give Buddy a bath when they smell like a dog or have rolled in something stinky. Heaven forbid they should have an encounter with a skunk. Many methods can neutralize skunk oils. Here is the most common de-skunking mixture:

1. **Mix 1 quart of hydrogen peroxide, ½ cup of baking soda, and 1 teaspoon of liquid dish soap.**

2. **Pour the mixture on a dry dog and then rub it in.**

3. **Allow it to sit for a few minutes and then rinse.**

4. **Repeat if necessary and follow up with a normal wash with your dog's regular shampoo.**

You can use the bathtub or the shower, or you can bathe them outside, weather permitting (see Figure 6-9). When you first put Buddy into the bathtub or shower, let them calm down before you turn on the water. When you finally turn it on, go slowly and let them look at it. (The water should be quite warm but not hot.) If you're using a sprayer, spray away from them first so they can get used to the sound and sight of the spray. Then, starting at the neck and shoulders, wet the body down to the back legs and tail. Continually tell them what a good dog they are. Keep your voice light and encouraging.

TIP

If your puppy is too bouncy, put a collar on them so you can control them with one hand. Or have a family member hold them by the collar while you bathe them.

FIGURE 6-9:
Bathing
your puppy.

After you wet the puppy, rub dog shampoo all over and lather their coat. (A good choice of shampoo is a coconut oil–based shampoo that has the correct pH for puppy skin and doesn't take the oil out of their coat.) Avoid Buddy's head; bathe only from the neck down. You don't want to get water in their eyes or ears; doing so will scare them. Rinse them carefully, making sure no soap is left in the fur; rinse them twice so you're sure they are truly soap free. Lift the puppy out of the sink or shower and put them on the same towel-covered table you're using for grooming. With a treat held just above their nose, make them sit and then gently rub them dry with a towel, as shown in Figure 6-10. While they're on the table, you can wash their face with a wet facecloth, but be sure to stay away from their eyes. After the bath, keep them in a warm area until they're completely dry.

FIGURE 6-10:
Drying puppy
after a bath.

Trimming the nails

Your puppy's nails need trimming when you can hear them coming on a hardwood floor. Trimming nails isn't as difficult as it sounds. First, get them accustomed to having their nails touched. To do so, wait until they're relaxed and then play with their feet, touching each nail.

After your puppy gets used to having their nails and toes touched, put Buddy on the table you're using to groom. Place them in a position in which they're comfortable, whether that be sitting or lying down. Using a dog nail clipper, cut just the tip of one nail. Chances are, your puppy will squeak, not so much out of discomfort, but because it's a new experience. Give them a treat. When they're comfortable with having one nail done, try doing just one foot this first session. Remember to clip the little dewclaws on the side of their front legs. Do one foot a day for four days, and you'll have all the nails trimmed.

You also can use a grinder, such as a Dremel tool, to grind the nails or to smooth out the edges after you've trimmed them. This type of tool makes quite a bit of noise, so it pays off to spend a little time letting Buddy see the grinder and smell it when it's turned off and when it's turned on without using it on their nails. Some puppies are sound sensitive, so we don't suggest using it for these pups. Have Buddy lie down on the grooming table, treats between their paws, and just try one nail at a time. Over a few days you can get all the nails done.

TIP

You may need a family member or friend to help you hold the puppy sufficiently still so you can clip their nails. Have treats ready.

Cleaning the ears

Part of your weekly grooming needs to include cleaning your puppy's ears. Prick-eared dogs, such as German Shepherds or Corgis, don't need ear cleaning as frequently as floppy-eared dogs. The earflaps of drop-eared dogs need weekly cleaning, and the ear canals need air.

To get started, get Buddy to sit or lie down on the grooming table and gently play with their ears. Lift up the ear flaps on the floppy-eared dog or stroke the prick ear before you start to clean them. Give Buddy a treat and tell them what a good dog they are.

When you and Buddy are both ready to start cleaning, combine in a spray bottle a mixture of half apple cider vinegar and half water. Spray a small amount onto a cotton ball and gently clean the part of the ear that you can see. If you don't know what you're doing, going farther into the ear canal is dangerous — leave that deep cleaning to your vet on Buddy's annual health exam or more frequently if Buddy has problems or their ears start to smell bad.

Cleaning the pearly whites

Buddy's mouth is the gateway to their overall health. First, get them used to their mouth being handled. Gently lift the lips on each side of their mouth and touch the teeth. At first, most puppies fight having their mouths handled. But be patient; Buddy will get used to the feeling.

With Buddy on the grooming table, put your arm around their neck and shoulders. After they're comfortably positioned, lift the lips on each side. Praise them for allowing you to look at the teeth on both sides. Then you're ready to wet a cotton ball with warm water and gently wipe their teeth. Give them a treat. By following this process, you're training Buddy to accept their mouth and teeth being touched. You can also wrap one of your fingers with an old nylon stocking and rub the teeth with your wrapped finger, which is good for massaging the gums as well as the teeth.

As Buddy grows older and is no longer a puppy, you can introduce a soft tooth-brush, which should be used weekly when they're an adult. A human toothbrush is suitable, but a dog toothpaste (which is flavored for their palate) makes the process more enjoyable for Buddy.

REMEMBER

Training Buddy to accept this routine is one of the most important things you can do for them, because as an adult, Buddy's teeth can get coated with tartar that will inflame their gums. Gum disease produces bacteria that have been implicated in heart disease, stroke, and some cancers.

Cleaning the eyes

Keep your puppy's eyes clean and wiped out if matter collects in them. Usually, a damp cloth to wipe the face off should be efficient. Eyes are a common place for dust or seeds to collect in the lower eye lids. A stream of contact eye saline can be enough to flush any debris from their eyes. Contact lens saline is rather cheap and a good thing to have in your medicine closet for such a need.

Spaying and neutering

The latest research has revealed that spaying/neutering a puppy at too young of an age has serious long-term side-effects on structure. Puppies and young dogs need the hormones that the reproductive glands produce for them to grow prop-erly. Research recommends that the puppy be fully grown before you take them for this surgery. Wait if you can until your puppy is at least 2 years old to avoid long-term side-effects from early spay/neutering. It's interesting that the United States is the only country where it's recommended to neuter young dogs. Research has disproven that neutering stops aggression and other behavioral problems.

Solving Perplexing Puppy Problems

Here are some of the more commonly asked questions in puppy classes about health conditions that interfere with housetraining and training in general:

» **My puppy pees small amounts frequently even though I take them outside regularly.** The stress of leaving their mother and littermates along with a long journey to their new home can cause a puppy to get an infection called *cystitis,* which is an inflammation of the bladder, making the puppy think they need to urinate frequently. What you see is the puppy straining and producing a few drops of urine. Don't ignore this symptom and think it will get better — it won't. Cystitis can wreak havoc with your housetraining efforts, so be sure to make an appointment with your veterinarian.

» **My puppy doesn't want to eat their food.** Find out what Buddy's previous owner or breeder fed the puppy before they left home. Try to get some of that food and see if merely the change in diet has affected their appetite. Also take a look at Chapter 4 for dietary suggestions.

A puppy on medication may have an upset tummy and not feel like eating. Try feeding small meals often. If your puppy is on certain antibiotics, the lack of appetite generally disappears after the medication is stopped. If all else fails, you can drop goat's milk or full fat organic yogurt mixed with honey (a half cup of goat's milk or yogurt to 1 teaspoon honey) into the side of their mouth with an eyedropper, to get them going. After they start to eat, they'll generally continue. Stop training until they feel better.

When a puppy is teething (anywhere from 4 to 6 months, depending on the breed), their mouth gets sore. Food can get stuck in the teeth, so you'll often see the puppy running their face along the floor or against the couch. Gently put your index finger into the puppy's mouth to clear out anything that's stuck. Provide lots of toys and bones to gnaw on during this teething period. Buddy needs to chew to loosen the baby teeth. If they have baby teeth that aren't coming out, an occurrence that's common, take them to your veterinarian. Again, stop training until your puppy feels better.

» **My puppy needs to take pills, and I don't know how to give them.** As a matter of course, teach your puppy to take food off a spoon. Put a little of their favorite food (peanut butter, yogurt, cheese, and so on) on the end of a teaspoon and encourage them to eat it. At first, they'll want to lick it off, but after several repetitions, they'll open their mouth. You can then scrape the food onto the back of their front teeth. Do this on a regular basis as a training exercise, and your puppy will readily take food from a spoon.

Now when you need to give them a pill, you can hide it in some food on the spoon, and they'll willingly take it.

>> **My puppy eats stools when outside.** Some dogs are partial to horse poop or cat poop. This behavior is objectionable to you, but it won't do Buddy any harm. With the Leave It command in Chapter 9, you should be able to stop it.

One way to stop the behavior is to keep the yard picked up.

>> **My puppy constantly bites me when I handle them.** When the puppy mouths you too hard, yell "Ouch" in a loud tone of voice. Then distract the puppy with a toy. In most instances, it takes only a couple times for the puppy to catch on that this mouthing isn't acceptable behavior. Some puppies are more persistent than others, in which case you may need to take Buddy gently by the scruff of the neck and lift their front paws off the ground.

>> **Should I worm my puppy frequently?** Don't worm your puppy without first taking a fecal sample to your veterinarian to be tested. If your puppy has worms, your veterinarian will give you the appropriate medicine for that particular worm. Stay away from wormers in supermarkets or pet stores. If you do find that they have worms and aren't feeling well, stop training until they feel better.

>> **Is it safe to use flea and tick products with my puppy?** Your veterinarian will give you their recommendations for flea and tick controls as well as heartworm preventions. Make an educated choice to keep your puppy healthy.

Ticks can carry Lyme disease. If you live in an area where ticks are prevalent, be vigilant with your puppy, especially in wooded areas. The most common symptoms of Lyme disease include muscle aches and fatigue. Use a flea comb to look for ticks after your walks in grass and fields. Flea combs have very small teeth that are close together, and you should be able to examine your dog for any ticks that they may have picked up by combing them with a flea comb.

Chapter **7**

Surviving Your Puppy's Critical Growth Periods

Everyone wants a super puppy, one that's well behaved and listens to every word you say — a Lassie. Of course, heredity plays a role, but so does early upbringing and environment. From birth until maturity, your dog goes through a number of developmentally critical periods. The many scientists and behaviorists who've studied dog behavior over the last century have made important discoveries about puppies' developmental periods and how they relate to their ability to grow into well-adjusted pets. What happens or doesn't happen during these periods has a lasting effect on how your dog turns out, their ability to learn, their outlook on life, their behavior, and how they respond to your efforts to train them.

In this chapter, we explain the developmental periods your pooch will go through and how to begin training them according to the stage they're in. We also discuss how spaying and neutering can affect your dog and their trainability.

Understanding Your Puppy's Early Development

Puppies go through distinct critical periods in the first 12 weeks of life. What happens during this time influences not only their temperament but also their health and overall development. In the following sections, we discuss each of the puppy periods your pet will go through so that you can begin training appropriately.

Birth to 7 weeks: The Canine Socialization Period

The first puppy period is from birth to 49 days. During this time, the puppy needs their mother and the interaction with their littermates. They also need to interact with humans. All these interactions are important because they lay the foundation for the puppy's future with their ultimate human family and what they will encounter as they grow.

WARNING

Be wary of obtaining a puppy who has been taken away from their mother prior to 7 weeks of age, because it not only deprives the puppy of important behavioral lessons but also can affect the puppy's future health. For example, the puppy obtains antibodies to many diseases by feeding from their mother. Every sip of milk is like a vaccine that protects the puppy for many weeks after they leave the litter and are placed in their new home.

One of the *most important* times is between 3 to 7 weeks of age, when the mother teaches her puppies basic doggy manners. She communicates to the puppies what behavior is acceptable and unacceptable. For instance, after the puppies' teeth have come in, nursing them becomes a painful experience, so the mother teaches them to take it easy. She does whatever it takes, such as growling, snarling, and even snapping, and she continues this lesson throughout the weaning process when she wants the puppies to leave her alone. After just a few repetitions, the puppies get the message and respond to a mere look or a curled lip from the mother. This teaches authority and what it looks like to the puppy. You want to have leadership and authority, and this early lesson aids you when you start to teach leadership to your new puppy. The puppy learns dog language — or lip reading, as we call it — and bite inhibition, an important lesson for when they go home with their new human family and have a new parent to listen to. During the mother dog's training, the puppy learns that there is an authority figure and what that authority looks like. These lessons transfer to you more easily because of what the mother dog has taught her puppies. If they leave the litter when they are too young and have not had these lessons, the puppies will not recognize authority and they will think that they are the center of the universe. This is very unfortunate for the new owners.

Besides learning from their mothers, puppies also learn from each other. While they are playing, tempers may flare because one puppy bites another too hard. The puppies discover from these exchanges what it feels like to be bitten and, at the same time, to inhibit biting during play. (See Figure 7-1.)

FIGURE 7-1: Puppies discover valuable lessons while playing.

REMEMBER

Puppies that are separated from their canine families before they've had the opportunity for these experiences with their mother and littermates tend to identify more with humans than with other dogs. To simplify, they don't know they're dogs, and they tend to have their own set of problems, such as the following:

>> Aggression toward other dogs

>> Difficulty with housetraining

>> Separation anxiety

>> Excessive barking

>> Mouthing and biting their owners

>> Nervousness

>> An unhealthy attachment to humans

At about the 49th day of life, when the puppy's brain is neurologically complete, that special attachment between the dog and their new human owner, called *bonding*, takes place. Bonding is one of the reasons that the 49th day is the ideal time for puppies to leave the nest for their new homes.

Bonding to people becomes increasingly difficult the longer a puppy remains with their mother or littermates. This brings us to the next critical period, the Human Socialization Period. The dog also becomes more difficult to train. In addition, with delay, the puppy has the potential to experience built-in behavior problems, such as the following:

>> The pup may grow up being too dog-oriented.

>> The pup probably won't care much about people.

>> The pup may be difficult to teach to accept responsibility for his own behavior.

>> The pup may be more difficult to train, including housetraining.

Getting to know everyone: Weeks 7 to 12, the Human Socialization Period

Your dog is a social animal. To become an acceptable pet, the pup needs to interact with people, you and your family, as well as with other humans and dogs during the 7th through 12th weeks of life. If denied these opportunities, your dog's behavior around other people or dogs may be unpredictable — your dog may be fearful or perhaps even aggressive. For example, unless regularly exposed to children during this period, a dog may be uncomfortable or untrustworthy around them.

TIP

Socializing your puppy is critical if you want them to become a friendly adult dog. While your puppy is developing, expose them to as many different people as possible, including children and older people of all shapes, sexes, and sizes. Let them meet new dogs, too. Introduce them to different surfaces — grass, carpet, wood floors, sidewalks, gravel, and so on. These early experiences will pay off big time when your dog grows up.

Your puppy needs the chance to meet and have positive experiences with those persons and activities that will play a role in their life. The following are just a few examples:

>> Your relative who has visiting kids that occasionally come by: Have your puppy meet children as often as you can.

>> You live by yourself but have friends that visit you: Make an effort to let your puppy meet other people, particularly members of the opposite sex.

>> You plan to take your dog on family outings or vacations: Introduce riding in a car. Getting in and out of a car is something people often forget to teach at an early age. It should be fun and not always end up at the vet for a scary visit. You can have the car ride end back at home, occasionally, because all you did was go for a ride.

You can set up all these encounters by taking them to the local park. Most people love to meet puppies. And they can get used to the ride on the way there!

Not being able to do this during the COVID-19 pandemic caused so many problems with young dogs that continued throughout their lives. This is referred to as the COVID Puppy Syndrome. Lack of this critical socialization is long term and permanent. Too often people learned this too late. Prior to 12 weeks of age is the Human Socialization Period, and once this time is past, it's gone.

WARNING

A common but incorrect way for people to greet a puppy or an adult dog is to pat it on top of the head, just as they do with children. Puppies and adult dogs don't like this form of greeting any better than kids do. Patting a dog on the head encourages jumping, the very behavior most owners don't want. Instead, stand up straight or kneel down, and then greet the puppy with a smile and a hello. Put the palm of your hand on his chest and calmly stroke it in a massaging motion. Doing so will calm him. When meeting a puppy or dog for the first time, slowly put the palm of your hand toward him and let him smell your hand. This is considered an honest open gesture that you are a safe person.

Socialization with other dogs is equally important to socialization with humans and should be the norm rather than the exception. Puppies learn from other dogs but can only do so if they have a chance to spend time with them. Make it a point to introduce your young dog to other puppies and adult dogs on a regular basis. Many communities now have dog parks where dogs can interact and play together. If you plan to take your puppy to obedience class or to any dog event, or eventually day care, they definitely need to have the continual chance to interact with other dogs. Time spent now is well worth the effort — it will build their confidence and make your job training them that much easier.

Socialization is important for Buddy at this time, but so is training. Begin training your puppy as soon as you get them. The puppy will learn whether you teach them or not, so you may as well teach them what they need to know. Start teaching the exercises listed in Part 3. At this age, it's much easier to physically manipulate the puppy than after they have grown into an unruly teenager.

TIP

During this development period, your puppy follows your every footstep. Encourage this behavior by rewarding the puppy with an occasional treat, some petting, or a kind word. Taking advantage of your puppy's willingness to follow makes teaching the Come command that much easier (head to Chapter 10 for more details on this command).

Suddenly they're afraid: Weeks 8 to 12, the Fear Imprint Period

Weeks 8 through 12 are called the Fear Imprint Period. During this period, any painful or particularly frightening experience leaves a more lasting impression on your pup than if it occurred at any other time in their life. If the experience is sufficiently traumatic, it can literally change your puppy's life.

TIP

During this period, avoid exposing the puppy to traumatic experiences. When you need to take your puppy to the veterinarian, have the doctor give them a treat before, during, and after the examination to make the visit a pleasant experience. Although you need to stay away from stressful situations, do continue to train your puppy in a positive and nonpunitive way.

REMEMBER

During the first year's growth, you may see fear reactions at other times. Don't respond by dragging your puppy to the object that caused the fear. On the other hand, don't pet or reassure the dog either — you may create the impression that you approve of this fearful behavior. Rather, distract the puppy with a toy or a treat to get their mind off whatever scared them and go on to something pleasant. Practice some of the commands you've already taught so that they can focus on a positive experience. After a short time — sometimes up to two weeks — the fearful behavior will disappear.

Now they want to leave home: Beyond 12 weeks, "Been there, done that"

Sometime between 4 and 8 months, your puppy begins to realize that there's a big, wide world out there. Up to now, every time you called, Buddy probably willingly came to you. But now they may prefer to wander off and investigate alone. Buddy is maturing and cutting the apron strings, which is normal. They're not being spiteful or disobedient; they're just becoming an adolescent.

While they're going through this phase, make sure that you keep Buddy on a leash or in a confined area until they have learned to come when called. Otherwise, not coming when called becomes a pattern — annoying to you and dangerous to Buddy. If calling Buddy over and over again becomes a habit, breaking it will become difficult; prevention is the best cure. Teaching your dog to come when called (before they have developed the habit of running away) is easy. Practice calling them in the house, out in the yard, and at random times. Have a treat in your pocket to reinforce the behavior you want. (For more on teaching the Come command, check out Chapter 10.)

TIP

When you need to gather in a wandering Buddy, don't, under any circumstances, play the game of chasing them. Instead, call their name in an excited tone of voice. If that doesn't work, run the other way and get Buddy to chase you. You also can kneel on the ground and pretend you've found something extremely interesting, hoping that Buddy's curiosity brings him to you. If you have to, approach them slowly in an upright position, using a nonthreatening tone of voice until you can calmly take hold of their collar. Better still, lay down on the ground and look at the sky and giggle. Puppies must come over and see what you are up to and you can give them a hug and take their collar. Of course, this only works if they are staying close and not fully running from you.

Your puppy also goes through teething during this period and needs to chew anything and everything. This chewing behavior is a physical need. Puppies have the irritating habit of going for shoes left out. If one of your favorite shoes is demolished, keep your cool. Look at it as a lesson for you to put your possessions out of reach. Scolding Buddy won't stop the need to chew, but it may cause him to fear and mistrust you as you unintentionally teach him *not* to come when called

Your job is to provide acceptable outlets for this need, such as chew bones and toys. Real dog bones from the butcher are favorite chew bones for some dogs. A dog can't easily break them and they provide hours of entertainment. They also keep your dog's teeth clean. Kong toys (www.kongcompany.com) are another favorite, especially the hard rubber ones that are virtually indestructible and can be stuffed with peanut butter or yogurt. They come in different sizes appropriate to the size of your dog and can keep most dogs busy for hours. Just be sure that the toy is large enough so that your dog can't accidentally swallow it.

WARNING

Stay away from soft and fuzzy toys. Chances are that your dog will destroy them and may ingest a part of them. Rawhide chew toys can be dangerous because they're often treated with chemicals and can become soft and gooey when chewed; therefore, the dog can swallow them and get them stuck in their intestines. If you do provide these toys for your pet, be sure to supervise them so that they don't ingest pieces.

When Buddy is going through this stage, you may want to consider crating them when they're left alone. Doing so keeps your dog and your possessions safe, and both of you will be happy. Crating them during this growth spurt helps with their housetraining, too. With all the chewing they do during teething, accidents sometimes happen (chewing stimulates bowel movements in puppies). See Chapter 8 for more on housetraining.

The Terrible Twos: Managing the Adolescent from 4 Months to 2 Years

The adolescent stage of your dog's life, depending on the breed, takes place anywhere from 4 months to 2 years and culminates in sexual maturity. Generally, the smaller the dog, the sooner they mature. Larger dogs enter (and end) adolescence later in life.

Adolescence is a time when your cute little puppy can turn into a teenage monster. They start to lose their baby teeth and their soft, fuzzy puppy coat. They go through growth spurts and look gangly either up in the rear or down in front; they're entering an ugly-duckling stage.

REMEMBER

Depending on the size of the dog, they achieve 40 to 70 percent of adult growth by the time they're 7 months old. If you haven't done so already, you'd better start training now, before the dog gets so big that you can't manage them. As Buddy begins to mature, they start to display some puzzling behaviors, as well as some perfectly normal but objectionable ones.

Because adolescence can be such a tricky time in a pup's life (and yours!), we provide some information to help make the transition as smooth as possible.

Understanding the juvenile flakies

The term *juvenile flakies* most accurately describes what's technically known as a second Fear Imprint Period (see the earlier section "Suddenly they're afraid: Weeks 8–12, the Fear Imprint Period" for more information on this period). Juvenile flakies are apprehension or fear behaviors that are usually short-lived. They're caused by temporary calcium deficiencies and hormone development related to a puppy's periodic growth spurts.

Understanding how hormones affect behavior

During the period from 4 months to a year, the male puppy's hormones surge to four times his adult level, and this surge can have important effects on his behavior. You can usually tell when he's entering this phase. The most obvious sign is that he stops listening to you. He also may try to dominate other dogs in the household or ones he meets outside. Fortunately, after this enormous surge, his hormones ultimately return to normal.

REMEMBER

Hormones drive behavior, which means that the intensity of behaviors increases in direct proportion to the amount of hormones coursing through his system.

TIP

Doing leadership exercises and training your puppy at this age is definitely a good idea. When Buddy experiences a surge of hormones during training, do some heeling or retrieving to get him back into the proper frame of mind.

Females go through hormonal influences when going through their heat cycle. These hormones can change the female's attention span and willingness to do training. Be patient during her cycles. The female is a bit older than the male puppy when they develop into puberty.

A female's age when going through their first heat cycle will vary by breed — the bigger the breed, the later they may go through a heat cycle, meaning they mature more slowly than a smaller breed. However, every dog is different; there is no absolute. Between 6 to 18 months may be when you first notice physical hormonal changes in a female dog. The physical changes are a swelling of the vulva and possibly a bloody discharge, but even that isn't necessarily always the case during their first heat cycle. It may only last a few days and the dog may keep themselves clean enough that you may not notice. An adult dog's cycle typically lasts three weeks and happens twice a year. Talk to your veterinarian about the benefits of spaying your female dog. Frequent heat cycles can be challenging to live with.

A SAD FACT OF LIFE

The majority of dogs in animal shelters are delivered to those shelters at around 8 months of age, when they're no longer "cute" and have "stopped listening." Millions of dogs are surrendered annually because their owners didn't want to spend 10 to 15 minutes a day training them when they were young.

During this time, the necessity for training and protection increases. The freedom that the puppy had before now becomes limited. The better trained they are, the easier this transition will be, but it requires a real commitment on your part.

Meeting the mature adult when your dog finally grows up

No matter how much you wish that cute little puppy could remain as is, your pup is going to grow up. It happens anywhere from 1 to 4 years of age, depending on the breed. Smaller breeds mature faster than larger breeds. If you trained Buddy as a younger dog, they'll now become the perfect pet you always wanted. Figure 7-2 shows a pup on the way to adulthood.

FIGURE 7-2:
Yes, your pup will grow up.

© John Wiley & Sons, Inc.

Spaying or Neutering to Help with Behavior and Training

Unless you intend to exhibit your dog in dog shows or to breed your dog, you need to seriously consider neutering or spaying. However, current research shows that neutering too early affects structure as the dog ages. The correct age to think about neutering your dog is after the growth plates are intact, somewhere between 18 months and 3 years. This opinion may differ with everyone you ask.

We suggest you discuss this with your veterinarian to help you decide the ideal age. We just want to give you things to think about and to help with your discussions with others.

When an intact male becomes aware of a female in season anywhere in the immediate area, chances are he'll be oblivious to any commands you have taught him. View such situations as training opportunities to remind Buddy that you still expect him to obey. After all, what better distraction is there? If you find you have difficulty controlling Buddy under such circumstances, see Chapter 5 for information on training equipment and Chapter 3 for more on the adrenaline effect. The *adrenaline effect* is when whatever your dog is doing affects his ability to "hear" you. A beagle pursuing a rabbit will not hear you call him. But a beagle in the house at dinner time will hear you every time you call. What equipment you need to aid your call with each example is affected also. No leash or collar is needed inside at dinner time, yet a training collar and long leash is a must when Buddy is running after a rabbit outside.

In the following sections, we show you both the pros and cons of spaying or neutering your pooch, including the effect the procedures have on your pet.

Heeding the advantages

For both males and females, the advantages of altering your pet generally outweigh the disadvantages. For the male, the advantages of altering include the following:

>> Keeps him calm and less stressed around a female in season

>> Reduces the tendency to roam

>> Diminishes mounting behavior but may not stop it completely

>> Makes training easier

>> Helps to prevent marking behavior in the house

In short, he'll be easier to live with and easier to train. Neutering also curbs the urge to roam or run away. So if the front door is left open by accident, he won't go miles to find a female in season.

TECHNICAL STUFF

It isn't true that dogs that have been altered lose their protective instincts — it depends on the age when the dog is altered. Generally, dogs altered after a year of age retain their protective instincts.

If you spay your female, she, too, will stay closer to home. Perhaps even more important are these benefits:

>> You won't have to deal with the mess that goes with having her in season — often referred to as *in heat*.

>> You won't have to worry about unwanted visitors camping on your property and lifting a leg against any vertical surface.

>> You won't have to worry about accidental puppies, which are difficult to place in good homes, yet will be your moral responsibility.

Finally, and most importantly in the context of training, she'll be more even keeled, a distinct benefit.

Acknowledging the disadvantages

Altering changes the hormone level in a dog's body. Some dogs that are altered develop hormonal deficiencies that can produce arthritis and bone disease and can affect joint and bladder function. Researchers have specifically evaluated the effect on clinical orthopedic disease (hip dysplasia, elbow dysplasia, and cranial cruciate ligament disease), neoplasia (lymphosarcoma, mast cell tumor, osteosarcoma, hemangiosarcoma, and mammary cancer), urinary incontinence, and pyometra, according to studies stated in *AKC Canine Health Foundation* (February 2019).

The most common deficiency seen is hypothyroidism. It's thought that around 70 percent of all purebred dogs have hypothyroidism. Detected in dogs as young as 6 months of age and all the way up to the age of 8 and beyond, hypothyroidism requires a special blood test for diagnosis.

Hypothyroidism can cause these problems:

>> Dull, oily, thinning, and smelly coats

>> Increased shedding

>> Separation anxiety

>> Skin problems

>> A tendency to gain weight

REMEMBER

Regardless of these disadvantages, we recommend altering a dog that isn't going to be bred simply because altered dogs are so much easier to live with. However, remember, spaying or neutering too early also causes long-term problems. See the preceding section for the advantages of altering.

Knowing when to spay or neuter

If you decide to alter your dog, think about having the surgery after 18 months of age for both sexes, but discuss this with your veterinarian and heed their recommendations as you make your decision.

Depending on the breed and size of the female, she'll go into her first season any time after 7 months of age. For a toy breed, it's apt to be sooner, and for a giant breed, it's likely to be later, sometimes as late as 18 months of age.

If you want a dog to show more adult behaviors and take more responsibility — like being a protector or guard dog, training for competitive events, or working for a living — think about altering males or females between 18 months and 2 years of age.

REMEMBER

A dog that hasn't been neutered until after a year of age, or a female that has gone through two seasons, is generally easier to train for competitive events, such as obedience or agility trials. Dogs have become fully grown by that time, are emotionally mature, have learned more adult behaviors, and can accept more responsibility.

TO BREED OR NOT TO BREED YOUR DOG? THAT'S THE QUESTION

Don't even contemplate breeding your dog unless

- Your dog is purebred and registered.

- You didn't get your dog from an animal shelter or pet store.

- You have at least a three-generation pedigree for your dog.

- Your dog has at least four titled dogs, such as conformation or working titles, in the last three generations.

- Your dog is certified free of genetic disorders applicable to the breed.

- Your dog conforms to the standard for its breed.

- Your dog has a stable temperament.

(continued)

(continued)

The correct reason to breed dogs is to better the breed. Breeding should never be done because it sounds fun or you want to make money. That always backfires. Health certificates, C-sections, vaccines, and health guarantees are all part of a good breeding program. Not to forget, feeding and nursing care of the mother dog and puppies is also very expensive. You should have potential puppy homes lined up before you breed, too; at least half of the puppies you expect should be lined up with forever homes before you decide to breed your dog.

Breeding dogs for the purpose of exposing your children to the miracle of birth is *not* a good idea. The world already has enough dogs that don't have homes, and finding homes for your puppies will be much more difficult than you think, if not impossible. Look on YouTube and the internet if you want your children to understand the birthing process.

IN THIS CHAPTER

» Becoming housetrained requires three things to know

» Crate training your dog

» Setting up a feeding and elimination schedule

» Dealing with accidents

» Exploring an alternative to crate training

Chapter **8**

The Ins and Outs of Crate Training and Housetraining

e strongly recommend that you use a crate or similar means of confinement. Dogs consider crates their dens. Because dogs are den animals, dens give dogs the feeling of safety, coziness, security, and comfort. A crate is your dog's bedroom inside of your house. A crate is also their home away from home when you travel, and it provides safety for both of you when they're with you in the car. The closest comparison to leaving your untrained dog in a crate would be if you were told to go back to bed for a few hours and then promised evening entertainment when everybody returned home later. Sounds good, doesn't it? And here's a book (chew bone) in case you wake up and need something to occupy your attention.

Crates ideally are solid airline-type crates rather than open wire crates. The solid sides add to the den feeling and concept whereas a wire crate forces the dog to be out in the open and can actually cause them more stress. Humans may view a solid, dark crate as a prison, but dogs don't view it that way because they are instinctively den animals. Confinement is security to a dog. Most puppies look for spots to nap, such as under a coffee table or behind furniture. Dogs are trying to reproduce the den environment. A solid crate works wonders as a den.

This chapter covers the keys to successful housetraining:

>> Appropriately using a crate or X-pen

>> Setting a schedule for feeding and exercising and sticking to that schedule even on weekends — at least until your dog is housetrained and mature

>> Practicing vigilance, consistency, and patience until your dog is trained

REMEMBER

If you've obtained an adult dog from a shelter or other source, they may not be housetrained. The rules for housetraining an adult dog are the same as for a puppy, but the process will likely go much more quickly. The adult dog's ability to control elimination is obviously much better than a puppy's. The things you must watch for are surface preferences and the ability to hold elimination. Dogs who have lived outdoors all their lives may never eliminate in the house because of grass and dirt preferences. But they also may eliminate at will, because they've never had to hold it before, ever. This chapter offers advice for all tendencies.

Helping Buddy Get Used to Their Crate

No matter whether Buddy is a puppy or a new adult dog you adopted, crate training Buddy provides peace of mind for you and a safe place for your dog when they need some peace and quiet and want to get away from the hubbub of family life.

To help get Buddy comfortable with their crate, follow these steps:

1. **Set up the crate in the family room and leave it open, which allows Buddy to investigate it.**

   Bring a container of treats over and plan to spend some play time around the crate.

2. **To get them to go inside, toss a treat or two in the crate and allow Buddy to reach in and eat them.**

   You may need to have the treats land just inside the door but gradually have them land farther toward the back. Allow them to eat the treats and come out on their own. Don't shut the door yet.

3. **To help them accept the door being shut, toss another treat into the crate and slowly swing the door shut, but don't latch it; just praise them for being inside and eating the treat.**

   Open the crate door and say, "Okay," as your release word and let them come out. At this point, introduce a command for getting in the crate. You can use any command you want but be consistent. Here are a few good choices:

   - Get in

   - Kennel up

   - Crate crate

4. **Next, train not to come out until you've given permission. Say, "Get in," as you toss a cookie in the crate.**

   Doing so introduces the concept that you own the crate and the door of the crate, and therefore the passage through the door is yours, too. Hence, Buddy shouldn't come charging out of the crate but rather politely wait for your command to exit.

5. **Swing the door closed, but hold onto the door because you won't be latching it just yet.**

   When Buddy is at the door, slightly open the crate an inch and then close it again. The visual pressure, not actual pressure of the door coming closed toward Buddy, will stop any forward motion out of the crate.

   The point is not to allow Buddy to burst out of the crate. They should politely wait for you to say "Okay" as the release word to exit the crate. As you continue to practice, slightly opening the crate, then closing it again, they'll start to respect the opening and even look up at you instead of inching out the door. Smile and say, "Okay." This command lets them out of the crate, and you can praise them.

REMEMBER

You also can feed Buddy in the crate to make the crate experience even more positive. Place their bowl in front of the crate and let them eat. The next time you feed, place the food just inside the crate. With every successive meal, put the bowl farther inside the crate until it's at the far end. Leave the door open as they eat, because feeding them in the crate with the door open is just one more way of teaching Buddy how wonderful the crate is. Plus, if you have more than one dog, feeding them in the crate gives them each a place to eat without worrying about protecting their food dish. Take a look at Figure 8-1 to see a dog enjoying a meal in a crate.

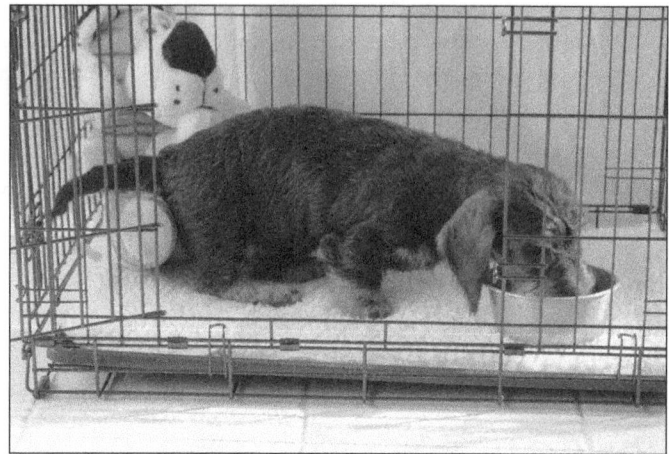

FIGURE 8-1:
Feeding a puppy
in a crate.

© John Wiley & Sons, Inc.

TIP

Be sure to give Buddy something to occupy their attention when you leave. Interactive toys stuffed with treats, such as a Kong toy, are a wonderful way to distract them should they be awake during their time in the crate. Usually, they sleep, learning your routine, while you're gone.

Balance crate time with energy outlets because exercise, training, walks, and so on are important to burn off the energy that they have, especially if they have spent a lot of time in the crate while you're away.

REMEMBER

How long can you ultimately leave Buddy in his crate unattended? That depends on your dog and your schedule. Adult dogs can stay in a crate for up to four to six hours. Puppies can't last that long, though. Over the course of a 24-hour period, puppies need to eliminate more frequently than adult dogs. A puppy's ability to control elimination increases with age, at the rate of about one hour per month starting the count at 2 months of age. Until they're 6 months of age, don't expect a puppy to last for more than four hours during the day without needing to eliminate. When sleeping, most puppies can last through the night, usually because they are crated in the room with you and you set a good example of quiet.

Training a Dog to Eliminate Outside

The following sections examine the three factors that are crucial for Buddy to know when you're training them to eliminate outside.

1. Buddy needs to know when to hold it; that is, not to go in the house.

2. Buddy needs to know why they're outside.

3. They also need to know that you'll be trustworthy to allow them outside often enough to eliminate when they need to go.

These are the big three factors that teach a dog to be housetrained.

Holding elimination when inside the house

When training Buddy to eliminate outside, the most important lesson is that they understand to hold elimination when they're inside the house. Go here but not there is a huge concept. It can be taught early in the whelping box with the mother dog and the breeder, but not all dogs have that early training opportunity. So, it's up to you now. In the whelping box, they learn to eat, sleep, and play here and eliminate over there. When the litter is large, this is easy to understand for the breeder, but when the litter is tiny with a tiny breed, it takes extra effort. This is why toy breeds can be harder to train to go outside; they never had two places, one to live in and one to eliminate in.

When you're home and Buddy is awake and with you, keep them confined in the room with you. A properly trained puppy that learned that there is one place to live in and one place to potty in will wander off to a different area to eliminate. Even though holding it is the goal, the fact that they know to go to a lesser-used area of the house or room is proper knowledge and good dog behavior that you can capitalize on. Keep them close to you so that you can watch them and make sure they don't slip out to eliminate. You also can close the door to the room you're in with your puppy or you can use a baby gate to close off the room.

After you have your puppy home or you get Buddy as an older dog, a crate is the best tool to teach them to hold their elimination. See the earlier section "Helping Buddy Get Used to Their Crate." When you aren't able to supervise Buddy or when you're leaving the house, the babysitter is the crate. Buddy will sleep while you're gone, which is the goal. When you return, take them outside to eliminate.

REMEMBER

The leash is another great device to help you teach your new dog to hold elimination. Use the leash inside the house as an umbilical cord to keep him tethered to you until you've established a routine with Buddy and you can read their need to eliminate. If they're on leash, they'll never be more than 6 feet away from you and you can monitor their need to eliminate.

TIP

When you keep your new dog on a leash tethered to you, keep a chew bone handy to offer something correct to chew on rather than unwittingly allowing them to find something of yours to destroy. Doing so is another benefit of using the leash to train your dog inside the home.

TAG-TEAM TRAINING WITH MOTHER DOG

We always say there is no better dog trainer than another dog, and the best trainer is the mother dog. Allow her to teach her lessons to her litter.

If Buddy is a puppy, do everything you can to learn how they were raised while still with the litter. Even as early as only a few weeks old, while still with the mother dog in the whelping box, puppies learn that there are two places in their lives:

- One where they sleep, eat, and play
- One where they potty

These areas aren't the same place. The mother dog will usually try to set this distinction if given the opportunity.

The area where the puppies are raised should be large enough to allow for two such areas. The litter with mom should stay together at least until 7 weeks, longer in some cases. Your new puppy has a lot to learn from the mother dog as well as socialization from their littermates.

Knowing why they're outside — to eliminate

Teaching your dog why you're both outside is super important. Look at it from your dog's point of view:

- » **Inside:** Your attention is about 95 percent on your life, working on your computer, watching TV, reading, talking, sleeping, whatever you like to do, whereas 5 percent of your attention is on your dog. What are they up to? Oh, they're sleeping or chewing on a bone. What a good dog. You don't want to interrupt them.

- » **Outside:** This is the reverse. Five percent of your attention is on your life: your yard or the weather and 95 percent of your attention is on your dog, playing together, sniffing the grass, walking around interacting, and so on. The dog is having fun enjoying all of your attention, but then they eliminate, and you go back inside where you go back to your life. *In other words, the dog's fun ends.*

If you were the dog, what would you have learned? The fun ends when you eliminate, so don't eliminate if you're having fun outside with your owner. Of course, that's the last thing you want them to learn, but indeed that's the lesson you accidently taught — unintentional training.

REMEMBER

To train your dog to eliminate when they're outside, you need to reverse these percentages. When you're outside with your dog, watch them and ignore them. Avoid the temptation to play with them. Instead, quietly stroll around to encourage them to sniff and then eliminate. Eliminating first is the most important thing you want to teach your dog — hurry up and go potty. When he does eliminate, then the fun can start. Praise, play, chase, treat, pick them up if possible, and make a huge party out of their elimination. Then and only then should you go back inside — after the party. And even then and only then should you start your walk with them. The walk is the party, and the elimination is the purpose of going outside. Dogs love to take walks. If you walk first, you're teaching your dog never to potty on a walk, because when they potty, the walk ends. Always look at it from your dog's perspective.

Make sure that you go outside with them to eliminate, no matter whether your yard is fenced or the weather is bad. Dogs are pack animals and love being with people. If you put your dog outside, most dogs will sit by the door waiting for you to open the door to come out and join them until trained to do otherwise. Dogs don't just empty because they're outside. During the housetraining process, you need to know when your dog is empty and when they aren't, when they actually went potty and when they haven't. If they haven't eliminated and you let them in the house, they'll empty inside because they truly did need to eliminate and were holding it, waiting for you to come out and join them. Go outside with them every time and keep track of whether they have eliminated or not. As your dog becomes trained and trustworthy, going outside with them won't need to be the case forever. You may be inconvenienced during this time of their training, but you'll eventually have a fully trustworthy and trained dog for the rest of their life.

Proving to Buddy that you're trustworthy to take them outside

Buddy needs to trust that you'll take them outside so that they can take care of business. You being trustworthy can be the hardest part because you need to be attentive. Mary Ann recommends a kitchen timer or the alarm app on your phone. You need to actually be reminded to take your dog outside often enough.

Most dogs quickly learn to hold elimination for eight hours at night and then another eight hours while you're at work and they're in the crate (as soon as they're old enough to hold it that long), but they can't then hold it for another eight hours while you're home and the household is active.

When you're home and Buddy has access to water and activity, their metabolism will speed up, producing urine and the need to have a bowel movement. That's when the alarm is important. When Buddy is new to you and you're home and all are awake, take them out every 45 minutes because small bladders need to be emptied often. As we already mentioned, the night time is different and Buddy will learn to hold it longer, because all is quiet and their metabolism slows.

As Buddy gets older, you can keep adding 15 minutes a week to your timer, but don't be too quick to make it more than 90 minutes when everyone is home and the puppy is active. You can always adjust it, but having that alarm can help you remember to take them outside.

Special care is required when it's raining or it's cold because many dogs, particularly those with short hair, don't like to go out in the wet any more than you do. Make sure your puppy actually eliminates before you bring them back into the house. If not, it will be as if you have a loaded gun walking around in your house. Take them out again and keep them on leash in the house if necessary or even return them to the crate if you can't watch them. They have to go, even if it's raining. You don't want to find eliminations in your house, so be alert.

REMEMBER

Housetraining can be inconvenient, but if you use a crate, baby gate, leash, and timer, you can do it in no time. Just be diligent and consistent. A few months of being inconvenienced will give you a lifetime of a housetrained dog you can trust.

Establishing a Regular Feeding and Elimination Schedule

Being diligent with Buddy's feeding schedule and their ensuing elimination schedule will make housetraining go much smoother. Keep the following schedule in mind:

>> **From 7 weeks to 4 months of age:** Puppies need to be fed four times a day. Set a time to feed the puppy that's convenient for you, and aim to feed at the same time every day. Depending on your schedule, you may establish a comfortable routine of feeding at 7 a.m., noon, 5 p.m., and 9 p.m. This schedule works well if you go to bed around 11 p.m. and can take the puppy out before you retire for the night. Adjust the schedule to the time you normally get up in the morning.

>> **From 4 to 7 months:** Three daily meals are appropriate. From then on, feed twice a day. Feeding frequent small meals keeps your puppy calm, helps them grow evenly, and controls the time when they relieve themselves. Also give your puppy a dog biscuit before bedtime to help them sleep through the night.

>> **Older than 7 months:** For many adult dogs, feeding two meals a day is best because it satisfies hunger throughout the day. Historically, some people choose to feed once a day, so talk to your veterinarian to help you decide what is best for you and your dog.

REMEMBER

Feed the right amount. Loose stools are a sign of overfeeding; straining and dry stools are signs of underfeeding or a poor diet. Be sure to keep Buddy's diet constant and feed the same kind of food at every meal. Abrupt changes in food may cause digestive upsets that won't help your housetraining efforts. See Chapter 4 for more feeding options.

WARNING

For the sake of convenience, you may be tempted to put Buddy's meal in a large bowl and leave it for him to nibble on as they see fit, a practice called *self-feeding.* Although self-feeding is convenient for you, for purposes of housetraining, don't do it. You won't be able to keep track of when and how much Buddy eats. You won't be able to time their intake with their need to eliminate. Don't prolong mealtimes, either: After ten minutes, pick up the dish and put it away. Feeding meals is healthier for your dog, and it helps you know their eating habits. You need to know if they go off their food when they are sick.

REMEMBER

Have fresh water available at all times during the day when Buddy is outside of the crate. Two hours before your bedtime, remove the water dish so that they can last through the night without having to make a trip outside. As an adult, most dogs won't drink at night. So not having water in the bedroom is a practice that you can continue into adulthood.

If you're following a regular feeding routine, you're promoting a regular elimination routine, too. A puppy's biological clock is astonishingly consistent. A puppy usually has a bowel movement several times a day and urinates perhaps six to eight times. Same goes for an adult — dogs will eat, then eliminate. Dogs will drink, then eliminate shortly thereafter. Dogs are routine animals and will hold elimination to specific times if your routine is consistent enough; they'll become comfortable with the same routine themselves.

Take Buddy to their toilet area after they wake up, shortly after eating or drinking, and after they have played or chewed. Of course, you need to be aware of their unique elimination needs, too. Some puppies need to eliminate more than once in a relatively short period of time. In fact, it isn't uncommon for a dog to eliminate first thing in the morning and then again about a half-hour later, because their metabolism speeds up after the long night of rest and quiet. You'll discover your dog's routine by being aware and by being an active part of the solution. Keep a log if that helps.

TIP

An easy way to become aware of Buddy's elimination routine is by keeping a notebook or chart each time they go potty. When you see your puppy sniffing and circling, take note! They're letting you know that they're looking for a place to go. Take them out to their toilet area so that they don't have an accident in the house.

Designating a Regular Toilet Area

No matter whether you live in a house or an apartment, you need to start by selecting a toilet area in your yard, along a path, or in a park. Always take Buddy to that spot when you want them to eliminate. The designated place shouldn't be too far from the house. Walk directly to that area and then ignore them until they have eliminated.

If you and Buddy live in an apartment or condo, you probably have to jump through a variety of hoops, including taking elevators and stairs, to take out Buddy. Moreover, if you're mobility impaired, going outside with Buddy may be a real challenge.

TIP

The easiest way to housetrain an apartment or condo dog is to first follow the regiment by using a crate. If you're using a pee pad and tray (available at pet stores or online) in the apartment or condo, take them to the tray, just as you would take them outside. Usually pee pads aren't recommended unless you have a tiny toy breed. Even then, going outside is so much better, but pee pads and trays can work for you if you aren't able to take Buddy out of your apartment (see Figure 8-2 for an example of a potty tray). When training to a potty tray, do the same thing as we discuss in the previous section. Take Buddy to the potty tray just as you'd take them outside. Keep a timer going to remind yourself to direct them to their potty tray so that you don't let too much time go by without taking them to their pee pad.

FIGURE 8-2:
A potty tray to hold pee pads.

© *John Wiley & Sons, Inc.*

BALTO: AN EXAMPLE OF A STAR HOUSETRAINING PUPIL

First thing in the morning, Robert takes his 12-week-old Yorkie puppy, Balto, out of his crate and straight outside to his toilet area. Fifteen minutes after Balto's morning meal, Robert takes him out again. Robert then crates Balto and leaves for work.

On his lunch break, Robert goes home to let Balto out to relieve himself, and he plays with him for a few minutes. He then feeds Balto and, just to make sure, takes him out once more. For the afternoon, Robert crates Balto again until he returns. When he gets home, he walks and feeds Balto and allows him to spend the rest of the evening in the house where Robert can keep an eye on him and train him. This is an important part of the day for Robert because Balto needs lots of socialization and Robert gives Balto all he needs. Before bedtime, Robert takes Balto to his toilet area one more time and then crates him for the night in the room where Robert sleeps.

When Balto turns 7 months old, Robert will drop the noontime feeding. From that age on, most dogs only need to go out immediately upon waking (or soon afterward) in the morning, once during the late afternoon, a few times in the evening, and once again before bedtime.

REMEMBER

No matter where you live — in the city, in a neighborhood, or in the country — you also need to pick up after your dog. Even in your own yard, unless you have oodles of land, you need to pick up after them, for obvious sanitary reasons. And don't let them do their business in a neighbor's yard; to have good neighbors, you need to be a good neighbor.

TIP

You also may want to teach Buddy a command, such as Hurry Up, so that you can speed up the process when necessary. Time the command to just before they start and then lavishly praise when they have finished. After several repetitions, Buddy will associate the command with having to eliminate. The Hurry Up command is useful when you're traveling with Buddy, and it gets them used to eliminating on leash.

When Accidents Happen — Knowing What to Do

No matter how conscientious and vigilant you are, your puppy will have accidents. Housetraining accidents may be simple mistakes or may indicate a physical problem. The key to remember is that, as a general rule, dogs want to be clean. Also remember that accidents are just that — accidents. Your dog didn't do it on purpose. The following sections give you tips on what to do when accidents happen.

Avoiding punishment

When Buddy has an accident in the house, don't call them to you to punish them. It's too late. If you do punish your dog under these circumstances, it won't help your housetraining efforts, and you'll make them wary of wanting to come to you (thus hampering learning the Come command).

A popular misconception is that the dog knows "what they did" because they look "guilty." Absolutely not true! They have that look because, from prior experience, they know that when you happen to come across a mess, you get mad at them. They have learned to associate a mess with your response. They haven't made — and can't make — the connection between the urge that caused the mess and your anger. Discipline after the fact is the quickest way to undermine the relationship you're trying to build with your dog.

Dogs are smart, but they don't associate what happened some time ago with belated consequences. When you come home from work and yell at your dog for having an accident in the living room, all you're doing is letting them know that you're upset on your return home. This reaction will cause undue stress on Buddy as they worry about your return home each day.

TIP

Instead, change the freedom you've given too early to Buddy and return to using the crate, not as a punishment, but as a training tool, to teach them to hold elimination longer. You can also go back to shortening the length of time you're gone. As soon as you stop using the crate, you can still come home at lunch to allow for an extra outing for elimination. Be fair and kind to your dog; remember, you're a big part of your dog's success.

Dealing with the accidents

Depending on the situation, you should handle accidents in different ways. Consider the following:

>> **When you come upon a belated accident:** Keep calm and put your dog out of sight so they can't watch you clean up (seeing you clean up attracts them to the spot). See the next section for more on cleaning.

>> **When you catch your dog in the act:** If you see Buddy squatting in the living room, sharply call their name and clap your hands. If they stop, take them out to their toilet area. If they don't, let them finish and don't get mad. Don't try to drag them out, because that will make your clean-up job that much more difficult. Until your puppy is reliable, don't let them have the run of the house unsupervised.

Regressions in housetraining do occur. Regressions after 7 months of age may be a sign that your dog is ill. If accidents persist, take them to your vet for a checkup.

When traveling with your dogs, make it a point to keep the regular feeding schedule and exercise routine as close as possible to the same routine you have at home. Sticking to a customary daily rhythm prevents digestive upsets that can lead to accidents.

Cleaning accidents

To adequately clean an area used by mistake inside, use an enzymatic cleaner to neutralize any urine odor. All sorts are available on the market. Buy one that neutralizes as it cleans. Soak up any urine with paper towels or a rag before you clean. Then saturate the full extent of the area with your cleaner and soak it up again.

Having a good rug shampooer is a good idea. Dogs will often have accidents or illnesses during their lifetime, and shampooers are wonderful appliances for cleaning up diarrhea, vomit, mud, or spills that you also make, especially that red wine.

Using an Exercise Pen for Housetraining

Although a puppy can last in their crate for the night when they're asleep, you can't leave a puppy in their crate for purposes of housetraining for longer than four hours at a time during the day. Your puppy will soil their crate, which definitely isn't a habit you want to establish.

If your schedule doesn't allow you to keep an eye on Buddy during the day or come home to let the puppy out in time, the alternative is an exercise pen, or X-pen. An X-pen (see Figure 8-3) is intelligent confinement and uses the same principle as a crate, except that it's bigger and has no top. An X-pen also can be used outdoors.

FIGURE 8-3:
An X-pen is
another form of
containment.

© John Wiley & Sons, Inc.

First, you need to acquire an X-pen that's appropriate for the size of your dog. For a dog the size of a Labrador, the X-pen needs to be 10 square feet. For a smaller dog, 6 square feet should be plenty. Set up the X-pen where the puppy will be confined during your absence. If your dog is a super athlete who either climbs over or jumps out of the X-pen, you need to cover the pen with a piece of plywood or pegboard.

To get your dog comfortable in their X-pen, follow the same procedure as you did when introducing them to their crate (see "Helping Buddy Get Used to Their Crate," earlier in this chapter). When Buddy is feeling at home in the X-pen and you're ready to leave them for the day, cover one-third of the area with pee pads. Buddy will get the hint and eliminate on the pee pads. Cover one-third of the remaining area with a blanket, adding some interactive toys or a biscuit. Finally, leave one-third uncovered.

As they get older and their ability to control the elimination process improves, gradually reduce the area covered with pee pads until you can remove it altogether. Because a dog's natural desire is to keep their den clean, the process should be completed by the time they are 6 months of age.

Leave while they're occupied with their toys or biscuit. Don't make a big deal out of leaving — simply leave.

Some people try to rig up confinement areas by blocking off parts of a room. Theoretically, doing so works, but it does permit Buddy to chew the baseboard, corners of cabinets, or anything else they can get their teeth on. You may want to confine your dog to a part of the room with baby gates. This option works well for some people and some dogs, but remember, confinement in a small room allows access to the room and potential destruction to the room. Lots of chew toys are a must! Dogs have a second chewing stage around 9 months of age. That's when the adult back teeth set into the jaw bone. Keep your dog confined until older than 12 months, but to be safe, crate until 18 months of age.

WARNING

Whatever barrier you decide to try, don't use an accordion-type gate — dogs can stick their heads through it and possibly strangle themselves. Also, leaving a dog on a concrete surface isn't a good idea. Something about concrete impedes housetraining; many dogs don't understand why it can't be used as a toilet area. Concrete also wreaks havoc on the elbows of large breeds.

TIP

You'll find that, in the long run, your least expensive option — as is so often the case — is the right way from the start. Don't be penny-wise and pound-foolish by scrimping on the essentials at the risk of jeopardizing more expensive items. Splurging for an X-pen or a good solid crate now will probably save you money on your home improvement budget down the road.

DOING YOUR DOODY

Being a good dog neighbor means not letting Buddy deface the property of others, including eliminating in their yards. When Buddy's got to go, only use areas specifically designed for dog elimination. Even diehard dog lovers object to other dogs leaving their droppings on their lawn, in the streets, and in similar unsuitable areas. They also object to having their shrubbery or other vertical objects on their property doused by Buddy when they lift their leg. If Buddy must potty in someone's yard, you need to be ready for poop-scooping duty. Always carry a bag to pick up after your dog. After all, part of responsible dog ownership is cleaning up after them. Don't let Buddy become the curse of your neighborhood. Do unto others. . . .

3

Tackling Training Basics

Train your dog to come to you when they're called. Before you can do that, they first need to learn their name and what you mean for them to do when you say that name.

Teach your dog to go away from you on command, another important concept. Most people have never thought of how useful this command can be.

Train Buddy on the fundamentals for all dogs — Sit, Lay Down, and Stay. Nothing can be simpler when you have a plan.

Teach Buddy how to walk politely beside you, which is the number one behavior most people want from their dogs.

Instruct your dog to go to their bed — a dog bed nearby where they can lie down and hang out with the family.

Make your home as safe as possible for your dog. Safety begins with openings to the outside, such as doors and gates. Teaching your dog not to bolt out an opening can save their life.

IN THIS CHAPTER

» **Comparing praise and petting — there is a big difference**

» **Releasing from work with "Okay" every time**

» **Teaching Buddy to recognize their name — the Name Game**

» **Introducing Hello as a greeting and sitting command**

» **Showing your dog the Leave It command can save their life**

Chapter **9**

Focusing on Some Basic Training Commands

S tarting to train the basics is when the fun really begins. Training requires Buddy's focus on you, and they need to know a few basic words that lead to all future training. In this chapter we cover getting Buddy to focus on you and how you can praise them while they're working and after they're released. The relationship you have with Buddy is already starting to develop, and as you continue to work together as a team, you'll be the coach and Buddy will be the team player. It's all about team work, and you are the leader of the team.

Training for Attention: Praise Versus Petting

To train your dog, you must have their attention. Without it, you can't teach them anything. How to get their attention requires some good food, a big smile on your face, lots of nice words of praise from you, and a leash to keep them with you.

Easier said than done, right? The following sections tell you how to differentiate praise from simply petting your dog, and then show you how to incorporate praise into your training plan.

Understanding the difference between praise and petting

As you continue training your dog, it's very important to distinguish praise from petting. Keeping the following in mind will help:

>> **Praise** is happy words *said* with a smile, which makes your dog's tail wag and gets them to look at you. In other words, you *say* praise. Your dog responds with a wiggle and a look, which means they're engaged with you and doing what you asked. You give praise while Buddy is doing a command you gave them.

>> **Petting** is *touching* your dog and massaging their ears, head, or body. You pet after they are done working and you've released them from their command with an *Okay* release word. Petting is the *party* you have after you say the release word. It is all about you and your dog interacting.

Petting in general is distracting to your dog and can change the dynamics between the two of you. You don't want to be seen as working for Buddy, being their massage therapist because you're petting them. Instead, by using verbal praise while they're working for you, petting becomes pleasing to your dog and something for which they strive.

For example, you command Sit and help them get into a sitting position. You then *verbally praise* them with a smile and get your dog to wag their tail and look at you, pleased with themselves. Then you say, "Okay," and move your dog out of their sitting position by stepping away, petting and partying with them, and giving them a massage and rubdown.

You *give praise* while your dog works. You *pet* after they're done doing each command.

REMEMBER

Using Okay to release from work

Every command must have an end command. For example, "Buddy, do this" until you're released with the Okay command. This is the basis for all training used in this book. You teach Buddy who is in charge — you. Here is an example: "Here is what Down means, now hold the position until I release you with the Okay release command."

Teaching Okay is easy. Just follow these steps:

1. **Standing next to your dog on leash, say, "Okay," in an excited, happy voice and take a few backward steps.**

   Reach for your dog and start petting them, which we call "partying with your dog."

2. **Repeat and review.**

You can also use a treat at the same time to help motivate their enthusiasm. The important part of this command is to make Okay all about you and your dog. Saying Okay is fun because you play together for a bit. The work is over, and now you've released Buddy. Always take a few steps, moving your dog out of position and connect with them by petting them. Party with your dog.

Practice getting your dog's attention

As you practice the Okay release word, Buddy's focus on you is the result of each exercise. You need your dog's attention to train them. Buddy needs to be attentive to you and try to understand what you're asking. By starting with praise and petting and the Okay release word, you're well on your way to gaining Buddy's attention and joy of working together as a team.

You can help get your dog's attention with food after the release word, but use it wisely. You should never try to find a dog's mouth or to chase them down to eat a treat. If they don't care about a treat, forget it and don't chase them to give the food; this would be rewarding their nonattention to you.

The best way to offer a treat is in your open hand with the treat laying in your palm or on your fingers. Figure 9-1 shows the correct way to offer a treat to your dog. The open hand allows your dog to gently take the treat from you without biting it out of your fingers.

FIGURE 9-1:
Offer your dog a
treat with an
open hand.

© John Wiley & Sons, Inc.

Using the Yes command

Practice giving a treat with a Yes command. The word *yes* means perfection — the moment your dog is absolutely correct when learning a new lesson, say, "Yes," which means a treat is soon to follow. Practice this routine a dozen times until your dog looks for the treat after you say, "Yes." Such practice prepares your dog for future training. To do so, follow these steps:

1. Look at your dog, and when they look at you, say, "Yes," and give them a treat.

2. Say, "Okay," to release them and pet them and have a little party.

3. Stand still again and wait for them to look at you; when they do, say, "Yes," and give them a treat.

4. Release with "Okay" and pet and party together.

Practicing Name Recognition or the Name Game

You have probably said your dog's name a thousand times a day in the past. Now, it's important that you're aware that their name is a command. Their name means: "Look at me, move towards me, and see what I want you to do. Basically, stop what you're doing and come to me." For a dog to know their name is a crucial lesson. Your dog's name means something, so don't say it and expect nothing from your dog. Show them what you want. Don't keep saying it over and over again. Rather, teach them that when you say their name, they're supposed to come to you and look at you.

REMEMBER Your dog should love their name and get excited when they hear it. Always use their name as a good thing and never as a precursor to punishment.

These sections explain how you can teach your dog their name.

Sequence 1: Having Buddy move toward you when they hear their name

The purpose of this step is for your dog to look at you and move in. Follow these steps:

1. **With Buddy on leash, walk around.**

   Don't let Buddy notice you. Move slowly around.

2. **When they aren't looking at you, say, "Buddy," and start walking *backward* while reeling in the leash.**

   As you walk backward and you reel in the leash, they will turn toward you and start moving toward you.

3. **Say, "Yes," as they turn and offer them a treat while you happily praise them.**

4. **Say, "Okay," and pet them.**

5. **Repeat until your dog stays focused on you.**

After they have mastered this first sequence, try for a freebie response to the treat. *Freebie* means that you don't actually use a verbal command yet, but by moving your hand up and over their head with the treat in it, you get a freebie response. More than likely you'll get a response that you want. By moving the treat upward as Buddy gets to the treat, they'll look up at your hand and they may sit. This is the freebie: getting a Sit, yet not giving a command for it.

REMEMBER Here, you're concentrating on teaching Buddy what you expect when you say their name. You want them to immediately come toward you and ideally sit when they arrive. The important thing at this moment is for them to learn to come when you use their name.

Now, repeat Sequence 1 with the freebie added at the end of Step 3. Praise them whether they sit or not. See if you get the freebie sit, without a Sit command. Say, "Okay," pet them, and repeat.

Sequence 2: Adding Come after their name

The steps in this sequence add the command that they're already doing, moving in to you after you say their name. Fundamentally, you always want the individual whose name you say to bring their attention around to you. This is true of your dog as well. Follow these steps:

1. **With Buddy on leash, walk around.**

   Don't let Buddy notice you. Move slowly around.

2. **Say, "Buddy, Come," and start walking backward while reeling in the leash.**

3. **When they come, say, "Yes," and offer a treat, lifting the treat slightly as they get close to your hand.**

4. **Praise them whether they sit or not.**

   See if you get the freebie sit, without a Sit command.

5. **Say, "Okay," and pet them.**

   Praise them whether they sit or not.

6. **Repeat.**

Sequence 3: Making Sit mandatory

After they get good during the Name Game, it's time to make the Sit a requirement and not just a freebie. Follow these steps:

1. **With Buddy on leash, walk around.**

   Don't let Buddy notice you. Move slowly around.

2. **Say, "Buddy, Come," and start walking backward while reeling in the leash.**

3. **When they come, say, "Sit," and offer them a treat slightly lifting the treat as they get close to your hand.**

4. **Say, "Yes," as they sit.**

   Help them, if necessary, by lifting their collar with one hand and tucking their tail with the other hand.

5. **Say, "Okay," and pet them.**

6. **Repeat.**

Well done. Practice until it becomes second nature for you and your dog.

Teaching Your Dog the Touch Command

Touch is an easy command to teach that Buddy should know and understand for many reasons. The purpose of the Touch game is that your dog should move toward you, look at you, and allow you to touch them. Never should your dog avoid your touch. Use the Touch command anytime you want your dog to move with you or toward you. Just follow the sequences in these sections to teach your dog this command.

Sequence 1: Getting Buddy to move toward you

The steps in this sequence get Buddy to move toward you:

1. **Put a treat in the palm of your hand snuggly between two of your fingers and have your hand flat like a plate, as shown in Figure 9-2.**

2. **Show your palm to your dog a few inches from their nose, so they have to step toward it.**

   Your hand holding a treat between the fingers is referred to as *being loaded*. Don't move your hand toward your dog. Make sure your dog has to move toward your hand. If Buddy doesn't walk toward your open hand loaded with the treat, hold still or make it harder by moving your hand farther away from them. This encourages Buddy to move toward the hand; making it easier won't have the same result.

3. **Say, "Touch."**

4. **As your dog moves toward your hand to get the treat, say, "Yes," and allow them to get the treat from between your fingers.**

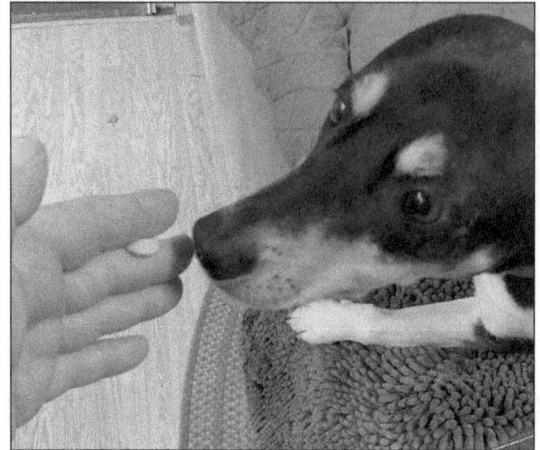

FIGURE 9-2:
Offer the treat
between two
fingers with your
hand flat.

© John Wiley & Sons, Inc.

Sequence 2: Increasing the distance Buddy needs to move toward you

This sequence increases the space that Buddy must move toward you:

1. **Hold your loaded hand a few feet, not just inches, from your dog and say, "Touch."**

   Your dog now has to walk to your hand to get the treat.

2. **Say, "Yes," and allow them to get the treat from between your fingers.**

3. **Release with "Okay" and praise.**

Sequence 3: Not offering a treat in the flat Touch hand

In this sequence, you don't have any treat in your Touch hand.

1. **With a few treats in your other hand, hold the treats ready to use close to your waist, as if that hand were a cup and then offer your free empty hand, flat like a plate as before (see Figure 9-3).**

2. **Say, "Touch," and make sure your dog moves toward your hand, not you toward the dog.**

184   PART 3 Tackling Training Basics

3. When they nuzzle your empty hand, say, "Yes," and then with the Touch hand, reach up and take a treat out of the cupped hand.

4. Give the treat to your dog and say, "Okay."

5. Repeat over and over again.

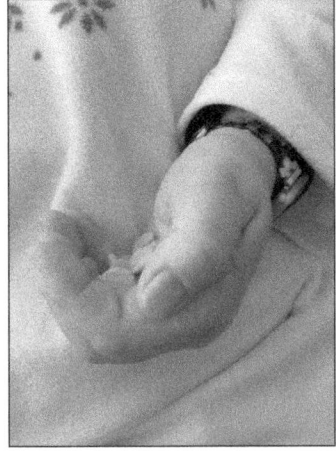

© John Wiley & Sons, Inc.

FIGURE 9-3:
Hold the treats in your other hand as if it were a cup of treats.

Sequence 4: Moving the Touch hand in different positions

In the steps of the following sequence, you move around and your hand moves around. Buddy comes to your hand when you say, "Touch":

1. Repeat Sequence 3, but move around now and back up between each repetition.

2. Move your hand, held flat like a plate, and hold it in different positions, higher or lower, to one side or the other.

   REMEMBER

   Make sure your dog always moves toward your hand on the Touch command and touches your palm before they get the *Yes* praise word and then a treat. Always reach up into the other hand held as a cup with treats and pick one out and give to your dog.

3. Release and repeat.

   See Figure 9-4 for an example.

FIGURE 9-4:
Your dog moves
to your hand any
time you give the
Touch command.

© *John Wiley & Sons, Inc.*

Sequence 5: Mixing up the hand you offer

Here, you mix up the hand you offer to Buddy, and you skip giving the treat every time:

1. **Alternate between your left and right hand as the Touch hand.**

Buddy should come to either hand offered to them. You can keep backing up or moving along beside them, but each time you say, "Touch," they should nose the hand that is offered to them.

2. **Say, "Yes, good dog."**

Do two in a row and then give a treat. Advance to three in a row and then give a treat. Make it lots of fun by smiling and praising and randomly giving them a treat.

Greeting and Sitting with the Hello Command

No matter how many people you ask, having a dog not jump up on them seems to be the most desired behavior. The easiest way to teach this behavior is to teach it as a default behavior. This means your dog should automatically go into a sitting position as soon as someone looks down at them and reaches for them in a greeting manner. To get this behavior, teach Buddy to go into a sitting position when someone reaches for them and says, "Hello," which allows that person to pet him without Buddy jumping up. Buddy will learn the only way to get someone's attention will be to sit at their feet, not by jumping on them.

In essence, you have two commands that tell your dog to sit:

» Sit, which we discuss in Chapter 11

» Hello, which means to sit and allow this person to touch you while you keep your bottom on the ground

The following sections break down the Hello command into easy steps.

Sequence 1: Focusing on the treat

You're going to use the dog's focus on the treat to get them into the sitting position. Stick to these steps:

1. **With Buddy standing, offer a treat by stepping up to them and leaning toward them. Lift the treat over their nose and up, and say, "Hello." The movement of the treat should be like a McDonald's arch up and over their head.**

   You want the dog's nose to come up and look up over their head slightly. Your action gets them to look up and back. As you offer them the treat and lift it up and slightly over their head, step and lean into them, which should entice them to sit. The Hello command signals them to sit for the cookie.

2. **As they sit, say, "Yes," and give them the treat and praise them verbally.**

3. **Say, "Okay," and step directly into the dog, forcing them to back up a bit and therefore reinforcing the no-jump behavior.**

Sequence 2: Greeting and praising

Here, before you release them, you want to touch them on their head and praise. Steps 1–3 are the same as Sequence 1, but you add touching the top of their head as they eat their treat at the end of Step 2:

1. **With Buddy standing, offer them a treat by stepping into them and leaning toward them, and then lift the treat over their nose and up and say, "Hello."**

2. **As they sit, say, "Yes," and give them the treat and praise them verbally while you touch the top of their head as they eat the treat.**

3. **Say, "Okay," and step directly into the dog, forcing them to back up a bit.**

Sequence 3: Training Buddy to hold the sitting position longer

This sequence is the same as Sequence 2, except that the Sit should last longer and longer before you release them.

1. **With Buddy standing, offer them a treat by stepping into them and leaning toward them, and then lift the treat over their nose and up and say, "Hello."**

2. **As they sit, say, "Yes," and give them the treat and praise them verbally while you touch the top of their head as they eat the treat for a few more seconds each repetition.**

3. **Because you're probably leaning over them as you hand Buddy the treat, stand up straight while they eat the treat.**

   Buddy must hold the sitting position longer and longer.

REMEMBER

   If they get up before you say, "Okay," put them back into the sitting position. The Sit should have been 5 to 10 seconds, but Buddy is working and shouldn't get up until you release them. Putting them back into the Sit requires you to pull up slightly on the collar and tuck their tail back into the sitting position.

4. **Say, "Okay," and then step directly into the dog, forcing them to back up a bit.**

REMEMBER

   We don't recommend you give the dog another treat to get them to sit again. If you do that, you'd be rewarding them for getting up, which isn't your intention. Instead, you want them to realize the oops in their actions. They must learn to not get up until you release them.

Sequence 4: Having a friend help

To advance teaching the Hello command, ask someone else such as a family member or a close friend to help. Show that person what you want them to do, such as lift up the treat over Buddy's head, step toward the dog, and so on. Pet Buddy's head and then stand up straight and release Buddy. By showing your friend what you want them to do, you're reviewing the exercise for Buddy. The review is always a good idea when someone acts as a greeter and gets Buddy to cooperate. Reviews are something you should always practice and reinforce with Buddy. When someone bends over your dog's head and says, "Hello," Buddy should always sit and allow that person to pet their head. After all, a polite dog is a pleasure to be around.

Leave It: Getting Your Dog to Leave Stuff Alone

The Leave It command means: "Back off what you're looking at." It can be something gross on the ground or something you may have dropped and you don't want your dog to get, such as a pill or food that isn't safe for them. It can even be a cat or another dog on a walk. Leave It means not only to look away from what you're looking at, but also look at you. That command is important, fun, and easy to teach.

Before you start, you need to remember a few important rules:

>> Never give a treat after you've said, "Leave it," without giving the permission word for your dog to take the treat, which is "Okay."

"Yes" means perfection for the sequence you're working on. So in Sequence 1, you say, "Yes," when your dog pulls their head away from the treat. In Sequence 2, you say, "Yes," when they look at you, rather than when they pull their head away.

You want more from the dog at that point, so watch your dog and read carefully to make sure you know what perfection is in each sequence.

>> Keep the sessions short — no more than five minutes at a time — and follow the steps in these sections (you can either sit or stand).

Sequence 1: Introducing Leave It

The purpose of the steps in this sequence is to acknowledge that backing away is what you want Buddy to do. Follow these steps:

1. **Hold out your hand with your palm facing up, showing Buddy the treat.**

2. **When they go for it, say, "Leave it," while you snap your hand closed into a fist.**

   You can turn your fist so that your palm now faces down if Buddy starts to paw at your hand for the treat.

3. **Observe your dog's reaction.**

   They may stare fixedly at the back of your hand, they may try to get to the treat by nuzzling or nibbling your hand, or they may start barking. Ignore all these behaviors and don't repeat the command. You're looking for the first break in their attention away from your hand. Most dogs at this point either look to the right, to the left, or they back up.

4. **The instant Buddy breaks their attention away from your hand, say, "Yes," at the moment of perfection, and then say, "Okay," as the permission word and hand them a treat. Use your other hand to give the treat reward.**

REMEMBER

Always give the *Okay* word for them to take the treat from you. Okay is the command that gives Buddy permission to eat the treat after the Leave It command.

The most difficult part of teaching this exercise is for you to remain silent and not to repeat the command. Be patient and wait for the correct response. Then say, "Yes," praise them, release them, and reward them with a treat from the other hand.

5. **Keep practicing this sequence until your dog is really good about backing off your fist for the Leave It command and praise.**

Sequence 2: Looking at you

This sequence teaches Buddy that you reward them with a treat by looking at you — and not at your hand. Follow these steps:

1. **Do Steps 1–3 from Sequence 1.**

   You now want more from Buddy, and the Yes perfect moment won't be when they back off the food hand, but rather when they make eye contact with you by looking at your face.

2. **When Buddy looks at you, say, "Yes," and then reward them from the other hand.**

TIP

   To get Buddy to look at you, praise them verbally for backing off your hand. Then you can say, "Yes," when they look at you.

3. **After Buddy moves their head away, but hasn't looked at you yet, reopen your hand to show the treat.**

   Doing so makes it even clearer that Buddy must leave the treat when you say, "Leave it." If they go for the treat, shut your fist again, but don't pull your hand away. Just leave it against your leg. Keep closing your hand if they move toward the treat, reopen your hand if they pull away, and praise them. Don't let them get the treat even though it's right under their nose. Simply close your fist again.

4. **To get the treat from you, Buddy must look at you while the treat is still visible in your hand.**

   When they do look at you, remember to say, "Yes." Then pick up the treat, say, "Okay," and give them the treat.

If they go back to your hand, make a fist and stop praising. When they back off again, open your hand and praise them. You're waiting for them to look at you now. This step is important. The trick to helping them to learn to look at you is the praise you verbally give them for not going toward the treat. Your praise should be exciting and interesting — smack your lips and make kissing noises, anything to cause your dog to look up at your face.

Sequence 3: Moving the treat from your hand to the floor

The purpose of the steps in this sequence is to get Buddy to understand that anything may become a Leave It command. Follow these steps:

1. **Sitting or kneeling comfortably on the floor, show Buddy a treat, put it on the floor, and cover it with your hand.**

2. **When their attention is on your hand or they try to get to the treat, say, "Leave it."**

3. **When they back off your hand, uncover the treat and praise them quietly, but wait for them to look at you before you give them the "Yes" command and then the _Okay_ release word.**

   Don't release them directly to the treat on the floor, but rather pick it up, say, "Okay," and then let them have it. This detail can help Buddy understand that, when they're told the Leave It command for something on the floor, they don't get it, ever. When something is bouncing across the floor and Buddy is in hot pursuit of it, the Leave It command means, "No, you don't get that unless I hand it to you. Ever."

Sequence 4: "Leaving" a dropped food item

The purpose of these steps is that even a dropped food item bouncing across the floor isn't to be had if you say, "Leave It." Follow these steps:

1. **Put Buddy on leash and stand next to them. Neatly fold the leash into your left hand, and hold your hand as close to his collar as is comfortable without tension on the leash.**

   You need to make sure that the amount of slack in the leash is short enough that Buddy's mouth can't reach the floor.

2. **Hold the treat in your right hand, show it to Buddy, casually drop it, and say, "Leave it."**

   If they hold back, praise them, pick up the treat, and from your pocket give them a different treat, not the one you told them to leave alone, with the *Okay* permission word.

   If they go for the treat, pull straight back on the leash, pick up the treat, and try again. Give the command immediately after letting go of the treat and before they want to make a dive for it. Repeat until they obey the command.

Test Buddy's response by taking off the leash, dropping a container of food, and saying, "Leave it." If they make a dive for it, they're telling you that they need more work on leash. If needed, practice more repetitions on leash.

Sequence 5: "Leaving" a found item on the ground outside

The purpose of these steps is to ensure that Buddy will leave alone anything they are looking at, no matter where you are or what it is. Follow these steps:

1. **Go outside and drop four or five pieces of food in the area where you're taking Buddy for their big test.**

   Use a food item in the grass or on the ground that's readily visible to you, such as some crackers or a few kernels of popcorn or cheese puffs.

2. **Put some of your regular treats in your pocket, and then walk Buddy on leash in the area where you left the food.**

3. **As soon as their nose goes to the food, say, "Leave it."**

   If they respond, praise enthusiastically, pick up the treat, and reward them with a different treat from your pocket. (Don't reward Buddy with the object you said to leave alone.) If they don't leave it, check straight back on the leash.

   If Buddy manages to snag a treat, your response is too slow. Practice walking around the food-contaminated area until they ignore the food on command.

REMEMBER

4. **Repeat until Buddy ignores the food on command.**

Buddy should now know and respond to the Leave It command reliably. Test them off leash to see whether they have mastered this command or need more work. You may need to review it with them periodically on leash.

TIP

If your dog is anything like most other dogs, they won't be far when you're in the kitchen preparing a meal. Their presence there is a wonderful training opportunity. Casually drop a piece of food on the floor — maybe a small piece of bread or cheese, a little broccoli or carrot, or anything else they like. When they try to nab it, say, "Leave it." If they do, pick up the food and reward them with something else. If they do nab the food, consider it a freebie and put Buddy on leash and try again.

Understanding other uses for Leave It

Teaching Buddy a reliable response to this command also transfers to other situations, such as chasing a cat and guarding a cabinet or dish. You also can use this command for excessive barking. Remember to reward correct responses with praise and a treat.

This command can save your dog's life if they become really reliable. Things you drop, such as medications or some foods, can potentially cause liver damage or kidney failure. Things you come across on walks can also be dangerous and potential life hazards, such as rotten food or other suspicious unknown things. More importantly, this command reinforces your leadership that you own all things.

IN THIS CHAPTER

» Being the leader you need to be
   for your dog

» Teaching the Come command

» Adding distractions and the different
   degrees of distractions

» Teaching the Go command

Chapter **10**

Coming and Going: Two Essential Commands to Teach

Most everyone recognizes that having a dog who comes when called is valuable. Equally valuable is to have a dog who goes where you direct them to go. Run ahead toward the house, the car, or an arriving friend are just a few examples. Furthermore, helping Buddy understand that they need to leave you and go with someone is also useful. This chapter works on both the Come and Go commands and the leadership needed to train them both. Plus, if you aren't aware of what Buddy is understanding, you may be teaching the wrong thing. Get on the same page and watch out for unintentional training.

Understanding the Importance of Leadership: Okay Is the Word

To get your dog to leave something they're looking at or sniffing, you must have their respect. To gain a dog's respect, you need to make sure your dog sees you as the pack leader, coach of the team, the mom, the dad. Use whatever word you feel best defines your relationship with your dog. Just remember more than anything that you aren't a littermate or a sibling. *You* are in charge. You decide what your teammate does, when they do it, where they do it, and for how long they do it. This is leadership.

For example, if you say, "Down," you expect your dog to get down right there, no matter what is going on around them, and you expect your dog to hold the Down position for as long as it takes until you say "Okay," releasing them from that position. You are the leader.

The Down, Sit, Stand, Stay, and Heel exercises are all considered to be leadership exercises, and each one can help get you to the point where your dog will listen to each and every command you say and therefore come when called, which this chapter focuses on. Although this chapter is about coming and going, we discuss leadership first. The command that teaches leadership and is therefore, in our opinion, the most important command we teach, is the release word *Okay*, which means, "Buddy, hold the position until you're released from it."

Follow these steps to teach the *Okay* release word; here is an example using any command:

1. **Say, "Sit," "Good dog," or any other command you want to reinforce and praise while Buddy is doing the said command.**

   If Buddy gets up before you give the release word, replace them back into the Sit or whatever command without repeating the command. Help them be successful.

2. **Say, "Okay," play, and party with them.**

   The *Okay* release word is crucial for clear leadership coming from you. (See Chapter 11 for the Sit and Down commands.)

Heel is the other leadership exercise. *Heeling* is walking with your dog while your dog is beside you walking on a loose leash. Heeling is a great leadership exercise because you decide where you walk, how fast or slow you walk, and which way you go. In other words, you're the leader of the pack. You set the pace and the direction. See Chapter 12 for the Heel command.

DOWN AND HEEL ARE ESSENTIAL TO COME

An elderly farmer once contacted me (Mary Ann). I don't know why the farmer seemed elderly, but it was probably because what he was saying depicted a stubborn old man. He worked independently, so he wasn't used to being told what to do. He also had land, lots of land, where his dog didn't need to be on leash, but the dog needed to come when called.

One day this farmer called me.

"My dog won't come when I call him," the farmer said. "He'll never need to be on leash. I only need him to come when I call him, and I don't need to teach him any of those newfangled commands like Down or Heel. I just want him to come. All else will be fine after that."

"I understand what you're saying," I said. "But what you need to understand is that the very first thing we must teach your dog is to Down on command and to Heel precisely by your side."

In frustration, he grumbled at me and said something about me not getting what he was saying. "I just want to teach him to come when I call him," he said.

Again, I agreed. "I understand you. You're right," I continued. "Down and Heel have nothing to do with the Come command, but *they have everything to do with the dog's coming.*"

He seemed to get what I was saying. In the end, the farmer taught his dog how to do a Down until he was released and to walk by his side when told to do so. The farmer and dog worked on the Come command and coming around distractions, and his dog became a champ at coming and watching the farmer while the two of them worked together all day on the farm.

Teaching Your Dog to Come When Called

Come is one of the most important commands for safety. The truth is, "If you don't have a dog that comes . . . one day you won't have a dog!" That's why this book is full of different ways to teach your dog to come: Name Recognition, Recall, Touch. Every command you teach your dog helps them want to be with you and helps them come when called. The following sections focus on the actual way you can teach your dog to come when you call them and some important points to remember when using the Come command.

Teaching Buddy the Recall Game

Before you teach Buddy how to come, Buddy needs to master Name Recognition and Touch, which we discuss in Chapter 9. When you're ready to teach Come, follow the steps later in the section. But first, a few thoughts on teaching Come.

REMEMBER

You must do these exercises so that you're sure your dog understands what Come means. When you say, "Buddy, Come," there must be no doubt that they *know* what you expect of them. If they don't come when called, you need to be sure that it isn't because they don't know what the command means, but rather because they couldn't hear you over the distractions of life.

Here's how to play the Recall Game and teach your dog the Come command. You'll need a partner because you'll be playing this game with another person. See Figure 10-1.

FIGURE 10-1:
Learning Come with the Recall Game.

1. **With Buddy on leash, hold the handle of the leash with your partner holding Buddy by the collar. Say, "Buddy, Come," and use the leash to guide them to you.**

   At this point your partner who's holding the collar lets go of Buddy. Avoid the temptation to reach for your dog. The next step is very important. Make sure both of you have treats easily accessible in your pocket. You'll need one at a time.

2. **When Buddy comes to you, show them the treat when they arrive while putting your hand through their collar, and only then give them the treat, pet them, and praise them enthusiastically.**

    You can — and should — pet Buddy when they reach you so that coming to you is a pleasant experience. This situation is different from teaching the Sit or Down commands when you want them to remain in place and petting them would cause them to get up (see Chapter 11.

3. **Hold onto Buddy's collar and pass the leash to your partner, who says, "Buddy, Come." Your partner puts a hand through the collar while showing them the treat, gives the treat, and then praises them.**

    Keep holding Buddy after you call them until your partner calls them again. Back and forth. Each of you is first the leash person and then the holder of the dog. You alternate. The leash person calls the dog.

    Keep working on this exercise until your dog responds on their own to being called and no longer needs to be guided with the leash.

REMEMBER

4. **Repeat the exercise with Buddy off leash, gradually increasing the distance between you and your partner to 12 feet.**

    Remember to keep showing Buddy the treat as you reach for the collar. Doing so is crucial for them to come all the way in, be touched, and then taken by the collar.

5. **Have your partner hold Buddy by the collar while you go into another room, and then call your dog.**

    Keep in mind all the tips about showing the treat before touching their collar and holding onto them until the next person calls.

6. **When they find you, put your hand through the collar, give them a treat, and praise them.**

    If they can't find you, *slowly* go to them, take them by the collar, and bring them to the spot from where you called. Reward and praise.

7. **Have your partner go into another room and then call Buddy.**

8. **Repeat the exercise until Buddy doesn't hesitate in finding you or your partner in any room of the house.**

    Add stairs and a second floor if you have one. Only go halfway up or down the staircase so Buddy learns that area is part of the playing field.

9. **Take Buddy outside to a confined area, such as a fenced yard, tennis court, park, or school yard, and repeat all the steps there.**

Now, you can practice alone. With Buddy on leash, go for a walk. Let them sniff around, and when they aren't paying any attention to you, call them. When they get to you, give them a treat and make a big fuss over them. If they don't come, firmly tug on the leash toward you, backing away as you call and then reward and praise them. Repeat until Buddy comes to you every time you call them. After Buddy is trained, you don't have to reward them with a treat every time but do so randomly. Always use praise lavishly.

TIP

You can add a whistle to the Recall Game or reteach the game using a whistle, especially if Buddy has accidently learned to ignore your calls. Blow the whistle and then say, "Buddy, Come." Do everything else the same way except add the whistle to your call.

Even changing your command from Come to Here or another word can help to reteach the Come command. It is possible to unintentionally train Buddy to not listen to the Come command by using it too often and ignoring their response to it. Consider reteaching the Recall Game using a new command.

Remembering what's important when you use the Come command

The Come command is arguably one of the most important commands you teach your dog. When you train your dog with the Come command, keep the following points in mind.

Exercise, exercise, exercise

Many dogs don't come when called because they don't get enough exercise. At every chance they get, they run off and make the most of this unexpected freedom by staying out for hours at a time. One of our mottos in life is: "A tired dog has happy owners," or "A tired dog is a happy dog." Either way, everyone is happy when the dog gets enough exercise. The problem though is that *you* don't get to decide how much exercise is enough.

For instance, exercise requirements between a Border Collie and a Basset Hound are huge. A Border Collie can work all day and needs to do so, or they will be a crazed lunatic looking for an outlet for all that energy. On the other hand, a Basset Hound is happy hanging out all day, sharing the sofa, and taking short walks; that's plenty. If you're a Basset Hound person and you get a Border Collie, you need to figure out what enough exercise is for your dog or more than likely your dog will develop behavior problems. But if you throw the Frisbee for an hour, walk or jog for several miles, and do agility every night, your Border Collie will be the best-mannered, well-titled dog that has no issues, and you'll be proud. You and your Border Collie will both be happy. What is enough exercise for every dog will be different.

REMEMBER

Consider what your dog was bred to do, and that background tells you how much exercise they need. Just putting Buddy out in the backyard isn't good enough. You have to participate. Dogs are social animals. Most likely a dog left alone in the backyard will sit near the door waiting for your return.

When your dog comes to you, be nice to them

One of the quickest ways to teach your dog not to come to you when called is to call them to punish them or to do something the dog perceives as unpleasant. Most dogs consider it unpleasant to be called when their owners are leaving them alone in the house. In these circumstances, go and get Buddy instead of calling them to you. If you're still crating your young dog, call them to you for a treat or a special reward that goes in the crate with them and then release them and continue getting ready for your day. Calling them to you and releasing them several times before you actually leave for the day is great practice and won't make your departure seem so bad. Review going in the crate and releasing them from the crate multiple times a day. (See Chapter 14 discusses how to teach getting into a crate.)

Another example of teaching your dog *not* to come is taking them for a run in the park and calling them to you when it's time to go home. Repeating this sequence several times teaches the dog that the party is over once called. Soon, they may become reluctant to return to you when called because they aren't ready to end the fun. You can prevent this kind of unintentional training by calling them to you several times during their outing, sometimes giving them a treat and other times offering just a word of praise. Then, let them romp again. Ending the fun is punishment for your dog, so calling them to you and ending the fun will result in a dog that doesn't come when called.

Teach Buddy the Come command as soon as you get them

Start right away. But remember, sometime between 4 and 8 months of age, a puppy begins to realize there's a big, wide world out there (see Chapter 7). While they're going through this stage, keep them on leash so that they don't learn that they can ignore you when you call them.

Dog training centers often get calls about training when dogs hit 8 months of age. What used to be a dog that always came when called is now a dog that ignores you. To the dog you've become boring. (Been there, done that, but look at this now!)

Using a leash to counteract that trend during this short period of time avoids the unintentional training you don't want. Unintentional training is when you accidently teach the opposite of what you expect to be teaching. You may think, "Buddy used to come, so let me call them again. Maybe they didn't hear me, so I'll call them again and surely they'll come." In this case, what you're really teaching them is that you don't mean what you're commanding, and you don't have any control when they are off leash, which is the last thing you want your dog to think about you. Instead, keep your dog on the leash for a while; you're simply stepping back to reinforce your previous training.

When in doubt, keep them on leash

Find out how to anticipate when your dog is likely not to come. You may be tempting fate by trying to call them after they have spotted a cat, another dog, or a jogger. Of course, sometimes you'll goof and let them go just as another dog appears out of nowhere. See the next section for how to deal with distractions.

TIP

Resist the urge to make a complete fool of yourself by bellowing "Come" a million times. The more often you holler, "Come," the quicker your dog learns they can ignore you when they're off leash. Instead, patiently go to them and put them on leash. Don't get angry with them after you've caught them or you'll make them afraid of you, and they'll run away from you when you try to call them the next time.

Touch his collar before you reward

Touching their collar prevents them from developing the annoying habit of playing "Catch me if you can" — coming toward you and then dancing around you, just out of reach. Teach them to let you touch their collar before you offer them a treat or praise. Watch your body language also; reaching out toward them can push them away from you. Turn to the side or even walk away for a few steps as they come toward you. This body language will encourage them to get close to you.

Training Your Dog to Handle Distractions

The following sections break up distractions into three degrees or levels. As the degrees go up, the distractions seem harder, although that may not be totally true. For example, if you have a ball-crazy dog versus a dog that doesn't ever want to retrieve something, the ball distraction isn't equal in difficulty to each dog. If your dog is a person-crazy dog that never met a stranger versus a one-person dog that never wants to be with anyone except you, then a person walking by and saying

"Hi" isn't much of a difficulty. Know your dog when you choose your distractions. You want to gradually make distractions more difficult; start easy and then gradually increase the difficulty.

Assuming that you've done the training for Come, you're ready to call your dog around a distraction. We do suggest that you work through the easier distractions first before moving to the more difficult distractions. For the purpose of this discussion, we refer to these distractions as first, second, and third degree.

Teaching Come with first-degree distractions

First-degree distractions are things in the nearby area that do not relate directly to the dog. Examples include going to the park, going to the neighborhood convenient store and training outside, and working in a new location from where you usually train. To handle these distractions, follow these steps:

1. **Put your dog on leash and start down the street for a walk. When your dog sees something that interests them, such as someone walking on the other side of the road, set yourself up to call your dog by backing up to the end of your leash and keeping it slightly loose. Say, "Buddy, come," and wait a second to see if they turn and come.**

   If they do, really lay on the praise and party hardily. If they don't come, give a quick check on the leash and back up a little to encourage them to move toward you.

   A *check* on the leash is when you have a loose leash and you quickly snap it tight for a half second and then let it go slack again. This check should bring your dog's attention around to you. When they do have their attention focused on you, praise enthusiastically, squat down, and welcome them into your arms for a party of praise.

   REMEMBER

2. **Repeat calling Buddy several times on your walk until, no matter what they're looking at, they always turn and come to you, or they get a check on the leash, followed by praise and a party.**

   If Buddy needs more training, see the earlier section "Teaching Buddy the Recall Game."

3. **In a fenced area, let your dog off leash and call, "Buddy, come."**

   Allow Buddy to become involved in a smell in the grass or a tree. Keep the distance between you and them no more than 10 feet apart. After you call them, praise them enthusiastically and reward their success if they respond. If they don't, don't call them again no matter what. Buddy heard you, but they chose to ignore you. Instead, slowly walk up to them and reattach the leash to the collar and trot backward to the spot where you called them. Then praise them and reward them even though you helped them be successful.

TIP

Rather than bending over Buddy, walk up to them and put the leash on them so that you can be standing up while backing up and bringing them to where you called them. Doing so is important because, if you bend over your dog too much, your body language may seem too defensive. Your dog will respond better to you standing and reeling them in. Be aware of your body language and what it is saying.

Teaching Come with second-degree distractions

Second-degree distractions are things that are related directly to your dog. Examples include when people stop and talk to you while out or want to see your dog. People coming and going right beside where your dog is working is really distracting. Someone calling commands to your dog, but *without* using your dog's name, is fair as a distraction.

The distracter using your dog's name isn't fair. Having the distracter say, "Down," while your dog is sitting is a second-degree distraction; your dog shouldn't go down but rather stay seated because that's the command you left them under. You've said, "Sit," to your dog and have not released them from that Sit. Your dog should hold that position no matter what goes on around them.

To teach Buddy to deal with second-degree distractions, have a friend help you work on them and follow these steps:

1. **Start with Buddy on leash and put them in a Sit-Stay if you've not trained the Stay command (see Chapter 11 for this command).**

    Use a secured area such as a fenced yard if you have one available. If you don't have a secured area, use a longer leash or put two leashes together so that you can be farther than 6 feet away. If Buddy hasn't perfected the Stay command, simply have them mill around on the long leash.

2. **Ask your friend to talk to your dog but not to touch them and not to use their name.**

    When your friend says something like, "Here, puppy, puppy," and looks inviting, this is a second-degree distraction.

3. **After your friend has talked to Buddy, you should call them, "Buddy, come."**

   Buddy has a choice now: come to you or go to your friend. If your dog comes to you, praise them, give them a treat, and party hard. If they go to your friend, reel in Buddy and then praise them for coming, even though you helped them to be successful.

4. **Repeat the steps on leash a couple of times, and after Buddy has been successful at this level of distraction, move to off leash.**

   You want to handle the off-leash distraction if your dog goes to your friend the same way as if Buddy were on leash. Go to them, take them by the collar, and back up to where you called and then praise and reward.

5. **Repeat these steps until your dog comes to you, even with your friend talking to them.**

Teaching Come with third-degree distractions

Third-degree distractions are things being offered to your dog, such as a toy or food, while they are working for you. For example, if your dog is in a Sit and someone offers a cookie and says, "Down," that distraction is third degree. If you throw a Frisbee next to your dog in a Stay, it also would be a third-degree distraction.

To teach Buddy how to deal with third-degree distractions, stick to these steps:

1. **With your friend sitting on the ground, have them offer Buddy a treat.**

   Make sure that the treat is small enough that they can hide it in their hand. They can use a container with a lid loosely placed on it if Buddy is too distracted by the food. You can have the lid loose. You don't want the dog to actually get any of the food from your friend, but you want the dog to think they may get some food. Hope springs eternal.

2. **On leash, you and Buddy walk up to the friend offering the treat.**

   Your friend doesn't give Buddy the treat but offers it to them. Let Buddy interact with the food and your friend while you quietly back up to the end of the leash.

3. **Say, "Buddy, come," and then wait one second.**

   If Buddy doesn't turn and come to you immediately, back up and check the leash. Even if you had to help, praise Buddy enthusiastically and give them a treat of your own.

4. **Repeat the third-degree distractions on leash until Buddy readily turns and comes each time you call them away from the food and your friend.**

   After you've had success on leash, you can try it off leash just as in the second-degree section. If Buddy goes for the food or your friend, walk up to them and take them by the collar (or reattach the leash), back up, and bring them with you. Praise them as if they bypassed your friend.

REMEMBER

A friend can offer a treat to your dog anytime, but when they're doing so while you're saying, "Buddy, come," Buddy should come to you and not take the treat from your friend, which is a very important part of distraction training. You calling Buddy to come is the most important command that your dog must comply with immediately. Buddy must ignore a friend with food, a bunny running in the field, or a car on the road. Come can mean life and death if they don't always come when called.

Doing all of these repetitions on and off leash around distractions can really pay off. After all, you want your dog to come to you no matter what.

Focusing on the Opposite of Come — Go

A command that few people think to teach their dogs is Go, which is quite useful in several ways: Get up into the car or Go. Go with the person taking your dog away from you at the veterinary office or Go. Get the ball the dog didn't see you throw or Go. At the park, send your dog out to play with other dogs or Go. When training alone and you want to practice the Come command, send your dog out so that you can then call them to you. We explain the sequences to train the Go command in the following sections.

Sequence 1: Teaching a target

Here, you want to teach Buddy to focus on a target, such as a lid from a butter container you have saved. You can even use a plastic plate; just make sure that it's unbreakable.

1. **Set the target on the ground in front of your feet and put your dog on your left and have your left hand in your dog's collar.**

   You want to teach your dog that the target is a place to find a treat.

2. **Place a treat on the target at your feet and then let go of the collar and with your left hand, point to the target, and release Buddy to the target with the Go command.**

   Use your left hand to point to the target, as shown in Figure 10-2. The best way to point or signal to the target is to always use the hand closest to the dog, so with Buddy on your left, use your left arm. Use your whole hand as a flat paddle, swinging toward the target with one large sweeping motion moving directly towards the target.

3. **Say, "Go," and let Buddy eat the treat.**

   Walk up to the target if Buddy doesn't realize it's loaded. Say, "Okay," and praise him.

4. **Do this sequence several times; remain close to the target, just in front your feet.**

FIGURE 10-2:
Use a hand
signal for Go.

© John Wiley & Sons, Inc.

Sequence 2: Add Come after the release

This sequence advances the Go command to include Come. Follow these steps:

1. **Hold Buddy with your left hand and load the target with your right hand.**

   Together with Buddy, step over the target and turn to face the target, still holding Buddy by the collar. You should be about a foot from the target.

Take your hand out of Buddy's collar and use your signal to command Buddy's attention to the target as you say, "Go." Buddy should go to the target and eat the treat.

2. **Say, "Okay," and back up, saying, "Come."**

Encourage Buddy to return to you. You have them on leash, so you can reel them in.

3. **Repeat this sequence until you no longer need to help Buddy find the target.**

Sequence 3: Increase the distance to the target

Now, you're ready to move farther away from the target with each successful repetition. Sequence 3 is a great exercise to work both Go and Come. Even better, dogs love to run and play with you, so your dog gets to run away from you to the target with the Go command and then gets to run toward you with the Come command. Here are the steps:

1. **Starting at 2 feet from the target, say, "Go," and signal Buddy.**

Always release with Okay after they have eaten the loaded treat, and call Buddy back to you with Come.

2. **Load the target and repeat at 4 feet away.**

Step over the target with Buddy, holding onto the leash instead of the collar.

3. **Point and signal to the target, and say, "Go."**

4. **Say, "Come," to call Buddy back.**

When Buddy gets to you, praise and release them with "Okay."

5. **Reload the target but set it up 2 feet farther away from the target each time.**

You can easily work at 10 feet still on leash; simply follow along with Buddy because your leash is only 6 feet long. Eventually, when you're working Buddy off leash, you can put the target farther away, up to 20 feet. Buddy must always go with the Go command directly to the target and return to you with the Come command. If not, you have progressed too rapidly, so decrease the distance of the target as a review.

Get on the Same Page: You and Buddy May Not Be Understanding the Same Thing

As you train a dog, be careful not to think one thing while your dog understands something different. For example, you say, "Come," but then you reach out and bend over to get your dog's collar. The dog will see body language that is saying Move Away and Keep Away. You are not on the same page. Your words say one thing and your body language says something else. (See Chapter 2 for all about drives.)

When your dog is on a leash, you should always work at keeping the leash slack, with no pressure on the collar. We often refer to this shape as a letter J or a J-leash (see Figure 10-3). If there is pressure on the leash, Buddy will consider this uncomfortable and interpret the pressure as either nagging or a constant correction when neither is intended by you. Therefore, unintentional training is occurring. A J-leash requires the dog to choose to be with you. If they pull away from you, give a quick check on the leash, which is a quick snap to the leash and then immediately letting it relax back to the J-leash. Praise with your voice as they are back on the J-leash. Buddy should look at you and you should smile and praise.

If the tug on the leash lasts too long, Buddy will continue to pull on the leash and neither of you will be happy, because both of you are tugging. It takes two of you to have a tight leash, Buddy pulling away and you pulling towards yourself. Get on the same page, use a quick check to give the information of don't pull, and then praise when the pulling ends because you slack up on the leash to have no pressure. Be aware of what your dog perceives.

Recently, I spent almost two hours with a client helping her to understand how she was pulling on the leash more than the dog was pulling. The dog was biting at the tight leash to make it stop and the client was getting angrier and angrier at what she called her "stupid dog." As I worked with her, helping her to understand how her participation resulted in the tight leash, the dog stopped biting at the leash. The owner relaxed and the dog started to enjoy their time together. By the time I left, she called me a miracle worker, and her dog was doing a lovely Down-Stay at her feet on a J-leash. The client's perception was that the dog had been stubborn and stupid. The dog's perception had been that the client was mean and didn't like dogs. Both were wrong, of course; it was all about that tight leash and unintentional training.

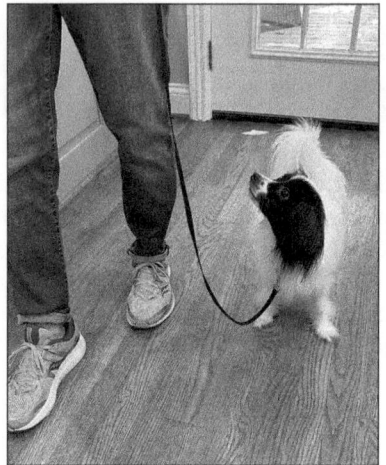

FIGURE 10-3:
Close up view of the J-leash. No one is pulling, neither you nor your dog. This is pleasant for both of you.

© John Wiley & Sons, Inc.

IN THIS CHAPTER

» **Identifying the importance of the Sit command**

» **Teaching the Sit and Down commands**

» **Mastering the three Down commands in your training**

» **Helping your dog to stay in place**

» **Being prepared makes a good dog trainer**

Chapter **11**

Mastering Some Fundamentals: Sit, Down, and Stay

For the most part, basic training is about teaching Buddy to do something you want them to do when they're doing something else. A great example is the Come command, which we discuss in Chapter 10. In this chapter we focus on teaching your dog a few new commands that are a foreign language to them, including Sit, Down, and Stay. A good example is when they sit, something that Buddy does often on their own, but now you use the Sit command. You want Buddy to know that when you say, "Sit," or any command, you want them to respond immediately the first time you say the command.

Understanding Why Sit Is So Important

The Sit command gives you a wonderfully easy way to control Buddy when you need it most. It's also one of the basic commands that you and your dog can quickly accomplish. In fact, Sit is one of the most useful exercises you can teach Buddy. You can use it for all of these circumstances:

>> When you walk in the street and stop at the curb or a traffic light

>> When you meet a neighbor and want to catch up on local news

>> Before Buddy goes up and down stairs

>> Before they go through doors

>> When they are running loose to make them stop

>> When guests arrive and you don't want Buddy to jump on them

>> As a default behavior to use anytime you want your dog's attention

REMEMBER

As your dog demonstrates that they have mastered sitting on command, start to reward the desired response with food every other time. Finally, reward them on a *random* basis — every now and then give them a treat after they sit on command. A random reward is the most powerful reinforcement of what your dog has learned. It's based on the premise that "if you work really well, you'll get a treat, so keep working harder." To make the random reward work, all you have to do is randomly give a treat, never after each and every command. Also, not every other time either, which would be a fixed pattern that your dog will learn to anticipate.

When Buddy wants to greet you by jumping up, tell them, "Sit." When they do, praise them, scratch them *under* the chin (dogs don't like being patted on the head especially if they're high in defense-fight drive; see Chapter 2 for more on drives), and then release them. By following this simple method consistently, you can change your dog's greeting behavior from trying to jump on you to sitting and being petted. (In Chapter 9 we introduce the Hello command to use instead of Sit for politely greeting guests.)

Introducing Down and Its Commands

The Down command is a very important command, similar to Sit. Down represents a submissive position to a dog. For a dog to willingly comply to the first Down command and go into that position completely is the sign of a well-trained dog and a sign of respect to the leader who is the person who gave the command. Dog trainers often argue which command is the most important for a dog to know. There will always be a group that chooses Down to be that command.

The Down exercise is divided into three parts:

» **The Down:** This obedience command means "lie down here and now" and should be taught in each of your daily training sessions. We explain how to teach it in the next section, "Training Your Dog Sit and Down Sequentially."

» **The Long-Down:** This exercise is taught for impulse control, holding a Down position for 30 minutes. You can teach this exercise as soon as you bring your puppy or dog home. It's designed to teach Buddy that you're in charge in a nonthreatening way. Dogs taught this exercise right from the start fit into the family routine and train much more easily. We suggest teaching it in the evening when your dog is tired or your puppy is just about to go to sleep. (A tired dog is more easily trained to be still for 30 minutes than a hyperactive, energized dog.) We explain how to teach this command in the later section "Warming Up with the Long-Down Exercise."

» **Go Lie Down or Go to Your Bed:** This is a natural extension of Down. This exercise is used when you sit down for dinner or any time you don't want to interact with the dog. We discuss this command in Chapter 13.

Training Your Dog Sit and Down Sequentially

In this chapter, we show you two techniques for teaching Buddy the Sit and Down commands. The first is a place-and-show sequence, and the second is a luring sequence. The place-and-show technique is taught first because you want to teach Buddy how to hold their position until they're released. If you start with the luring technique first, you won't be able to replace them into position without giving another lure. The following are two techniques for teaching the Sit command:

» **Placing and showing:** With this technique (Sequence 1), you place Buddy into a sitting position and label it "Sit" by tucking their tail under their hind legs with one hand while you hold their chest still with the other hand. You then hold them in the Sit position while you verbally praise them. Then, you release them with a happy *Okay* release word and play with them for a few seconds while you continue to pet them.

>> **Luring:** The *luring style* (Sequence 3) uses a treat or cookie, and if the dog is interested in the treat, they will follow it into a different position. For Sit, raise the treat up and back over your dog's head slowly while they sniff it; the action of moving the cookie lures them into a sitting position. The motion of the treat over your dog's head is similar to the McDonald's arch.

Teach the Sit command with place and show first and then do it with a lure. Here are the full sequences in detail. The same pattern goes for the Down command, so you can teach them simultaneously.

Sequence 1: Placing and showing

Using the place-and-show method as the first sequence for Sit and Down is critical because of the release word *(Okay)* and the concept of training Buddy to comply when you want them to obey. When you teach this method to sit on command and remain until you release them, if Buddy moves or gets up before you release them, you simply stop praising and replace them back into the sitting position. Then, you resume praising them only while they're sitting. Then, you say, "Okay," and get them to move while you play with them for a few seconds.

REMEMBER

With Buddy standing next to you on your left side, you can either kneel next to them, sit in a chair next to them, or put Buddy on a table or garden wall if they're small enough. Training a small dog on an elevated surface is useful because you don't want to bend over them. In chapter 2 we explain how your body language affects your dog's interpretation of what you're saying or doing. Follow these steps:

1. **Put your right hand on Buddy's chest and your left hand on their shoulder blades; slide your left hand down their back and around their tail and tuck their knees up under them as you keep your right hand on their chest, folding them into the sitting position.**

2. **Say, "Sit," as you hold them in the sitting position and verbally praise them for a few seconds.**

3. **Say, "Okay," and start to pet them as you release them from the sitting position.**

4. **Do this sequence several times in a row, for several days in a row.**

Sequence 2: Adding the Down

In these steps, as you place and show Buddy how to sit, you add the Down command before the release word. In other words, you string the three commands in a row: Sit, Down, and then Okay:

1. With Buddy in the Sit position next to your left side, put your left hand on Buddy's shoulders. Reach with your right hand and slide out one of the front feet, sliding Buddy into the Down position. It doesn't matter which front foot you reach for, usually the one baring the most weight; try either front foot, keeping your left hand still on the shoulders. Buddy needs to stay in the Down position. See Figure 11-1.

2. As Buddy stays in the Down position, you can replace them by sliding out the leg again, if they should get up. You can also apply a small amount of pressure on the shoulder blades to encourage the Stay in the Down position. Your left hand on the shoulders should only be applying pressure if Buddy tries to get up; otherwise, remove all pressure and then your hand completely.

3. Praise Buddy while they are still in the Down position, and then say, "Okay," and start to pet them.

4. Do this sequence several times in a row, for several days in a row.

   Do both the Sit and the Down together along with the Okay release. Buddy must hold each position for a few seconds before you do the next command. Sit, praise, and pause. Down, praise, and pause. Okay and release.

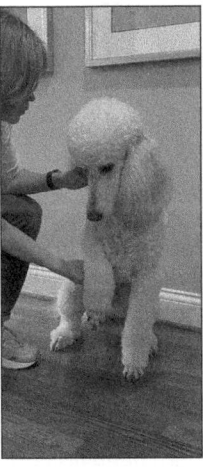

FIGURE 11-1:
Gently slide your dog into the Down position.

© John Wiley & Sons, Inc.

Sequence 3: Luring into the Down

When you use the luring method to teach Buddy the Down position and they move or get up before you release them, don't give them another treat to get them back into the Down position, which would be rewarding them for getting up.

Rewarding Buddy for getting up without being released is the last thing you want them to think you're doing. This is why you teach the luring sequence after the place-and-show sequence. If Buddy gets up without being released by you, you then immediately revert to the place-and-show sequence, return them to the Down position, and resume praising them until you actually do release them with "Okay." Follow these steps:

1. **With Buddy in a sitting position (see Sequence 1) on your left side, place your left hand on their shoulders, take a small enticing treat in your right hand, and present it to their nose.**

2. **Slowly lower the treat from their nose to the floor directly in front of their feet, moving _slowly_, and saying, "Down."**

   As Buddy follows the lowered treat with their nose, they fold themselves into a Down position.

3. **Give them the treat and praise them, but don't release them.**

   If they get up, slide them back into the Down, as in Sequence 1 above. Because you haven't released them, they should hold the Down position.

Sequence 4: Luring into the Sit

When you use the lure to move between the Down and the Sit commands, you must be ready to reposition or replace Buddy into the correct position if they change their position without a different command from you or a release from you. Using the lure is easy, but it can be tempting to grab another treat if your dog moves out of the commanded position. Always reinforce the command after you've used a lure by reverting to Sequence 1. Follow these steps:

1. **While Buddy is in the Down position, keep your left hand gently on the shoulders as you praise them quietly, reach for a treat with your right hand, and then move your left hand to the collar between the ears.**

2. **Present the treat with your right hand at Buddy's nose and slowly raise the cookie up and back in a 45-degree angle over and above the head. Gently lift the collar if necessary as your right hand lifts the treat up and over the head, and then say, "Sit."**

   When Buddy is up in a sitting position, let them eat the treat.

3. **Hold Buddy still with your left hand still in the collar, praise them softly, and then say, "Okay." Release them and play with them for a few seconds.**

4. **Repeat Sequences 3 and 4 together several times in a row for several days in a row.**

   Buddy should hold each position for a few seconds before you do the next command.

TIP

Vary the time between the Sit and the Down commands, but remember that Buddy must hold each position until you release them. You want your dog to comply because they were commanded to do so, not because they learned a pattern of Down, Sit, Down, Sit in sequence. If they get out of any of the positions, go back to Sequence 1.

Sequence 5: Adding collar pressure

The steps in this sequence introduce collar pressure in the presence of food, so upward collar pressure for Sit and downward collar pressure for Down won't be a problem for Buddy. Follow these steps:

1. **Place Buddy into a Sit in front of you.**

   You can be kneeling in front of them, you can be in a chair, or you can place Buddy on a table, as in Sequence 1.

2. **Put your left-hand fingers in the collar under the chin while you hold a treat in front of their nose with your right hand.**

3. **As you lower the cookie with your right hand, press the collar toward Buddy's chest and down at the same time with your left hand in the collar.**

   By applying pressure toward Buddy, they should fold into a Down, and because the cookie is there helping their head to lower, they should go right down.

4. **Say, "Down," simultaneously and let them eat the treat.**

   Don't release them yet.

5. **While Buddy is in the Down position, reach for another cookie in your right hand and put your left hand in their collar between the ears.**

6. **Lift Buddy by the collar into the "Sit" as you raise the cookie from their nose up and over their head, as you did in Sequence 4.**

7. **Say, "Sit," simultaneously and give them the cookie and praise them.**

8. **Say, "Okay," and release them.**

9. **Practice several times in a row for several days in a row.**

REMEMBER

Sit and Down are two of the most important commands that prove your dog sees you as the leader of the pack, the mom, the dad, the coach of the team. Practice makes perfect, and perfect practice makes perfect training.

Sequence 6: Foregoing the treat

The last sequence of teaching the Sit and Down commands together uses only the collar pressure if necessary and no food. You need only use the collar pressure if Buddy doesn't follow the command the first time you give it. Buddy should wear the leash in these steps:

1. **Place Buddy in a Sit, as in Sequence 1.**

   Be close enough to reach out and touch your dog.

2. **Say, "Down."**

   Buddy should start to go down. If they don't, reach and take the collar from under the chin and apply slight pressure in the collar back, down, and toward them. They have felt this type of pressure many times, but this time you didn't start with your finger in the collar before you gave the command, plus you don't have a treat in your other hand. Buddy should respond because of all the practice you have done. If not, apply the pressure and praise them for going Down even though you helped.

3. **Practice doing more repetitions and in different locations.**

   Dogs learn well in one location. Practicing in different locations is extremely important and is the first step of distraction training.

4. **With Buddy in the Down position, stand up with the slack leash in your hand and say, "Sit."**

   If Buddy doesn't sit, use the leash to apply a slight amount of upward pressure on the collar, which lifts Buddy into the sitting position. Release with Okay and party together.

Warming Up with the Long-Down Exercise

One of the best impulse control exercises is the Long-Down. Practice the Long-Down exercise under the following conditions to start, and then you can use this exercise anytime:

>> When your dog is tired

>> After they have been exercised

>> When interruptions are unlikely

>> When you aren't tired or frustrated

If the situation allows it, you can watch television or read, as long as you don't move while you're training during the first two weeks. Stick to this schedule:

>> **Week 1:** Three times during the course of a week, practice the Long-Down for 30 minutes at a time as follows:

1. **Sit on the floor beside your dog.**

2. **Say, "Down," and place them in the Down position.**

   This is the only time you say the command during the 30 minutes, no matter how many times they get up and you put them back. This exercise is not about teaching Buddy how to Down on command but rather that you decide what they do and when and where and for how long. You are the leader of the team.

3. **If they get up, put them back without saying anything.**

4. **Keep your hands off of them when they're Down, other than to replace them back into the Down position if they get up.**

5. **Stay still.**

6. **After 30 minutes, release them, even if they have fallen asleep.**

   Well done. Even if Buddy gets up every 5 seconds, keep putting them back down; this is a crucial leadership exercise, and you're doing a great job if you put them back each time they get up.

TIP

   As a general rule, the bouncier the dog, the more frequently they'll try to get up and the more important this exercise becomes. Just remain calm, and each time they try to get up, place them back in the Down position. If your dog is particularly bouncy, put them on leash and kneel on the leash so that your hands are free to put them back.

   Some dogs cooperate relatively quickly, whereas others need more time. If your dog is in the latter group, your first experience with the Long-Down will be the most challenging, and you'll be quite busy putting Buddy back into the Down position. As they catch on to the idea and gradually accept the procedure, each successive repetition will go more easily.

>> **Week 2:** Practice three 30-minute Downs while you sit in a chair, such as a kitchen chair next to your dog.

>> **Week 3:** Practice three 30-minute Downs while you sit across the room from your dog. Start with Buddy 3 to 4 feet in front of you, the second time 10 feet in front of you, and then the third time on the other side of the room.

>> **Week 4:** Practice three 30-minute Downs while you move about the room but stay within sight of your dog. You can be cooking or cleaning or simply walking around the room occasionally.

REMEMBER

After Week 4, practice a Long-Down at least once a month; you can be working at home or simply relaxing while you do it. Either way, Buddy needs to be in a Down position within sight of you, but not necessarily near you. If they ever get up, simply go back to them and replace them into the Down. Don't try to direct them from a distance, which will only break down their belief that you can control them from a distance. Go to Buddy, put your finger in their collar, and return them to the Down position. No command is necessary because you've already given them the command.

Staying in Place: Sit-Stay and Down-Stay

You have two position choices when giving the Stay command to Buddy. First, give Buddy the position command and make sure that they take that position. Then, give them the Stay command while they're in the correct position. Always release Buddy from the Stay with the *Okay* release word when you're done by stepping forward to insist that they move out of position.

The following are the two position choices:

>> **Sit-Stay:** This command is used for relatively short periods.

>> **Down-Stay:** This command is for longer periods and is taught as a safety exercise to get Buddy to stop wherever they are and stay there. For example, suppose Buddy gets loose and ends up on the other side of the road. They see you and are just about to cross the road when a car comes. You need a way to get them to stay on the other side of the street until the car has passed by.

When working on Stay, no matter which position, you can use these three Ds to make the Stay more solid and reliable:

>> **Duration:** This is how long you do the Stay. Work on duration first before the next two Ds.

>> **Distance:** How far away from Buddy you practice the Stay is next important. After you successfully have worked on length of time, do Stays longer and longer and then practice on moving farther away from your dog, but go back to shorter periods to help them be successful.

>> **Distractions:** The third D stands for distractions, which includes what's going on around them that makes Buddy concentrate on maintaining the Stay. Distractions, such as the ones we mention in Chapter 10, include a person talking to them, another dog, or you eating. No matter the distraction, Buddy needs to remain in the Stay.

In the following sections, we explain how you can add these two Stay commands to your dog's repertoire.

REMEMBER

After Buddy understands what you want, alternate between the Sit-Stay and Down-Stay every other day. Whether you start with Buddy in the Sit position or the Down position when you say Stay, they should remain in that position. If not, replace them back into the starting position and continue working on the length of time you're having Buddy stay.

Teaching the Sit-Stay

The Sit-Stay is one of the most useful exercises you can teach. When you have guests, when your doorbell rings and Buddy rushes barking to the door, when you want Buddy not to dash through open doors, the Sit-Stay exercise is what keeps Buddy safe. It's also useful for stair manners and for stopping him from jumping out of the car when the door is opened (we discuss door and stair manners in Chapter 14). Overall, use this command when you want your dog to remain quietly in one spot.

To teach the Sit-Stay, Buddy needs a training collar and a 6-foot training leash (see Chapter 5 if you need to pick one). Before you proceed to another step while teaching the command, make sure that Buddy is solid on the previous one. Here are the steps to follow:

1. **With your dog on your left side, place your dog's collar high on their neck, directly behind their ears. Neatly fold half of your leash accordion-style in your left hand, and place it against your belly button, allowing 3 feet of slack.**

2. **With Buddy sitting, say, "Stay," and take a step out directly in front of your sitting dog and turn them so that you face each other.**

3. **Count to ten, return to Buddy's side, pause for a few seconds, and then release with "Okay," taking several steps forward as you release them from the sitting position.**

   The *Okay* release word needs to actually move them from the sitting position. That's why you must move forward after you say, "Okay."

While doing the Sit-Stay, if you see that Buddy's attention is drifting, they're probably about to move. You can tell that your dog is thinking about moving when they start to look around and begin to focus on something other than you. Any time you see that lack of attention, reinforce the Stay command by taking a step toward your dog with your right foot and with your right hand bring the leash straight up to a point directly above their head (see Figure 11-2).

FIGURE 11-2: Reinforce the Sit-Stay.

© John Wiley & Sons, Inc.

4. **Bring your right foot and right hand back to their original position without repeating the Stay command, count to 30 and pivot back to your dog's right side, pause for a few seconds, and then praise and release with "Okay" while you move forward a few steps taking Buddy with you.**

   Doing so guarantees that Buddy releases from the Stay position.

   You can then add the three Ds.

5. **Increase the duration and work on longer and longer Stays as your dog is learning to Sit-Stay.**

6. **After Buddy is successful with duration, start to add distance in small increments when you practice.**

   Say, "Stay," and then place yourself 3 feet in front of your dog, keeping your left hand at your belly button and your right hand at your side, palm open, facing your dog. Put them back if you think they are about to move or if they do change positions.

7. **After Buddy is successful with distance, start adding distractions to your Sit-Stay practice.**

   Repeat over the course of several training sessions until your dog is steady on this exercise and practice on a regular basis. See Chapter 10 for the different levels of distractions.

8. **Buddy is ready to practice off leash, so take off the leash and put it in your pocket.**

   Start close to them again and always keep your attention on your dog. If they move or change position, slowly go to them and put them back into the Sit, but don't repeat Sit or Stay. You aren't starting over again; you're fixing the command you were working on. Then, release them with "Okay."

TIP

Until you read the signs that Buddy is thinking about moving, chances are you'll be late reading their intentions. When that happens, without saying anything, put them back to the spot where they were supposed to stay, stand in front of them, count to ten, return to their side, pause for a few seconds, and release them with "Okay."

Teaching the Down-Stay

The object of the Down-Stay command is for your dog to remain in a comfortable position for a long period of time (see Figure 11-3). That's where the Down-Stay command comes in — the theory being that the dog is least likely to move from the Down position. Just as with the Sit-Stay command in the previous section, you work through the Stay sequentially.

FIGURE 11-3: A dog doing a lovely Down-Stay at their owner's side.

© John Wiley & Sons, Inc.

1. **With your dog on your left side, give Buddy the Down command (see Figure 11-3).**

   Review the Down command from earlier in this chapter. By this time, Buddy should be able to do a Down at your side for long periods, as long as 30 minutes with you nearby.

2. **Next, say, "Stay," and take a step out directly in front of your downed dog and turn them so that you face each other. This works on distance, not just duration, of the Down-Stay command.**

3. **Count to ten, return to Buddy's side, pause for a few seconds, and then release with "Okay," taking several steps forward as you release them from their Down position.**

   Your *Okay* release word needs to actually move them from the Down. That's why you must move forward after you say, "Okay."

TIP

   While doing the Down-Stay, if you see that Buddy's attention is drifting, they're probably about to move. Any time you see that lack of attention, reinforce the Stay command by taking a step toward your dog with your right foot and with your left hand reach for the collar under the chin and apply just enough pressure down and toward the chest to return them to the Down position.

4. **Stand back up without repeating the Stay command, count to 30 and pivot back to your dog's right side, pause for a few seconds, and then praise and release with "Okay" while you move forward a few steps, taking Buddy with you.**

   Doing so guarantees that Buddy releases from the Stay position.

   You can then add the three Ds.

5. **Increase the duration and work on longer and longer Stays as your dog is learning to Down-Stay.**

6. **After Buddy is successful with duration, start to add distance in small increments when you practice.**

   Say, "Stay," and then place yourself 3 feet in front of your dog, keeping your left hand at your belly button and your right hand at your side, palm open, facing your dog. Put them back if you think they are about to move or if they do change positions.

7. **After Buddy is successful with distance, start adding distractions to your Down-Stay practice.**

   Repeat over the course of several training sessions until your dog is steady on this exercise and practice on a regular basis. See Chapter 10 for the different levels of distractions.

8. **Buddy is ready to practice off leash, so take off the leash and put it in your pocket.**

   Start close to them again and always keep your attention on them. If they move or change position, slowly go to them and put them back into the Down, but don't repeat Down or Stay. You aren't starting over again; you're fixing the command you were working on. Then release them with "Okay."

Being a good dog trainer requires you to be prepared

While you are training your dog, be prepared by having the leash ready in your hand, having the collar where it should be, high on your dog's neck, and having a treat close at hand or in your pocket. Yelling out commands to your dog and not setting up for that command means that you aren't ready to reinforce the command should Buddy not respond correctly. If you are not prepared and set up to act on your command, you will be untraining your dog. A delayed response or no response at all will be the result.

Have your leash folded in your hand, loose against the collar, if necessary; set up with a finger in the collar, depending on what you are working on; and be prepared before you give a command. This will make you a great dog trainer. Your dog will see you as a coach and will follow you everywhere waiting for the next command.

Remember that praising after the *Okay* release word is also being prepared. Play with your dog and keep them engaged with you — it is all about the relationship you are building with your dog. Make it fun, meaningful, consistent, and fair.

Well done!

IN THIS CHAPTER

» **Relying on the right leash for walking**

» **Teaching your dog to walk**

» **Recognizing the difference between a pleasure walk and heeling**

» **Including distractions**

Chapter **12**

Going for a Pleasant Walk

Taking your dog for a nice, long walk is music for your soul and good exercise for both of you — or it should be when you both know how to walk together. Teaching Buddy to walk on a loose leash makes your strolls a pleasure rather than a chore or a safety hazard.

In this chapter, we provide you with everything you need to know in order to take a pleasant walk or romp in the park, including how to end Buddy's pulling and how to deal with distractions.

Using the Right Leash and Collar When Walking Your Dog

Studies show that people who regularly walk their dogs get more exercise than those who go to the gym. What could be more fun than sharing that exercise routine with Buddy? Sometimes Buddy may pull. To end the pulling, you need to teach Buddy to walk on a loose leash. For that job, you need the right equipment. The sole purpose of using any equipment at all is to communicate between you and your dog. The leash and collar need to provide a means for you to get Buddy's attention that results in them looking at you and, therefore, gives you a reason to praise them. It's really as simple as that.

REMEMBER

The best way to get that attention is a quick check on the leash and collar. A *check* is a snappy pull on the leash that starts with no pressure and ends with no pressure. The shorter the pressure lasts, the better a check it is. Repeating the check or checking twice is better than pulling so hard and long on the leash that you end up simply dragging each other. It takes two to get the leash to become tight — you pulling and the dog pulling on each end at the same time.

Different collars provide different results. The collar you need depends on the drives of your dog (see Chapter 2 for more information on drives). For example, a high prey drive usually needs more of a check than a high pack drive. Thus, having the right leash for walking is imperative. No matter how much of a check you need or provide, your dog's attention should be brought around to you, and you must praise them for looking at you. The praise is more important than the check, but a tight leash is the worst result. If the collar you're using isn't bringing your dog's attention back to you when you give a quick, snappy check on the leash and collar, then you need to try another type of collar. Chapter 5 discusses the basics about your choices. The following focuses on selecting a leash and collar for walking:

>> **Snap-around collar:** The best choice is a snap-around collar, which is similar to a slip collar except it has a snap that allows the collar to snap around Buddy's neck, right behind their ears, instead of being so large as to go over their head. When fitted snuggly behind a dog's ears at the top of their neck, this collar is effective because a check won't hit their trachea, and the check will be more of a guide to bring the dog's attention around to the owner.

>> **Web leash:** For a leash, our preference is a 6-foot cotton web leash when walking with your dog. It's light yet strong, comfortable to hold, and easily folds up when you want a shorter length or want to put it in your pocket.

>> **Buckle collars:** They stay the same size all of the time, whether you're checking the collar or not and no matter whether your dog is pulling or not. Most dogs can quickly ignore this collar. If anything, it becomes a nagging collar providing little to no results. Plus, because a buckle collar is a collar that your dog may wear all the time with identification on it, it most likely rests too low on their neck, which is where Buddy has a lot of muscle, and their trachea would get too much pressure if you were to yank on a buckle collar too much.

>> **Prong collars:** When used correctly, prong collars are effective and humane because they provide a quick check with little effort other than just enough to bring Buddy's attention immediately back to you. If held too tightly instead of loosely, though, when a check is needed, a dog can ignore a prong collar.

Prong collars are used when your dog isn't responding well enough to a snap-around collar. Often, a prong collar is referred to as *power steering* because, when used correctly — that is, well fitted high on the neck and with little effort on the leash — it is an amazing tool to achieve focus from your dog.

Here are a few reasons you may want to consider using a prong collar:

- When you have a small dog with a lot of prey drive. The extra power steering allows for hardly any pull on the leash to get your dog's attention.

- When you have a large, strong dog and you don't want to use too much effort to get your dog's attention.

- When you aren't very steady on your feet and you want your dog to quickly respond to a quick tug on the leash.

A friend who uses two hearing aids equates a prong collar to a hearing aid for the dog.

Dogs pull on a leash because they're more interested in the sights and scents in their environment than in you. Your job is to teach Buddy to become aware of your existence at the other end of the leash and to respect your presence. Praising them when they look at you and rewarding them with your joyful praise makes the walks fun for Buddy, too.

Taking a Pleasure Walk with Your Dog

The No. 1 rule to walking your dog is that it's *Buddy's* responsibility to pay attention to you, not the other way around. Even though they may be several feet away from you eagerly pursuing a scent, they must be aware of where you are, never straining on the end of the leash but adjusting their speed to your pace and direction. They don't need to pay 100 percent attention to you — but they must be aware of where you are and how you are walking. A *pleasure walk* is fun for both you and your dog. It allows your dog to sniff as long as they're nearby and pacing themselves to your pace and direction. It's like two friends enjoying each other's company.

To teach Buddy to walk nicely with you, you need their collar and their leash. Take Buddy to an area that's familiar to them with no distractions; your backyard or a quiet street are good places. The command to use for a pleasure walk is Let's Go.

The following sections help you teach Buddy how to go on a pleasure walk.

Using a clock face to train your dog to walk

Imagine that you're standing inside the center of the clock face, which can help you train your dog. Figure 12-1 helps you prepare to train your dog to take a pleasure walk.

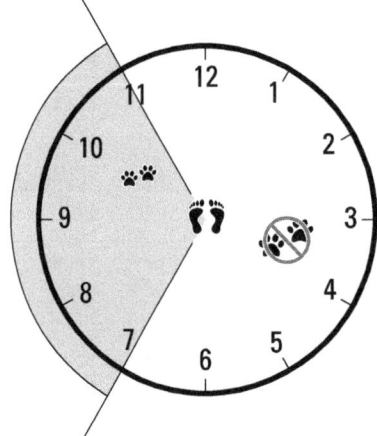

FIGURE 12-1:
Use this clock face to learn your dog's walking zone — 7 o'clock to 11 o'clock.

The following breaks down Figure 12-1:

>> **You are in the center of the clock facing in the direction you are to walk.**

>> **The 12 is in front of you.** This area belongs to you — the team leader — and not Buddy. As a result, the 12 spot is off-limits to Buddy.

>> **The 6 is directly behind you.** You can't see it, so the 6 is off-limits to Buddy because you want to be able to see them without turning completely around.

>> **The 11 on the clock face is slightly to your left, and moving down to the left you pass the other numbers until you come to the 7.** This zone is Buddy's zone to start. The 7 to 11 on your left side is where you want Buddy to walk with you on a pleasure walk. For a pleasure walk to be pleasant, Buddy shouldn't wind the leash around you, so they need to stay to one side of you as you walk.

TECHNICAL STUFF

Why do dogs walk on the left of all dog trainers? They traditionally do this because people used to lead their horses on their right, and people might have carried their hunting weapons on their right.

>> **The 3 is on your right.** Just to orient you, this is the no-dog zone.

>> **The 9 is on your left.** This is the Heel position (see the following section, "Teaching Buddy How to Heel at Your Side," for more information).

The leash is 6 feet long, so the clock face or Buddy's zone must be smaller than the leash is long. Therefore, Buddy can never go outside the 5-foot zone of 7 to 11 on the clock face. You must know exactly where you want Buddy to be in order to teach them where they should be. If you aren't specific in your own mind, how can Buddy learn their place to walk with you?

Training the pleasure walk

Follow these steps when you're training your dog to go on a pleasure walk:

1. **Know Buddy's zone on the clock face and start in the 7–11 area (see the previous section for clarification).**

2. **Hold the leash loosely with both hands.**

   Have the loop of the leash over your right thumb, and hold the leash across your legs with your left hand but keep the leash loose for Buddy as you walk together, the dog on your left. This is a pleasure walk, so no tight leashes and use the check to bring Buddy back to zone 7-11 by your side. Figure 12-2 shows you how this should look.

FIGURE 12-2: Hold the leash over your right thumb and float the rest of leash through your left hand. Notice the loose J-leash shape.

© John Wiley & Sons, Inc.

3. **Say, "Let's go," and start walking.**

   Make sure Buddy is on your left, inside their zone when you start. As you walk, keep an eye on where Buddy is walking. If they are in the 7–11 zone and less than a few feet away from you, that's great — keep walking and praise. If Buddy moves too far out in front or anywhere other than the 7–11 zone, check the leash back to you quickly, bringing Buddy back into their zone and immediately praise them for being back in their zone. Keep walking. Use the bring-back check while you keep walking.

   Unintentional training can result if you keep the leash too tight for too long. When your dog is on a leash, you should always work at keeping the leash slack, with no pressure on the collar. We often refer to this shape as a letter J or a J-leash. If there is pressure on the leash, Buddy considers this uncomfortable and interprets the pressure as either nagging or a constant correction when neither is intended by you. Therefore, unintentional training is occurring. A J-leash requires the dog to choose to be with you; if they pull away from you, give a quick check on the leash, which is a quick snap to the leash that immediately relaxes it back to the J-leash. Praise with your voice as they are back on the J-leash. Buddy should look at you and you should smile and praise. It takes two to pull out of the J-leash; both you and Buddy are pulling each other. Relax the leash back into the J-leash shape. See Figure 12-2.

4. **Change your direction as you walk.**

   The clock face turns with you, but Buddy's zone is still on your left even though you're now walking in a different direction. Buddy needs to learn that you determine their zone. Everything is in relationship to you. Say their name as you make a turn to give Buddy a reason to look your way just as you did when doing the Name Game (see Chapter 9). Practicing in your yard makes it easier to vary your direction because there aren't sidewalks to restrict your direction as you walk.

   If Buddy decides to stop and sniff within their zone, that's fine; you can stop, too. After all, it's a pleasure walk for both of you. When you're ready to move on, say, "Let's go," and start walking again, making sure Buddy is in their zone.

   The trick to a pleasure walk is that you walk where you want to go, as fast as you want to get there, while Buddy hangs out on your left on a loose leash. If they need reminding where their zone is because they left the zone, check them back into their zone and praise them for being back. The praise after the bring-back is vital to the communication that you're teaching Buddy how to walk nicely on a walk.

   The first few times you practice using the leash to keep Buddy in his 7–11 zone, you'll likely be a little late — Buddy will already be leaning into their collar. If so, extend your elbows a tiny bit to give the leash some looseness before you give a quick check on the leash. Concentrate on Buddy and figure out how to anticipate when you're about to make a turn. If you haven't taught Buddy to look at you when you say their name, then visit Chapter 9.

5. **Practice this sequence over the course of several sessions until Buddy responds reliably to the Let's Go command.**

   Keep the sessions short — no more than five to ten minutes to start. Make it fun. Eventually, you'll be walking around the block and then for a few miles a day. Buddy should always be in their zone of the clock face.

   As Buddy gets better with your pleasure walk, you can shrink their zone on the clock face. Whatever zone you choose is fine as long as you communicate the change to Buddy by being consistent as you bring them back with a check and praise them afterwards. For example, change or shrink his zone to be 8–10 on the clock face.

Teaching Buddy How to Heel at Your Side

Heeling is ideal when you cross the street, pass another pedestrian, or walk through a marketplace. Heeling is a controlled walk with Buddy directly at your side, moving smoothly together as one, whereas a pleasure walk is pleasant on a loose leash with Buddy freer to move within their zone.

By teaching Buddy how to go on a pleasure walk in the preceding section, you're ultimately starting the process of teaching Buddy how to heel. The distinction is Buddy's location. The Heel position is on your left at 9 o'clock with Buddy walking with full attention with his ears in line with the seam on your pants, walking at the same pace and in the same direction as you. While heeling, Buddy learns to stop and sit at your side when you stop walking.

As you practice and teach Buddy to heel, make your sessions short. If you're taking a walk around the block, make the majority of the walk be a pleasure walk and interrupt the walk with short sessions of heeling for a few yards or so, and then release with Okay and go back to your pleasure walk with the Let's Go command. The following steps help you teach Buddy how to heel:

1. **Put Buddy on the training collar and leash, start with them on your left side, and throw the handle of the leash across your chest and over your right shoulder.**

   Your hands should be loosely funneled around the leash in front of you. When needed, you can take the leash in your hands by squeezing your hands shut around the leash and bringing Buddy back to the Heel position if they leave the 9 o'clock spot as you walk. See Figure 12-3.

FIGURE 12-3:
With the leash over your right shoulder, have your hands funneled around the leash in front of you.

2. **Say, "Buddy, heel."**

   By saying their name before the Heel command, Buddy should look up at you. By saying, "Buddy, heel," *before* you step off to walk, they'll be ready to move with you, not after you start to walk.

3. **Praise Buddy as they're moving nicely with you.**

   Do so as you walk with Buddy at your left side, still at 9 o'clock on the clock face. If they leave your side, check them back to your left side by taking hold of the leash with your hands that are circled around the leash across your chest. The check brings them back to your left side as you continue to walk and praise them enthusiastically. Repeat this sequence as you walk around your yard, house, or sidewalk.

4. **Add a change of direction by turning around and going the other way by turning away from Buddy or to the right.**

   Say your dog's name before you turn around so they look at you and see that you're turning. Praise them in the new direction as they remain by your side. Repeat turning around, always to the right and saying their name first. Also, take hold of the leash as you turn to help keep Buddy with you.

5. **Add a change of pace, such as walking faster or slower, and then going back to a normal pace for you.**

   You don't need to give a command to Buddy as you change your pace; simply use your leash to keep them with you and praise when they're beside you. Make sure Buddy learns to change their pace to match your pace, not the other way around.

6. **To end the exercise, say, "Okay," and then release by running five steps straight forward and end by partying with Buddy.**

    Start again with Buddy on your left, leash over your shoulder, and say, "Buddy, heel." Release after a few yards by saying, "Okay," and then start over.

The other option instead of releasing is to teach Buddy to automatically sit at your side when you stop, which means that Buddy notices that you've stopped and then sits directly beside you in the Heel position. Initially, there is nothing *automatic* about sitting in the Heel position because you're helping them see where to sit and how, but eventually Buddy should stop and sit when you stop and they are on the Heel command.

TIP

To teach the Automatic Sit, before you stop walking, take hold of the leash by reaching across your body with your right hand, close to the top of Buddy's head, and lift the leash up slightly as your left hand tucks their tail under their hind legs as you say, "Sit." Praise them for any attempt at a sit in the beginning and then release them to fun and praise with you.

As you practice the Automatic Sit, you and Buddy will get better at this, and the Sit should happen squarely at your side in the Heel position. Saying "Sit" each time you ask for the Automatic Sit helps Buddy know what you expect from them when you stop. Eventually, saying "Sit" won't be necessary, and as you stop and lift the leash slightly, they'll automatically sit.

Adding Distractions

As you practice the Heel command, do so in a distraction-free environment. As you and Buddy get good at heeling, you're ready to teach Buddy that it's their responsibility to pay attention to you while you say, "Heel." You use the Heel command when you need more control, usually around distractions, such as in the marketplace, with kids on bikes and other pedestrians, and so on.

Training with distractions

Follow these steps when incorporating distractions while teaching Heel:

1. **Start your session, still without distractions, by reviewing Buddy's response to Heel with two or three about-turns.**

2. **Say Buddy's name as you make your turns.**

   During the first several tries, Buddy will likely experience a tug on the leash before they turn to follow you. After several turns, however, they'll catch on and respond to your turn. When they do, praise lavishly and stop for that session. Review this sequence for several sessions.

3. **When Buddy's comfortable with the routine and follows you without hesitation when you make a turn, you can move on to introducing distractions.**

   For this sequence, you need a distracter — a family member or anyone willing to stand still long enough. The distracter's job is just that: to distract Buddy with any object that may interest them. Food usually works. Of course, the distracter doesn't let Buddy obtain the object, because doing so would defeat the purpose of the exercise. Figure 12-4 shows a distracter at work.

   The distracter holds the object — for this exercise, you can assume that it's food — close to his body, without waving it about or talking to Buddy. Because this is a new exercise for Buddy, you start at the beginning: You reintroduce the Heel command.

FIGURE 12-4:
Heeling with distraction.

© John Wiley & Sons, Inc.

4. **From a distance of about 10 feet, say, "Heel," toward the distracter.**

    When Buddy is aware of the food held by the distracter, say, "Heel," again and do an about-turn. If Buddy fails to respond, they'll experience a tug on the leash because of the natural force of the turn at the distracter. Repeat the procedure until Buddy responds by following you on command and no tug occurs. When they remain with you, praise lavishly and end the session.

    At your next session, review the same sequence; when Buddy responds correctly, end the session with lots of praise. Eventually, follow the same sequence but eliminate saying "Heel" during the distraction and the about-turn because avoiding the distraction is the lesson Buddy has learned.

Going to places with new distractions

Buddy should now have a pretty good idea of what to do while heeling and avoiding distractions, so you're ready to take them to new places. Chances are, on a walk in the park, you'll meet a number of new distractions, including other dogs. Exposing Buddy to a variety of new circumstances is a wonderful teaching opportunity. Practice in those settings both the Let's Go and Heel commands, and alternate between the two different commands.

The Heel command is more precise, and Buddy should avoid all distractions while you use it. Let's Go is less precise. While Buddy is on the Let's Go command, as long as they don't pull you toward a distraction, they're able to be beside you showing interest in something other than you for a few seconds. Buddy should never be allowed to stop being aware of where you are at all times.

To find out if Buddy has learned their lessons, try the ultimate tests. Go to a secure location, your fenced backyard, a fenced ballfield, or fenced tennis court.

Try this first test: When Buddy isn't beside you when you command them, they should join you when you say, "Buddy, let's go."

1. **Go into the fenced area and remove the leash.**

2. **Let Buddy wander around a bit and then say, "Buddy, let's go."**

3. **Turn your back toward them and walk away.**

    If they come to you, enthusiastically praise. If not, do a little more practicing. Praise them for joining you as you walk around the fenced area. The Let's Go command means, "Come with me. We are going." When Buddy comes to you and moves on with you, well done. Praise Buddy for being such a great friend.

Try this second test: Buddy starts by sitting next to you. They should get up and move with you because you say, "Buddy, heel."

1. **Go into the fenced area and sit Buddy next to you, and then remove the leash.**

2. **While Buddy sits there, pet them on their head to put them into pack drive (see Chapter 2 about drives).**

3. **Smile and say, "Buddy, heel," and then start walking; Buddy should move with you.**

   Give Buddy the Heel command off leash and start walking forward. Praise them as they move with you. Don't go more than a few steps the first time. Say, "Okay," to release and have a big party together. What a great dog Buddy has become.

   If they don't move with you, you need more practice on leash. The best way to teach a dog to work off leash is on leash. If you step off saying, "Buddy, heel," and they don't move with you, reach back with an open palm for their collar to guide them up, and encourage them to move with you.

REMEMBER

Often, the reason a dog won't move while off leash is because the leash has been too tight while you trained and they have become used to the feel of the leash. (This is why the J-leash is so important. See "Training the pleasure walk" above and Figure 12-2.) Practice more, going back to using the leash, but be careful to keep the leash loosely placed over your right shoulder. Keep your hands off the leash but in place ready to use as necessary to bring Buddy back to your side with a check.

Training with your dog, spending time with each other, and working as a team is not only fun, but also it results in a dancing team. As you and Buddy heel together, you're dancing together. It's easy to see why heeling looks like dancing. When this is done well, you're a team working in sync — a beautiful sight. Praise that beautiful dog.

Chapter **13**

Going to Bed and All of Its Practical Uses

A dog who knows the Go to Your Bed command is a wonderful dog and well trained (see Figure 13-1). This command is useful because it teaches your dog a place to hang out for long periods of time, such as when you're hosting guests. Another wonderful use for this command is to teach your dog where you want them to go when someone comes to the door or when you come home instead of jumping up on you or your guests. It can even become a default behavior for when the door bell rings.

One of the uses of the Go command is to teach Buddy the Go to Your Bed command. We explain the Go command in Chapter 10.

Your dog needs to understand that when you say, "Go to Your Bed," you mean these three things:

» Get on the bed when commanded "Go to Your Bed."

» Don't *get off* the bed until given the release word or you say, "Okay."

» Find your bed in the face of distractions or from anywhere in the house.

FIGURE 13-1:
A well-trained
dog showing off
their good
manners.

REMEMBER

Your dog having a useful understanding of the Go To Bed command doesn't mean that Buddy can't simply choose to get on his bed at will. The difference between being commanded to "Go to your bed" and your dog getting on their bed themselves is how and when they can get off the bed. If you say, "Go to your bed," they can't get off the bed until you release them with "Okay." This is crucially important. When they choose to go to bed on their own, they can come and go at will. Your command is what makes the difference of how long they remain on the bed. You being the coach of the team dictates that getting on the bed at this moment is a requirement based on the fact that you commanded them to get on it.

In this chapter we explain the importance of having a bed for your dog and what steps you can take to teach Buddy how to respond to the Go to Your Bed command.

Selecting a Bed for Your Dog

Before you teach your dog the Go to Your Bed command, you need to choose the bed you want to use for Buddy. A well-trained, mannerly dog should be able to be sent to and remain on their bed when you have guests and when you need to deal with someone at your door.

Here are a few options:

>> **Elevated cot:** An elevated cot, shown in Figure 13-2a, makes a good choice because it has an actual border to clearly define being on the bed or off the bed.

Elevated beds or cots can be found all over the internet and are often made with PVC pipe as the framework. These beds come in all price ranges and all sizes (see Figure 13-2b). Look around and find one that works for your wallet and the size of your dog.

>> **Foam mattress:** A covered foam mattress, shown in Figure 13-2c, is wonderful for older dog's joints. These beds can offer more warmth and definitely more cushioning. They can come with removable covers, which make for easy washing.

>> **Pads:** Any type of pad can make a nice bed that is easy to take along if you travel, as shown in Figure 13-2d. A pad can be a sponge mat, a throw rug, or an old blanket.

(a)

(b)

(c)

(d)

FIGURE 13-2: Different types of dog beds.

© John Wiley & Sons Inc.

An elevated bed isn't mandatory; you can use any dog bed, blanket, or towel, even a mouse pad or place mat, to signify your dog's place, spot, or bed.

Deciding When and How You Want to Use the Command

You need to answer this important question before using the Go to Your Bed command: Should you command Buddy to lie down while they are on their bed?

>> If Buddy knows to lie down on their bed each time they get on their bed, it will add one more layer of stability to the Go to Your Bed command. If so, the answer is yes.

>> If Buddy can choose his own position on the bed, it adds a freedom to Buddy to move around on their bed as long as they remain there. If so, this choice is no.

You need to choose only one option. The option you select is a personal one and depends on you, the owner. You can add the Down command later (see Chapter 11) if you choose not to put Buddy in a Down to start. Some dogs struggle with Down, and that struggle takes away from the Go to Your Bed command, which is otherwise relatively easy to teach. The fact that Buddy must remain on their bed after you've sent them there is crucial for Buddy to understand. If you allow them to choose their position, that's fine. If they lay down on their own and you reward them for that position, without a Down command given, that's okay, too. To reward the Down position if Buddy chooses it on their own, simply say, "Good, Down," and give them a treat.

If you choose "yes" and you want Buddy to lie down each time, start this behavior at Sequence 2 in the next section and continue giving the Down command with each subsequent sequence. After Buddy is on the bed, tell them, "Down," and give them the treat for getting down on the bed. If they sit or stand up while on the bed at any time, you must go back to them and reinforce the Down position by using collar pressure down.

Training Buddy the Go to Your Bed Command

Set up the dog bed in the location you want to use it. Ideally, it's a place where Buddy can still see you hanging out with guests or still see the front door if you're going to use it as the default behavior for answering the front door. You may need to have two beds, one in the foyer and one in the family room.

Sequence 1: Starting with the Bed command

In these steps you begin with the command and use a food lure to encourage your dog onto the chosen bed:

1. **Put the bed in a logical spot in your house, conveniently out of the way yet easy to access.**

   Have plenty of small but visible treats in your pocket.

2. **Use a cookie in your hand, show Buddy the cookie, lure Buddy onto the surface of the bed, and say, "Bed."**

3. **Feed him and then say, "Okay," and move to the side so that your dog can get off the bed.**

   You're teaching Buddy not only to get on the bed, but also not to get off of the bed until you release them. They need to understand these two things.

   Feed them while they're on the bed, not after they have gotten off the bed. You want the reward to be for getting on the bed, not for getting off of the bed.

REMEMBER

4. **Practice Sequence 1 until they are easily lured onto the bed for the treat.**

Sequence 2: Adding the Go, Bed command

This sequence teaches Buddy to willingly get on the bed by using the Go command (see Chapter 10). Follow these steps:

1. **Place a treat on the bed while holding Buddy back a few inches from the bed, and then let go of his collar and signal with your closest arm to Buddy and say, "Go, Bed."**

   Use these two commands rather than the whole phrase "Go to Your Bed" to start. Buddy knows the Go command, and you're teaching them the Bed command, so you now want these two words to stand out to them.

   If Buddy can reach onto the bed to eat the treat without actually getting on the bed, turn the bed to be longways on their approach and put the cookie at the far end, making it necessary for them to step onto the bed to get to the treat.

TIP

2. **Block their exit from the bed by stepping in front of them if they go to get off without permission.**

   Then, release them with "Okay" to let them get off of the bed. Praise them, but don't give them a treat for getting off.

3. **Practice Sequence 2 until they are readily going to the bed on their own and not getting off until you release them.**

Even if you're still body blocking them, that's fine. If they get off the bed by accident without being released, take them by the collar and gently return them to the bed by walking back to the surface of the bed with them.

Sequence 3: Increasing your distance from the bed

In the first two sequences, you and Buddy are close to the bed. Now, step back a foot and follow these steps:

1. **Load a cookie onto the bed as if it were a target, and then you move Buddy back a foot and signal and say, "Go to your bed."**

Don't step forward with them but let them move toward the bed on their own. (We discuss using a target in Chapter 10 when you teach the Go command.)

WARNING

Stepping forward *with* your dog as you want them to move away from you is called *bowling* with your dog. Don't bowl with your dog. Be aware that moving with your dog is unintentionally teaching them that you'll both be going together all the time. In actuality, you want your dog to move forward alone. Watch that your dog independently moves on to the bed without you.

2. **As you load the bed with a target piece of food, walk away with Buddy while holding onto their collar.**

As the distance increases, move back a step on each repetition until you are both across the room from the bed when you send Buddy to bed with the Go to Your Bed command.

Sequence 4: Foregoing the food lure

In these steps, rather than preloading the bed with a treat, you keep the treat in your pocket and then give it to them after they obey your command:

1. **Start close to the bed again without putting a treat on the bed, signal with the arm closest to your dog, and say, "Go to your bed."**

2. **After Buddy steps onto the bed, go to them and give a treat from your pocket.**

This change relies on Buddy learning the command, not just going for the food.

Make sure that the treat isn't in your hand before you command him. If it is, Buddy won't want to leave you and the treat. Instead, put the treat in your pocket or on a dish near the bed on a table that Buddy can't reach. Go to Buddy while they're on the bed and give them the treat from your hand. Body block them so that they don't get off until you release them.

REMEMBER

If your dog is snatching food from your fingers, head to Chapter 9 to discover how to stop your dog from biting at your fingers for food.

Work this way until you successfully get across the room again, as in the previous sequence.

Not loading the bed with a treat is very different from preloading the bed as a target. Buddy will be getting the treat from you for doing what you just asked them to do. The difference is that Buddy is now working without a lure or target and working for you instead of for getting a treat.

3. **While you're working on distance, randomly make the time spent on the bed change from a few seconds to 10 or 20 seconds before the release.**

REMEMBER

Don't give a treat for getting off the bed when asked. Say, "Okay," to release and praise and play with them with no food. Give the treat only while they're still on the bed.

Sequence 5: Increasing the time spent on the bed

Now that Buddy is getting really good at getting on their bed, you want to instill in them that they must remain there until you release them. You have already been consistent with this point but only for short amounts of time (less than a minute). In these steps, you increase the amount of time your dog stays on the bed before you release him:

1. **Send Buddy to bed, reward them with a treat, and body block them from getting off the bed.**

While you stand close, keep them on their bed for a full minute. Praise them quietly while they're on the bed. You can repeat the treat during this minute. If Buddy lies down, definitely reward the behavior of choosing to lie down on their own with a treat. After a minute, say, "Okay," to release and step aside to allow Buddy to get off, but make sure that the release word is what prompts them to get off the bed, not your body language of moving to the side. Praise and pet them for getting off, but give no food.

2. **Increase the time on the bed to 90 seconds, 2 minutes, and so on.**

They should be able to work up to 30 minutes on their bed with you nearby.

TIP

If they get off the bed, take them gently and quietly by the collar and replace them by guiding them onto the bed. After they're back on the bed, start to praise them again. Don't repeat the Go to Your Bed command because they got off without permission. By getting off without you saying "Okay," they have ended the command, not you, so put them back into position without a command. By not using the command again, it lets Buddy know they did an oops. If you repeat the command at this point, they'll think you're starting over again, and that there was no oops on their part, which only adds confusion because they won't learn that you and only you end their work with "Okay."

3. **Practice until they remain on the bed with no mistakes for as much as 30 minutes.**

Sequence 6: Moving around while they're on the bed

In these steps, you start moving away from the bed after you reward them for getting on the bed.

1. **From a distance, say, "Go to your bed."**

2. **After they leave you and get on the bed, go to them and give them a treat.**

By slowly moving around them, moving away from the bed, and then stepping back to the bed, you're making your location not important for Buddy while they're on the bed.

3. **Work up to being able to step to the other side of the room to mill around but still keep a close eye on Buddy while they're on the bed.**

Always stop them from getting off the bed or return them to their bed if they should get off. Stay in sight of Buddy at this sequence.

4. **Sit down in a chair and keep an eye on them.**

As you sit down, they'll be tempted to get off and come to you. Immediately get back up and gently guide them back to the bed if that happens.

Sequence 7: Adding distractions

Adding distractions is fun to do with any behavior; however, don't add distractions until you feel that your dog understands their job without distractions. Keep the distractions sequential and see the different degrees of distractions in Chapter 10.

For the Go to Your Bed command, you can add distractions in two different places:

>> **Buddy's on the bed, and the distractions may pull them off the bed.** As you work on these distractions, you can put a leash on Buddy to help guide them back to the bed. Some examples of distractions are other people coming and going from the room; you sitting down, eating food, dropping food, throwing a toy; shaking hands with someone who enters the room; a knock on the door; the doorbell ringing; and so on. All of these distractions are appropriate for Buddy to learn to remain on their bed.

>> **You haven't given Buddy the Go to Your Bed command yet.** For example, you go outside alone and then come back in and say, "Go to your bed" to Buddy. Or someone else is assigned to come to your door and ring or knock on the door, and then you send Buddy to their bed with "Go to your bed."

Having a leash on their collar while you practice these distractions will be helpful. The leash allows you to better control them and help guide them to the bed while you're standing. Furthermore, with a leash you don't need to catch Buddy while they're so distracted.

Don't practice these distractions until Buddy has become successful in remaining on their bed and finding their bed from a distance. Don't rush into distractions until Buddy is ready to deal with them. That's why adding distractions is Sequence 7.

REMEMBER

Distraction training is meant to build your dog's confidence. You need to know that Buddy completely understands this command before you work the command under distracted conditions.

Sequence 8: Finding the bed from another room

Teaching your dog to find a specific bed from anywhere in the house may not be something you need to do. The bed by the front door and the bed in the family room may not be the same bed; therefore, which bed you mean may be confusing to Buddy. As long as they find a bed that you have trained them to go to, they can go to either bed. For example, if you need to corral Buddy for whatever reason, you can use the Go to Your Bed command. In such a situation, you may want to use the Get In command for the crate command from Chapter 14.

Calling your dog to you or sending your dog to their bed or crate are choices you have, and your dog should be well versed in all commands.

To practice this sequence, stick to these steps. Always remember to follow through with the reward and release before trying another suggested location to send Buddy from.

1. **Go to the doorway or arch of the room your dog's bed is in and say, "Go to your bed."**

   If Buddy needs help, you may need more practice with earlier sequences.

2. **As Buddy is successful, move farther into the next room and send them from there.**

   Always follow them without bowling them. Let them leave you before you move to follow.

   This sequence is fun because Buddy gets to run to their bed. Running is fun for dogs, plus they get a food reward after they're there.

3. **Move from room to room as you vary the location from which you send Buddy.**

   Also vary the time of day you practice this command. Simply stand up from somewhere in the house and say "Go to your bed" to Buddy. You may not have been training them at this time of day, but surprise them.

   By varying the times and the locations, Buddy will become well versed in watching you and listening to you at any and all times. Remember in the relationship you have with Buddy, you are the coach, and they are the player. Making training fun is great, but adding training into any part of the day really keeps Buddy waiting and watching for a command from you.

WHEN THE DOORBELL RINGS, USE THE GO TO YOUR BED COMMAND

If you want Buddy to always go to their bed when the doorbell rings, you can make this their default behavior for the bell ringing. To do this, get another person to help you. Have this person be outside and text them to ring the bell when you want it to ring.

Start with Sequence 1, but add the doorbell ringing first and then lure Buddy onto the bed. Then train Sequence 2, 3, and so on. If Buddy goes crazy for the doorbell, you need to do this step on leash. You should do the doorbell as a default Go to Your Bed command only after you've already taught all of the sequences in the earlier section "Training Buddy the Go to Your Bed Command." Don't start with the doorbell as your command if you haven't already taught the Go to Your Bed command.

The Go to Your Bed default command became true for my Australian Shepherd when I drove into the driveway. She would peek out the door window, see my vehicle, and by the time I got to the door and opened it, she would be on her dog bed, waiting for her hello and maybe a cookie. Remember, you get the dog you train, so train for the dog you want!

IN THIS CHAPTER

» Training Buddy how to get in
  and get out

» Focusing on Buddy to get on
  and get off

» Dashing your dog's dashing habits
  by teaching them door and
  stair manners

Chapter **14**

Getting In, Out, On, and Off and Mastering Door and Stairs Manners

Almost as annoying as unrestrained greeting behaviors, but far more dangerous, is a dog's habit of dashing through doors just because they're open, or racing up and down stairs — ahead of or behind you — or jumping in and out of the car without permission. These behaviors are dangerous to your dog because they may find themselves in the middle of the road and get hit. These behaviors also are dangerous to *you* because Buddy may knock you over going down the stairs or through the door.

REMEMBER

You can prevent such potential accidents by teaching Buddy not to go through a door and to wait until you tell them it's okay to go through. For the exercises in this chapter, Buddy doesn't need to sit, but many dogs do so on their own after a few repetitions. Instead, Buddy must stop at the door and wait for permission from you to cross the threshold.

Getting In and Out

Get In is an extremely useful command when you're training Buddy. You can say, "Get in," for the crate, the car, the door, the gate, and so on. Other variations are just as important. The Move Ahead of Me command is the basic concept, which is similar to the Go command (see Chapter 10 for more information). Go means move on, go with someone else, or go without me. The difference is that the Get In command means getting into a smaller opening or confined space.

Starting with a crate is an easy way to begin teaching the Get In command. (Chapter 6 describes crates and the benefits of using them.) Even if you already use a crate, you must teach Buddy that you own the door opening. You, the leader, own the opening and give permission for them to exit. They should enter when you tell them and not exit until you tell them. Bolting out of the crate isn't acceptable; plus, they should never avoid getting in.

To teach the Get In and Get Out commands, break them down into these sequences and steps:

Sequence 1: Eating the reward

The steps in the first sequence motivate Buddy with a cookie to go inside the crate:

1. **Go to the crate and open it and hold onto Buddy's collar.**

2. **Open the crate door, toss a cookie inside, and say, "Get in."**

3. **Let go of Buddy's collar, allowing them to go in and eat the cookie without any rules of remaining inside at this point, and leave the door open while they eat the treat.**

   They can bring the treat out or stay in and eat it. No rules yet. Repeat several times until Buddy is excited to get inside for the treat.

Sequence 2: Making Buddy wait for the treat

The steps in this sequence make Buddy wait for their reward:

1. **Open the crate door.**

2. **Say, "Get in," and release Buddy's collar to allow them to move inside.**

3. **Hand Buddy the treat through the door opening for getting inside.**

They can eat the treat and leave because you're not yet making any rules about remaining inside.

Sequence 3: The rules of the exit begin

Now you're ready for Buddy to exit only on command. Follow these steps:

1. **Say, "Get in," and go back to tossing a treat into the crate.**

2. **After Buddy is inside, swing the crate door shut while they eat the treat. No need to latch it; simply hold it closed.**

3. **When they're finished eating, make eye contact with Buddy, say, "Okay," open the door, and let them out.**

If they won't look at you, make a kissy sound to encourage them to look up at you.

4. **Repeat Step 1 and start controlling the door with your hand by only opening it slightly and then immediately swinging it shut again if Buddy goes to exit.**

You have not said "Okay" yet, so they have no permission to exit the crate.

The action of the door swinging shut puts visual pressure on Buddy, and they'll move back inside. Remember, you haven't said the release word yet.

Repeat swinging the door shut until Buddy doesn't try to exit while the door is ajar. At that point, with the door ajar, wait for them to look at you and then say, "Okay," and have a big party outside the crate. You Own The Opening!

REMEMBER

These rules remain throughout their life. They should never bolt out of a crate without your permission. If Buddy is crated in a public place, you should be able to reach in and leash them before you release them from their crate.

As Buddy gets better about entering and exiting the crate on command, they next need to find the crate on your command.

5. **Move a bit away from the crate and have them practice running into the crate on command for their cookie from a slight distance.**

They should then turn around, but wait for you to either close the door behind them or hand in a cookie, so you can then release them from the crate.

These distance reviews give you an opportunity to keep practicing this sequence. Initially, you were right outside the crate, but are now two feet away, then four feet, and so on. They should get into their crate when you say, "Get in," from any distance, even from another room. Then, walk up to the crate and review the exit by saying, "Okay."

Well done. Review each and every day and each and every time you put Buddy into the crate. These are lifelong rules of living with your dog. Never allow them to exit the crate without controlled permission and always say, "Get in," on your command.

Getting On and Off

As you live with Buddy, you'll find the need for them to move off of the sofa, off of your lap, off of a piece of furniture, out of the car's back seat, and so on. The Get Off command is useful in all instances. When you say, "Get off," Buddy should jump immediately off of whatever they are on. You can work on both the Get On and Get Off commands together using a sofa or big foot stool or garden wall, something that has a big upper surface that Buddy would love to get up on but can easily and safely get off of when you ask.

REMEMBER

Get On and Get Off are two commands that should bring immediate response to Buddy's actions. Your body language and immediate movement plays a big role in impressing this on them each and every time you give the commands. Use your body language each time, moving toward the object when you say, "On," and turning and moving away from the object when you say, "Off."

These two commands are especially useful when getting in and out of the back of the car. Take your lessons to the car and get Buddy jumping in and out of the car on command. Remember your part in making this go well — turning your back and moving away for getting off and stepping toward the elevated surface for getting on.

Sequence 1: Getting Buddy on something

Follow these steps to teach Buddy how to get on something, such as a sofa:

1. **Put Buddy on a leash and bring them to the sofa or surface you'll be using and have some good treats, small and easy to eat, with you.**

   Treats should always be small when training multiple repetitions.

2. **Offer them a treat on the edge, pat the sofa, and say a happy "Yes," allowing them to eat the treat.**

   "Yes" means Buddy is performing the command perfectly and correctly.

3. **Repeat, moving the treat a few more inches back away from the edge, pat the surface, and say, "Yes," when he reaches for the treat to eat it.**

If Buddy willingly jumps up on the sofa, great, praise them; if not, then put your hand gently in their collar and use the treat in your other hand to encourage them to move closer to the sofa.

4. **Place the treat on the sofa and say, "Get on."**

If they need help, use your body language and turn and walk along the front edge of the sofa to help bring them up and on the sofa. Gently bring Buddy up onto the sofa and let them eat their treat. Say, "Yes," when they step up and praise them while they eat. Body block them to keep them on the sofa.

Sequence 2: Getting Buddy off something

These steps help you train Buddy to get off something, such as a sofa:

1. **With Buddy on the sofa, on leash, turn your back to them, say, "Get off," and step forward and away from the sofa. Never look over your shoulder back at them. That look will stop them from moving with you and will lock them in place.**

The most important thing is for you to keep your back to Buddy while you say, "Get off," and walk a step away from the sofa with a slight tug on the leash. Say, "Yes," for stepping off and play with them and praise them on the floor.

2. **While you're still a step away from the sofa, say, "Get on," and step toward the sofa and give them their treat while they are on the sofa.**

3. **Say, "Yes," pet them while they are up, and body block them from getting off until you command them to do so; then turn away, step away, and say, "Get off."**

When they do, say "Yes," and party together on the floor.

REMEMBER

Turning your back to Buddy for the Get Off command is important. Stepping toward the elevated surface is critical for Buddy as well, especially in the early stages.

4. **Review until you no longer need to move with Buddy — until your words are the only command needed to get Buddy to move up and on or off.**

Training Threshold Door Manners

Teaching door manners doesn't require any prior training and is a good introductory exercise. This exercise is fun to teach because you can see the wheels in Buddy's brain turning. Your dog will learn quickly that the only way out of the door is with the release word, such as Okay. This command is meant for doors to the outside: front door, back door, gate in the fence, and so on.

REMEMBER

You don't use a verbal command for stopping your dog from going through the door; the door is always there, so the threshold becomes the living command. You're teaching Buddy never to cross the threshold without permission.

Sequence 1: Opening the door

Training Buddy door manners should be a breeze. Here's what to do:

1. **With Buddy on leash and at your side, hold the leash so it's loose with no pressure on the collar.**

   The leash should have some slack, but not so much that when Buddy starts to bolt out the door, you can smoothly "check" them from stepping over the threshold (see Figure 14-1).

   Choose a door that opens to the outside (or your front door that opens into a hall like in an apartment or condo) and approach it right up to the threshold.

2. **With your free hand, open the door a crack; when Buddy moves, close the door quickly.**

3. **Praise them for stepping backward when the door moves toward them as you close it.**

4. **Start over; open the door a little, and, when they move, close it. Praise them again for stepping backward.**

   If you have an overly enthusiastic dog, you may need to apply a little backward tension on the leash to keep them from moving forward. After several tries, Buddy may look at you as if to say, "Exactly what are we doing here?" The little wheels are turning. Try again, and this time they shouldn't move toward the door. When they stand still, close the door and verbally praise them with "Good dog."

5. **Repeat this process several times, each time opening the door a little wider before closing it again.**

FIGURE 14-1:
Practicing
door manners.

The entire sequence takes three to five minutes. You can end the session here and pick it up again at another time (after practicing this sequence), or, if your dog is still interested, continue with the next sequence.

Sequence 2: Adding some outside distraction

Distractions outside add a new layer of enticement to Buddy going through the door. Follow these steps when Buddy is distracted:

1. **When Buddy is distracted, apply a little leash pressure in the form of a *check* (a snappy, crisp jerk back) if Buddy goes to cross the threshold.**

   The action of the door has been enough to stop Buddy from crossing the threshold without distractions. In the presence of a distraction, there must be a consequence if they step over the threshold without your permission.

TIP

If you're holding Buddy back from moving through the door opening, they'll never learn this exercise. The pressure of the leash is keeping them from making a mistake. They need to control themselves. Giving Buddy a verbal command, such as Wait or Stay or Sit, may be tempting, but for their own safety they must learn to respect the open door as an invisible command and wait until you've given permission to exit. If you train a verbal command, you will always need to be present to stop Buddy from crossing the threshold, which is not ideal. Others may be coming and going or the door may be left ajar. You want Buddy to always stop at the threshold whether you are there or not.

2. **If Buddy steps toward the threshold, check them back and show no negative reaction.**

   The doorway caused the check back, not you, or that's what you want Buddy to think. Praise them for stepping back when the check occurs though. They're correct when they step back away from the door.

3. **Release them through the open door with the Okay permission command.**

   With the door open and Buddy on the inside of the house, look at Buddy and say, "Okay." Step through with them and make sure you party on the outside.

4. **Repeat coming back inside and use Steps 2 and 3 to come back inside. The command of waiting at the threshold is true for going both directions.**

Wait to release Buddy through the door only after they've looked at you. This is the leadership part of this exercise. The opening belongs to you — the leader of the pack. Waiting for them to look at you before you release may take seconds or much longer. If it's taking longer than you want it to, make a kissy sound to encourage Buddy to look your way. Then smile, praise, and say, "Okay."

Sequence 3: Leaving Buddy behind at the door

Buddy shouldn't follow you through a door just because you're going out. Only with the permission word should they go through the opening. Follow these steps to teach that concept to Buddy:

1. **Open the door and step over the threshold, leaving Buddy behind inside; prepare the leash in Sequence 2 and be ready to check them back.**

   When or if Buddy moves, check them back with the leash, close the door, and start over. When they're committed to wait on the inside of the door, step over the threshold again. If they move, step back, close the door, and try again.

   As you step over the threshold, you need to let out enough leash so you don't inadvertently pull on it, thereby causing Buddy to follow. Remember to praise for every correct response.

When Buddy holds their position after you've crossed the threshold, praise, pause, and release them with "Okay," and then let them exit. Remember, praise isn't an invitation to move! Okay is their only release command.

2. **Approach the door, exit, and close the door behind you.**

You decide when Buddy can follow or when they have to stay. After that, your success depends on consistency on your part. After Buddy has become solid at this exercise, review the entire sequence off leash.

3. **Move to the gate in a fence and repeat the preceding steps for the gate.**

REMEMBER

It takes a little time to teach Buddy that all openings to the outside are active openings and that they must respect them because you own all openings. Put a sticky note on the door frame to remind everyone that you're teaching Buddy door manners. Everyone needs to be consistent in Buddy's training.

4. **Repeat the above sequences for the door into a retail store you allow Buddy to visit.**

They should always look to you for permission to enter and exit.

The time invested in teaching door manners is well worth it, considering the exercise's application of other situations, such as stairs and gates. The exercise also applies to entering the house. It makes no difference whether you prefer to go through the doorway first or whether you want the dog to go through first, as long as they wait until you release them and they look to you for permission to go through. Practice going through all doors your dog uses regularly.

WARNING

Motion means more to dogs than words, so make sure you stand still when releasing your dog. You don't want them to associate your moving with the release. Also, be aware that dogs have an acute sense of time. Say you usually wait for two seconds before you release them. They will then start to anticipate and release themselves after one second, defeating the purpose of the exercise. You need to vary the length of time between opening the door and the release so that they learn to wait for you to release them.

Teaching Stairs Manners

If you have stairs, start teaching Buddy to stay at the bottom while you go up. First, tell them, "Stay." (See Chapter 11 to teach Stay.) When they try to follow, put them back and start again. Practice until you can go all the way up the stairs with them waiting at the bottom before you release them to follow. Repeat the same procedure for going down the stairs.

Practice on a short flight of stairs first, just a couple of steps. Then move to a whole flight of stairs. Starting with a short flight makes it easier for Buddy to understand this command.

After Buddy has been trained to wait at one end of the stairs, you'll discover that they'll anticipate the release. They'll jump the gun and get up just as you're thinking about releasing him. Before long, they'll stay only briefly and then release themselves. Put them back and start all over. Few things are more irritating and potentially dangerous than the dog rushing past you as you are descending stairs, especially if you're carrying something.

REMEMBER

Teaching stair manners sounds like a lot of work and exercise for you. In the beginning, it does take a little time, but you'll be surprised by how quickly the routine becomes a habit for Buddy. The best part is that you're teaching them to look to you for direction and rite of passage. Also, we think it's important that each member of the family is consistent in following these directions. Doing so makes it easier for Buddy to understand that each family member enforces the same rules. To help remind everyone to use the training commands, add a sticky note on the staircase. Consistency is important for Buddy and for people, too.

4

Taking Training to the Next Level

IN THIS PART . . .

Dealing with common doggie don'ts; be my pride and joy and not my delinquent four-legged child.

Play fetch with your dog, which is one of the greatest forms of exercise that can lead to so much more. Discover how to play retrieve step by step.

Make your dog the star of the party by teaching them to perform trick after trick for fun or for an audience.

Chapter **15**

Dealing with Common Doggie Don'ts

Does your dog have what you think is a behavior problem? Does Buddy bark incessantly, but otherwise behave like the perfect dog? Do they jump on people when they first meet, but are perfectly well behaved the rest of the time? Does Buddy chew on your favorite possessions when left unattended? Do you feel Buddy should know what's yours is yours?

The first line of defense is basic training (see Chapter 9). You'll find dealing with undesired behaviors easier to handle after you've established a line of communication with Buddy through training.

Where to start? If you haven't done the Long-Down exercise, let's start there. The purpose of the Long-Down exercise is to teach Buddy in a clear way that you're in charge. For this reason, the Long-Down is the foundation of all further training.

Training your dog is next to impossible unless they accept that you're the one who makes decisions. It takes four weeks to get the Long-Down established as a routine. But, as soon as you've accomplished the Long-Down, it can go a long way toward helping you establish your role as the coach. Teaching Buddy the Long-Down shows Buddy that you decide what they do, where they do it, when they do it, and for how long they do it. In other words, you're the coach of the team.

The majority of doggy don'ts are relationship problems rather than behavior problems. These behaviors often are the result of insufficient exercise, not enough time spent with the dog, or the need for more training. In this chapter, we discuss some of the most common doggie don'ts and provide you with some workable solutions.

REMEMBER

Behavior problems don't arise overnight. Working toward a solution may take time, patience, and training, but it's well worth it.

Preventing Bad Habits — The Five General Prescriptions for Good Behavior

Many dogs form bad habits or behavior problems that possess a common cause or a combination of causes. In order of importance, they include the following:

>> Boredom and frustration due to insufficient exercise

>> Mental stagnation due to insufficient quality time working and training with you

>> Loneliness caused by too much isolation from human companionship

>> Nutrition and health-related problems

REMEMBER

Loneliness is perhaps the most difficult problem to overcome. By necessity, many dogs are left alone at home anywhere from eight to ten hours a day with absolutely nothing to do except get into mischief. Fortunately, in addition to spending quality time with your dog, you can do some things to help them overcome their loneliness.

The following sections point out five general prescriptions for good behavior you can use as a guide for Buddy.

Good exercise

Exercise needs vary depending on the breed and energy level of your dog. Many dogs need a great deal more exercise than their owners realize. Working dogs are a good example. If the owner of a working breed (Shepherds, Border Collies, Retrievers, and Terriers to name a few) lives in an apartment in a large city and the dog doesn't get enough free-running exercise, they're bound to develop behavior problems. These behaviors can range from tail spinning, which is a neurotic behavior, to ripping up furniture and destruction. This kind of dog would show none of these behaviors if they lived in a household where adequate exercise, both mental and physical, was provided. The dog determines what is enough exercise, not the owner. For example, a Bassett may be satisfied with a short walk every day, but a Border Collie needs a real job: running, chasing, and getting exhausted daily to be content.

REMEMBER

The dog trainer's maxim is: "Tired dogs have happy owners." After all, dogs that get adequate exercise and can expend their energy through running, retrieving, playing, and training rarely show objectionable behaviors. Dogs denied those simple needs frequently redirect their energy into unacceptable behaviors. Figure 15-1 shows a well-exercised pet.

FIGURE 15-1:
Tired dogs have happy owners.

© John Wiley & Sons, Inc.

When your dog engages in behaviors that you consider objectionable, the problem can be vexing. Sometimes the behavior is instinctive, such as digging. Sometimes, it occurs out of boredom. However, it's never because the dog is ornery. Before you attempt to deal with the behavior, you need to find out the cause. The easiest way to stop a behavior is by addressing the need that brought it about in the first place rather than by trying to correct the behavior itself. And if there's one single cause for behavior problems, it's the lack of adequate exercise. For example, when dogs destroy things because they're not getting enough exercise, trying to "correct" the destructive behavior instead of supplying more exercise will cause more stress and anxiety for the dog, which will not fix the problem, but rather make it worse.

Good company

The *single-dog syndrome* refers to the behavior problems that develop because a dog doesn't get enough social interaction. These dogs can run away from their owners more frequently than those dogs living in multi-dog households. They may growl around their food bowls, be picky eaters, be possessive about toys, and be much more unruly than dogs living in homes with other dogs. In other words, dog ownership may be easier if you owned two dogs. Dogs are social animals and need companionship, if not from you, then from another dog.

If you can't bear the thought of being a two-dog household, good company is even more important. *Good company* means not only that you act as a companion to your dog but also that your dog shares the company of other dogs as frequently as possible. Some possibilities include taking regular walks in parks where they can meet other dogs, joining a dog club where dog activities are offered, or putting your puppy into doggie day care several days a week. Socialization of your pet is a continuing process. If you can, get another dog to be Buddy's companion. Dogs are pack animals and thrive in the company of other dogs. If you can't get another dog, give yourself to your dog and be their friend by playing more and being together more. The simple act of moving your dog into your bedroom counts as quality time together. Your dog will be aware of your presence, your scent, and your breathing. This easy bit of advice has fixed so many behavior problems in my many years of behavior counseling that it's impossible to count. Letting your dog sleep in your bedroom counts as hours of social time.

Good health

A dog in pain can become aggressive as a means of protecting their own space. If your dog starts to show aggressive behaviors that they have never shown before, take your dog to the vet for a complete physical before doing any behavior modifications. Treat the hidden condition first, because without treatment, their behavior won't improve.

REMEMBER

Health-related conditions are often confused with behavior problems. Buddy may ingest something that upsets their stomach, causing a house-soiling accident. They may develop a musculoskeletal disorder, making changes of position painful and causing irritability and sometimes snapping. These concerns obviously aren't amenable to training solutions — and certainly not to discipline. Owning a dog that has constant health problems — from minor conditions, such as skin irritations, fleas, smelly coat, and ear infections — to more serious conditions that affect their internal organs, such as the kidneys, heart, liver, and thyroid — is no fun! Not feeling well can cause your dog to develop behavior problems. For more on your dog's health, see Chapter 4.

Good nutrition

The saying "You are what you eat" applies equally to dogs as it does to people. Properly feeding your dog makes the difference between sickness and health, and it has a profound effect on their behavior. With the abundance of dog foods on the market, figuring out what's best for your pet can be difficult. Chapter 4 discusses in greater detail the ways you can correctly feed your dog and the importance of sound nutrition.

Good training

Behavior problems don't arise because your dog is ornery or spiteful, and discipline is rarely the answer. Instead, mental stagnation often can be a cause of unwanted behavior. Training your dog on a regular basis, or having them do something for you, makes your dog feel useful and provides the mental stimulation they need. (To get started with basic training, see Chapters 9 and 10.)

REMEMBER

Use your imagination to get your dog to help around the house. You'll be surprised by how useful Buddy can become. If you've taught Buddy to retrieve, they can help you bring in groceries from the car. They can carry a package of frozen food, a cereal box, or whatever you think they can hold in their mouth. Encourage them to take it into the kitchen. You can use Buddy to take the dirty laundry to the washing machine. They can carry their leash out to the car. (Chapter 16 shows how to teach a dog to retrieve.) Retrieving and carrying is regarded by Buddy as a reward — dogs love to work — so giving them a treat each time isn't necessary. Remember to always give lavish praise, though.

Handling Your Dog's Objectionable Behavior

Like beauty, objectionable behavior is in the eye of the beholder. Playful nipping or biting may be acceptable to some and not to others. Moreover, different degrees of objectionable behavior exist. After all, getting on the couch in your absence isn't nearly as serious an offense as destroying it.

Dogs like to please, and most behaviors can be changed with a little good training. Knowing a dog's Personality Profile (see Chapter 2) helps you understand why your dog does the seemingly irritating things that they do. What's objectionable, however, is when you visit friends and their untrained dog jumps up and scratches you in the process. Other critical negative behavior patterns include dogs who

>> Don't come when called, which is dangerous (see Chapter 10 for more on the Come command).

>> Don't stay when told (head to Chapter 11 to find out how to teach Stay).

>> Chase cats, squirrels, joggers, bicyclists, or worse yet, cars (see how to manage prey-drive behaviors in Chapter 18).

>> Bark incessantly (see the section, "Quieting the Incessant Barker," later in this chapter).

By investing a mere ten minutes a day, five times a week for about four weeks, you can eliminate all these irritating behaviors. After that, brush-ups several times a week in different locations for the rest of the dog's life keeps the behaviors you want sharp. Training is a lifetime process. Training takes such a small amount of time and energy to get a wonderful dog for which you can be proud. Trained dogs are free dogs — you can take them anywhere, and they're always welcome.

REMEMBER

When you believe your dog has a behavior problem, consider the following options:

>> You can tolerate the behavior or manage it, for example, by crating your dog when guests come over.

>> You can train your dog to change the behavior.

>> You can find a new home for the dog, one which may be more suited for their needs.

>> You can take your dog to the shelter, but do know that this could be a one-way trip for them.

We discuss each of these topics in the following sections.

Tolerating your dog's behavior problems

Considering the amount of time and energy that may be required to turn Buddy into the pet you always wanted, you may decide it's easier to live with their annoying antics than it is to try to change them. You tolerate them the way they are, because you don't have the time, the energy, or the inclination to put in the required effort to change them.

TIP

One tool that aids in tolerating any kind of inappropriate behavior is a crate. Leaving Buddy in a crate when you're at work saves you from worrying about house-training, chewing, and digging. When properly trained to stay in a crate, Buddy will think of it as their den or bedroom. They'll always be safe (and feel safe) in their crate. With a crate, they can go anywhere with you, from the car to a friend's house. Today, lightweight crates can be bought for even the largest of dogs. You can even take crates on vacation with you. They'll also be comfortable any time you must leave your dog at the vet, where dogs are kept in crates during treatment.

Crates are a good aid in working toward the solution of many problems. While you are working on other issues of training, using a crate for your dog's alone time can be invaluable.

WARNING

Behaviors you shouldn't tolerate are those that threaten your safety or the safety of others, such as biting people or aggression. True aggression is defined as unpredictable — without warning — and unprovoked biting (see Chapter 18 for more). You also shouldn't tolerate behaviors that threaten the safety of your dog, such as chasing cars or stealing and gulping your possessions (check out the later section "Contending with Chewing — The Nonfood Variety" to curb this behavior).

GOING DIRECTLY TO THE SOURCE

If you want to stop a negative or annoying behavior, you must deal with the need that brought it about in the first place. When your dog goes through teething, for example, you need to provide them with suitable chew toys. When your dog has an accident in the house, ask yourself whether you left them inside too long or whether the dog is ill (and in that case, a trip to the vet is in order). If your dog is left alone in the yard and continuously barks out of boredom, don't leave them out there. When your dog needs more exercise than you can give, consider a dog-walker or day care.

Every behavior has a time frame and a certain amount of energy attached to it. This energy needs to be expended in a normal and natural way. By trying to suppress this energy, or not giving it enough time to dissipate, you help cause most behavior problems.

By using the Personality Profile in Chapter 2, you can find out where your dog's energies lie. For example, are they high in prey drive? These dogs need more exercise than dogs in other drives. They're attracted to anything that moves quickly and want to chase it. Finding an outlet for these behaviors, such as playing ball, throwing sticks, or hiding toys and having Buddy find them, goes a long way to exhausting the energies of this drive.

Trying to solve your dog's behavior problems

You've decided that you can't live with your dog's irritating behaviors and that you're going to work with them so that they'll be the pet you expected and always wanted. You understand that doing so will require an investment of time (at least ten minutes a day, five times a week), effort, and perhaps even expert help. But you're willing to work to achieve your goal — a long-lasting, mutually rewarding relationship. Good for you! This book can help.

Obedience training, in and of itself, isn't necessarily the only answer to your problems. Still, when you train your dog, you're spending meaningful time with them, which in many cases is half the battle. Much depends on the cause of the problem (see the earlier section "Preventing Bad Habits — The Five General Prescriptions for Good Behavior" for more information).

When all else fails: Finding a new home for your dog

Sometimes a dog's temperament may be unsuitable to an owner's lifestyle. For example, a shy dog or a dog with physical limitations may never develop into a great playmate for active children. A dog that doesn't like to be left alone isn't suitable for someone who's gone all day. A dog may require a great deal more exercise than the owner is able to give them and, as a result, develops behavior problems. Although some behaviors can be modified with training, others can't — the effort required would simply be too stressful for the dog and/or the owner.

In instances like these, the dog and the owner are mismatched, and they need to move on to live a happier existence. Whatever the reason, under some circumstances, placement into a new home where the dog's needs can be met is advisable and is in the best interest of both the dog and the owner. This isn't a failure but rather an acceptable outcome to an unacceptable situation.

If all reclamation efforts fail — you can't live with this dog, and they can't be placed elsewhere — your final option is to take them to a shelter or to the veterinarian to put them to sleep. This option isn't to be considered lightly, and you should only follow through if you've really tried to work it out and truly see no other alternatives. If you choose to take them to a shelter, don't kid yourself; most shelters are overwhelmed by the number of unwanted dogs and can find new homes for only a small percentage of those homeless pets. But this unhappy fact doesn't mean that you must live an unhappy life and your dog live an anxiety-ridden one, as well. There is no fault here; there is no burden that you should live with if the match was completely wrong.

Teaching Buddy to Keep All Four on the Floor

In many instances, dogs are systematically rewarded for jumping on people. When a dog was a cute puppy, for example, they received much oohing and awing; everyone was petting them and getting them all excited. Naturally, they learned to jump up to get all that attention. As Buddy got older, relatives and friends would reinforce the behavior with lively petting, especially on top of the head, causing the dog to jump up. They quickly learned to anticipate this greeting ritual and to jump on anybody and everybody that came through the door. Figure 15-2 shows a dog jumping for attention.

FIGURE 15-2: Does your dog jump on people?

Now that they're a 50-pound (or more!) energetic and enthusiastic one-year-old, these assaults are no longer acceptable. Establishing a line of meaningful communication with the dog is your first approach. However, if the behavior has become severely habituated, you need to take the lead. It's never too late to do so. You can use the following two commands to prevent Buddy from jumping on your guests.

Greeting people — using the Hello command

When someone greets Buddy out and about or at your door, people usually bend forward over them, reaching out to pet them, and say, "Hello." You can train this action as the cue for Buddy to sit and be still for the petting. The Hello command and bending forward are the dual command. Stepping toward the dog often applies enough visual and physical pressure to remind the dog to back up, rather than to jump forward toward the person. This is part of the Hello command training. See Chapter 9 for specifics on teaching this command.

Using Sit and Stay as an alternative to jumping up

A more formal approach is to teach Buddy to sit on command and follow with the Stay exercise (see Chapter 11). After they're reliable with the Sit and Stay, enlist a helper and follow these steps:

1. **Before your helper comes to the door, instruct them to avoid eye contact with Buddy and to ignore them when the door is opened.**

2. **Ask the helper to ring the doorbell or knock.**

3. **After the knock, leash Buddy, tell them to "Sit" and then say, "Stay," before you open the door.**

   Chances are, Buddy will get up to greet your helper. Reinforce the Stay command by checking (lifting straight up on the leash) to make Buddy sit again. If they don't respond, they may not be ready for this level of distraction while practicing the Stay exercise. You can also review the training equipment you're using (see Chapter 5).

   REMEMBER

   Buddy's response to a check with the leash depends on the extent to which they're distracted and their distraction threshold. (See Chapter 3 for more information.)

4. **Keep practicing.**

   Repeat the preceding steps until Buddy holds the Stay position on a loose leash when you open the door, which may take several repetitions. As soon as you're both successful, stop the session for now and repeat later.

5. **Add distractions, such as the doorbell or knocking on the door.**

   Other distractions can be that the arriving person is wearing a hat or carrying a box. Before the next session, remind your helper to ignore Buddy and to avoid making eye contact with them. Review the steps from the beginning and invite your helper into the house.

When Buddy stays, quietly tell them what a good dog they are and end the session. If they don't stay, reinforce the Sit with a check on the leash, putting them back into the sitting position.

You need to continue this routine until Buddy sits politely when someone comes to the door. When they reliably sit and stay, you can try the exercise off leash. Their response will tell you whether they need more training. If Buddy gets up out of the stay while off leash, you must reach in for their collar and replace them into the sitting position again. No command is necessary, but you should praise them quietly when they are indeed sitting again. Remember: Training is often a matter of who's more persistent — you or your dog.

Putting an End to Counter Surfing — Leave It

Buddy is *counter surfing* when they put their nose on the counter to sniff out anything edible within reach (see Figure 15-3). Use one of the following techniques, or a combination thereof, to stop this behavior when they're thinking of sniffing the counter's edge or jumping on the counter.

FIGURE 15-3:
A puppy showing early signs of counter surfing.

© *John Wiley & Sons, Inc.*

Here is a list of some additional things you can put into practice when working on counter surfing issues.

>> **Teach Buddy the Leave It command.** This is the most important thing you can do. See Chapter 9 for the how-to specifics. Buddy must know that sniffing the counter's edge isn't acceptable, so as your first step, teach them the Leave It command.

>> **Physically remove them by taking them by the collar and moving them away from the counter.** Set them up with food hanging half off the counter or extending off the edge of the counter, while you're nearby. They'll know you're there, but they need to first learn what is wrong before you can teach them from a distance without you being in the room.

>> **Use the startle response of a penny shake or an air horn as a deterrent.** Just as Buddy sniffs at the counter's edge or the food hanging off the edge, shake the penny can or blow the air horn, and the noise should interrupt and stop them in their tracks. Remember to use the noise *as* Buddy moves toward the counter and sniffs, not after they have done so or grabbed the food. If it's after they sniff, the response is too late because Buddy has already enjoyed the stolen reward.

>> **Practice on a lower surface such as the coffee table in the family room.** Buddy should leave all snacks alone on that table even though it's within easy reach. You shouldn't need to put away to-go containers, pizza boxes, chip bowls, and so on just because Buddy is in the room with you. Practice Leave It there as well. You need to police the table and their actions, but this work will result in a dog you can trust around food that isn't theirs.

>> **Put several emptied soda cans with pebbles or pennies inside on the counter.** Tie them loosely together with a light string. Have the cans set close enough to a food or bag of food so that the dog will disturb the cans and they will all fall like dominoes if touched. This method works well if you've already trained the previous lessons while you are present.

TIP

One little trick that helps Buddy think you're psychic, and to reinforce your Leave It command, is to place a mirror in such a way that you can see the counter from another room. You can bait the countertop with something very tasty, go into the other room, and wait for Buddy to sniff. When you say, "Leave it," Buddy will be amazed at your ability to catch them in the act. And for the persistent and dedicated counter surfer, you may consider an indoor containment system to solve the problem (see Chapter 5).

Quieting the Incessant Barker

On the one hand, few things are more reassuring than knowing that your dog will sound the alarm when a stranger approaches. On the other hand, few things are more nerve racking than a dog's incessant barking. Dogs bark for three reasons:

>> In response to a stimulus or distraction

>> Because they're bored and want attention — any attention — even if that attention involves the owner's being nasty to the dog (scolding or physically punishing)

>> When someone comes to the door

Therein lies the dilemma: You want the dog to bark, but only when you think they should. We cover each of these situations in the following sections.

Here are a couple general ways to get your dog to stop barking incessantly:

>> **Use a remote bark collar or an air collar.** The remote bark collar causes a slight stimulus, such as a shock, vibration, or tone every time they bark, whereas an air collar sprays a puff of air in the direction of the dog's nose when they bark.

These tools work well in a single-dog household. (See Chapter 5 for more info on these collars.) When the dog barks, the collar goes off. Some collars reset to a lower level if the dog is quiet for a length of time and may increase if they keep barking continually. Buddy needs to learn how to shut the collar off by being quiet. You must help him when you initially put the collar on, especially if they bark again because the collar has startled them. When your dog is quiet, it will stop vibrating or emitting citronella. You can praise them for their silence.

>> **Use a command.** Some good ones include Quiet, Shhh!, or That's Enough. The best time to give the command is when you're with the dog and you can say your command and immediately put your fingers into the collar and turn them around, away from the visual distraction. Praise if they stop barking. If you start commanding from a distance, Buddy will simply think you're barking, too. If you're too far away from them, your command will be meaningless. They'll think you're in agreement and barking along with them.

Barking as a response to a stimulus or distraction

Your dog is outside in the yard and some people walk by, perhaps with a dog on leash, so Buddy barks. Barking is a natural response of defending their territory. After the potential intruders pass, they're quiet again. People and dogs passing are the stimuli that cause barking, and after they're removed, your dog stops. The problem here is that Buddy will think their barking moved the people away, which rewards their perception of the barking having worked.

If the people had stopped by the fence for a conversation, your dog would continue to bark. To get your dog to stop, remove the stimulus from the dog or the dog from the stimulus. If you live in a busy area where people pass by frequently, you may need to change your dog's environment. In other words, you may not be able to leave your dog in the yard for prolonged periods. Putting up a privacy fence is one alternative, if you want your dog to be outside, or putting them in a crate in the house can successfully remove them from the stimulus. You also can use a remote bark collar in this situation, but first you must train them on how the collar works. The collar will come with a how-to manual.

Barking for attention

Sometimes, it's as if your dog is barking for no apparent reason. However, even though the motivation isn't apparent to you, your dog always has a reason for barking. It can be due to any or all of the following:

>> Anxiety

>> Boredom

>> Attention seeking because they're lonely

Although Buddy's barking may be unacceptable to you, to them it's the only way they can express their unhappiness and frustration. Using a doggie day care service a few times a week can help with the loneliness and boredom. Starting a new training hobby with Buddy, including agility, obedience, and retrieving, is helpful. If your dog knows that an activity will occur every day at around the same time, they will stress less knowing you'll attend to their social and mental stimulation needs.

REMEMBER

Theoretically, none of the preceding reasons is difficult to overcome if you work to eliminate the potential causes. Spend more time exercising your dog. Spend more time training your dog. Don't leave your dog alone so long, and don't leave them alone so often.

As a practical matter, however, overcoming these reasons isn't that easy. Most people work for a living and must leave their dogs at home alone for prolonged periods. If you live in an apartment, your dog certainly can't bark all day. The stress on the dog is horrendous, not to mention the fact that your neighbors will soon begin to despise you and your noisy dog. Remember your dog has needs and spending quality time with you is one of them. (Chapter 19 can help if you suspect that your dog's barking is due to separation anxiety.)

Barking when someone comes to the door

Most dogs bark when someone comes to the door. Although you may appreciate being alerted that someone has comes to the door, you probably want Buddy to stop when you tell them "Thank you. I've got it from here." Some dogs don't stop, however.

Take control of the situation. Training your dog at the front door is necessary, but you must do the preliminary work first before you apply the distraction of someone at the door. Keep a leash and collar near the door as a helpful tool to aid you, especially in the beginning of your training. Use your Quiet command, turn your dog away from the door, and give them a command to sit and stay before you open the door.

Contending with Chewing — The Nonfood Variety

The main reasons that dogs chew are physiological and psychological. The first is understandable; it could be that a puppy is teething. The second isn't so understandable. Both are a nuisance. In the following sections, we explain both reasons and provide some guidance if you're having problems with chewing.

"I'm teething!" Examining the physiological need to chew

As part of the teething process, puppies need to chew. They can't help it. To get through this period, provide your dog with a soft and a hard chew toy, as well as a canvas field dummy, which is quite chew resistant. Real bones (soup bones are ideal) are great hard toys. You can get them at the butcher; ask them to cut the ends off the long bones because the ends can break off bits and be swallowed. You can also purchase smoked long bones from vendors on the internet. These are less messy than bones from the butcher but just as popular among dogs.

Hard rubber Kong toys (www.kongcompany.com) with some peanut butter (make sure the peanut butter doesn't contain sweeteners) inserted into the center will also keep a dog amused for a long time. Don't give them anything they can destroy or ingest unless they're food items. Carrots, apples, dog biscuits, or ice cubes are great to relieve the monotony; otherwise, they may select other interesting things to chew on, such as those new shoes you left lying around or the rugs.

REMEMBER

When your dog is going through their period of physiological chewing, make sure they don't have access to your personal articles, such as shoes, socks, and towels. Think of it as good training for you not to leave things lying around the house. And don't forget that a lonely dog may chew up anything in their path. So, make sure your dog gets enough attention from you — and that they get some strong chew toys! When you can't supervise them, crate them (see Chapter 6.)

"I'm bored!" Recognizing the psychological reasons that dogs chew

Chewing that takes place after a dog has gone through teething is usually a manifestation of anxiety, boredom, or loneliness. This oral habit has nothing to do with being spiteful. If your dog attacks the furniture, baseboards, and walls, tips over the garbage can, or engages in other destructive chewing activities, don't become angry. Instead, recognize that you probably aren't providing them the stimulation they need and give them some solid chew toys.

Use a crate to confine Buddy when you can't supervise them. Confining them saves you lots of money, and you won't lose your temper and get mad at the poor baby. Even more important, they can't get into things that are a potential danger. (We discuss crates in detail in Chapter 6.)

REMEMBER

Confinement is a problem-solving approach of last resort. Ideally, the dog isn't left alone so long and so often that they feel the need to chew in order to relieve their boredom. Your dog doesn't need you to entertain them all the time, but extended periods of being alone can make your pet neurotic. Crating is one of the many tools you need to use to solve behavior problems. See the "Preventing Bad Habits — The Five General Prescriptions for Good Behavior" section earlier in this chapter. Good nutrition, exercise, training, socialization, and health are all part of the solution. The crate can be viewed as a babysitter when you aren't around, but it shouldn't be the only solution you apply to your dog.

Dealing with a Digger

A favorite pastime of many breeds, such as Dachshunds, is digging, or *landscaping*. They engage in this activity at every opportunity and with great zest. Because Dachshunds were bred to go after badgers that burrow into hillsides, this behavior is instinctive. Does that mean you must put up with a yard that looks like a mine-field? Not at all, but you do need to assume the responsibility for

>> Expending the digging energy, which involves exercising Buddy

>> Providing an outlet for it, which means giving your dog a place where they can dig to their heart's content

>> Supervising your dog to make sure they don't get into trouble

REMEMBER

The good news is that most behavior problems are under your direct control, but you need to get involved. The cure to digging is rather simple. Don't leave your dog unattended in the yard for lengthy periods.

Recognize that digging is part of prey drive (see Chapter 2 for more on the drives). Because it's part of prey drive, all the tips we give you about exhausting the behavior apply here. You can't make a dog dig until they're exhausted, but you can tire out your dog by playing ball or running with them so that they're too tired to dig!

TIP

Here are some other suggestions to help curb Buddy's digging:

>> Install or hammer along the bottom of your fence a fencing barrier that stops any chance of digging under the fence (see Figures 15-4 and 15-5).

>> Put up a small, fenced area for them where they can dig. You can supply sand if that helps. Bury things for Buddy to find.

>> Cover existing digging areas with pegged-down fencing or barriers. Using tent pegs, for example, peg down plastic or metal fencing that cannot be dug through. This will discourage repeat digging in those areas. Grass can grow through the staked down fencing, and if you really hammer in the pegs, you can even mow over it if your mower is set at the right height to allow it to easily go over it (see Figure 15-6).

>> Give your dog interactive toys with food inside that they must roll around to find the treat to drop out and eat.

>> Take your dog for hikes in the woods, on a farm, or in the park. Let them dig at the dog park where they can search for critters.

>> Exercise your dog.

FIGURE 15-4:
Hammer a wire fencing barrier into the ground.

FIGURE 15-5:
A wire fencing barrier in front of your regular fence.

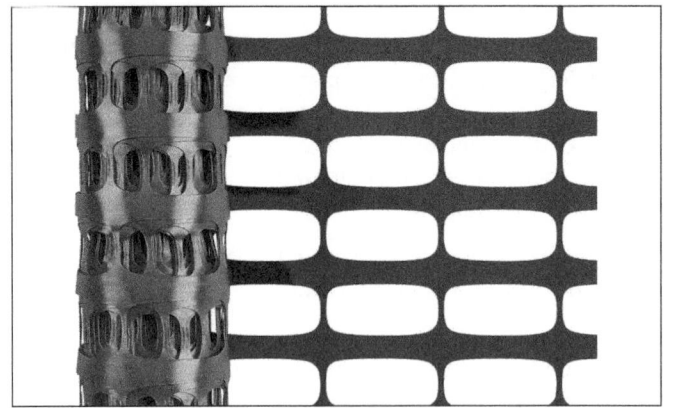

FIGURE 15-6:
Staked-down fencing.

Uline

UNDERSTANDING THE REASONS FOR DIGGING

Although some breeds, such as the small terriers, have a true propensity for digging, all dogs do it to some extent at one time or another. Take a look at some of the more common reasons for digging:

- To participate in mimicking behavior. In training, this practice is useful, but it may spell trouble for your gardening efforts. You plant, your dog digs. If this is the case, don't garden with your dog present. Put them in the house or close the gate to your garden.

- To make nests for real or imaginary puppies. This reason usually applies to female dogs.

- To bury or dig up a bone.

- To see what's there, because it's fun, or to find a cool spot to lie down.

- To relieve boredom, isolation, or frustration.

If you think you have a championship digger who's digging for mice, moles, or other critters in the ground, consider getting them involved in Barn Hunts where dogs are encouraged to hunt among hay bales for the scent of rats. The game of Barn Hunt has become quite popular in some areas of the country.

Managing Marking Behavior

Marking is a way for your dog to leave their calling card by depositing a small amount of urine in a particular spot, marking it as their territory. The frequency with which dogs can accomplish marking never ceases to amaze. Male dogs invariably prefer vertical surfaces, hence the fire hydrant. Males tend to engage in this behavior with more determination than females, though both can and do mark.

Behaviorists explain that marking is a dog's way of establishing their territory, and it provides a means to find their way back home. They also claim that dogs can tell the rank order, gender, and age — puppy or adult dog — by smelling the urine of another dog.

People who take their dogs for regular walks through the neighborhood quickly discover that marking is a ritual, with favorite spots that must be watered. It's a way for the dog to maintain their rank in the order of the pack, which consists of all the other dogs in the neighborhood or territory that come across their route.

Adult male dogs lift a leg, as do some females. For the male dog, the object is to leave their calling card higher than the previous calling card. This can lead to some comical results, as when a Dachshund or a Yorkshire Terrier tries to cover the calling card of an Irish Wolfhound or Great Dane. It's a contest.

When this behavior is expressed inside the house, it becomes a problem. Fortunately, this behavior is rare, but it does happen. Here are the circumstances requiring special vigilance:

>> When you get a new dog or a cat

>> When taking Buddy to a friend's or relative's house for a visit, especially if that individual also has a dog or a cat

>> When you've redecorated the house with new furniture or curtains

>> When you've moved to a new house

TIP

Distract your dog if you see that they're about to mark in an inappropriate spot. Call their name and take them to a place where they can eliminate. When you take Buddy to someone else's home, keep an eye on them or keep them leashed until they settle into their new surroundings. At the slightest sign that they're even thinking about lifting a leg, interrupt their thought by clapping your hands and calling them to you. Take them outside and wait until they've had a chance to relieve themselves. If this behavior persists, you need to go back to basic house-training principles, such as the crate or X-pen, until you can trust them again. (See Chapter 8 for more on housetraining.)

Chapter **16**

Retrieving: Time to Fetch

Playing fetch is a fabulous exercise for you and your dog. If you have a natural retriever, then you already know. A natural retriever is a dog that was born retrieving — a dog that retrieves for the joy of the chase. Every dog needs an exercise outlet — some more than others. Retrieving is a good and easy way to entertain and burn off all that energy, tiring out your dog. Even on a rainy day, you can throw the toy down the hall or down the stairs. Remember our motto: A tired dog has a happy owner.

REMEMBER

Play retrieve for as long as your dog is having fun. End the game while your dog still wants to play a bit longer so that they don't get tired of the game. For a lot of dogs, this isn't an issue, but keep in mind, you never want to call and call your dog back to you as they wander off. Doing so is unintentional training, and it backfires. *Unintentional training* is when you accidently teach something you don't want your dog to learn, such as calling your dog over and over again and not reinforcing the fact that your dog must come to you when called. Retrieving is fun and you want your dog to love it.

In this chapter we look at all the different elements of retrieving for you and your dog. Whether your dog is a natural retriever or not, teaching all these elements is important as you play this game with your dog. What are the rules of the game and what are you going to call the different parts of the game. Think it through and then go play.

Introducing the Common Retrieving Commands to Your Natural Retriever

The main task about a trained retrieve is for your dog to bring the item back to you and actually give it to you. Here are the three retrieving commands and elements of the retrieve:

>> **Take It:** If you have a natural retriever, whether they bring it back or not, you need to have a command for them to chase the toy. We recommend Take It. (You may prefer a different command, such as Get It or Fetch. Choose one and stick with it.) Say this command to mean, "Go after what I just threw."

>> **Bring It Here:** If your dog chases the toy but doesn't return it to you, then the Bring It Here command is perfect.

>> **Give:** If you have a natural retriever, then trading the toy for a treat is an easy way to get them to give it back. Just exchange a small treat you have in one hand as you reach with the other hand to get the toy. Repeating "Give" each time you do this will teach the dog to release the toy.

If you have a natural retriever, a dog who willingly wants to get the toy, incorporate these three commands to the game of retrieve:

1. **Using a long leash or long rope, toss the toy a shorter distance than the line is long and say, "Take it."**

   You don't want the leash to tighten up as your dog chases the toy.

2. **When your dog has the toy, gently pull the line into you as you praise your dog and say, "Bring it here."**

3. **As your dog gets to you, offer a treat in exchange for reaching for the toy and say, "Give."**

REMEMBER

   The timing of the treat being offered should ideally have you reaching and getting the toy as the treat goes toward Buddy. In a perfect world, Buddy doesn't drop the toy for you to then pick it up.

Explaining the Basics of Retrieving

If your dog is a natural to retrieving — you throw a ball, and they love getting it — then teaching these steps will be easy. If you don't have a natural retrieving dog, you can still teach your dog how to fetch. It just takes patience and practice. Plus, it takes a really wonderful, special treat that you use only for retrieving. As you teach the retrieve, you'll want to also teach the Hold command, because the dog must hold onto the toy or the dumbbell as part of the retrieve. They must hold the toy while walking with it in their mouth.

Here's what you need to start teaching your dog to retrieve:

>> **Treat:** You want to be in a playful mood with a hungry dog who wants what you have to offer, such as a high value treat or a dumbbell toy.

>> **Dumbbell:** A *dumbbell* is a wooden or plastic article used in obedience. It looks like a dumbbell, thus the name, and it has two ends that bell out, held together by a dowel in the center. The dowel should be a comfortable length for your dog to pick up behind their canine teeth without squashing their whiskers. Dumbbells are readily available online, in pet stores, and at other training outlets (see Figure 16-1). You can use any toy, but dummies or dumbbells are great for retrieving. Dummies are canvas cylinders for retrieving. The canvas is tough enough to stand up to lots of play.

>> Work in an area that won't cause a loud noise when the dumbbell hits the floor or ground; you don't want the noise to be a fearful negative consequence.

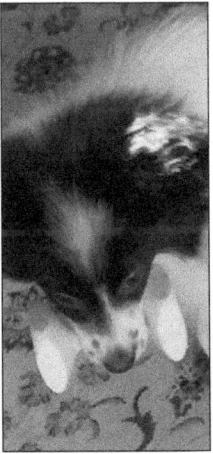

FIGURE 16-1:
The dog holds the dumbbell from the middle dowel.

© John Wiley & Sons, Inc.

In the following sections we explain the steps to teach a retrieve to any dog, regardless of whether they are a natural retriever or not. Have fun with the different steps. Do a few repetitions each evening until you have the whole list done. Retrieving is worth the time, because it's a great way to have fun and exercise with your dog.

Sequence 1: Play the retrieve game by making the toy or dumbbell enticing

Follow these steps to begin teaching Buddy how to play the retrieve game:

REMEMBER

1. **With your dog in the room with you, show them the toy in your hand, shake it around for two to three seconds, and then bring it behind your back and hide it.**

   Shaking the toy makes the toy look alive and interesting. This is Prey Drive Stimulation.

2. **Bring it out again and shake it for two to three seconds, and then quickly hide it behind your back a second time.**

3. **Bring it out in front of you one last time and then hide it again.**

4. **Bring it out and toss it a few feet onto the floor and say, "Take it."**

   Use an excited voice and praise them when they go for it.

5. **Back away and say "Bring it here." Trade them for a cookie and say "Give."**

   By backing up, your body language is enticing your dog to come to you. Even if they come without the toy, praise them for returning to you. If you have complete success, praise and party and be excited.

If your dog goes to the toy but doesn't pick it up, repeat the hide and shake three times and then toss it again. If your dog picks it up, praise, back up, and use a high-pitched tone to your voice while you praise. Offer them a cookie and say, "Give."

Take a break and put the toy away. Let your dog think about it for a bit. This is called latent learning. Hug your dog, go for a short walk, and hang out before you repeat the game above.

Sequence 2: Play the retrieve game and keep it high prey drive and fun

Play this game every day but only for a few times. You want to stop while your dog still wants to play the game. Only repeat two to three times before you put the toy away and take a break.

Repeat this sequence until your dog becomes proficient with the game. Always pick up the toy from the floor and repeat the shake and hide if they lose interest.

Sequence 3: Increase the distance that you throw the toy

Now comes the fun part, where you get to throw the dumbbell or toy farther and Buddy gets to chase it and bring it back. Follow these steps:

1. **Throw the dumbbell a few feet away, and at the same time, send your dog to the dumbbell with the command, "Take it."**

2. **As soon as they pick up the dumbbell, say, "Come. Bring it here," and tell them how terrific they are.**

3. **When Buddy gets back to you, take the dumbbell, say, "Give," and reward them with a treat.**

TIP

   Sometimes, dogs get carried away by the fun of it all and don't come right back with the dumbbell. They may make a detour or just run around for the joy of it. If that happens, say "Come" as soon as they pick up the dumbbell. Then praise and reward them when they get back to you.

4. **Continue to gradually increase the distance you throw the dumbbell, and as they gain confidence, introduce Sit in Front with the command, "Hold it."**

   When Buddy gets back to you, say "Sit" and "Hold it." Because they haven't done this task before, you may have to hold your hand under their chin to prevent them from dropping the dumbbell. When they're successful, praise, remove the dumbbell, and reward. From then on occasionally make them sit and hold the dumbbell when they get back to you.

Congratulations! You now have a dog that retrieves on command.

TIP

You also can use the Retrieve command to have Buddy bring other things to you. Repeat the retrieve game above and try having Buddy pick up their leash or a set of keys or even a small basket. Only play retrieve games with things that are easy for Buddy to pick up and carry, yet impossible to swallow or choke on.

Sequence 4: Polishing and perfecting the retrieve by testing your dog's patience

In this section we show you how to put all the pieces of the retrieve together. You now introduce the Stay command when you throw the dumbbell. Slip a finger in Buddy's collar before you throw the dumbbell and after saying "Stay" to guarantee that they indeed do stay when the dumbbell is thrown. After waiting a short time, use the Take It command. Some dogs respond well to a voice command; others respond better to a hand signal given with the left hand toward the dumbbell. Practice with Buddy to see which one brings the kind of response you want.

Buddy must learn to stay while you throw the dumbbell and until you release them to get it. Making them wait can get them even more excited about getting to the dumbbell. Trying to teach your dog patience is almost like teaching a two-year-old child patience, but you can do it. Just follow these steps:

1. **Start with Buddy at your left side.**

2. **Put two fingers of your left hand through their collar, say, "Stay," and throw the dumbbell about 15 feet away.**

3. **Very slowly, let go of the collar, count to five, and say, "Take it."**

4. **When they return with the dumbbell, praise, remove, and reward.**

5. **Repeat these steps until your dog holds the stay without you having to hold them by the collar.**

REMEMBER

Give the Take It command in an excited and enthusiastic tone of voice to put Buddy into prey drive. Don't use a harsh or threatening tone because that tone may put your dog in the wrong drive and make it more difficult for them to learn. This is a prey drive game, and you want them in prey drive, which a high tone of voice will stimulate. You may also give a hand signal to Buddy to bring out even more prey drive. It goes from the left side of your body toward the dumbbell. If at any time your dog needs motivation, throw the dumbbell and at the same time say, "Take it," letting them chase after the toy again.

Sequence 5: Retrieving with distractions

After Buddy knows how to retrieve, they're ready for distraction training. Retrieving around distractions is important because almost everything is a distraction to a dog. Wherever you throw the dumbbell or toy, it will land near some kind of distraction, such as a smell, a noise, other people, or other visual distractions that can keep your dog from thinking they can retrieve the item and return to you. Systematically work through made-up distractions so Buddy learns that nothing can stop them from picking up the thing you threw and returning it to you.

Introduce your dog to distractions as follows (you need a helper for this sequence):

1. **Your helper stands about two feet from the dumbbell and assumes a friendly posture that's not threatening to the dog.**

2. **Send Buddy after the dumbbell, and as soon as they pick it up, enthusiastically praise and call them back to you.**

   The exercise is completed as soon as your dog picks up the dumbbell.

3. **As the dog gains confidence, have your helper stand a little closer, and then stand over the dumbbell.**

   You also can ask the helper to hide the dumbbell by standing directly in front of it with their back to the dog. Or you can use a chair as a distraction by putting the dumbbell under the chair and then on the chair.

REMEMBER

Continue to use food rewards for Buddy on a random basis; that is, instead of using them every time and in a predictable pattern, use them only often enough to maintain their motivation. This is called *random reinforcement*. This is the most powerful pattern, which is actually no pattern at all.

During distraction training, you may see the following responses or variations:

>> **Buddy hesitates and fails to retrieve**. They start going toward the dumbbell but then back off and fail to retrieve, meaning "I don't have the confidence to get close enough to the helper to retrieve my dumbbell."

   Without saying anything, slowly approach Buddy; put two fingers of your left hand through the collar, back to front, palm facing you, at the side of the neck; and take them to the dumbbell. If they pick up the dumbbell, back up, praise enthusiastically, and trade the dumbbell for a treat; if they still don't pick it up, repeat the shake and hide it right there by your distractor helper, back up, praise, and trade for a reward. Don't repeat the command.

REMEMBER

Keep trying and remember your dog's learning style and how many repetitions it takes before they understand. You may find that you need to help them several times before they have the confidence to do it by themselves. You can help by going over and pointing at the dumbbell, picking it up, and enticing their prey drive by shaking and tossing it. Aid in a nonconfrontational way. Your dog isn't wrong for not picking it up. They just need help to know that they can still do it with the distraction there. As soon as they have done it on their own, stop for that session.

>> **Buddy gives up.** They leave altogether and don't retrieve, saying, in effect "I can't cope with this." In this case, use the remedy from the preceding response, helping as needed.

>> **Buddy does nothing.** In other words, they're thinking "If I don't do anything, maybe all of this will go away." If Buddy does nothing, use the same remedy from the first response, helping them to be successful.

>> **Buddy becomes distracted.** They permit themselves to be distracted, meaning "I would rather visit than retrieve my dumbbell." If you experience this response, use the remedy from the first response.

>> **Buddy takes the dumbbell to the distracter.** Slowly approach Buddy without saying anything, put the leash on the dead ring of the training collar, and with a little tension on the collar, show them exactly what they were supposed to do by guiding them backward to you. No extra command is given.

>> **Buddy anticipates the retrieve without waiting to be told to do so.** In other words, they break the Stay and try to retrieve without the command. They're catching on and they want to show you how clever they are.

Whatever you do, don't shout "No," or do anything else that would discourage them from retrieving after you have just worked so hard to get them to pick up the dumbbell near the distractor. Simply take the dumbbell from your dog's mouth and try again. It could be a Stay issue and not a Retrieve issue, so don't correct it in any way.

>> **Buddy does it correctly.** At this point, stop training for that session.

When your dog confidently retrieves with the first level of distractions, introduce the next level. *Second-degree distractions,* which are visual and auditory, consist of having your helper crouch close to the dumbbell while trying to distract Buddy by saying, "Here, puppy, come visit for some petting." The distracter doesn't use your dog's name. After Buddy successfully works through the second-degree distraction, you can increase the level of difficulty to the *third-degree distraction,* which uses food or a toy. Have the helper offer Buddy a treat, a ball, or a toy about a foot away from the dumbbell. Of course, the helper never lets your dog have those items (see Figure 16-2). If Buddy goes to the distracter or tries to take the food, follow the preceding guidelines until Buddy does it correctly. Then stop for that training session.

TECHNICAL STUFF

Distractions add an extra dimension and take training to a higher level. Challenging Buddy to use their head with distraction training helps build your dog's confidence and teaches them to concentrate on what they're doing. This type of training is especially important for the shy dog, providing the confidence they need to respond correctly under different conditions.

FIGURE 16-2:
Retrieving with third-degree distraction.

During distraction training, keep in mind that anytime you change the complexity of the exercise, it becomes a new exercise for the dog. If Buddy goes for the food, you would treat that response the same way you did when you first introduced distraction training. No, your dog isn't defiant, stubborn, or stupid; they're just confused as to what they should do and must be helped again.

REMEMBER

When using distraction training, giving Buddy a chance to work out the situation is important. Don't be too quick to help by making it easier. Be patient and let them try to figure out on their own how to correctly handle the situation. After they do, you'll be pleasantly surprised by the intensity and reliability with which they now respond. It's fascinating to watch your dog think things through with distraction training. Enjoy the process and keep it reasonable.

You're now ready to work with different objects that you want Buddy to retrieve. When you do, you may have to review the first few sequences. Just because Buddy retrieves one object doesn't necessarily mean they'll retrieve others. They may need to get used to them first.

Chapter **17**

Trick Training for Fun and Bonding

very well-trained dog knows a trick or two that can impress your friends and family alike. The tricks you teach your dog can be simple or complex, depending on your dog's drives and your interest. You can teach some tricks in an afternoon whereas you'll need more time for others. With your help, each trick can be a showstopper with your dog's personality shining through.

As you increase the communication between you and your dog by doing delightful things, your dog will enjoy your time together even more. That bond will shine through every day. The benefits of training become so evident. Enjoy.

Tricks by definition are entertaining. In fact, teaching tricks is fun for both you and your dog. During the training, you'll use lots of cookies (or other tasty treats) and praise to keep the motivation going for your dog.

REMEMBER

The trick to teaching successful tricks is sequencing. *Sequencing* means breaking down what you want to teach your dog into steps small enough for the dog to master, which leads up to the final product. For example, if you want to teach your dog to shake hands, start by first taking Buddy's paw in your hand while saying the command you want to use and then praise and reward them. The next sequence is offering your palm first instead of taking their paw, and so on to the next sequence.

You don't need to teach these tricks in any order. Choose your favorite and have fun.

TEACHING BUDDY TRICKS IS WORTH IT EVERY TIME

A new client, Martha, contacted Mary Ann a few years ago to help teach her new dog Jax the basic skills needed to become a welcomed member of the family. For fun, at the end of the second lesson, Mary Ann taught Jax how to shake hands. The giggle that came out of Martha was infectious. She was beside herself with joy over Jax's ability to learn the trick. By the following week, Jax was a pro at shaking hands. Martha had practiced every day, making shaking hands with Jax a stellar trick.

Tricks are ideal to teach obedience clients because tricks give them a fun reason to practice obedience. Trick training also helps teach the dog how to learn. Before long, Martha and Jax had three AKC Trick Dog Titles, and they're still going strong, doing agility and advanced obedience. Martha had no intention to continue to train her new dog to such a level, but with the onset of trick training, she's now doing agility and advanced obedience and scent work. They're a great team, and it all started with that laugh of joy (see the attached figure of Jax).

Shaking Hands and Giving a High Five

This trick shows you how to teach Buddy to Shake and then add a High Five for extra flair. This exercise has four sequences. Sequences 1 through 3 teach Shake and Sequence 4 adds the High Five. For the High Five, the object is to teach Buddy to raise one front paw as high as they can on command.

Needed: Treats

Command: Sit (see Chapter 11)

Command: Yes (see Chapter 9), to mark the moment of success and compliance from your dog

Sequence 1: Introducing the concept of lifting the paw off the ground

Follow these steps to accustom your dog to shaking hands:

1. Sit your dog in front of you.

2. Reduce your body posture by kneeling or squatting in front of your dog so that you're not leaning or hovering over them.

   Better yet, sit on the floor in front of your dog.

3. Reach slowly for the dog's collar at the side of the neck. Praise them for allowing you to touch their collar. Praise and reward.

4. Reach again for the collar and slip a finger in the collar at the side of the neck and pull gently to that side, forcing the dog's weight to shift. As the dog leans that way, take your other hand and pick up the lifted paw and praise and reward.

5. Offer them your palm at mid-chest level as you reach for the collar to tilt the weight of your dog. Praise them as they allow you take their paw. Praise and release.

6. Repeat this step until your dog willingly lifts the paw to you. At this point you can ask them to "Shake."

7. Take the elbow of the front leg and lift it off the ground about two inches. Slide your hand down to the paw and gently shake, as shown in Figure 17-1.

8. Say, "Yes" and praise enthusiastically as you're shaking their paw.

9. Reward with a treat and say, "Okay," to release them.

FIGURE 17-1: Help by sliding your hand from the elbow to the paw.

Sequence 2: Lifting their paw

Keep following these steps for Buddy to lift their paw:

1. **Sit your dog in front of you and reduce your body posture.**

2. **Offer your palm at mid-chest level and say, "Shake."**

   You're looking for some sort of response. If nothing happens, touch their elbow and offer your palm again. Give them the chance to lift their paw. Be patient and smile.

3. **After Buddy lifts the paw on their own, take the paw, enthusiastically praise, reward, and release.**

   If nothing happens after offering your palm and saying "Shake," go back and follow Step 4 of Sequence 1. Doing so takes the weight off the leg you want to come up, and it will come off the ground. Say, "Yes," take their paw, and then praise, reward, and release.

REMEMBER

Stay with Sequence 2 until your dog is lifting their paw off the ground on command so that you can shake it. Move on to Sequence 3 when your dog is ready.

Sequence 3: Putting their paw on your palm

When you're ready for Buddy to put their paw in your palm, keep following these steps:

1. **Sit your dog in front of you and reduce your body posture.**

2. **Offer your palm at mid-chest level and say, "Shake."**

   At this point, they should put their paw on your palm. When they do, say, "Yes," praise enthusiastically, reward, and release.

   If nothing happens, go back to Sequence 2.

REMEMBER

Stay with Sequence 3 until your dog readily and without hesitation puts their paw on your palm. Then, if you want to teach your dog to add an impressive high five to their shake, you can move on to the last sequence.

Sequence 4: Adding the High Five

With this trick you want your dog to raise their paw as high as they can and touch your hand rather than you shaking their paw. These steps can help:

1. **Sit your dog in front of you.**

2. **Offer your palm at *chin* level not *chest* level.**

   By now your dog should readily and without hesitation put their paw on your palm with the command "Shake." When they do, say, "Yes," praise, and turn your palm so that your fingers are in a high-five position. Reward and release. If they don't put their paw on your palm, go back to Sequence 3.

3. **Raise your palm, in two-inch increments, until you have until your dog can't reach any higher.**

   At this point you can change the trick command to "High Five" and say, "High Five" instead.

REMEMBER

Your hand is in less in a shake-hand position and more in a high-five position with your fingers pointing up. Say, "Yes," as your dog touches your palm with their paw. Praise and reward with your release. After several repetitions, your dog will stretch their paw as high as they can. Praise, reward, and release. The high five is a faster trick because you don't take hold of the paw in your hand, you just touch each other's palms. Keep it fun.

Finding the Pea under the Right Cup

With this trick, your dog finds the right cup (out of three) that has the treat pea under it. This trick is fun for both you and your dog.

Needed: Three cups: You can use plastic or paper cups or small disposable flowerpots that new plants come in to repot later. Kids' hand bells, instead of cups, work wonders, too; just cut out the clangor because you don't need the noise from the bell. The handles on the bells help your dog to tip the bells over during the trick.

Treats: Dry treats that scoot along the floor without leaving crumbs or residue behind. Cereal or oyster cracker–type treats work best. The treat is called the *pea* in the final step.

Command: Stay (see Chapter 11).

Command: Stay with Distractions (check out Chapters 11 and 16).

Sequence 1: Establishing a pattern for the game

These steps in the first sequence help Buddy understand the pattern:

1. **Kneel in front of your dog on a Stay command with an ample supply of treats and your cups handy.**

2. **Put a treat on the floor and say, "Stay," and then release Buddy to the treat with "Okay."**

   If they go before the release, simply cover the treat with your hand before they get to the treat. This is a practice review for the Stay command around distractions

3. **Repeat the whole sequence.**

   By repeating several times you're teaching Buddy that this is a game they'll want to play; they need to get focused to play several times. Doing this sequence really teaches that Okay means you can get up from a Stay command. Even if food shows up first, Stay means stay no matter what is going on around them.

Sequence 2: Introducing the covered treat

The next steps focus on making the introduction. Buddy, meet the treat.

1. **Kneel in front of your dog on a Stay command, show them one cup, and put a treat on the edge of the upside-down cup, half under the cup and half showing.**

2. **Pause and then say, "Stay."**

3. **Release them to the cup with "Okay," and treat and praise again and again while you pet and party with Buddy for finding the hidden treat.**

4. **Repeat until Buddy knocks over or pushes aside the cup with ease to get at the half-exposed treat.**

5. **Now completely cover the treat so that Buddy can't see it.**

   Remember to enforce the Stay command.

6. **Release to the cup with "Okay."**

Sequence 3: Adding a second cup with no treat

You can now introduce an empty cup next to the loaded cup. This can be on another day after a review or you can continue playing if your dog is game for it.

1. **Have two cups upside down in front of the dog on a Stay, as shown in Figure 17-2.**

2. **Lift one cup at a time, and then make a big deal about putting a treat under one of them.**

3. **Pause and then release and let your dog find the treat.**

   If they go right for the correct one, or even if they don't, make a huge fuss of praise when they find the treat.

FIGURE 17-2:
Two cups, one is loaded, and one is empty.

© *John Wiley & Sons, Inc.*

Sequence 4: Moving the cups and changing their position

To keep building on this trick, follow these steps:

1. **Repeat Sequence 3, but after you've loaded one of the cups, slowly switch the cups' location by sliding them around on the floor, not lifting the cup to expose the treat.**

   Usually, the dog is fascinated by this while on the Stay. Pause before releasing Buddy to the cups.

TIP

2. **Repeat this step, but slide the cups back and forth a few extra times.**

   Try to determine whether your dog is simply crashing the cups over or using their nose or eyes to go to the right cup. Help them if needed by tipping over the cup.

   If your cups aren't tipping over, do this on a bit of carpet to allow for some traction. The hand bells help with this because they knock over more easily because of the handles.

Sequence 5: Finishing the trick

During this sequence you add the third cup, which is when this trick really gets fun:

1. **With Buddy on a Sit-Stay, place the three cups in front of them.**

2. **Load one with a treat and allow Buddy to watch you.**

3. **Slide the cups around in front of them and talk up the mystery of which one has the treat under it.**

4. **Sit back on your heels, say, "Okay," and watch Buddy sniff out the correct cup (see Figure 17-3).**

   Only one cup has the treat. Your dog may tip them all over, but eventually most dogs get it right, going directly to the correct cup.

TIP

If you want to make this trick a show piece, add some drama to your voice and act as if you have a crowd in front of you. Announce and show off "the Famous Buddy of the World, who can follow the cup to find the pea every time. As if by magic, Buddy will watch and concentrate and find the famous pea under the cups as they switch and move before their eyes." It's your show, so play it up.

FIGURE 17-3:
Watch Buddy
sniff out the
correct cup for
the treat.

Hiding in a Box

With this trick, you teach your dog to get in a big box and eventually hide in it by laying down.

Needed: A cardboard box and treats

Make sure the box is big enough for your dog to get into and lay down. Save one from a delivery or visit a store that lets you take one. Close in the flaps to add stability and so the box doesn't have a top or flaps to deter your dog. Make sure the box isn't so high that your dog can't leap into it later.

Use treats that are easy to toss, such as cheese-flavored corn puffs, popcorn, or something special and fun. Be careful about overdoing the snacks.

Command: Get In (see Chapter 14).

Command: Down (check out Chapter 11).

Sequence 1: Introducing the box on its side

The steps in this sequence help your dog get acquainted with the box:

1. **Set up your box and lay it on its side so that the opening isn't on top but rather easy to walk into.**

2. **Toss a treat into the box and say, "Get in," and then release with "Okay" as Buddy eats the treat.**

3. **Repeat over and over until Buddy willingly goes in the box for the treat.**

TIP

Turn the box if it isn't a square box so that they'll go into the box to get the treat from any side. You can move the box around the room, too, so that the box changing location isn't a concern for Buddy.

4. **Step behind Buddy as they go in the box so that they don't just back out.**

   You want them to wait until you say, "Okay."

Sequence 2: Standing the box correctly with the opening on top

This sequence may take a bit of help, especially if Buddy isn't a leaper. We find that helping them into the box and having them leap out is helpful. Just follow these steps:

1. **Without fear or frustration, gently put Buddy into the box, lifting them up and placing them inside.**

2. **Immediately give them a treat and then say, "Okay" to release them and give them another treat for leaping out.**

   The leaping out will only get a treat when you are putting them in the box by lifting them in. After they get in the box by themselves, you'll only treat them while they're inside the box, not after they come out. You want them to go in the box, so only reward them for going in, not for coming out.

3. **Drop a treat or two into the box and say, "Get in your box."**

   If they don't try, lift them in so they can eat the treats inside of the box. Then say "Okay" to release them and play with them outside the box.

   Dogs know when you're pleased if you let them know you're pleased. We often hear people say their dogs always repeat a behavior if they laughed at their dog for doing something because your dog reads your laughter as being pleased. Laughter is praise to a dog. Have fun with trick training.

4. **Keep practicing until Buddy gets into the box on their own. Toss treats inside and encourage them to leap inside, as shown in Figure 17-4.**

   If you're tossing treats and they won't go, and you've lifted them in a few times and they still won't do it, tilt the box over with the treats inside and have them go in for the treats. This reminds them that the treats are there waiting for them. Make it easier and don't get frustrated.

Get In Your Box is the command. Add it as your dog leaps inside. Okay is the release for your Get Out of the Box command.

© John Wiley & Sons, Inc.

Sequence 3: Adding the Hide command

You can wait for another day to work on this sequence. Make sure that your dog is willingly getting in and out of the box on your commands before moving on to the following sequence:

1. **Review the Down command outside of the box.**

   When they go down, they'll look like they're hiding in the box.

2. **Say, "Get in your box," and toss a treat inside.**

3. **Say, "Down, Hide," and raise your arm as your signal.**

4. **Praise and give another treat for them lying down.**

5. **Say, "Okay," to release them from the box.**

6. **Praise, praise, praise.**

7. **Repeat the Down, Hide combined command until Buddy starts responding to just the Hide command alone (see Figure 17-5).**

FIGURE 17-5:
Hiding in the box
by going into the
Down position.

© John Wiley & Sons, Inc.

Sequence 4: Putting it all together

Now that you have a dog that will get in the box, wait for you to release them with Okay to come out, and lie down in the box when asked, it's time to make it a performance. Follow these steps to put it all together:

1. **Have Buddy get in the box and raise your arm as you say, "Hide."**

   After they hide, say, "Okay" to release them to get out.

2. **You can use your imagination to make this into a bit of a celebration and put on a show by leaving your box out and playing this trick anytime you want.**

Trick training and training in general makes for a dog that is always listening and watching you.

REMEMBER

Picking a Hand

When it comes to showmanship, the trick in this section is a winner. You can profess that your dog can read your mind. You have both hands behind your back, one holding a treat. Then you bring them forward, and your dog noses or paws the hand that they want you to open. If they pick the correct hand, they'll find a treat. If not, no treat. But as a mind reader, they'll always pick the right hand, of course. (You know they're using their nose, but the audience will think Buddy is mind-reading.) Success is how you play your roll of showman for your audience.

Needed: Smelly treats, like beefy snacks

Command: Touch (see Chapter 9)

Command: Sit (see Chapter 11)

Sequence 1: Reviewing the Touch command

The steps in this sequence focus on mastering the Touch command, which requires your dog to nose your hand for a reward. Follow these steps:

1. **Put a treat between your fingers on the palm side of your hand and offer it to your dog as you say, "Touch."**

2. **Relax your fingers so that your dog can eat the treat.**

3. **Practice using both the right and the left hands.**

   Buddy should willingly nose both of your hands.

Sequence 2: Touching the back of the treat hand

The command you use isn't as important as the actions you use. Dogs learn actions and expectations first. In fact, commands are the easy part of trick training. What's important is that you're consistent with the commands you do use. These steps train Buddy to touch the back of the hand that's holding the treat:

1. **Have your dog sitting in front of you.**

   You can be sitting in a chair, too.

2. **Hide a treat in your hand, between your fingers again, show it to your dog, and then turn your hand over into a fist, offering it toward their face and say, "Touch, which one?"**

   When they nose your hand, say, "Yes," and flip your hand over and give them the treat.

3. **Repeat this again and use either hand.**

Sequence 3: Offering both hands for the dog to choose the loaded hand

The steps in this sequence work on showing both hands so that Buddy can select the hand with the treat:

1. **Have your dog sitting in front of you.**

2. **Place a treat in one palm, show both palms to your dog, and then make fists and turn them over.**

3. **Say, "Touch, which one?" and let them choose one with their nose (see Figure 17-6).**

   Open the hand they touch and give them the treat. Remember that at this point, they saw the treat and saw you turn your hands, so it's likely they'll pick the correct one. If not, just say, "Oops," and start again.

FIGURE 17-6:
Offer both fisted hands, but only one holds a treat.

REMEMBER

You'll show the treat in the one hand, turn the hands and cup them shut, and then ask, "Which one?" If you still need to say "Touch" first, that's fine, but you'll ween off from saying it and eventually only say, "Which one?"

Sequence 4: Putting your hands behind your back first

After your dog has consistently had fun and success with the last sequence, it's time in these steps to put your hands behind your back before bringing them out in front, already cupped shut:

1. **Have your dog sitting in front of you.**

   This sequence requires you to be a bit animated. You want your dog to keep playing. If you simply bring your hands around and ask which one, your dog may lose interest.

2. **Play it up, hold the treat in front of you and show it to your dog, and tease them a bit, but don't let them have it, and then bring your hands behind your back and put the treat in one hand.**

3. **Bring your hands in front of you with both hands cupped shut and then offer each hand, one at a time, for them to sniff, bringing the hand toward their nose, as shown in Figure 17-7.**

4. **Stop moving and ask, "Which one"?**

   Your dog should nose one of your hands. If they're correct, praise them and offer the treat. You can say, "Yes, Okay. What a good dog!" or something like that.

   If they touch the wrong hand, say, "Oops," show them the empty hand, and that's the end of it. No treat.

5. **Start over with Steps 2 and 3. Only the correct hand pays!**

FIGURE 17-7: Have them choose which one.

When you're ready, make a show of it with an audience. As you and your dog get better at this trick, you'll find what helps your dog get it right; let them sniff your hands, one at a time. Then hold them still and let them pick.

In your showmanship voice, make it fun and announce something like, "The Great Mind Reader, Buddy, traveled the world to learn this magical art. Buddy will think and think. Could it be this hand (let them sniff) or this hand (let them sniff)? Which one is it?"

Playing Shy

With this trick, you teach your dog to shove his face between your knees or thighs to hide his face, acting and looking shy. This is such a crowd pleaser every time. Asking your dog whether they are shy in front of friends and your dog hides their head is so adorable and funny. Well worth the time to train.

Needed: Any variety of treats

Command: Stay (see Chapter 11)

Command: Yes (see Chapter 9). *Yes* is the praise word that means the moment of perfection. Mark the moment that they do exactly what you wanted them to do.

Sequence 1: Putting their head between your legs

The steps in this sequence instruct Buddy to place their head between your legs:

1. **Standing up with your dog hanging around your feet, get your dog to focus on a treat in your hand.**

TIP

   Place your feet far enough apart to reach your arm around one of your legs and get your dog to reach through your legs to get the treat in your hand. Keep your dog in front of you. If your dog comes through your legs, that's okay but not exactly what you want. The only tough part of this is to keep your dog from going around your leg rather than through your legs. Have your dog on a leash at first or hold the collar so you have time to get the treat hand behind your legs before your dog follows it around your body.

   Ideally, they reach through your legs to get the treat. If you have to hold them back with the other hand initially, that's fine. Keep at it until your dog reaches through to get the treat from your hand held behind your leg.

2. **Use your Yes command the moment your dog reaches through your legs for the treat.**

3. **Repeat this often until your dog understands to go between your legs for the reward.**

Sequence 2: Holding your legs closer together

This sequence gradually gets your legs closer together until finally they're close enough that Buddy can only get their face and nose through your legs:

1. **Hold your legs closer together so that your dog can reach only their head through.**

   You don't want their shoulders to go through your legs (see Figure 17-8).

2. **Start using the Stay command as they press in between your legs.**

3. **Feed from behind you, with your dog's head only coming through your legs.**

4. **Say, "Yes," as you feed them.**

   Yes is the marker word. Continue to praise, and then release them from your legs.

FIGURE 17-8:
Only Buddy's face should be able to push through your legs for the Shy command.

Sequence 3: Holding their head pressed between your legs

To look shy, your dog needs to keep his head pressed between your legs as if they're hiding their head. In this sequence, you use the Shy command:

1. **Give the Shy command, even saying, "Shy, are you shy?"**

   As your dog puts his head between your legs but doesn't go through, say, "Shy," which means that you won't immediately give the treat. Instead, your dog should hold their head between your legs and wait for the release word to end the command.

REMEMBER

2. **After a few seconds, say, "Okay," to release your dog and give the food reward.**

   Still give your dog the food between your legs to reinforce the position.

   As your dog gets more practiced on the Shy command, you won't need to put the treat behind your leg first to entice your dog's head through your legs. You may need to hold the treat with your hand hanging in a natural position, slightly around your hip, but even doing so will be less necessary as your dog learns the Shy command more solidly. Practice every day to help Buddy learn it.

TRICKS — A GREAT WAY TO ENGAGE WITH YOUR AUDIENCE

My dog and I (Mary Ann) were contracted to do a short performance every 30 minutes at a huge holiday event at a big venue. We were the entertainment as people milled around. We would do a 20-minute performance of tricks and stunts and agility and obedience. Then, we would reset the stage and walk around inviting people into the auditorium for the next performance. This went on all night: Do the performance, chat up the audience, reset and walk around, repeat. After five shows, I forgot to do the Shy trick at its appropriate time during the performance, which turned out perfectly though, because for some reason, during that performance, someone in the audience, coughed quite loudly and startled my dog. They were usually stable and not sound sensitive, but that noise caused them to visibly startle and look around at the audience as if they just realized they were there.

It was amazingly perfectly timed. I immediately jumped in and laughed and asked the dog, "What? Did you just realize people were here? Are you going to be shy now?" Bam, they stuck their head in my legs and hid their head. It brought down the house.

This is what doing a stellar trick performance is all about; talking between your dog's tricks is just as important as having a great trick dog. You are part of the act. How you keep the audience engaged is all part of your success.

Rolling Over

Roll Over is always a crowd pleaser. This trick requires the dog to be on the floor and completely roll over sideways.

Needed: Yummy treats

Command: Down (see Chapter 11)

Sequence 1: Rolling over with a little help

First your dog needs to lie down, then go to their side, and then roll completely over. Take each part as a complete success before moving on to the next part; really be excited with each success. Your excitement and praise are so motivating for your dog. Follow these steps:

1. **Place your dog into the Down position.**

   Reduce your body posture by kneeling or squatting in front of your dog so you're not leaning or hovering over them.

2. **Hold the treat in such a way that your dog must look over their shoulder while lying on the ground.**

   Keep the treat close to their nose, slowly rotate their neck by moving the treat to look back over their shoulder.

3. **Say, "Roll over," and slowly make a small circle around their head, keeping the treat close to their nose.**

   As soon as your dog moves to their side, lying on their side instead of their sternum, say, "Yes," and give the treat. Even though Buddy didn't roll over yet, they rolled to their side, which is the first big success and step.

4. **Repeat Step 3. As they lie on their side, with your other hand, gently help your dog roll over completely in the direction they lay down, say, "Yes," praise, and party.**

   When the dog has completely rolled over, enthusiastically praise, reward, and release. Even though you helped them over, Buddy must be praised with a lot of enthusiasm. That last bit of the Roll Over, going over their backbone, is a huge deal, and you must make it a big party with lots of praise and food.

5. **Repeat these steps until your dog is completely relaxed with you helping them roll over.**

   TIP

   If you're having trouble with that final roll over, move your training to a softer surface, such as a bed or grass.

Sequence 2: Rolling over on their own

The steps in this sequence instruct Buddy to roll over by themselves:

1. **Place your dog into the Down position.**

2. **Say, "Roll over," and get them to follow the treat without any help from you.**

   REMEMBER

   Move the treat around their shoulder and over their back. When they roll over, praise, reward, and release. If they don't respond or need a lot of help, go back to Sequence 1. Remember that doing this on a softer surface, such as a bed or a quilt on grass, can really help with the backbone roll.

3. **Repeat the steps until your dog rolls over with little to no guidance from you.**

Sequence 3: Rolling over on command

As you follow these steps to help Buddy perform the final trick, don't have a treat in your hand, but be prepared to reward immediately after you get the correct response. Follow these steps:

1. **Say, "Down," and then, "Roll over."**

   The first few times you do this, you may have to use the same hand motion as though you had a treat in it. Praise, reward, and release when your dog does the trick properly.

2. **Reduce the hand motion until they do it on command alone.**

3. **Enthusiastically praise, reward, and release when they perform on command.**

Playing Dead

Playing dead is an old favorite and a logical extension of Roll Over (see the previous section.) It consists of aiming your index finger and "firing" at your dog with a command, such as Bang, and your dog falls on his side or back and plays dead.

Needed: Yummy treats

Command: Down (see Chapter 11)

Command: Roll Over (see above)

Sequence 1: Lying down on their side or back

The steps in the first sequence of this trick are to instruct your dog to lie down.

1. **With a treat in your "gun" hand, use the Down command, as shown in Figure 17-9.**

2. **Lean over your dog and in a deep tone of voice say, "Bang," as you point your index finger at them.**

   Some dogs will roll on their side or back simply because of your body language, and the low bang sound can elicit defense drive.

3. **Praise and give them a treat while they're in that position and then release them with "Okay."**

   If they don't roll on their side or back, use the treat as you did for Roll Over. Then praise, reward, and release them.

4. **Repeat this sequence until your dog responds to the Bang command.**

FIGURE 17-9: Load your gun (your pointed finger) with a treat in your hand.

Sequence 2: Playing dead from the sitting or standing position

After Buddy lies down from a Down command, they have to be able to "die" from any position. Follow these steps:

1. **Call you dog's name to get their attention.**

2. **Lean over your dog and in a deep tone of voice say, "Bang," as you point your gun (index finger and thumb in the form of a gun) at them.**

   If they lie down and play dead, say, "Yes," praise, reward, and release. If they don't, show them what you want by placing them in the Dead position by giving the Down signal and moving the treat around their shoulder (see Sequence 1 of "Roll Over"). Praise, reward, and release.

3. **Repeat this sequence until your dog responds to the Bang command from the sitting or standing position.**

Sequence 3: Playing dead at a distance

To make this trick into a skit, you need to train Buddy to "die" to a Bang command from a slight distance:

1. **With your dog about two feet from you, call their name to get their attention and then give the Bang command as you point your finger gun at them.**

   If they respond, praise, go to them, reward them, and then release. If they don't, show them what you want and start all over.

2. **Practice this sequence as you gradually increase the distance to about six feet. Have fun; this is a game.**

Sequence 4: Presenting the trick to an audience

This sequence is a favorite and a real crowd pleaser. Put a story to it and make it for an audience. For example

> "Buddy wants to win an Academy Award one day. I've explained to Buddy that the best way to do that is to have the perfect death scene, so Buddy is always after me to practice with them. Here we go again (with a John Wayne Western accent). Okay, Buddy, this town ain't big enough for the two of us. It's either *you* or *me,* and I'm not going to be leaving town anytime soon. *BANG! BANG!*

By time you get to the *BANG! BANG!* Buddy will already be spinning with excitement and will "die" immediately. As a back-up fix, should Buddy not die, you can claim a bad aim on your part or blanks loaded by mistake. Command again.

Jumping through a Hoop

A hula hoop makes a wonderful prop for this trick, which is suitable for medium- to small-sized dogs. Start by getting a hoop that's appropriate for your dog's size, and then follow the three sequences.

Needed: A yummy treat

Command: Come (see Chapter 10)

Command: Stay (see Chapter 11)

Sequence 1: Walking and jumping through a hoop

These steps teach your dog to walk first and then jump through a hoop on leash:

1. **Lay the hoop on the ground and walk your dog over to examine it.**

   Take your time with this step so that Buddy thoroughly smells the hoop and isn't frightened by it.

2. **Put your dog on leash and walk them over to the hoop.**

3. **Pick up the hoop and let the bottom edge rest on the ground.**

4. **Thread the leash through the hoop and encourage your dog to walk through to you by saying, "Come, Jump."**

   You can use a treat to get them to walk through the hoop. Repeat until your dog readily goes through the hoop with the Come, Jump command. Praise, reward, and release with Okay for successful attempts. By adding the Jump command immediately following the Come command that they know, Buddy will quickly make the association of the new command.

5. **Thread the leash through the hoop, raise it a few inches off the ground, and say, "Come, Jump."**

   If necessary, use a treat to get them through and then enthusiastically praise. As your dog gains confidence, begin raising the hoop in two-inch increments until the bottom is eye level in front of them.

Sequence 2: Jumping through the hoop off leash

The steps in this sequence train your dog to jump through the hoop off leash:

1. **Take the leash off and present the hoop in front of your dog with the bottom of the hoop no higher than the dog's knees.**

2. **Say, "Come, Jump," and let the dog jump through.**

3. **Praise and reward with a treat.**

   Repeat but change the position of the hoop so that the bottom is level with the dog's elbows and then their shoulders. The maximum height you can raise the hoop depends on the size and athletic ability of your dog. If Buddy is under a year old, you shouldn't allow them to jump higher than their elbows. Eventually, you can drop saying "Come" before the Jump command.

WARNING

Keep in mind that as soon as you get to about shoulder level (the dog's, not yours), you need a surface with good traction on which the dog can take off and land safely. Wet grass and slippery floors aren't good surfaces for this trick. They may wind up injured.

Unrolling the Red Carpet, or Any Carpet Runner

Find a carpet runner that is about 6 feet long. No requirement here, any throw rug will do.

Needed: Several smelly good treats

Command: Stay (see Chapter 11)

Command: Go (see Chapter 10)

Sequence 1: Load the rug with treats in front of your dog

Doing this in front of your dog shows them where to find the goodies.

1. **Put your dog in a Sit Stay command.**

   Lay out the carpet runner in front of your dog so that the dog is looking at the rug longways.

2. **With your dog still on a Stay command, start rolling up the rug from the far end, dropping a treat every 6 inches or so as you roll up the rug.**

   The rolled-up rug can't be too tight or too loose; you want the rug to unroll easily.

3. **Leave a few inches out with a treat exposed. It will be great if Buddy has a bit of the rug to stand on while they unroll the rug.**

Sequence 2: Encourage Buddy to find the treats with their nose

With you and Buddy close to the front of the rolled rug, encourage their focus onto to the rug.

1. **Give the Go command for Buddy to go to the rug and look for the treats by pushing the roll away from them.**

2. **Assist their efforts by encouraging a smooth head push to unroll the rug.**

3. **Praise success; the treats will come automatically to your dog.**

4. **As Buddy gets better and understands the game, you can put the treats farther apart when rolling up the rug.**

This is a great game for rainy afternoons — teaching Buddy to use their nose to find hidden treats. Make sure you shake out all the crumbs from the rug after playing and training.

Taking a Bow

Performers customarily take a bow after a performance to accept the applause of the audience. This trick teaches your dog to take a bow after they have performed the tricks you've taught them.

Needed: Treats, small, smelly, and easily eaten

Command: Down (see Chapter 11)

Command: Stand (see Chapter 19)

Command: Stay (see Chapter 11)

Command: *Yes* marker praise word (see Chapter 9)

Sequence 1: Bowing by using a food lure

These steps get your dog to bow by using food as a treat:

1. **Stand your dog next to you.**

   With a small dog, you can teach this trick on a table.

2. **Place your left hand, palm facing down, under your dog's belly with a little backward pressure against their hind legs.**

3. **With a treat in your right hand, slowly lower the treat from your dog's nose to the ground, keeping your left hand under their belly.**

   Move the treat slightly closer toward the paws, not out away from the dog — from their nose toward the ground, toward their elbows on the ground.

4. **Say, "Take a Bow," as you move the treat and Buddy gets into the correct bow position.**

   When they do, say, "Yes," and hold the treat, allowing them to lick it before eating it. Have them hold still for a few seconds before releasing and giving the treat.

   You want Buddy to lower their front end and remain standing with their rear end. When Buddy is successful, praise and say, "Okay," to release.

5. **Practice this sequence until they lower their front end on command without a treat.**

   You can use the movement of your treat hand even though it doesn't have a treat in it.

6. **Praise enthusiastically after each successful repetition.**

Sequence 2: Practicing until Buddy bows with little to no help

The steps in this sequence focus on practicing until Buddy bows on their own with little to no help from you:

1. **Stand next to your dog, keeping your left hand under their belly.**

2. **Say, "Take a bow," and pat the ground in front of them with your right hand.**

   When they lower their front end, praise and release. You can add the Stay command while they are in the Bow position. This will help them hold longer and longer.

3. **Practice these steps several times until they respond to the command without you patting the ground.**

Sequence 3: Taking a bow on command

The final sequence in this trick teaches Buddy to take the bow when you command them to do so. Do these steps in front of an audience:

1. **Stand next to your dog, point to the ground in front of them with your left hand, and say, "Take a bow" (see Figure 17-10).**

   When they do, praise and release. If they try to lie down, prop up their rear end with your left hand. Practice until you no longer have to prop up their rear to help.

2. **When they take a bow on command, say, "Stay," and release them after several seconds.**

   Be prepared for your audience's applause.

FIGURE 17-10:
Take a Bow to
thundering
applause.

© John Wiley & Sons, Inc.

USING YOUR DOG'S NATURAL BEHAVIORS TO YOUR ADVANTAGE

Teaching Buddy tricks that use their natural tendencies generally makes teaching tricks easier. If your dog has a quirky habit, you may find that you can turn it into a fun trick. When you see a behavior you want to turn into a trick, tell your dog how clever they are and give them a treat.

For example, when you see Buddy sneeze and you want to turn the behavior into a trick, praise them when you see them doing it and give them a treat and praise. Next, give the behavior a command, such as "Sneeze." When you see them doing it, give the command, praise, and reward. It won't take long before Buddy responds to the command.

5

Handling Special Situations

Understand what aggression is, where it comes from, and how to defuse it if your dog is aggressive.

Be prepared and know how to handle unique situations, such as thunderstorms and stressful situations, before you see them to keep a step ahead of life with your dog.

Keep your old dog's life full and fun. Learn what keeps your older dog young so it's as easy for them as it is for you.

Know when you need to look for professional help. Don't do so blindly. Know what to ask and what to look for when you do.

Saying goodbye is hard. How to survive the loss and figure out how to move on.

IN THIS CHAPTER

» Recognizing aggression and its causes

» Managing dogs high in prey drive, defense drive, and pack drive

» Dealing with a dog who's aggressive about their food bowl

» Working with a fear-biter

» Coping with aggression in everyday life

Chapter **18**

Addressing Aggression

ggression: Be not afraid. Aggression can be considered a normal behavior, not to be feared. You can manage it using basic commands and leadership as well as patience and observations. Don't wait and watch for aggressive behaviors to manifest. Instead, be proactive and directive to your dog. After all, *you* are the coach of the team. Be in charge and manage through obedience and training. This chapter discusses recognizing aggression, understanding what it arises from and how to manage it, and learning how to train to avoid it.

Understanding Aggression

The term *aggression* means different things to different people. For example, a passerby may consider a dog as being furiously aggressive when they run along the fence in a yard while barking and snarling. But if that's your dog, you may consider the behavior to be a perfectly normal reaction. The dog is protecting their territory, which is what you expect from them.

Of the many behaviors a dog expresses, perhaps the most misunderstood is aggression. With aggression goes health, self-confidence, survival, a good work ethic, ability to handle stress, a greater capability of bonding, and the ability to breed. Here we discuss the connection between aggression and your dog's drive and some causes for aggression.

Examining the link between aggression and drives

Aggression in Buddy can rise from any drive. Consider the following to help you grasp how aggression can show up in Buddy (in Chapter 2 we explain the different drives in greater detail):

>> **Prey drive:** This drive is considered the "killing" drive because the hunting of prey stimulates it. Although people see chasing and attacking as aggression, these behaviors are actually normal prey drive. We discuss how to manage prey drive later in the "Managing a Dog's Aggression — Prey, Pack, Defense Drives" section.

>> **Defense drive:** Aggression rises from defense drive, both fight and flight, because defense drive is all about protecting oneself. For example, if while walking your dog, a stranger approaches and your dog starts growling, they may be afraid of the unknown person, and the growl or aggression is referred to as *defense flight*. Conversely, if your dog wants to protect themselves or you and they're willing to fight, the growl is referred to as *defense fight*. In either case, it's now your job to manage the situation correctly.

TIP

Managing the environment and the dog is a great way to stop aggressive behavior. You can choose to cross the street, turn around and go the other way, or command your dog to "Heel" and pass the stranger, keeping yourself between the stranger and your dog. Basic training exercises such as Heel and heeling in a circle with the dog on the inside circle can help you manage the dog by giving them something on which to focus their attention: you. If your dog is on your left, circle to the left as if you're inside a hula hoop. Doing so forces your dog to look up at you, because you're coming into their space by circling with them and into them. If they're looking up at you, they won't be looking at the thing that's causing them to be aggressive. Under no circumstances should you make any effort to calm your dog by reassuringly petting them or telling them in a soothing voice, "There, there, it's perfectly okay." Buddy will misinterpret your soothing as praise.

>> **Pack drive:** Aggression rising out of pack drive is due to the hierarchy of those involved: possibly between you and your dog or between two dogs. When the aggressive behavior is directed toward you, ask whether you and Buddy have previously resolved this question of rank order: "Who is top dog?" Usually it hasn't been, and Buddy is convinced that they are top dog or can become top dog. They aren't a bad dog; they're just a pack animal and are looking desperately for leadership. If you don't provide that leadership, they'll fill the vacuum. Dogs are quite happy and content when they know their rank order.

If the aggression is between two dogs of your household, you need to support the more dominant dog such as by passing out treats and meals to the *alpha dog* (top dog) first. The more dominant dog is top dog; it may not be your favorite and often is not the first dog in the household. Alpha depends on which dog wants to be top dog more, who is monitoring doorways, which one is pushing past the other dogs, which dog is territorial about the best dog bed, which dog always wants the best of everything. That dog needs your support by letting them have the first of everything while you hold back the other dog. If you don't support the top dog by allowing them the rights of the top dog, then they'll become more adamant and pushy and therefore can potentially harm a dog who is taking away their rightful place or due. By supporting the true top dog, you're sending a message to the other dog that they indeed aren't top dog. Above all, you are leader of the pack.

If the aggression is between your dog and another dog, you need to manage your dog by putting them under command and not allowing them to make wrong choices on their own. You should command them to "Heel" and get your dog to focus on you. See Chapters 9, 10, and 11 for leadership exercises and basic obedience commands.

Looking at the causes of aggression

Many factors, including environment, poor health, or heredity, can cause aggressive behavior, such as biting and growling. Keep reading to see how each can cause aggression.

REMEMBER

Aggression is a natural and even necessary phenomenon. In the case of unwanted aggression, human mistakes or misunderstandings are the usual cause. The owner may be unintentionally rewarding the undesired behavior, causing it to occur again and again, or the owner may not have socialized the dog properly. Only when you're unable to manage aggression or don't understand its origin, does it become a problem.

Environmental causes

The most common cause for dog bites is environmental — the result of a misunderstanding or outright mismanagement of the dog. A misunderstanding can occur when a puppy or dog nips at the owner's hand during play or when the dog is playing retrieve and accidentally bites the hand when their owner tries to get the stick. Most dog owners can recognize when a bite occurred due to a misunderstanding — in this case, the dog will likely be just as horrified as the owner.

Bites occurring because of mismanagement are a different matter. For example, say a child is playing with Buddy and Buddy has had enough, so the dog retreats under the bed. When the child crawls after Buddy and tries to drag them out, Buddy snaps at the child's hand and may even make contact. This scenario isn't uncommon, and it's coming out of the defense-flight drive. Even though the dog may not have provided any warning, their behavior was predictable — the fact that Buddy retreated should have told the child that they'd had enough, that they're trying to flee. Similarly, when you stick your hand in the crate of a dog that isn't yours and they growl at you, you should know that you need to remove your hand. The dog is acting out in defense-flight drive. If you persist, they have given you ample warning that they may bite.

One scenario frequently encountered is when the dog, when told to get off the couch or bed, growls at the owner. When the owner is asked whether the dog has had any basic training, the answer invariably is "not much" or "none." In this case, the first order of business should be teaching the dog the basic impulse control exercises — Sit and Stay and the Leave It commands, along with door and stair manners. All are considered leadership exercises. See Chapter 14 about getting on and off the furniture, Chapter 9 for Leave It, and Chapter 1 for the beginner exercise.

Lack of socialization

Not socializing a puppy with different people, other animals, and different environments in the first weeks of owning them can cause aggression around strangers, so it's crucial that your puppy, from eight weeks on, gets out and meets people. The human socialization period is from seven to twelve weeks of age, and dogs must meet people during this time.

WARNING

Keeping your dog at home until they have had all their vaccinations at six months of age prevents proper socialization with people and other dogs and the lack of proper socialization can be a cause for aggression. During the critical socialization period, up to seven weeks of age and early puppyhood, Buddy learns dog language from other dogs, allowing them to behave appropriately around other dogs. After Buddy has had their first set of vaccines (for parvovirus and distemper), it's safe to take them out and about. The benefit of early socialization far outweights any risk. It's critical that Buddy be taken different places in puppyhood so that they learn to accept different environments. In Chapter 7 we talk about the human socialization period, which is up to 12 weeks of age. Training in different areas is helpful to the puppy because they discover that training is enforced not just at home but also wherever they find themselves. (See the nearby sidebar "Socializing your pup when they're young" for more information.)

Poor training plan on the owner's part

Inappropriate punishment can also cause aggression. Pulling a dog into a crate, pulling them through doors, treating them roughly, or punishing them for house-breaking errors can all cause high states of anxiety. Remember, a puppy is just a baby that hasn't been taught what you expect from them. Be patient, be kind, and have compassion. Take your puppy to local puppy training classes and learn how to treat them appropriately. Accidents are reflections on your inability to read your dog. It isn't their fault. Look to changing your behavior.

Poor health causes

If a dog is in poor health, they can become irritable and aggressive. If a dog that never has shown any aggressive tendencies before all of a sudden is growling or snapping, the first thing you must do is to get a veterinary exam. If a dog is in pain, they are going to protect their surroundings, and they will watch out for someone who may bump into them or touch them. Pain is a big cause of aggressive behavior. It you don't pinpoint the problem physiologically you will never fix the aggression behaviorally.

In these cases, the dog's action isn't a behavioral problem but a health problem. If you've never seen aggression in a dog that is several years old and, suddenly, they're becoming irritable, have a health check and bloodwork done at your veterinarian's office. The new behavior most likely is due to a new pain or illness.

Hereditary causes

Hereditary aggression, unless selectively bred for, is relatively rare, because it contradicts the whole concept of domestication. Dogs who are high in one drive over another produce offspring who are more likely going to be similar in their personalities or drives. Meet the parents of a puppy before you choose a puppy from a specific litter.

Managing a Dog's Aggression — Prey, Pack, Defense Drives

This section examines the triggers of aggression in the context of the three drives — prey, pack, and defense (which includes fight and flight drives). The triggers are different in each drive, and so is the management. Your dog's Personality Profile (see Chapter 2) tells you the likely triggers so that you can predict what Buddy will do under certain circumstances. Discovering how to anticipate your dog's reaction under certain situations is part of managing their behavior.

Other than ignoring or putting up with the behavior, you have three basic options:

>> **Expending the energy:** Each behavior has a time frame, or energy, and you can manage it by expending that energy, which means exercise specifically focused on that energy. The exercise can be playing ball (prey drive), jogging (pack drive), playing tug-of-war games (defense drive), or any game. Basic training is always essential for all drives.

>> **Suppressing the energy:** This option means that the dog isn't given an outlet for the energy. Suppression can be an effective temporary solution, provided that the dog has periodic opportunities to expend the energy.

Total suppression can be dangerous. Liken it to a bottle of soda that's shaken vigorously. When you take the top off, it explodes. So, a dog that has been bred to run (for example, a Greyhound or Whippet) but is suppressed will run for a long time and may not come back when they finally get loose. Working dogs that come from generations of dogs that have worked for a living don't make good pets when their natural behaviors are suppressed. Unless they have an outlet for their intelligence, they can become grumpy, irritable, and obsessive over toys. Some even indulge in self-mutilation. Training and working these dogs regularly is a necessity.

For example, a Malinois dog, which is bred to work, lived in a home as a pet with no job and only got to walk around the block two times a day, not nearly enough mental stimulation or release of prey drive or exercise. This dog had bitten its owners and kept running off. The solution was a job: obedience training and an outlet for prey drive. The trainer on the case walked around the perimeter of a fenced field and showed the dog where he had previously hidden a lot of toys. He brought the dog back to the entrance to the field and told her to find a toy. It took about 20 minutes for the dog to find them all, but the activity had expended the energy and mental stimulation she needed, and she was calm and happy for the rest of the day. She never showed any tendencies to bite when she was given the opportunity to work. Plus, the owners and the dog did basic obedience, which gave the dog even more of an outlet and leadership with the owner.

>> **Switching the drive:** When Buddy growls at another dog, for example, they're in defense drive. To manage the situation, switch them into pack drive. Give them a command, such as "Come," check the leash with a quick snap in your direction, if necessary to turn the dog toward you, and then lavish on calm praise for having come. Doing so should switch them into pack drive.

Depending on the situation, you're going to use a combination of the three options in your management program. In the following sections, we look at the triggers and management for aggression caused by the three different drives.

Dealing with aggression from dogs high in prey drive

You shouldn't be surprised that *prey behaviors*, those associated with chasing and killing prey, are one of the leading causes for aggression. In a sense, aggression coming from this drive is the most dangerous, because so many different stimuli can trigger it. Dogs high in prey drive are stimulated by sounds, smells, and moving objects. See Chapter 2 for help recognizing a dog that is high in this drive.

Triggers for prey drive

Anything that moves can trigger prey behaviors. Dogs high in prey drive chase cars, bicycles, joggers, cats, other dogs, squirrels, bunnies, you name it. And if they catch up with whatever they're chasing, that's when the problem becomes real. Running after a car, for example, can get your dog killed. Running after a cat can be dangerous if the cat stops, turns, and attacks your dog. They can lose an eye that way. Running after squirrels and other critters also needs to be stopped. Imagine that you're traveling with Buddy and stop at a rest stop that has trees, squirrels, and picnic tables with families enjoying an outing. If Buddy gets loose and chases a squirrel, you can run into trouble. If you're lucky, the squirrel goes up a tree and Buddy doesn't catch it. But the act of chasing can terrify the families and can lead Buddy to keep going out onto the highway.

Prey drive can be triggered in a training class situation when dogs are moving in the class, such as during the Heel exercise. Some beginner dogs get overly excited and start barking at the other dogs. This behavior makes it impossible for the instructor to guide the students, and it makes the other dogs in the class nervous and excited, too. Barking can be common in under-socialized dogs. To diffuse this situation, it's wise for the instructor to teach the owner and dog to do a circle left, heeling in a tight circle, about the size of a hula hoop during the moving exercises and have them work a bit away from the group. If you're the student in this situation, it's a good idea either to work on the sidelines or put your dog into the car if you can't manage them. Practice at home until the dog has become more confident and can rejoin the class.

Managing prey drive triggers

Play retrieve games on a regular basis, and make sure your dog gets plenty of exercise, as shown in Figure 18-1 . When you take them for a walk and they spot a cat or squirrel, distract them, redirect their attention on you by doing a circle left, heeling in a small circle together, or turn and go in the opposite direction. The Leave It command (see Chapter 9) may be sufficient, or you may need to give them a check on the leash to refocus their attention on you. Basic training is a must to control this kind of behavior in the long term.

REMEMBER

If Buddy doesn't reliably respond to the Come command, don't let them loose in situations where they may take off after something. Better yet, train them to come reliably on command. Whatever you do, don't let Buddy chase cars, joggers, or cyclists. This can lead to unintentional training as you will call and call with no response because the distractions are too great for the level of training your dog has.

© John Wiley & Sons, Inc.

FIGURE 18-1:
Releasing energy from prey drive.

Handling aggression from dogs high in defense drive

Survival and self-preservation govern defense drive, which consists of both fight and flight behaviors. Defense drive is more complex than pack or prey because the same stimulus that can cause aggression (fight) also can elicit avoidance (flight) behaviors. *Cornered flight drive,* in which the dog thinks that they have no escape, can even be more dangerous than fight drive because the dog feels they have nothing to lose, so they'll fight to the death.

After some basic training, dogs with high fight drive are terrific companions and protectors, great competition and show dogs, and a joy to own. As young dogs, they may start bucking for a promotion. You may see signs of aggression toward you when you want the dog to get off the furniture or in similar situations when they don't want to do what you tell them.

REMEMBER

If a puppy is allowed to grow up doing anything they like and isn't given parameters for what they can and can't do, they likely won't make a satisfactory pet. After all, they'll develop a sense that they can do anything they please.

Full-fledged signs of aggression don't just suddenly occur. The signs start with many warnings, from growling to lip lifting to staring at you. If you condone these behaviors and avoid dealing with them, your dog is on their way to becoming aggressive.

Buddy also may be aggressive toward other dogs. When meeting another dog, they'll try to lord it over the other dog. The classic sign is putting their head over the shoulder of the other dog. The dog of lesser rank lowers their body posture, signaling that they recognize the other dog's rank. When two dogs perceive each other as equal in rank, a fight may ensue. Left to their own devices (that is, off leash), chances are they'll decide that discretion is the better part of valor. Both know that there are no percentages to fighting. They will slowly separate and go their own ways.

A true dogfight is a harrowing and horrifying experience, and most people prefer not to take the chance that it'll occur. Discover how to read the signs and take the necessary precautions by keeping the dogs apart. Dogs are no different from people: not all of them get along. See the sidebar "Getting attacked by another dog." about being attacked by another dog.

WARNING

Some owners inadvertently cause dogfights by maintaining a tight leash on the dog. A tight leash alters your dog's body posture, thereby giving an unintended aggression signal to the other dog. Maintain a loose leash when meeting another dog so that you don't distort Buddy's body posture. And at the slightest sign of trouble, such as a hard stare from the other dog, a growl, or a snarl, happily call your dog to you and walk away. *Happily* calling is important because you want to defuse the situation and not aggravate it by getting excited. You want to switch the dog from fight drive into pack drive.

REMEMBER

A female dog is entitled to tell off a male dog who's making unwanted advances. She may lift her lip, a signal for the male dog to back off. If the male doesn't take the hint, she may growl or snap at him. This behavior isn't aggression but perfectly normal dog behavior.

TAKING SOMETHING OUT OF BUDDY'S MOUTH

At some point during your dog ownership, you'll need to remove something from Buddy's mouth. It could be a chicken bone from the garbage, your shoe, or anything else inappropriate. Don't yell at them or chase them. They'll redouble their efforts to eat whatever it is. Try the Leave It command (see Chapter 9). If that doesn't work, try a trade. Offer them a fair trade, such as a piece of cheese or a treat. As they reach for it, of course, the chicken bone (or whatever you're after) will drop out of their mouth. Remember, never chase Buddy and corner them. Doing so destroys the very relationship you've been working so hard to achieve. It's better to run away from Buddy making all sorts of happy sounds to get Buddy to chase you. Most likely, they will abandon the thing you wanted to retrieve from them during the game. Unintentional training will result if you chase Buddy instead.

Triggers for defense drive

Aggressive behaviors can be set off in a dog with defense drive (fight and flight) by a variety of triggers. Some of the more common ones are

>> Approaching the dog in a threatening manner or walking directly at a dog

>> Hovering or looming over the dog (bending at your waist is a very threatening posture)

>> Staring at the dog

>> Teasing the dog

>> Telling them to get off the couch or bed, which is a prime location

>> Trying to remove something from their mouth (see the sidebar, "Taking something out of Buddy's mouth")

You can avoid some of these triggers altogether — like teasing them, staring at them, or hovering over them. Just don't do any of that. Other triggers, though, you need to deal with.

Managing aggression triggers

If you've identified that your dog's aggression is triggered by defense drive, management is your solution. In the following sections we explain some ways you can manage your dog out of defense drive.

PROVIDE EXERCISE AND TRAINING

One way to manage aggressive behavior is to provide plenty of exercise and training. Exercise physically tires the body, and training tires the brain. If there is a lack of mental stimulation, the dog will get into trouble. Aim for two training sessions a day, each at least ten minutes long. If you keep to the same time schedule, you'll have a happy dog.

REMEMBER

Training doesn't stop just because Buddy grows up. They love to use their brains all the way into old age. Using their brains helps keep them young. Be inventive in your teaching. Get them to help you around the house — teach them to retrieve the newspaper or trash from the yard. They'll love the challenge. Periodically review door and stair manners, getting in and out of the car, and the Go and Come commands. A short obedience routine is always enjoyed, and teaching them tricks can be fun. (See Chapter 17 for tricks and games you can practice with Buddy.)

PLAY TUG OF WAR

Another way to manage aggression is to expend the energy in the fight drive by playing a good game of tug of war. This came enables your dog to growl, tug, and bite to their heart's content. Instead of trying to suppress the behavior, dissipate its energy. The absence of an outlet for that energy, or efforts to suppress it, only makes matters worse. Figure 18-2 shows a game of tug of war.

FIGURE 18-2:
The tug-of-war game.

© John Wiley & Sons, Inc.

Put aside ten minutes several times a week to play tug of war at the same time every day. A routine helps the dog learn to expect an energy outlet at the same time every day, which helps manage their excitability. Here's what you do:

1. **Get a pull toy, a piece of strong fabric, or a knotted sock to use for the game.**

2. **Allow your dog to growl and bite the object and shake it while you're holding it.**

   After a satisfying tug, let Buddy have the toy.

   Be careful not to tug too hard toward you; you can injure Buddy's mouth or loosen a tooth.

   WARNING

3. **Let them bring the object back to you to play again.**

4. **Be sure to let them win each time by letting them carry it to their bed or wherever they want to go.**

   Some people object to the approach of letting the dog "win." Win exactly what? You started the game; you ended the game. You made all the decisions.

5. **When you've had enough, walk away from this session with the dog in possession of the toy.**

   Remember that everything belongs to you, especially the affection, attention, and time that they seek from you. If your dog comes after you for more playtime, then simply turn your back on them and ignore them.

REMEMBER

The game effectively discharges the energy associated with that drive. Remove the game from regular training sessions and do it only when you and your dog are alone with no distractions. It's their time with you. You'll be amazed at how satisfying the game is to your dog and the calming effect it has on them. See the nearby sidebar, "A tug-of-war case in point" for more about using this game.

PRACTICE THE LONG DOWN

A third way to manage high-fight-drive aggression is with the Long Down (see Chapter 11). We can't emphasize the importance of this exercise enough. The Long Down is a benign exercise and establishes quite clearly who is in charge (that would be you) in a non-punitive way. For dogs who express any kind of aggressive behavior, go back to this exercise and do a 30-minute Down. Make this the last thing you do at night, and do it two or three times a week.

A TUG-OF-WAR CASE IN POINT

Historically, tug of war has been a taboo to play with your dog. The misconception was that the dog shouldn't be allowed to win and challenge you for the toy. Instead, what's really happening is that when the dog wins, they inevitably shove the toy back at you to keep playing the game. To prove that the tug of war is a good concept, we taught it to a class of students who were very advanced in their training. Many of them were training their second or third dogs, and all were experienced handlers. They had chosen dogs with a relatively high fight drive because they knew how well those dogs trained and how well the bonding is with high drive dogs, but they had to live with the dog's tendency toward aggressive behavior and always had needed to be careful in a class or when the dog was around other dogs.

For the entire eight-week session, the owners were told to put time aside daily to play tug of war with their dogs. By the third week, we noticed a big difference in the dogs' temperaments. When together in class, the dogs became friendly toward each other, played more, trained better, and were perfectly well behaved when away from home.

USE A MUZZLE

If your situation has reached the point that you're afraid of your dog, or they try to bite you, or you can't get them into the Down position, use a muzzle. You also may require professional training help (see Chapter 21).

When you're nervous or anxious about what your dog may do when encountering another dog or person, your emotions go straight down the leash, which can cause your dog to react in an aggressive manner. In a sense, your worries become a self-fulfilling prophecy. You can solve this dilemma with the use of a muzzle.

REMEMBER

Using a muzzle is a simple solution to a complex problem. It allows you to go out in public with your dog without needing to worry about them. A strange thing happens to a dog while wearing a muzzle. After you've taken away their option to bite, they don't even try. It's almost as if they're relieved that the decision has been taken away from them. Even better, it gives you peace of mind and allows you to relax. On the other hand, although your dog acts differently, so will people you encounter; a muzzled dog may make some people apprehensive, although other people may relax when seeing a muzzle because it shows that the owner is taking responsibility for what the dog may do. A muzzle can be a good tool as you work toward training a high fight-drive dog. But a muzzle isn't a substitute for seeking professional help.

Training to a muzzle should be done slowly and gently because at first many dogs panic from having something around their faces. But with diligence, common sense, and some compassion for the dog, you can train them quite easily to accept it. Here's what you need to do:

1. **Drop a treat into the muzzle and allow your dog to fish it out with their nose and tongue.**

2. **Repeat putting the treat in the muzzle, put the muzzle on your dog for a few seconds, and then take it off again.**

3. **Give them a treat and tell them what a good dog they are.**

4. **Repeat Steps 1 and 2 over the course of several days, gradually increasing the length of time your dog wears the muzzle.**

5. **When they're comfortable wearing the muzzle at home, you can use it when you take them out in public.**

In some European cities, ordinances require certain breeds to wear muzzles in public. Many of these dogs happily accompany their owners on walks. They're well behaved and seem to be quite comfortable with their muzzles.

REMEMBER

Many owners are reluctant to use a muzzle because of the perceived stigma attached to it. You need to make a choice: stigma or peace of mind? Something else to think about: Suppose that your dog actually bites someone. When you have such a simple solution, why take the chance?

Controlling aggression in dogs high in pack drive

Pack drive consists of behaviors associated with reproduction and being part of a group. Believing that a dog high in pack behaviors can be aggressive may be difficult to grasp, but you must accept the fact. This type of dog may

>> Show signs of aggression toward people

>> Attack other dogs with no apparent reason

>> Not stop the attack when the other dog submits

Triggers for pack drive

The problem with aggression stemming from pack drive is that few obvious triggers seem to exist. Aggressive behavior is frequently observed in dogs that are taken away from their litters and mothers before seven weeks of age. Between five and seven weeks of age, a puppy learns to inhibit their biting (see Chapter 7). They also learn canine body language at this time. In short, your puppy learns that they're a dog. Puppies that haven't learned these lessons tend to be overly protective of their owners and may be aggressive to other people and dogs. They can't interpret body language and haven't learned bite inhibition, which is learning not to bite down hard when a dog is mouthing someone or another dog.

WARNING

In a household with more than one dog, when one dog is being petted and the other is seeking your attention at the same time, the dog being petted may be aggressive toward the other dog. This overpossessiveness is common in dogs that were taken away from a litter too earlier, before the Canine Socialization Period.

Lack of adequate socialization with people and other dogs prior to six months of age also can cause subsequent aggressive behaviors. The owner and the dog haven't worked out leadership when partners of the owner can't show affection to each other in front of the dog. When growling occurs when one partner hugs their that partner, it shows the dog is taking ownership of the one person instead of seeing both people as leaders of the pack. At this point, you must do the Long Sit and Long Down exercises regularly, focus on basic obedience, such as heeling and quick compliance to all commands, and work with your dog every day.

Managing pack drive triggers

You can solve a lack of socialization with other people by gradually getting the dog used to accepting another person. As always, the job is made easier when the dog has had some basic training and knows simple commands like Sit and Stay (which we describe in Chapter 11). A trained dog is a free dog. Train your dog, and they'll be welcomed to go with you in public.

Aggression toward other dogs, especially if the aggressor has had a few successes in their career, isn't so simple to resolve. Prevention is the best cure here. Keep your dog on leash and don't give them a chance to bite another dog when you're away from home.

TIP

A holistic approach to calm dogs with aggressive tendencies is to get some essential oil of lavender from a health food store. Put a couple drops on a small cloth and wipe them onto your dog's muzzle and around their nose. Lavender has a calming effect and helps in class situations in which one dog aggresses at another dog. The lavender scent enables the dog to concentrate on their work. You can also use the oil in a spray bottle (four drops of oil to eight ounces of water), and spray the room before the dogs come in. It really works wonders with the dogs and even calms the owners. Students who have been in agility competition and have dogs that couldn't concentrate because of the number of dogs and people around them have found that wiping their dogs' muzzles and noses with the oil has made a dramatic improvement in their performances.

Coping with Aggression around the Food Bowl

Your dog may growl when you get close to their food bowl. From their point of view, they're guarding their food — an instinctive and not uncommon reaction. The question is this: Should you try to do anything about it? And if the answer is yes, what do you do?

Some owners unwittingly exacerbate the behavior by trying to take the dog's food bowl from them while they're eating. Doing so definitely isn't a good idea. Why create unnecessary problems? Don't attempt to take food away from them and then putting it back. Imagine how you'd feel if someone kept taking away your dinner plate and putting it back. In no time at all, you'd become paranoid at the dinner table. Removing food for no reason repeatedly creates apprehension and makes the guarding and growling worse.

Instead, put the empty food bowl down and add some food into the bowl a scoop or spoonful at a time, which will make your presence near the bowl more welcome because you're adding food to the bowl. For the first few times, allow them to eat the amount in the bowl before adding more. Then work up to adding more as they're still eating what you recently added.

REMEMBER

You can also change the environment. Make sure Buddy is fed in a place where the children or other dogs can't get to their food. A good place to feed them is in their crate. Give them their food and bones in their crate and allow them to eat their food and treats in peace and quiet. And make sure that when they're in there, everyone leaves them alone. In Chapter 8 we explain how to train your dog to a crate. Follow the directions and the food bowl aggression problem will be solved.

A lot of conflicting advice is available about the subject of feeding a dog. But one bit of advice that is always true is to leave your dog alone when you feed them. Give them a place where they can be quiet and enjoy — and more importantly — digest their food, without the stress of kids, people, or other animals around their food bowl. Respect their space. If you insist on taking their food away, you'll train your dog to be neurotic. It will destroy the very relationship you're trying to build, and doing so is one of the first steps in teaching Buddy to become aggressive.

Dealing with Fear-Biters

The term aggression for fear-biters is actually a misnomer. These dogs in defense-flight drive don't aggress; they only defend themselves. When they do bite, it's out of fear; hence they're called *fear-biters.* Anytime this type of dog feels that they're cornered and unable to escape, they may bite. Biting to them is an act of last resort. They'd much rather get away from the situation.

REMEMBER

Avoid putting this type of dog in a position where they think they have to bite. Use a similar approach to the one we describe in Chapter 19 for submissive wetting. Fear-biters are most comfortable when they know what's expected of them, as in training. Timid behavior can resurface when they're left to their own devices and not given clear instructions on how to behave.

Dogs high in flight drive can appear shy around strangers, other dogs, or new situations. They may hide behind their owners and need space. Keep them a good distance away from people and other dogs, and don't corner them for any reason. Use your body to reassure these dogs; squat down to their level, bending your knees and not hovering over them, and coax them to you with some food. Be patient to gain their confidence and never ever grab for them. A running release together can give your dog a sense of escape. Holding the leash in control position, folded in your hands so the dog is near your side, say "Okay," and take off running away together. This sense of release can calm your dog down. Repeat as needed.

TIP

A dog high in flight drive needs confidence building. Training with quiet insistence and encouragement is one way to achieve a more comfortable dog. To get the dog used to people and other dogs, enroll them in an obedience class. Be patient with this dog and figure out how to go slowly. If you try to force an issue, you may wipe out whatever advances you've made.

A high flight-drive dog needs a structured and predictable environment. Walk, feed, and play at certain times of the day so the dog knows what's coming. Dogs have a phenomenal biological clock, and deviations from the time of walking and feeding can make undesirable behaviors resurface.

GETTING ATTACKED BY ANOTHER DOG

What do you do when you're walking your dog down the street on leash and another dog comes out of nowhere and attacks your dog? You do this:

- No matter what, don't yell or scream. Remember, prey drive is stimulated by sound — especially high-pitched sounds. Screaming just escalates the intensity of a dogfight. Try to keep calm at all times.

- While your dog is on leash and you hold the leash, your dog is at the mercy of the loose dog approaching. Let go of the leash if a fight is about to start so your dog can either retreat or fend for himself.

- For your own safety, don't try to separate the dogs, or you may get bitten. In the vast majority of incidents like this, one dog gives up, and the other one walks away.

- Canvass the neighborhood to find out who the loose dog belongs to. Then visit the person in a friendly way and make them aware that their dog is running loose and scaring (or harming) your dog. Perhaps times can be worked out so that when you walk your dog, the other dog is confined. Under no circumstances should you try to see whether the dog has a collar or tag. You would lean over the dog to do this, which would trigger more aggression. If talking to the owner doesn't work, consider walking in a different location.

Handling Aggression in Different Circumstances

Aggression can happen to even the best-behaved dogs. Put dogs in a situation that triggers aggression and they can get into a fight. Be in charge and manage through obedience and training. Buddy may have demonstrated aggression in these situations. In the following sections we explain how you can deal with that behavior.

Aggression in a multi-dog household

If you have several dogs in your household, you may encounter aggression. To avoid it, separate them when you feed them or give them high value treats such as real bones that are fresh from the butcher. Make note of what triggers the aggressive behavior you see and try to avoid putting the dogs in those situations again. Aggression also can happen over toys, so be vigilant.

Doorways are a common place for fights to break out because dogs often see the doorway as a rite of passage with the top dog going first. If one of the dogs wants to push through the door while another dog does also, a fight can erupt. To avoid these fights, award and control aggression in multi-dog households when dogs are going through doors into the yard or out the door. Use the door manners we discuss in Chapter 14 to control the door. Teach each dog door manners separately, then two at a time, and then all of them together. After all, you own the door, not the dogs. Leadership exercises, basic obedience, and door manners are all necessary when you have multiple dogs who are all vying for status by going through the door first.

Dogs also get excited about going out either into the yard or on a walk, and the level of excitement builds and one dog can jump on the other. If that happens, go back to training the Stay command (see Chapter 11) and release the dogs individually by name to go through the door. If one dog breaks its Stay and runs toward the door, simply close the door on the dog, guide it back to its Stay location, wait a few seconds, and try again. Door manners takes constant practice, time, and patience, but they're worthwhile and bring peace to the household.

Aggression while grooming

We strongly recommend grooming a dog on a table. Any table will do — just put a towel on it, so that the dog doesn't slip. Clipping toenails, cleaning ears, and removing hair mats in your dog's coat are so much easier on both you and Buddy if you don't lean over them. Keep a handful of small treats in your pocket; each time you do something, such as cut out a mat or clip a toenail, give a reward. You soon will have a dog that looks forward to their weekly grooming instead of you both dreading it. If you start grooming Buddy as a puppy, you shouldn't have any problems. See Chapter 6 for help with grooming your puppy early.

Aggression at the veterinarian

If you know that your dog has had unpleasant or painful procedures done at the veterinarian in the past, chances are they won't be happy to be in that veterinarian's office again. If you have any doubts about your dog being aggressive when their blood is drawn or when they're having a physical examination, suggest to the vet that the dog be muzzled, thus providing peace of mind for all concerned. Also make sure that you take your dog in your car to places that have a positive influence — like a nice walk, obedience classes, hiking, vacation, and so on. That way they'll never know when it's time for the veterinary visit and they'll be much less anxious in the car.

Chapter **19**

Helping Buddy Handle Special Situations

D ogs can have a variety of phobias and other problems — some that are related to training and others that aren't. Depending on how severe they are, these problems can be solved with your help. In this chapter, we list some of the more common phobias and the approaches that have worked to solve them.

Reacting to Loud Noises and Thunder

Some dogs have keener senses of hearing than others, to the point where loud noises literally hurt their ears. Some dogs leave the room when the family starts yelling or someone is simply telling a story with a loud voice. Some dogs do the same thing — leave the room completely — because the TV has been turned on. Fear of thunder also can be the result of this type of sound sensitivity.

Under ordinary circumstances sound sensitivity isn't a problem, but it can affect a dog's ability to concentrate in the presence of moderate to loud noises. A car backfiring causes one dog to jump out of its skin, whereas it only elicits a curious expression from another dog.

Dogs that experience fear of thunder and lightning become agitated and apprehensive when they sense an approaching storm. They may try to get out of the house, hide under the bed, engage in destructive behaviors, or exhibit other neurotic signs. Attempts to console the dog only reinforce his fears.

TIP

One product that claims an 85 percent success rate in controlling these symptoms is the Thundershirt — a pressure wrap that applies a gentle, constant pressure on a dog's torso. For more information, see www.thundershirt.com. The security that the Thundershirt gives helps dogs cope in the face of stress caused by noise. The sensation is similar to the security that a den or crate gives to a puppy or dog. When the Thundershirt works, it's amazing. Dogs who usually pant and drool and leave the room now remain with the family and can cope with the family's help. Playing with and distracting a worried dog that is also wearing the Thundershirt is a great combo to get through the fear. You can also try pheromone therapy, which you can find on the Thundershirt website.

Coping with Separation Anxiety

With *separation-related behaviors,* also called *separation anxiety,* your dog becomes anxious and stressed when you leave them. They're emotionally responding to being physically separated from the person to whom they're attached. Dogs that experience separation anxiety usually are high in pack drive and low in defense (fight) drive. (See Chapter 2 for more information on the many drives your dog may have.)

The most frequent inquiries about separation anxiety come from individuals who have just adopted a rescue dog. With these dogs, a certain amount of anxiety on the dog's part is understandable. Everything is new, including the people, surroundings, and routine. Giving the dog a week or two to settle in and establishing a routine before becoming overly concerned is the first avenue of prevention. Start training and bonding with the new dog immediately. Trying a Thundershirt, as we mention in the previous section, with sound phobias can help with separation anxiety as well.

In some cases, having an overly solicitous owner makes the problem worse. As the owner prepares to leave the house, they make a big fuss over the dog: "Now don't worry. Mommy/Daddy will be back soon, but I have to go to work for now. You be a good dog while I'm gone, and I'll bring you a nice treat." Such reassurances only increase the dog's anxiety at the expectation of being left alone.

The owner then makes an equally big fuss upon their return: "Poor dog. Did you miss me while I was gone? I missed you, too. Were you a good dog?" These utterances increase the dog's excitement in anticipation of the owner's return.

The best way to leave the house and to return is to make your departure benign and with little fanfare. Put a special treat in the crate with your dog and leave. On your return, open the crate door quietly and head out to the yard for a potty break. No big party or greeting, simply push past your dog and head outside to go potty. The transition from being alone to not being alone for the dog needs to be less starkly different.

The most typical and obvious signs of separation anxiety are destructive behaviors (destructive chewing, scratching, and in severe cases, self-mutilation), vocalizations (whining, barking, or howling), house soiling, pacing, and excessive drooling.

One solution to Buddy's boredom and loneliness is to get another dog. They can keep each other amused, and two dogs are more than twice the fun of one dog. But be warned that two dogs can also mean double the trouble.

If you don't want to get another dog, try the approaches we discuss in the following sections. One of these may be just the trick to getting Buddy more comfortable at home without you.

Testing the desensitizing approach

People are just as much creatures of habit as dogs are, and they tend to follow a specific pattern before leaving the house. This pattern becomes the dog's cue that you're about to depart. Make a list showing your customary routine before leaving the house. For example, you may pick up your bag or briefcase, grab the car keys, put on your coat, turn off the lights, and then reassure and pet the dog.

At odd intervals, several times during the day, go through your routine exactly as you would prior to leaving, and then sit in a chair and read the paper or watch TV, or just putter around the house. By following this procedure, you'll begin to desensitize the dog to the cues that you're about to leave.

When your dog ignores the cues, leave the house without paying any attention to the dog. Leave for about five minutes and then return. When you return, don't pay any attention to them for about five minutes. After that, interact in a normal fashion with your dog.

Repeat this process over the course of several days, staying out for progressively longer periods. Turning on the radio or TV and providing suitable toys for your dog also may help. Whatever you do, make sure to ignore the dog for five minutes after your return. With this process, you want to take the emotional element out of your going and coming so your dog will view the separation as a normal part of a day and not as a reason to become apprehensive.

Trying the DAP approach

Another way to cope with separation anxiety is to use DAP — Dog Appeasing Pheromone — a product developed by vets that mimics the properties of the natural pheromones of the lactating female. After giving birth, a mother dog generates pheromones that give her puppies a sense of well-being and reassurance.

DAP is an electrical plug-in diffuser that dispenses the pheromone, which the dog's sense of smell detects (see Figure 19-1). The pheromone reminds the dog of the well-being they felt as a puppy. In clinical trials, DAP was effective in about 75 percent of cases in improving separation-related behaviors. To be effective, the diffuser must be plugged in 24 hours a day. DAP, which is odorless to people, is available at pet stores and from pet product catalogs.

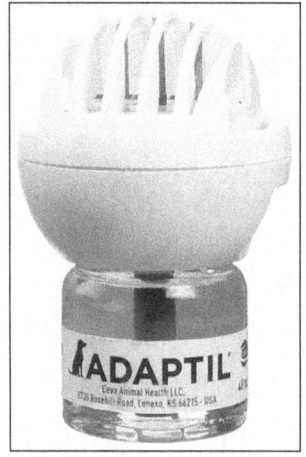

FIGURE 19-1:
A DAP dispenser.

© John Wiley & Sons, Inc.

Looking at some other options

Consider enrolling your dog in a doggie day care facility where they can meet and play with other dogs while you're away. It may take their mind off wondering where you are. Going to doggy day care can also provide more exercise for your dog. A tired dog is a happy dog and has happy owners. A truer statement has never been said. For more on your dog's social needs and the pros and cons of doggie day care, flip to Chapter 3.

For relatively mild cases of separation anxiety, a visit from a pet sitter during the time they're left alone may be enough to allay their anxiety.

Soiling the House

House soiling that occurs after you've housetrained your dog and that isn't marking behavior can have a variety of causes other than separation anxiety. Its usual causes are one or more of the following:

>> **You've left your dog too long without giving them a chance to relieve themselves.** As the saying goes, accidents happen, and that's just what it was — an accident. You know your dog's endurance and schedule, so don't blame the dog when for some reason you were unable to adhere to their needs. You may have had to work late, or some other unforeseen event prevented you from getting home on time. As long as it doesn't become a regular occurrence on your part, the behavior won't be a continuing problem. If it becomes a frequent occurrence, consider getting a dog walker to walk your dog at lunch and perhaps in the evening if you're going to be extra late. It also may be time to revisit using a crate while you are gone if you have stopped. By providing a smaller area to sleep and rest in, dogs will again be reminded to hold their potty routine to match your schedule.

>> **Your dog may have an upset stomach.** Abrupt dietary changes, such as changing dog foods, are the most common cause for an upset tummy. Any time you change your dog's diet, do so gradually by mixing the new food with their old food over a period of several days so that their system can get used to the new food.

Another cause of upset stomach may be from something they ate that didn't agree with them. Giving treats at holiday times that your dog ordinarily doesn't get, such as turkey and gravy or pizza, can create havoc with their digestive system. If the upset stomach continues, you need a trip to the veterinarian. Gastritis can be quite serious if allowed to continue.

>> **Your dog may have *cystitis,* or a bladder infection.** This condition is more common among female dogs than male dogs and may cause dribbling. Cystitis is an inflammation of the bladder wall that can be caused by a bacterial infection. It makes Buddy feel as if there's constant pressure on their bladder, and they think they have to urinate all the time, even after just relieving themselves. When they do urinate, it can burn, which in turn causes them to spend a lot of time cleaning themselves.

REMEMBER

Although not dangerous in and of itself, cystitis can cause all sorts of problems if left unattended, because the bacteria can spread up into the kidneys. If you see any of the preceding symptoms, a trip to your vet is a must. A short course of the appropriate antibiotics cures this inflammation quickly.

>> **If your dog is older, they may have developed urinary incontinence.** The slackening of the sphincter muscles that holds the urine in the bladder can cause incontinence, which often happens as your dog ages. So many dogs are put to sleep for this perceived problem, which although not easy to live with, can be solved in several ways, including being treated with medication.

A change in diet to a more natural diet also can often solve this problem (see Chapter 4). Finally, you can find many herbal and homeopathic remedies on the market specifically targeted at the kidney and bladder of older dogs. A good holistic vet can help you make the best choice for your dog.

>> **Your dog may be stressed.** Lifestyle changes, moving into a different house, work schedules changing, long-term company, or high levels of emotion in the household can all change a dog's routine to the point that anxiety causes changes for your dog. Be sensitive to the pets in your life. As your life changes, so does theirs. Stress is as real to dogs as it is to people. Give your dog what they need: exercise, mental stimulation, social time, and so on. Most behavior problems can be isolated to a change for the dog or a need not being met. Fix the need and you fix the problem.

TIP

While you're finding a vet to help you, you still have to live with the soiling problem. Put a tablecloth that's plastic on one side and soft on the other under your dog's blanket or bed. Doing so saves the furniture or floor, and both are easy to wash. You also can consider diapers, but only as a last resort because the urine may burn their skin. Don't give up on your dog friend — explore the alternatives and see how you can support Buddy.

Dribbling and Submissive Wetting

Dogs that are high in defense flight and low in defense fight drives are notorious for submissive wetting behavior. (See Chapter 2 for more on your dog's drives.) This behavior usually occurs upon first greeting the dog. He either squats or rolls over on their back and dribbles, dating back to their days as a puppy when their mother cleaned them.

REMEMBER

When Buddy dribbles urine, don't scold them, because it reinforces the submissive behavior and makes it worse. By scolding them, you only make them act even more submissively, which brings on the wetting. Also, don't stand or lean over your dog or try to pick them up, because that, too, makes them act submissively and causes wetting.

Fortunately, submissive wetting isn't difficult to solve. Follow these steps:

1. **When you come home, ignore your dog.**

    Don't approach Buddy; let them come to you instead. Go outside together and greet in the yard instead of inside the home.

2. **Greet your dog without making eye contact and by offering the palm of your hand.**

    This step is important. The back of the hand transmits negative energy, and the palm of the hand transmits positive energy.

REMEMBER

3. **Be quiet and let them sniff your palm.**

4. **Gently pet them under the chin, not on top of the head.**

    Be sure to pet under the chin rather than on top of the head, because dogs generally don't like being patted on the head. To them, it's much like a child being pinched on the cheeks.

5. **Don't reach for or try to grab the dog.**

    Reaching for or trying to grab them causes them to be afraid of you, creating anxiety and worsening the problem.

TIP

When friends visit you, they also can help you manage your dog's wetting behavior. Tell your visitors when they arrive to ignore the dog and let Buddy come to them. Instruct them about offering the palm of the hand and about not trying to pet or make eye contact with the dog.

Taking Buddy on the Road

Whenever possible, take your dog with you when you travel. Traveling with a well-trained dog is a real pleasure because you know they'll behave themselves around people and other dogs.

When you travel with your dog, you need to ensure that Buddy has the opportunity to stretch their legs every few hours, just as you do. The same rules of housetraining apply when you're traveling. If they're still a puppy, be prepared to stop about every two hours. An older dog can last much longer.

In the car, crate Buddy for their and your safety. For reasons not entirely clear to us, many people drive with their dog loose in the car. The problem with this situation occurs when you have to make an emergency stop — Buddy can be thrown, causing injury to them and possibly you and your passengers. If you drive a sedan that can't accommodate a crate appropriate for the size of your dog, at least get a barrier to install behind the first row of seats.

Start with a review of teaching Buddy door manners (see Chapter 14). After that, apply the same progressions teaching Buddy to enter and exit the car with particular emphasis on exiting.

WARNING

When given a chance, many dogs love to ride in the car and stick their head out of the window. Don't allow them to do this — it's dangerous! They may get hit by a pebble or stone thrown up by a car in front of you. They also can injure their eyes with flying debris.

TIP

When traveling with your dog, make a point to keep to their feeding schedule and exercising routine as closely as possible. Sticking to customary daily rhythm prevents digestive upsets that can lead to accidents.

Getting used to entering the vehicle

First, practice entering the car in the driveway or garage. Put Buddy's training collar on them and attach the leash to the live ring (see Chapter 5) to determine which is the live ring. Have them Sit and Stay, and then open the car door. If they move, reinforce the Stay command. (By now Buddy should sit on command; if they don't, head to Chapter 11.) Count to five and then tell them to get into the car with whatever command you have chosen — Get In for example. After they're in the car, take off the leash and close the door. If you're using a crate and they have been trained to get into the crate in the car, follow the same procedure except direct them to jump into their crate. Just remember to close the crate door so that it doesn't interfere with closing the car door.

REMEMBER

At first, some dogs may be reluctant to jump into the car or crate, in which case you have to lift them in. With several repetitions (and provided Buddy is physically able to jump into the car or crate), they'll do it on their own. Some dogs are too small to jump into the car without help. Ramps are great for those dogs who can't physically jump into the car or crate.

Staying put before exiting the vehicle

When taking Buddy on the road, an especially important exercise is teaching them to stay in the vehicle when you open the door from the outside. That way you can leash them before letting them out. Your dog should never exit the car or crate without your permission word. See Chapter 14 for door manners and getting out of a crate. An open door isn't an invitation for your dog to leap out. Put on Buddy's leash before giving them the Okay exit command.

If Buddy tries to make a move to get out of the car, close the door. (Be careful that you don't slam their tail or any of their limbs in the door!) Repeat opening and closing the door until they stay so that you can attach the leash to their training collar. Then, count to five and release them with "Okay" to exit the car.

Review these sequences over several sessions until both of you are comfortable with the procedure and the rules. When Buddy reliably remains in the car, you need to practice around distractions. On a weekend, go to the local park when it's busy with people and dogs. Exit the car, crack open the door through which they'll exit, and close it again, open a crack, close it again, repeating until they remember their job isn't to leave without permission. Then open the door all the way, and they'll tell you whether they need more training.

Getting ready for your road trip

In preparation for your road trip, you need to train Buddy to ride in the car and to get in and out of it as we describe in the preceding sections. You don't want to be in a position of having to take Buddy out of the car at a busy interstate rest stop for a potty break and have them get loose.

If Buddy is used to relieving himself off leash, you may want to teach them to eliminate on leash on command. (A good phrase is the "Hurry up and go potty. Hurry up.") After all, when you stop during your trip at a busy rest stop and are looking for a few blades of grass, you certainly can't have Buddy off leash. Dogs need to practice going potty on leash if they're used to relieving themselves in a fenced yard. This is the only time a flex or retractable leash can come in handy. A retractable leash allows Buddy to get farther away from you and move more freely to find the perfect spot to potty. A good practice is to leave a retractable leash in the vehicle for such needs.

Make sure you also pack all their possessions needed for the trip, such as their collar and leash, water and food, blankets, bowls, toys, towels to dry them off in case they get wet, cleanup material if they throw up or have an accident, baggies for multipurpose cleanup and disposal, and any medications. You may want to make a list so that you don't forget anything. Buddy needs their own suitcase or bag to store everything.

If you're planning to visit relatives or friends and Buddy is going to stay in their home, about a week before the trip start reviewing Buddy's basic exercises — Sit and Stay (no jumping up on people), Down, Come (you can use the Touch command), and Leave It. (You can read about all these exercises in Chapters 9 through 11.) Your hosts will be impressed with (and appreciative of) how well-behaved Buddy is.

When you arrive at your destination and are finished with the hugs and hellos, immediately take Buddy to an area where they can relieve themselves. If necessary, clean up after them, too. Above all, try to stick to Buddy's daily routine as much as possible, especially their feeding and elimination schedule. It would be most embarrassing if they had an accident in the house.

TIP

A good habit is stopping a mile or so from your destination beforehand to allow Buddy to relieve themselves. Arriving at the homes of friends and family or at hotels often distracts us for too long and we forget to see to Buddy's needs in a timely fashion.

Easing carsickness

Some dogs get carsick, which manifests itself in excessive drooling or vomiting, and can be attributed to

>> True motion sickness

>> A negative association with riding in a car

Dogs that tend to get carsick usually aren't taken for rides very often. And when they're taken for a ride, it's usually to the vet. You can compare their reaction to that of a child who, every time they get in the car, goes to the doctor for a shot. It doesn't take many repetitions before your dog makes an unpleasant association with your car.

Some dogs get sick in vans because they *can't* see out of the window, and others get sick in cars because they *can* see out of the window. In the latter case, covering the crate may solve the problem.

REMEMBER

Whatever the reason for the dog's reaction, you can create a pleasant association with the car. By working with your dog to make car rides a positive experience, you can tell how well they're taking to the car and how much time you need to spend at each sequence.

Throughout the following remedial exercise, maintain a light and happy attitude. Avoid a solicitous tone of voice and phrases such as, "It's all right. Don't worry. Nothing is going to happen to you." These reassurances validate the dog's concerns and reinforce their phobia about the car. Buddy will think you're praising them for their anxiety. Here's what to do:

1. **Open all the car doors and, with the engine off, lure or put Buddy in their crate (see Chapter 14 for crate training), which is in the car.**

You also can feed them in their crate. After they're in the crate (no matter how they got there), give them a treat, tell them how proud you are of them, and immediately let them out again. Repeat this step until they're comfortable in their crate in the car.

2. **When Buddy is confident getting into the crate, close the doors on one side of the car, with the engine still shut off.**

3. **When they're comfortable with Step 2, tell your dog to get in the crate, give them a treat, and close all the doors.**

   Let them out again and give them a treat. Repeat until they readily go into the crate, and you can close all the doors for up to one minute.

4. **Tell your dog to get into the crate, close all the doors, get into the car with them, and start the engine.**

   Give your dog a treat. Turn off the engine and let them out.

5. **Now it's time for a short drive — no more than once around the block or out the driveway and back in.**

   Increase the length of the rides, always starting and ending with a treat or a game they love.

When Buddy is comfortable riding in the car, make it a point to take them for a ride on a regular basis. You want the ride to be a pleasant experience for them, like going for a walk in the park — not just the annual trip to the vet. Even taking a ride that ends back at home can be a positive trip.

WARNING

You need to be careful about leaving Buddy unattended in the car for more than 10 minutes when the outside temperature is greater than 60 degrees Fahrenheit and the sun is shining. The temperature inside a car, even with the windows partially open, rises quickly.

TIP

If you discover that they truly have motion sickness, give Buddy a ginger cookie when you start your journey in the car — the ginger will help to calm their stomach.

Going to Doggie Day care

Doggie day care has become almost as popular as day care for children and with good reason. The dog isn't left alone at home alone for the entire day with nothing to do (except possibly get into mischief). At doggie day care they get to play with other dogs and have a good time for most of the day (Figure 19-2 is a great example). When their owners pick up Buddy in the afternoon, they're sufficiently tired and don't make any other demands on them except dinner.

FIGURE 19-2:
Dogs getting the
exercise and
social interactions
that they need
and want.

© John Wiley & Sons, Inc.

Dogs don't have to be trained for day care, but most likely they'll be evaluated beforehand. For their own convenience in handling the dogs, the staff may train the dogs to understand at least the Sit and Stay commands. The environments that day care facilities offer vary enormously; they may be spa-like or spartan. Most have an indoor facility, but many also have an outdoor area. Some offer grooming, bathing, and training as well. Some even have swimming pools. Check ones in your area to see if you like how the staff interacts with the dogs and how much exercise your dog will get.

REMEMBER

Before committing to a day care facility, you should have a chance to evaluate the facility and its program, and the facility will have the opportunity to evaluate Buddy. For you, things to look for are cleanliness, supervision, the number of dogs in a given space, indoor and outdoor areas, ratio of staff to the number of dogs, appropriate rest times for the dogs, and how they're housed during this time (they're usually crated). Rest breaks between play sessions are also important. Don't forget to ask about rest for your dog during the day. You and Buddy both have to be comfortable with your choice, but Buddy's opinion is particularly important. Do they look forward to going to that facility, or do they balk? Pay attention to how *Buddy* feels.

Minding Your Manners at the Dog Park

Many communities have dog parks — designated areas where dogs can run and play off leash. Some parks are fenced, and some aren't. Some municipalities make the park available to the community; other parks are privately operated. Both may restrict entry, either by residency requirements or fees. All dog parks have rules, which are posted at the entrance (if the park is fenced).

REMEMBER

The two main rules require you to pick up after your dog and to control them at all times. Unfortunately, both rules often are ignored. It never ceases to amaze how many so-called "conscientious" dog owners seem to be oblivious to these rules. One of the main reasons for the nation's growing anti-dog sentiment stems from the fact that so many dog owners don't clean up after their dogs and don't keep them under control. The gyrations some owners go through to get their dogs to come to them when it's time to go home are prime-time comedy.

Before you ever take Buddy to a dog park, make sure you have distraction-trained them to come when called. And keep in mind that when you take them to the dog park for the first time, it's best to take off the leash; the vast majority of dogfights occur when one or both dogs are leashed. The "regulars" at the park will have formed a pack, which will rush up to Buddy, the newcomer, to investigate. Although perfectly normal, the experience can be overwhelming for Buddy. Fortunately, it rarely results in an altercation as long as everyone stays calm. After the initial greeting ceremony is over, everyone will go their own way. Promise Buddy and yourself that you won't enter a dog park if you think too many unruly dogs are inside. Stand outside your car for a minute and watch what's going on inside. Go back home if you don't feel comfortable.

Almost every park has a bully, so it's your responsibility to keep your eye on Buddy to intervene, if necessary. The owner of the bully is usually singularly oblivious to what their dog is doing — and much less interested in correcting the undesired behavior. Because bullies "teach" other dogs bullying behaviors, the owner needs to correct the bully's behavior.

WARNING

Even under the best of circumstances, dog parks contain some hazards. After visiting a dog park you should thoroughly clean your shoes or take them off before you go into the house. (You can even reserve one pair just for the dog park.) Before letting your dog into the house, thoroughly clean their feet (consult your vet for a safe disinfectant). Moreover, if you regularly visit a dog park, you should get biannual fecal examinations for your dog from your vet.

Keeping Your Canine Calm at the Vet's Office

Most dogs don't like to go to the vet's office, whether it's something serious or just for the semiannual or annual checkup. People experience similar feelings about their own annual physicals.

For the untrained dog, the anxiety level of going to the vet is increased by the owner, who's fidgeting with the dog, telling them not to do this, to quit doing that, to behave themselves, to calm down, to sit still, to not visit, and on and on. Because the dog hasn't been trained, they don't have a clue what their owner wants, so they have an increase in apprehension.

For the trained dog, the owner's message is reassuring — "Sit," "Down," "Stay," and "Good dog!" are all commands they're used to. Instead of hearing "Don't do whatever you're doing," he hears "Good dog." (See Chapter 9 for basic training.) And keep in mind that the trip in the car to the vet's office may also be traumatic if the dog isn't used to the car. To avoid this problem, check out the earlier section "Taking Buddy on the Road."

Being Patient with the Rescue Dog

The main problem with rescues isn't that they're inherently different from a puppy you may get from a reputable breeder; the issue is that you don't know their background. Many dogs are brought to the shelter for no other reason than that they've outgrown that cute puppy stage. Others are turned in because they've become unmanageable — read this to mean they suffer from a "lack of basic training." The reasons vary, some legitimate though most not.

The majority of rescue dogs turn out to be fine pets with training and good health. After several weeks of getting used to their new homes, most are happy to be where they are. Even so, some come with behavioral baggage of unknown causes. The most common is separation anxiety, ranging from mild to severe. (You can read more about this behavioral issue in the earlier section, "Coping with Separation Anxiety.") Another one is unexplained aggressive-appearing behavior (see Chapter 18). Many of the quirks of rescues can be solved, but it starts with basic training.

Chapter **20**

Keeping Your Senior Dog Young: Teaching an Old Dog New Tricks

Old dogs are wonderful to have around. They have known you for so long, have shared so many memories with you, have been there for you through good times and bad, and know your every move. They're precious resources and loving family members, and they deserve the best you can give them. Some good souls also adopt older dogs; these dogs can be wonderful pets as well. Older dogs require less exercise as a rule and are often trained to a certain degree.

In this chapter, we discuss the best ways to train these senior citizens so that they stay healthy, happy, and young at heart. We also provide some reminders about the importance of keeping your older dog well groomed. If you want to introduce a young canine friend to your senior dog, we provide tips on the best ways to do that as well.

REMEMBER

Older dogs thrive on knowing their daily routines. They wake up at a certain hour and go to the door to be let out for their morning or evening walk. They like to eat at set mealtimes. In fact, you often can set your clock by their habits. Adhering to Buddy's customary routine is extra important if they're losing their sight and/or hearing. If they're becoming deaf, remember that they can't hear you when you approach. To avoid startling them, make sure you gently touch them when approaching them. Old dogs startle quickly and may get irritable if they're woken up abruptly. Changing Buddy's routine can cause needless anxiety to your old friend.

Old Gray Muzzle: Exploring the Signs of Aging in Dog Years

What does "old" really mean? In the case of dogs, old is breed-specific; the aging process is related to the size of the dog. The life expectancy of giant breeds, such as Mastiffs or Newfoundlands, is often only 7 to 8 years, whereas smaller dogs live older than 15 years. Medium to large dogs live 10 to 13 years. If these dogs have been fed a species-appropriate diet (raw food), they then become old much later — giant breeds around 12, medium size dogs around 14, and small or toy dogs around 16 to 18. See Chapter 4 for Wendy's advice on feeding healthy food.

A number of factors affect life expectancy in dogs. At the top of the list is diet, which shouldn't come as a surprise. A dog's muzzle doesn't have to turn completely gray with age unless there's a genetic component. They'll have some white hairs for sure, but if you feed and supplement Buddy correctly, they can age without looking old at all. (The later section "Taking Care of Your Older Dog's Health and Nutrition Needs" provides some pointers.)

REMEMBER

Another factor is spaying and neutering. Recent studies show that spayed females lived longest of dogs dying of all causes, whereas nonspayed females lived longest of dogs dying of natural causes. Although neutering protects your male dog against testicular cancer, studies have shown that neutered males have the shortest life-span, probably as a result of prostate cancer.

Depending on the breed of your dog, you may see the signs of aging beginning from 7 years on and sometimes even before. Signs are graying of the muzzle, loss of hearing and vision, arthritis, an inability to get around, weight gain and decreased energy. Some of these changes can be delayed by following the simple preventative steps that we suggest in this chapter.

TIP

For more information on how to take care of your older pet, see *Senior Dogs For Dummies* by Susan McCullough (Wiley).

Teaching Exercises to Keep Buddy's Mind and Body Sharp

The value of exercise as your dog ages can't be overemphasized. Just as humans have less energy, less muscle mass, and less ability and endurance as they age, dogs experience the same things. Humans can enroll in classes at the gym to keep themselves supple, but your dog relies on you for help.

In the following sections, we show you some exercises for your dog that involve the use of most of Buddy's muscles, tendons, and ligaments. Remember that muscles keep bones in place. So, keeping Buddy's muscles flexible will strengthen their skeletal system and their heart and lungs, improve their circulation, and help to keep their immune system strong. We also make suggestions on how to keep their mind sharp. Training your old friend can be fun for you and your dog, and it can add years to their lives.

REMEMBER

Do be careful that you don't ask too much from Buddy. If you find they're stressing or unable to do a certain exercise because it's painful, have your veterinarian check them out.

TIP

Many of these exercises require you to use treats as motivation. Treats should be small and not too hard and should provide very few calories. Look for treats that have only three or four ingredients in them or whole food treats like dehydrated liver or jerky treats. Stay away from food made in China, because there is no assurance that what is listed in the ingredients in the treats is actually accurate. Plus, treats made in China have no quality control and have been recalled many times, causing sickness and even death.

Begging

The balancing act in this exercise makes use of most of the muscles along Buddy's back as well as stomach and side muscles. Balancing strengthens Buddy's *core,* or center body muscles. How your dog is built determines whether they're able to achieve perfect balance without help or whether you may have to assist them by holding their front paws. Strong core muscles allow Buddy to run and turn more easily. Here's what to do:

1. **With your dog sitting in front of you, hold a treat about an inch above their nose.**

   You can find out more about the Sit command in Chapter 11.

2. **As they stretch their neck to reach the treat, slowly elevate the treat until Buddy is sitting on their haunches.**

   Getting themselves balanced takes a while, so be patient. After they balance themselves, give them the treat.

3. **Increase the time that Buddy holds the begging position until they can hold it for about 15 seconds.**

   Repeat four times each session.

Crawling

Crawling stretches the back and neck muscles, which helps Buddy to remain limber and able to look up, down, and to the right and left. Practice this exercise on a soft surface so Buddy doesn't graze their elbows or stifle (knee) joints. Nearly all breeds of dogs can do this exercise. Follow these steps to help your dog do the crawling exercise:

1. **With a treat in your right hand, have Buddy sit at your left side.**

2. **Put your left-hand palm down on Buddy's shoulders and slowly lower the treat between their front paws.**

   As Buddy follows the treat, slowly, an inch at a time, pull the treat forward with your right hand.

3. **As they lower their body, keep your left hand on Buddy's shoulders so they can't get up; they should start to crawl towards the treat.**

REMEMBER

   Be careful not to apply too much pressure on their back, because doing so will stop their ability to crawl forward and it may hurt them.

   Aim for four crawls and then reward them. Repeat four times during a session, each time starting from the sitting position. As Buddy gets the hang of this exercise, you can increase the number of crawls before rewarding them.

Walking backward

Walking backward strengthens the muscles of Buddy's back legs. As we mention earlier, muscles keep bones in place. With older dogs, their hips and back legs often become arthritic. *Arthritis* occurs when bone grinds on bone and inflammation appears, causing pain and discomfort. To help if they already have some arthritis, or to help prevent it, keep back leg muscles in shape. (You also may want to check with your veterinarian about getting monthly Adequan shots, which are excellent for relieving arthritis in dogs. Or consider using Myristin, which is an arthritis supplement.) The muscles and nerves in this part of the body control the bladder and rectum. Keeping them strong helps Buddy to avoid incontinence in old age. Try these steps to teach Buddy to walk backward (see Figure 20-1):

1. **With Buddy standing in front of you, take a treat and hold it at their nose level.**

2. **Slowly take tiny steps toward them, and when they step backward, reward them.**

   Do it again, aiming for two steps. Reward each increment. Your goal is to reach 25 steps per training session before rewarding. Build up to 100 steps, rewarding every 25 steps. Be careful to keep your hands still and in the same position.

FIGURE 20-1:
A 12-year-old dog walking backward.

© John Wiley & Sons, Inc.

Doing neck and head stretches

The following head and neck stretching exercises help keep Buddy's muscles in their head and neck region supple. The nerves to the eyes, ears, and mouth are all contained in this area of the body, so keeping the muscles along their cervical spine stretched will keep their head, neck, mouth, teeth, and gums in good shape. If you start these exercises around the age of 8, they can go a long way to preventing loss of hearing and sight as Buddy ages. If your dog is older than 12 when you start these exercises, they'll probably be stiff in the beginning, so go slowly. If you're persistent and do these exercises with Buddy daily, you'll be surprised at how quickly the flexibility comes back.

Here's how to do it:

1. **With Buddy sitting in front of you, take a treat and slowly lower it between their front legs.**

   Don't let them lie down, but allow them to stretch their neck far enough down to reach the treat. Reward them when they reach the treat.

2. **Take another treat and slowly move it past their shoulder, first to the right and then to the left, having Buddy stretch their neck as far as they can.**

   Reward each stretch. See Figure 20-2 to see this step in action.

3. **Take the treat and hold it just above their head so they stretch upward.**

   Reward them when they stretch for the treat.

FIGURE 20-2:
Neck stretches to keep Buddy in shape.

© John Wiley & Sons, Inc.

Using the coffee table stretch

The coffee table stretch is an important one to do because it helps stretch Buddy's spine. When their spine is in good shape, they'll move around much more freely and easily. Follow these steps:

1. **Tell Buddy to lie down just a few inches in front of a coffee table.**

   To find out more about the Down command, head to Chapter 11.

2. **Put a treat on the edge of the table and tell Buddy to stand and stretch forward for the treat.**

WARNING

   Be careful not to put the treat too far from them. You don't want them to walk toward it; rather, you want them to stand up from the down position and stretch. This exercise goes slowly in the beginning because Buddy has to figure out what to do, but be patient.

Walking, sitting, and downing

Walking, sitting, and downing are all great for keeping Buddy in shape. Simple as these activities seem, they go a long way to exercise all the muscles in Buddy's body. You can do them inside around the house, but it's better if you can take them for a ten-minute walk and practice daily. It makes their daily walks more fun, and it's good for you, too. Have a pocketful of treats before you leave! Here are the steps to take:

1. **With Buddy on leash at your left side, walk ten steps forward and say, "Sit."**

   If Buddy doesn't sit, use a treat to help them sit. See Chapter 11 for details.

2. **Go ten steps and say, "Down."**

   If they won't, head to Chapter 11 to see how to teach Buddy the Down command. Each session you can alternate between a Sit and a Down, two times each. Make sure you make a big fuss over them and reward them by giving them a treat when they're successful.

Swimming

One of the best exercises for Buddy is swimming. It allows them to use their entire body without putting pressure on their aging joints. More and more facilities now have hydrotherapy pools for dogs. These pools have a current that can be adjusted. (Figure 20-3 shows a senior dog enjoying a swim.) If Buddy doesn't know how to swim, look for a facility where a qualified instructor is in the pool with your dog.

Start slowly, building up Buddy's stamina to 20 minutes, two to three times per week. Most of swimming facilities insist that Buddy wear a life jacket, and they have a selection for you to choose from that will fit. This is a good safety requirement.

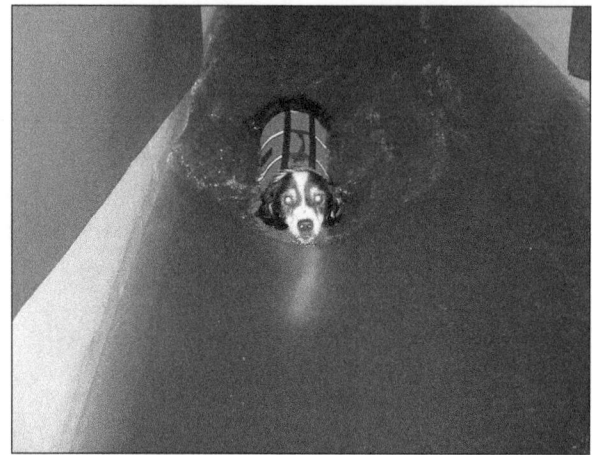

FIGURE 20-3:
Swimming is a great activity for your senior dog.

REMEMBER

You can find facilities close to you by using your favorite browser to search for hydrotherapy pools for dogs. Be sure to enter your town and state in the keywords. Visit the facility before you book an appointment for Buddy to swim. You want to make sure that the facility is clean and that a qualified person will be swimming with your dog. Avoid pools that are dirty or where dogs are left to swim around by themselves. Also avoid those where the dogs are tethered across the pool to make them swim in place. This setup is used only at pools in veterinary facilities where qualified instructors are supervising the swimming and monitoring the heart rate of the dogs.

Another possibility is taking Buddy to a local lake or pond, but do due diligence. Check the body of water thoroughly before you allow Buddy to swim in it. Many ponds and lakes are in rural areas and serve as a runoff for farm fields or contain deadly algae. These farm fields are heavily fertilized, and the runoff goes into the pond or lake. Also, the bacterial count in most ponds is very high, especially around the muddy edges. If you find that Buddy is scratching and gets runny eyes after swimming in one of these areas, don't go back. Bathe them immediately and take them to your veterinarian to determine whether they have picked up a staph infection.

If you have your own swimming pool, and it has steps where Buddy can get in and out, let them have the occasional swim. However, be aware that the chlorine in the pool can irritate their eyes, making them red and runny. Too much swimming in a chlorinated pool can dry out their coat, so you may have to add extra oil to their food. (See www.volharddognutrition.com for the oil we recommend.) Also, keep in mind that dogs that are not used to swimming can tear the liner of the pool.

Applying mental stimulation

Treat dispensers are a great way to keep any dog amused and mentally sharp. These toys range from puzzles to simple rubber toys with holes for treats. Most rely on the concept of putting a treat in the toy and letting the dog figure out how to get the treat out of the toy. Whether pushing around the toys with their noses or using their paws, these toys can be great fun for dogs. Our only objection to some of them is that they can be really noisy when pushed around on a hardwood floor.

TIP

You can find many complex interactive toys and puzzles on Amazon.

Playing games indoors also can be helpful for stimulating your dog mentally. In the winter, you may not be able to exercise Buddy outside, so having several games and toys that can be played indoors is necessary to keep Buddy exercised both physically and mentally.

TIP

To exercise your dog's mind, play the Find It game, which is really easy to do. Follow these steps:

1. **Show your dog their favorite toy, leave them on a Sit-Stay, and place the toy close to the door of the room.**

   To read about the Sit-Stay, check out Chapter 11.

2. **Return to your dog and point to the toy with your hand closest to your dog while telling them to "Find It" and bring it back to you.**

   After they have learned Find It, start placing the toy around the corner and send them to fetch it. Gradually increase the level of difficulty by putting the toy in different places around the house. Dogs love this game, and it keeps them mentally stimulated.

Last but not least, take Buddy to a new area to walk once a week. Make sure it's safe to let them off leash and to do all the normal doggie things like smelling and wandering around. If you have a friend who has a dog that's a friend of Buddy's, make a date so the dogs can walk together. These weekly walks will give Buddy something to look forward to, and both dogs will be content. Being mentally stimulated and being allowed to be a dog are two of the kindest things you can do for your old friend.

Taking Care of Your Older Dog's Health and Nutrition Needs

To understand why good nutrition is vital to the health and well-being of your dog (which in turn affects their ability to learn and your ability to train them), you need to think of Buddy's body as a machine that has an engine. For the engine to work correctly, all the component parts of the engine must be in good order. It must be given the correct fuel (that is, food); for example, if the fuel given is of the wrong blend, the engine may splutter and lose power. If the fuel is totally incorrect, the engine may stop working altogether. As your dog ages, their engine needs to be given the very best fuel you can afford. In the following sections, we provide you with information regarding feeding your senior pup and keeping them healthy with supplements.

Maintaining Buddy's slim and trim figure with a satisfying diet

How much and what kind of food you feed Buddy as they age depends on you. You're in charge of how much and what Buddy eats. Keeping them slim to the point you can feel their ribs (but not see them) is your contribution to keeping them healthy. Studies show that a decrease in caloric intake can add years to Buddy's life. Vets report that more than 50 percent of all older dogs they see are grossly overweight. Just as obesity in humans creates all sorts of health hazards, the same applies to dogs. Heart disease, diabetes, cancer, and joint problems are all associated with Buddy being overweight.

Buddy has an uncanny knowledge of what's good for them and what isn't. If they become a picky eater on the food you're currently feeding, head to Chapter 4 and review some healthy alternatives. If Buddy isn't getting the exercise that they need and they're overweight, you need to cut down the amount of food you're feeding. Try decreasing the food by about 10 percent for a week and see if that helps. Add in some fresh raw foods to satisfy their hunger. If they maintain their weight, you're putting in more calories than they're burning on a daily basis. Cut back 25 percent and see if that decrease trims them down.

REMEMBER

Be careful not to give high-calorie treats. Use fresh vegetables like pieces of carrot, cucumber, or broccoli instead. Raw fruits can be used in moderation. Apples are favorites with many dogs, but peel them first to remove the skin, which harbors the insecticide sprays used in growing them.

Here's one of our favorite sayings: "If your dog is overweight, *you're* not getting enough exercise." Get your dog moving to help keep their weight in check. Take them for walks and play games with them. See the earlier section "Teaching Exercises to Keep Buddy's Mind and Body Sharp" for some tips.

If you haven't switched to a balanced, raw food, or a supplemented commercial diet, now may be the time to do so. In terms of prolonging Buddy's life, a balanced, raw food diet is the best you can feed. Raw food is easy to digest, and you control Buddy's caloric intake with this type of diet. It provides all the nutrients needed in old age and breaks down and converts to energy.

The diet we recommend is called NDF2. All you have to do is to add water and the meat your dog likes best. In fact, this diet is used by a lot of the top-winning show and working dogs in the country. If you watch the Westminster Dog Show, you'll see many dogs that are fed this way. Chapter 4 provides information on all these diet options.

WARNING

According to a study by Tufts University of 100 commercially available foods, so-called "lite" or weight-management dog foods for older dogs have shown a wide variance of calories recommended to maintain a dog. In fact, many of them recommend more calories than an older dog requires. With most of these foods, pets would actually gain weight if the owners adhered to the feeding directions on the labels. These foods generally are full of indigestible grains. These make Buddy's body work harder to break down the food in their stomach that doesn't give them energy. And often poor Buddy experiences gas when on these foods. Not what we recommend for your old friend.

If you must use a dry kibble for your dog, at least add some fresh foods and supplements so that their digestion works better and they feel better. If you feed Buddy correctly, they'll feel like a puppy again.

Making life easier with supplements

As Buddy ages, they'll need some supplements so they can digest and break down their food and medications. For example, chances are high that they'll need a supplement to support their aging joints. You'll also want to use supplements to boost their immune system and improve their cognitive abilities.

The $5 billion yearly supplement industry produces thousands of products. It's overwhelming to the average dog owner and almost impossible to make an informed choice. We've made the job easier by listing in the following sections the supplements we have used successfully over the years. Unless otherwise noted, these products are available through www.volharddognutrition.com.

Digestive enzymes

To readily absorb food and utilize it, senior dogs (those older than 8) need to be supplemented with digestive enzymes. Enzymes help practically all body systems function better. Digestive enzymes specifically break down food particles for storage in the liver or muscles and are used when the body needs them. They're naturally secreted along the digestive tract and help the nutrients in food to be absorbed into the bloodstream.

REMEMBER

As Buddy ages, the production of these enzymes slows down and the food they eat isn't as well absorbed and turned into energy. Supplemental digestive enzymes are particularly useful for dogs who experience digestive upsets, such as vomiting and diarrhea, and who have gas and have problems with weight control. Digestive enzymes also help older dogs that are on medication; they make it easier to absorb and cause it to work better.

Immune booster

To rebuild the immune system, the Immune Booster supplement is a vitamin/mineral mix that contains colostrum. *Colostrum* is the yellowish fluid that's secreted by the mammary glands of mammals after they've given birth. It contains high levels of proteins and immune factors that help to protect the newborn from infection. Sources used in supplements generally come from either cows or pigs. Colostrum boosts the body's immune system, burns fat, and builds lean muscle. It's especially useful in healing the body, so you can use it for any dog who has experienced surgery, illness, or trauma of any kind. It also can be used before and after vaccination. Colostrum works quickly, and we recommend its use for only three weeks. Too much colostrum can make your dog very itchy. Look on Amazon for this type of supplement.

Myristin (arthritis formula)

Cetyl myristoleate is a unique fatty acid ester incorporated into the fat layers of cell membranes. It's often referred to as the WD-40 for joints because of its lubricating qualities. Myristin helps to reduce pain and inflammation caused by bone grinding against bone. It helps over a period of a month or so to rebuild the synovial fluid that stops bones rubbing together. We recommend this arthritis formula for dogs with weak rear ends, dogs who limp, and all older dogs experiencing arthritis.

System Saver

The System Saver supplement is an herbal anti-inflammatory that contains frankincense, green tea, turmeric, and orange-peel flavonoids. It's effective for use with hip dysplasia, arthritis, tendonitis, dermatitis, autoimmune and degenerative disorders, and inflammatory bowel and respiratory diseases that haven't responded to traditional medications. It has shown amazing results in skin problems that have genetic tendencies and that are impossible to cure otherwise.

RNA

Ribonucleic acid (RNA) is one of the substances used successfully for aging and degenerative diseases. By taking a capsule twice a day, RNA has been found to increase skin elasticity and to energize the body. It's antiviral and has cognitive enhancing effects. The idea behind using RNA is that you provide the cells with an abundance of their basic building materials to repair any damage caused by aging. Look for it on Amazon.

Keeping Up with Grooming

Grooming Buddy as they get older is critical to their well-being. If they feel well, they're easier to train. Simple things like keeping their nails short, their coat brushed out, and their ears and teeth clean makes them feel good.

REMEMBER

As Buddy ages, it's not as easy as it was for them to take part in self-grooming. Older dogs aren't as flexible as they used to be. So reaching their rear ends or tummies to clean may not be possible for some dogs, especially if they're overweight. As a result, their fur can get matted easily. Look under Buddy's arms to make sure that their freedom of movement isn't curtailed by mats.

In addition to your normal grooming for Buddy, here's a rundown of the things you should get in the habit of doing for them every week when they're older:

>> **Put some time aside to give Buddy a really good brush (and wash) from top to toe.** Brushing stimulates the skin by bringing blood to the surface and keeps it healthy by removing dead fur. Just because you have a smooth-haired dog or one that goes to the groomer every six weeks doesn't mean that a weekly brush isn't necessary. Pay particular attention to the rear, the underside of the tail, and the back of the hind legs. Look for any discharge from the genitals and any fur mats that may make it uncomfortable for your older dog to get up and down easily. They may get some feces stuck on the fur around their rectum or urine on their back legs, but frequent washing of this part of their body will prevent skin burns. We suggest using a coconut oil shampoo, which is gentle and doesn't take the oil out of their coat. Trimming the hair around these areas makes it easier to keep clean for both of you.

» **Check Buddy's ears for any odor and clean them.** If they have a musty odor, Buddy may have a yeast infection, which can be painful. And if it isn't treated, it can cause deafness. As a weekly cleanser you can use apple cider vinegar and water (half and half) on a cotton ball and wipe out the ears. Or, as long as Buddy has no sore spots, rubbing alcohol on a cotton ball does a great job for overall cleansing.

Be sure not to poke around too far in the ear — just clean the part you can easily see. Avoid using cotton swabs and sticking your finger into the ear canal. Not only is this painful for Buddy but you also can damage the ear.

» **Trim their nails regularly.** Buddy's nails don't get the wear and tear they did when they were young, so they don't wear down as easily. Allowing nails on the front feet to get too long forces the dog to walk on their nails and pushes their weight onto their shoulders, weakening them. As a general rule, when you can hear your dog's nails clicking along the floor when they walk, they're too long. If you feel you can't trim their nails by yourself, take your dog to the groomer or your vet for a trim on a regular basis. (See Chapter 6 for tips on getting a dog used to this practice.) Figure 20-4 shows a well-groomed set of nails. You'll notice that it's difficult to see the nails on this dog's foot. If you can see the nails sticking out, they're likely too long.

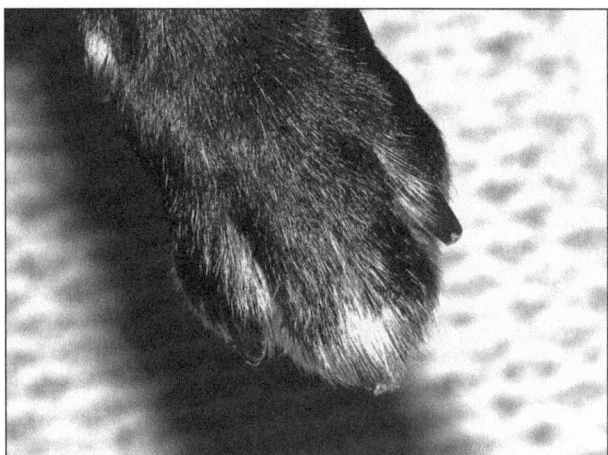

FIGURE 20-4:
Keeping your
senior's nails
short is a must.

© John Wiley & Sons, Inc.

» **Check Buddy's teeth.** Buddy's mouth is the gateway to their overall health. When the teeth get coated with tartar, their gums will become inflamed. Gum disease produces bacteria, which drains into their stomach and has been implicated in heart disease, strokes, and some cancers. To clean their teeth, you can use a toothbrush and some doggie toothpaste. Both are available at any pet store. An effective tartar remover is a gel called Petzlife (available at petzlife.com), which you rub onto Buddy's teeth daily. Petzlife also puts out an oral mist that you spray on their teeth. Both products work to dissolve the tartar in one month. This product is a good alternative to putting Buddy under anesthesia at the veterinarian for a teeth cleaning. With the correct diet and raw appropriate bones twice a week, Buddy's teeth should stay clean throughout their life (see Figure 20-5).

REMEMBER

If your dog's teeth are badly stained and their gums are inflamed, the only alternative is to take your dog to the veterinarian and have them put under anesthesia to have their teeth professionally cleaned. Anesthesia is a risk for Buddy at any age, but they could have an adverse reaction if they're older. Sometimes, you just can't avoid a professional veterinary teeth cleaning. Make sure that Buddy's blood panel is taken before they're put under anesthesia. This panel indicates the health of their liver (which has to metabolize the anesthesia), kidneys, heart, and so on. It can tell you whether it's safe for Buddy to have this procedure done. After their teeth are cleaned, use oral brushing or gel products on a regular basis.

FIGURE 20-5:
Clean teeth keep your old dog healthy.

© John Wiley & Sons, Inc.

>> **Keep Buddy's eyes clear and clean.** Homeopathic eye drops are a good choice for when Buddy's eyes get watery or weep liquid. This can happen when running in a different park or out in the country and can be a sign of allergies. We use Similasan Allergy Eye Relief, available at any large drug store. Even eye saline available where you buy contact supplies is a great flush for cleaning and rinsing out Buddy's eyes.

WARNING

Yellow or greenish discharge in Buddy's eyes usually indicates an infection and a trip to your veterinarian may be necessary. Don't let this go thinking it will resolve itself. It can lead to a more dangerous condition.

Bringing Home a Puppy to Help Rejuvenate Buddy

Raising a young dog and teaching them life's lessons in the presence of your older dog can help Buddy stay young. Plus, puppies brought up with older dogs are easy to train because they usually mimic the older dog's good behaviors. Figure 20-6 shows an older dog playing with a new puppy.

FIGURE 20-6:
Playing with a puppy keeps an older dog feeling young.

© John Wiley & Sons, Inc.

Don't wait too long to introduce a puppy to Buddy. Bring one in when your older dog is young enough to enjoy them. If your dog has been fed, trained, and exercised well, they really won't age that much until they're 11 or 12. Before Buddy is having trouble getting around is an ideal time to bring in the puppy. Buddy can still get around okay, teach the puppy manners, and enjoy their new companion's company. If your dog is showing signs of aging at 8 or so, don't wait any longer. Do it now, because the older dog, if they aren't feeling well, won't enjoy a puppy under foot.

REMEMBER

You can introduce a puppy into a household that has an older dog by following our suggestions in Chapter 6. The main thing to remember is that it's Buddy's house, and they have to invite the youngster to come in. Introductions are best done on neutral territory, such as the front lawn, the sidewalk, or somewhere away from the house. Let both dogs sniff each other all over. Buddy knows by smelling the puppy that they aren't a small grown dog but rather something tiny that needs help in learning to be a dog. Then, tell Buddy to take the puppy home. Let Buddy in the house first and have puppy follow them in. Make sure you always feed, brush, and train Buddy before the puppy. Buddy is number one, and peace will reign if they're treated that way.

Using a crate with the puppy is the best way to stop the puppy from jumping all over Buddy when they're taking their nap. When Buddy is teaching the puppy manners, its normal for Buddy to growl at times, just leave them alone to teach the lesson. However, don't let puppy take liberties with Buddy, and crate the puppy when it becomes obvious that Buddy dislikes the attention.

Looking Into Dog Beds, Ramps, Wheelchairs, and Carts

As Buddy ages, you need to provide a soft bed for them to sleep on so that their elbows, knees, and other joints are protected from hard surfaces. A soft bed is especially important if they're becoming arthritic. And if their back legs get weak and they have difficulty getting up and walking, you may need to purchase a product to help them maneuver higher places or simply stay mobile. In the following sections, we provide some information on products that we and our students have used over the years.

Making Buddy cozy: Beds

With a plethora of beds to choose from, you may find it difficult to determine which one is the best one for Buddy. The right one is mostly dependent on your dog's size. Make sure it's soft to protect their joints. When you have dog beds all over the house, you'll find at different times of the day the dogs will be stretched out on them enjoying their naps. Buy beds with washable outer covers. In the dog crates for traveling, a great idea is to use sheepskin-topped beds that are filled with either a microfiber pad or sponge in a waterproof casing that can be washed.

TIP

You'll find an enormous price difference in beds from different sources. Search the internet to comparison shop before investing in new beds. See Chapter 13 for other dog bed ideas.

The detergent you use to wash your dog beds is also important. Many of the popular brands contain chemicals that can cause contact allergies on the skin around the joints of older dogs. As Buddy ages, they sleep more than they did when they were younger and spend more time on their bed. So, if your dog gets a red rash where their body contacts the bed, changing your detergent may be in order. Look for hypoallergenic detergents, which should keep your dog from experiencing any contact allergies.

Making heights more manageable with ramps

Ramps aren't as important for smaller dogs as they are for dogs weighing more than 50 pounds. Small dogs can be lifted onto the couch or bed, into the car, or into the bathtub. However, the larger the dog, the stronger your back has to be. With the giant breeds, it's next to impossible to move them if you're alone.

TIP

We advise using a ramp while Buddy is still stable on their feet. Introduce it to them when they reach 8 years old or so. Train large dogs to use the ramp for getting into the vehicle and into the bathtub. Doing so is much less stressful for Buddy (and you) than trying to get them to jump up with their front legs so that you can lift up the rear.

Look for a ramp that is lightweight and telescopes down to a third of its size. These features make it easy to pack on top of or next to the crate in the car. One place to look is www.amazon.com. Dog ramps can be pricey. There are many economic choices on Amazon. Look around for features that are to your liking and fit your dog.

Helping the handicapped dog: Wheelchairs and carts

Having your beloved dog become paralyzed in the rear and unable to move is heartbreaking. Disease, trauma, or old age can cause the paralysis. However, paralysis doesn't mean the end of life for your pet. A number of companies have designed wheelchairs or carts with wheels to support the rear end of your pet.

Wendy once had an old German Shepherd who became paralyzed at age 14. She never gave up on them, and it was her first introduction to using carts with wheels.

The cart was made to their measurements. The dog lived two more years using their cart and had a very happy life.

Your handicapped dog also can be fitted with a cart made to measure by an orthopedic veterinarian. Check out k9carts.com to find their products. At this company's website, you can see a video of how dogs manage to retrieve, run, and go for long walks in their carts, enjoying every moment. You can also find similar canine wheelchairs on Amazon.com and Chewy.com.

A TRAINED DOG EQUALS A GREATER BOND

The house seems empty. I (Mary Ann) lost my dog to cancer. The heartache is a pain that many understand, yet some don't, because they've chosen to live without a pet. I don't really understand people who don't live with pets in their lives. Of course, owning a pet is a true lifestyle change; I do understand that. Having no pets and losing out on the love you get from them, no matter how short lived, is something I would never choose.

My husband and I lost one of my dogs, my show dog, an obedience, agility, rally, trick dog — a dog that went with me to schools to meet children and be an ambassador of her kind, a good, well-trained dog, my beloved Australian Shepherd Benna (see the photo). Training a dog completes the bond you can have with a dog. After you've trained a dog, they are yours forever. My life's goal is to share the knowledge of training with everyone I can so they too can know the love of a well-trained dog.

© John Wiley & Sons, Inc.

(continued)

(continued)

Benna came into my life while I still had my last show dog working and doing well in his field. I didn't realize it, but Benna would be held at bay by him until I began to think she was a bit of a loner. When we lost him though, Benna blossomed into her own. It's not that she wasn't there by my side before he died. It was just that she occupied his place next to me after he left it, which was nice. She was special, beautiful, and loving. And she was a big presence, too. She was a guard dog, protecting us from the daily postal carrier, the neighbor's driveway usage, and every stray squirrel that dared enter her domain. And now that presence is gone.

I don't have that sidekick, that 50-pound hunk of gorgeous hair nestled by my desk. She wasn't ready to go; she was in perfect health, or so I thought. But silent cancer crept in and yanked her from me while I was traveling abroad. It was hemangiosarcoma, which is the silent cancer because with it, the dog feels just fine, until the day she didn't. And that was the day we lost her. I'm glad to think she felt fine until that day, but I'm sad that I wasn't with her the day she didn't. She wasn't alone though. Others were there and that's what matters. The choice was made during emergency surgery, which was the right and only decision. My friend was keeping her during our travels, and she immediately noticed the change in Benna's attitude. Benna was rushed into surgery and was cared for all the way. But now the house is empty.

My Aussies didn't care about their own comfort as long as they were near me. That's the difference I feel — palpable with the emptiness in my heart and at my feet.

I can't imagine living without her presence. Sure, the house is cleaner without a dog, and the house is quieter and my guests are easier to host without managing the dog as well. But my heart is emptier, and it's not just the house. My life is emptier, my office is emptier, and my day is quieter. How long can I let this go on? I need to miss Benna. I need to mourn the quiet. Then I will look around and find another heart dog. I can't live without my partner in life. I feel doing so is a tribute to the dog I loved and lost, to not ever want to live without the love of a dog in my life. My husband feels the same way about his dog and knows how I'm feeling without mine. We're a perfect match.

My previous dogs, the ones that came before Benna, each hold a special place in my memories, filling my life with stories and laughter. I choose life with a trained dog, and I suffer the loss without her. It hurts, but having the moments of loss are worth it because I had the moments of joy. The time spent training your dog will give you the joy of dog ownership. Every training moment is part of that journey. My motto is and always will be: Know dog, know joy; no dog, no joy!

Chapter **21**

Saying Goodbye: Losing Your Old Friend

You have lived your dog's lifetime together. How lucky you are to have known Buddy for so long. Whether it's been years or decades, it's never long enough.

Whether from old age, illness, or worse — an accidental death — when you lose your friend, not everyone will understand how deeply you hurt. Surround yourself with other dog people if you can. Sharing your loss can be helpful and can ease your pain. But if you hear, "it was just a dog," move on and share with someone else; these people just don't understand and won't be able to help you right now.

Writing has always helped me (Mary Ann) — in a journal or a blog or to a friend. Here is something I wrote after the loss of one of my beloved dogs.

An Empty Collar

I now have an empty collar, sitting on my desk. It used to hold my laughing dog. Now it sits, at the base of my desk lamp, empty. What do you do with such mementos? They are priceless, with the DNA that surely is attached, microscopically to the leather. But instead of hugs and kisses, romps in the yard, rides in the car and days together, it will sit there on my desk and simply collect dust. I can't let that happen, but its usefulness is no longer required. My dog is gone. He hung on as long as he could, but we lost the battle yesterday. I have an assortment of these collars in my house. They have moved from beloved necks, to spots on my desk, then to memory boxes on the shelf. I cannot let them go. I can't imagine the day that this collar will go into a memory box. I want the neck back. I want to slip it over those ears and hear the jingle of the tag as it bounces along beside me. I am not ready to let it sit quiet, in its new spot. My desk is a good spot, though, I think. That collar was always within arm's reach, lifting if I looked its way, moving if I moved along. Now it will be right here, watching over me, helping me remember, as if I needed a memento to do that. I will miss having that collar along for the ride. I can hardly stand it, how I feel the ache in my fingers, with no hair to get tangled into. My eyes can now rest on that motionless tag as it hangs from the lamp. Right there, a breath away from me now. A beloved breath gone. Help me process the loss. Help me remember the love. Rest peacefully and please, wait for me, I have the collar which says on its tag, that you were mine.

FIGURE 21-1:
A dog's collar before it is empty.

As you can feel from this writing, grief is painful. Sometimes, when the loss is about to happen, it is obvious, but sometimes it isn't always clear. I have always felt that knowing that the time is now is the last gift we can give to our beloved pet. The end of suffering is a gift.

REMEMBER

Some can see it's time when others can't accept it and are therefore blind to the inevitable. Once, after looking at photos taken before the passing of an old dog, my husband could *now* see what he couldn't see then. He made me promise to never let him be blind again if it ever came to that once more. I said I would help him see, but that wasn't possible. He could never see past the love in his eyes. So being supportive was my job. It is important to give the support others need.

Deciding When the Right Time Is to Say Goodbye

When deciding on the right time, the quality of life is important to evaluate. Is there joy in your old or ailing pet's days? Even if they sleep most of the day and night away, do they still seem joyful when seeing you or at mealtimes or during bonding time? Keeping an ailing pet with you needs to be for them, not just for you because you can't face the loss. As we mention earlier, being able to say goodbye is a gift.

Having worked in veterinary medicine for over 40 years, I always wanted to cry and then scream when someone would say something like, "I keep hoping I will find that they have passed when I check on them." I am always in disbelief at that statement. I think of the ailing pet — alone, confused, possibly in pain — and that is why I cry, because the owner can't face the decision and then the loss, so they want the animal to suffer alone so they can escape that decision. Having a pet is a lifelong commitment and making those difficult decisions are part of that — holding your pet until the end, being there, making them comfortable, and smiling into their eyes. Help them, please.

Planned euthanasia at your veterinary office can be made tolerable. These days some vet offices have special rooms to allow visiting before and after as long as you need. The process can be made more peaceful by using pre-tranquilizers and catheters, and the staff can give you plenty of time to say goodbye. Some cities even have veterinarians who make home visits and this is all they do, home euthanasias.

TIP

After the death of a pet, it's helpful to allow your other pets to sniff and visit the deceased. Don't expect your other animals to sit and grieve next to the body, though that can happen. What does happen is they sniff and realize that their friend is different and is now gone. This awareness stops your other pets from looking for the missing pet and therefore won't wonder where they went. Visiting the deceased helps the living realize the other dog is gone and won't return, so no need to look for them. This is also helpful when you lose a human family member. Dogs miss their people and they understand death is different from disappearing so seeing and sniffing helps them to know that the family member didn't just disappear. It is amazing how much emotion pets have. It isn't anthropomorphic; it is true emotion that pets have, different from us, yes, but they feel loss, too.

A poem that circulates on the internet is called "The Last Will and Testament of a Dog" (author unknown). You can find it on the Dog Lovers Corner website: dogloverscorner.com/a-dogs-last-will-and-testament/

We reprint it here:

Before humans die, they write their last will and testament, giving their home and all they have to those they leave behind. If, with my paws, I could do the same, this is what I'd ask . . .

To a poor and lonely stray, I'd give my happy home; my bowl and cozy bed, soft pillow and all my toys; the lap, which I loved so much; the hand that stroked my fur; and the sweet voice that spoke my name.

I'd will to the sad, scared, shelter dog the place I had in my human's loving heart, of which there seemed no bounds.

So, when I die, please do not say, "I will never have a pet again, for the loss and the pain is more than I can stand."

Instead, go find an unloved dog, one whose life has held no joy or hope, and give my place to him.

This is the only thing I can give . . .

The love I left behind.

— Author Unknown

FIGURE 21-2: A well-trained and well-loved best friend showing off ribbons earned in the show ring.

© *John Wiley & Sons, Inc.*

Basically, having a dog whom you've loved before means you can't imagine living without that relationship again. That is what the dog is trying to say in the poem above: "Once you have loved such as me, say you can't live without such a love again. I bequeath my owner's love to the next dog." That is what makes this poem special to me. The greatest tribute to your previous dog is just that — you will give that love again to another.

Where to Look for Your Next Dog

That has become somewhat of a politically charged question. Breeders? Rescues or shelters? The internet? Friends of friends? Pet stores? So many opinions. It seems like every one of these options has a potential problem attached to it.

Breeders

Some say breeding contributes to the overpopulation problem, adding more dogs to the world when there are so many already out there. So, you need to do your homework. Finding a reputable breeder is your challenge. Someone who breeds to better the breed is what you should be looking for. Ask these questions when looking for a breeder:

>> Do they do the necessary genetic testing? Bad hips are considered hereditary, and your veterinarian can schedule the breeding pair to be tested for hip issues. The same with eyes; different breeds can have genetic concerns about the breeding pair's eyes, and these concerns can be tested for through your veterinarian. Here is a good source for information: www.allaboutvision.com/eye-care/pets-animals/genetic-eye-conditions-dogs. Have a good talk with a veterinarian about any genetic concerns with your breed specifically or breeding at all, based on the physical makeup of your dog.

>> Do they breed dogs that have been tested in the breed ring to show that these dogs meet the breed standard?

>> Do they have working titles for the tasks that the breed is meant to do, such as hunting, herding, obedience, scent work, and so on, in the dog's lineage?

>> Are they what is referred to as a "backyard breeder"? That is, simply someone who is trying to make money selling dogs?

>> Does the breeder you are interviewing have health guarantees?

There are so many questions you should ask, just as there are many questions they will ask of you to make sure you will be a committed owner. Similar questions will be asked of you at a rescue facility as well.

Rescues and shelters

Shelters can be a great place to find your next dog, but there are questions to ask here also.

>> **Are they a kill shelter or not?** There really isn't a correct answer here because there are always two sides to every coin. Some no-kill shelters turn away dogs from their facility, because they don't feel a dog is adoptable, so they refuse to take the dog. Fine, but what happens when the person trying to rehome their dog is turned away? It is a concern; does the owner simply dump the dog on the side of the road or in the countryside? If so, these dogs won't add to the no-kill shelters numbers, but they could end up sick or injured, and starving and lost.

>> **Why did a dog end up in a shelter in the first place? Is it a problem dog? What emotional baggage does it come with?** Again, do your homework. Don't just pick a dog, interview the dog, meet with it, take it for a walk. Consider whether you think it will be a good fit for your life. You will be interviewed as well; the shelter wants to make sure you will be this dog's forever home.

No reputable breeder wants a dog from their line to be found in a shelter. Preferably, breeders want a dog that doesn't work out to be returned to them instead. This is not always the case, and you can find purebred dogs often in shelters and rescues. Therefore, it's common for some people to look down their noses at those who buy dogs from breeders instead of rescuing dogs from shelters. This is a personal choice and one that can be argued from several points of view. Recently, we saw a Facebook comedy clip that had the speaker talking about a confrontation he experienced with someone on the street when he was walking his purebred dog. The stranger was chastising him for having purchased a purebred dog from a breeder when he should have rescued a dog. The speaker quickly came back with the argument that he just cut out the middleman and committed to the purebred dog from the start and didn't allow it to end up at a rescue. It was amusing. There are many sides to this problem.

Friends of friends and the internet

These options can elicit the same concerns as breeders and shelters. Why does your friend have this dog and why are they trying to rehome it? You don't want to become home number three or four. You want a lifetime commitment with this dog. Are you ready to commit? Are you using your head and not only your heart?

Pet stores

Opinions differ, but some think this is the worst place to get a dog (see Figure 21-3). Often puppy mills use pet stores to sell pups they themselves can't sell. Early socialization and enrichments are critical (see Chapter 7 about critical periods of development). Puppies who miss out on these enrichments suffer emotionally their whole lives. Be smart. Research. Don't impulse adopt or purchase. Dogs are a 10- to 18-year commitment, we hope. Pet stores often can't offer these enrichments and don't do what is necessary to help potty train their puppies. It can be a nightmare if a puppy spends days or weeks or more there.

FIGURE 21-3:
Puppies can be left at pet stores without proper socialization and companionship.

© John Wiley & Sons, Inc.

6

The Part of Tens

Discover how training your dog is fun when you have a plan and know how to identify certain traps you want to avoid falling into.

Find out why dogs do some of the silly things they do.

Chapter **22**

Ten Reasons Dogs Do What They Do

Who knows why your dog does some of the things that they do? Or more important, who *wants* to know why your dog does some of the things that they do? Well, if you're curious, this chapter offers answers to a few of these questions.

Why Do Dogs Insist on Jumping on People?

The behavior of dogs jumping on people goes back to the weaning process. As puppies grow, the mother dog begins to feed them standing up so puppies have to stand on their hind legs to feed. Then, as her milk decreases, the puppies jump up to lick at the corner of her mouth, trying to get her to regurgitate her semi-digested meal. When she does, it's the puppies' first introduction to solid food.

As dogs grow, jumping becomes more of a greeting behavior, as in, "Hi, good to see you," much like people shake hands when they meet someone. Because the behavior is so instinctive, modifying it is sometimes difficult. Although you're probably pleased that your dog is happy to see you, you'd also probably prefer a more sedate greeting, especially if Buddy is a large dog. Because jumping on people is a friendly gesture from the dog's point of view, we suggest modifying the behavior in a positive way by teaching a reliable Sit command (see Chapter 11) and petting only when Buddy is sitting.

Why Do Dogs Sniff Parts of Your Anatomy That You'd Prefer They Didn't?

When two dogs meet each other for the first time, they often go through what looks like a choreographed ritual. After some preliminaries, they sniff each other's respective rear ends and genitals. Dogs "see" with their noses and gather important information in this way. They can identify another dog's gender, age, and rank order — information that dictates how they interact with one another.

When meeting a new person, a dog wants to know that same information. Some are confirmed "crotch sniffers," but others are more subtle. Although embarrassing for the owner and the "sniffee," the behavior is harmless enough and easily remedied with the Sit command. (Head to Chapter 11 for information on teaching Buddy to sit on command.)

Why Do Male Dogs Lift Their Legs So Often?

All dogs *mark* their territory by leaving small amounts of urine — the male more so than the female. You can liken the behavior to putting up a sign or billboard; it lets other dogs in the neighborhood know others have been there. The scent enables dogs to identify the age, gender, and rank order of every dog that has marked that spot.

When you take Buddy for a walk, they intently investigate various spots and then lift their leg to deposit a few drops of urine to cover the area, thereby reclaiming their territory. Male dogs have a special fondness for vertical surfaces, such as a tree or the side of a building. Corners of buildings are a special treat. Height of a particular marking is important because it establishes rank. Comical contortions can be the result, such as when a Yorkshire Terrier tries to cover the mark of a Great Dane. Females don't seem to have that need, which explains why they can do their business in a fraction of the time it takes a male. Both males and females also may scratch at the ground and kick the dirt after urinating to spread their scent, thereby claiming a larger amount of territory.

REMEMBER

If your male dog starts to mark things in your house, it may be because something new is introduced into the household. The regression in this housetraining may occur when a baby or another pet is added to the family, or even when a new piece of furniture or drapes are added to the household. If this happens to you, see Chapter 8 and follow the instructions for potty training.

Why Do Dogs Mount Each Other?

Both female and male dogs can display mounting behavior. Even though this behavior is more normally associated with males trying to flirt or breed with a female, it also can be seen male to male, female to female, and female to male. Most people think it's only related to sex, but it also can be a dominance display with dogs of the same gender — the one on top reminding the other who is in charge — or it can be a behavior that's displayed when dogs that know each other well have been separated for some time. The behavior is then a form of bonding, like a hug, meaning, "I missed you."

Instead of discouraging this behavior, we have found it better to leave the dogs alone; they work things out well between themselves. They have to, because they're pack animals and know exactly the message they're trying to convey, usually to bring harmony back to the household or situation. However, if this behavior goes on too long, distract with food or a squeaky toy or take Buddy for a walk.

REMEMBER

The time mounting behavior can be construed as abnormal is if a female has some vaginal discharge indicating some sort of infection, which smells as if she's in season. In that case, other dogs won't leave her alone, and a visit to the vet is the appropriate remedy.

Why Do Dogs Like to Chase Things?

Dogs chase things for a variety of different reasons:

>> To chase intruders, be it people or other animals, off their property — this is Defense Drive.

>> Chasing is usually associated with Prey Drive; movement elicits Prey Drive.

>> To chase a potential meal, such as a bird, rabbit, squirrel, or chipmunk — Prey Drive.

> » To chase just because the object is moving, such as cars, bicycles, or joggers — Prey Drive.

> » To chase because it's fun — Prey Drive.

WARNING

Whatever the reason, chasing usually isn't a good idea because it can endanger the safety of people and the dog. Unless you're prepared to keep Buddy on leash under circumstances where they're likely to chase, you need to train them to come when called, especially around strong distractions. (Chapter 10 provides tips on how to successfully teach the Come command.)

Why Do Dogs Roll in Disgusting Things?

Dogs delight in rolling in the most disgusting stuff, such as dead fish, deer or rabbit droppings, and similar decaying debris. To make matters worse, the urge to roll seems strongest just after Buddy has had a bath. Do dogs *like* to smell putrid?

Behaviorists believe that because dogs are pack animals, they're merely bringing back to the pack the scent of possible food sources. The pack can then track down a meal. The behavior is instinctive. Most dogs roll at one point or another, some to a greater extent than others. It's just part of being a dog. If you have taught a reliable Leave It command (see Chapter 9) and/or Come command (see Chapter 10), you can interrupt the behavior. But here's another solution if you have a constant roller: Keep several bottles of shampoo handy.

Why Do Dogs Eat Weeds or Grass?

Dogs come with many instinctive behaviors. One of those behaviors is the incredible knowledge of what weeds to eat and when. One reason a dog eats grass is to induce vomiting. They may have eaten something that disagrees with them, and the grass goes into the stomach and binds whatever it contains, which is then expelled. It's an adaptive behavior that protects the dog against indigestion and food poisoning. New grass is also sweet and tasty to dogs. Dogs eat it as a treat, and it won't make them throw up in those cases.

REMEMBER

Just make sure you don't expose your dog to areas that have been sprayed with chemicals. If your dog insists on eating a plant that you know is not good for them, use the Leave It command (see Chapter 9).

Why Do Dogs Hump Humans' Legs?

Some believe that humping humans' legs is a sign of dominance, but this is doubtful. Often, it is due to bonding. Puppies often hump their littermates. Many dogs continue humping humans' legs or other dogs even after they're spayed or neutered. The explanation is probably as simple as they have learned the behavior feels good. Distract with either food or a squeaky toy to change the behavior.

Why Do Dogs Scoot on Their Rear Ends?

Once in a while, your dog may appear to be sitting and then will suddenly drag themselves around on their front paws, with their rear end on the floor. It looks as if they're trying to clean (or scratch!) their rear. This behavior can mean that their anal glands — small scent sacks just inside the rectum — are full and need emptying. When they need to be emptied, you need to take them to your vet so that they can express the glands. With some breeds, these small glands have to be emptied a couple of times a month. With other breeds, you never see this behavior.

Another reason for this behavior is tapeworms. The segments of these worms are pushed out through the rectum and irritate the dog. To rid themselves of the segment, they scrape their rectum on the carpet or on the grass outside. If you think your dog has worms, visit your vet with a small fecal sample and let them make a diagnosis.

Why Do Dogs Circle Before Lying Down?

In the wild, dogs had to trample down the grass to make a bed for the night. Even though this tamping down is no longer necessary, the behavior is instinctive. You can still see when your dog makes small circles stomping on their bed. The behavior is harmless — let them be a dog.

REMEMBER

You may have to intervene when they're tearing up your bedspread or your couch. If that should happen, you need to deny Buddy access to the bed or couch or consider covering them with something that you don't mind being damaged.

Chapter **23**

Ten Training Traps and How to Avoid Them

A *trap* can be a situation that you've gotten into and is unpleasant or difficult to escape from, specifically a trap between you and your dog. A *training trap* is often referred to as *unintentional training*. This is when you think you are training one thing but instead you teach your dog something else. In this chapter we explore some examples.

Procrastinating on Basic Training

As soon as you get your puppy or older dog, you need to start immediately training them. Puppies are like a sponge, hungry to learn. They learn even if you don't actively train them, so make sure you're aware of what they are learning. If your dog ever comes willingly to you, praise them, never correct them or do something unpleasant to them, like grabbing and bathing or brushing them if they don't like those experiences. If you call them to you because you found something wrong they have done, you can't correct them at that moment; they just came when called. Watch your timing and praise them for coming. You must be the joy zone. Never put this lesson off until later; this is the number one, the most important lesson for your new dog.

Start with crate games, tossing food and toys into their crate. Teach them to go into the crate and then come out again on the *Okay* release word. See more on crate training in Chapter 8. The Name Game is early training, too. Dogs have no idea the name you chose for them. Early training is forever, so make it fun and rewarding. Visit Part 3 for all the basics. Do it now and have permanent learning for life with Buddy.

REMEMBER

All these exercises should be taught in an area free of distractions. No other people or dogs should be present. When Buddy understands a command, you can begin to add distractions.

Buying into Attention-Seeking Behavior

Barking for attention is the most annoying form of attention-seeking behavior. The same applies to jumping up on people. The dilemma is that in your efforts to get Buddy to stop, you're giving them the attention they seek. For a dog, negative attention — such as yelling at them to stop — is still attention. It can be seen as a party, a fun game, which is unintentional training. If what you are doing doesn't end the unwanted behavior, it's not working. Instead, concentrate on teaching the desired behavior. Teach a Sit On command, such as a Hello command.

When dealing with attention-seeking behavior, remember that your attention belongs to you. You decide when to dispense it and when to withhold it. The first rule is to interrupt the unwanted behavior and redirect your dog's attention. Turn your back on them for a moment and walk away. This approach requires a bit of patience, but most dogs realize quickly that their way didn't produce the desired results, and they will stop. As you walk away, wait for and notice the quiet, the end to the barking, and then praise and interact with your dog. Instead, work on training the Touch command or the Name Game or give them a toy to tug. Your dog needs exercise and mental stimulation.

REMEMBER

This advice doesn't mean that you should neglect your dog. Just the opposite — give them plenty of attention by stepping up your basic training routine. The difference is that you decide when to initiate the interaction and when to end it, not Buddy. And don't forget to determine whether Buddy is barking or jumping up for another reason, such as needing to go out.

Forgetting to Release Your Dog from a Stay

The quickest way to undermine your efforts to teach and maintain a reliable Stay is to overlook releasing your dog. You release a dog by saying, "Okay." When you forget to release Buddy, they'll begin to release themselves, which isn't acceptable. You're the decision-maker, and you decide when they can move, not the other way around.

TIP

During the day you have several opportunities to reinforce the Stay command. For example, reinforce Stay when you feed your dog and when entering doorways. (In Chapter 11 we provide more info on teaching Stay.)

Eliminating Rewards Too Soon

During the teaching of various exercises, most dog owners use rewards like treats and verbal praise. Oftentimes, however, owners stop using treats as the dog masters commands, and then the dog stops obeying those commands. To avoid this behavior, after the dog is familiar with a command, begin to reward correct responses on a random basis so they won't know when they're going to be rewarded. Random rewards are powerful motivators because they rely on the principle of "hope springs eternal." Always carry treats in your pocket to reinforce desired behaviors now and then.

We like to use random rewards for the life of the dog. Compare it to your paycheck — would you continue working if you didn't get paid?

Using Your Dog's Name as a Command

Your dog's name is used to focus their attention on you and is followed by a command, such as, "Buddy, Come." Their name isn't an all-purpose command to control or direct their behavior. If you're repeatedly yelling their name in frantic and varying tones of voice without getting a response, it means that you have to get back to basics. Unfortunately, it also teaches your dog to ignore you and to ignore their own name, which is definitely unintentional.

REMEMBER

When you call your dog's name, ask yourself, "Exactly what am I trying to communicate?" Do you want Buddy to stop doing what they're doing? Do you want them to come to you? Be specific and use a command. For example, use the Come command if you want your dog to come to you. Use the Down command if you want your dog to lie down. A command should follow your dog's name. Joy should follow your dog's name always.

Having to Repeat Commands Away from Home

When you give a command and nothing happens, you probably repeat it and hope it will produce the desired result. Repeating commands, however, isn't a good training practice. More often than not, you're systematically teaching your dog to tune you out. They're telling you that there are gaps in their training and it is too much to obey these commands around these new distractions. Review for a bit and back up in the sequences you are teaching away from home. Review and then reward.

We frequently hear, "Well, they always do it at home," and that is probably true. Whatever the command involved, chances are it was taught at home, a location familiar to the dog and usually without distractions. But obeying at home doesn't mean that Buddy will generalize the learned behavior to new and different locations with serious distractions.

To avoid this training trap, you need to review in new locations those commands you've taught them at home. After that, you must review the commands around distractions, such as other dogs. One of the built-in benefits of obedience classes is that they provide a different place with plenty of other dogs as distractions. (See Chapter 21 for more information on obedience training classes.) Buddy will learn to focus on you and to ignore the distractions that come with class.

REMEMBER

Are you home free after teaching Buddy in obedience school? Not quite, but training will become much easier. After the first class, the location is familiar to Buddy, and after several classes the other dogs will be, too, so you still need to practice in new locations with new distractions.

Punishing Your Dog When They Come to You

The quickest way to cause a problem with the Come command is by punishing your dog, either verbally or physically, when they come to you. And that's one problem you don't want to create.

An important rule to always follow: Whenever your dog comes to you, be nice to them. In other words: Whenever your dog comes to you, don't do anything the dog perceives as unpleasant. What your dog perceives as unpleasant may be entirely different from what you think they will perceive as unpleasant. Some dogs don't like to be bathed, in which case you wouldn't call your dog to you to give them a bath. Instead, you simply go get them, clip on a leash, and using a happy tone of voice bring them to the tub. Under no circumstances should you drag your dog to be bathed or groomed. The same applies giving medications.

WARNING

The absolute worst thing you can do is to verbally or physically punish your dog when they come to you after having enjoyed a romp around the neighborhood. No matter how mad or upset you may be, welcome them home with lots of praise. The last thing your dog does is what you're punishing them or praising them for. Allowing themselves to be touched or caught while running loose is what they did last. Praise them profusely because you always want them to come to you when they are loose outside.

Running after Your Dog

If you want your dog to come to you, chasing after them is counterproductive to your goal. Instead of chasing after your dog, consider some common situations and the solutions:

>> If your dog is chasing a rabbit (or anything else), you need to review teaching your dog to come when called (see Chapter 10).

>> If your dog is running from you because they're not bonded to you, play the Recall Game that we explain in Chapter 10.

>> If your dog is running from you because they think it's a game of chase, run the other way and have them chase you. As soon as they do, stop with your back to them and intently examine the ground as though you've found something of particular interest. Dogs are curious creatures, so they'll want to see what you've found. At that point, slowly take them by the collar and attach the leash. If you try to snatch them too quickly, they'll just bolt again.

Under no circumstances should you ever verbally or physically punish your dog when you finally corral them.

WARNING

Expecting Too Much Too Quickly

Many dog owners become frustrated with training because they feel the dog isn't progressing quickly enough. But keep in mind that dogs learn the same way that everybody else does — through experience, clear and concise instructions, and repetition. What we all must realize is that learning can be fun for both of you, so make it fun. Experienced trainers, for example, can train a dog in a fraction of the time that it takes a beginner. In an obedience class, the budding trainer is guided step by step, so basic training is usually accomplished within several weeks. Consistently applying the techniques in this book will yield similar results. The key is patience, persistence, and, above all, never blaming the dog — they're trying just as hard as you are.

Ignoring the Principle of Consistency

When training your dog, consistency counts, so don't ignore the principle; otherwise, you'll end up with a poorly trained dog. A maxim that trainers use says, "Don't give a command unless you're able to reinforce it." For example, if you tell Buddy to sit and they ignore you, you need to reinforce the command. Show them exactly what you want them to do by placing them into a sit. Failure to do so will result in unreliable responses to the command in the future. Be prepared before you give Buddy a command. Be ready to reinforce the command you give. Then be ready to praise, release, and party with your dog. End with joy. But be ready to help Buddy be correct with the command that you give.

Of course, you'll encounter times when you don't or can't follow that maxim, such as when you're in the shower. Just make a mental note that you need to review Buddy's response to the command.

Consistency results in a pattern of behavior that becomes habitual. Consider the following examples:

>> After Buddy has grasped the concept that they must wait to eat their meal until you've released them (see Chapter 1), they'll dutifully wait until you release them. In fact, after a while, you won't even have to tell them to wait.

>> After you've introduced door manners to Buddy (see Chapter 14), you'll see the same results as with waiting for their food. As you approach the door, they'll stay, again without having to be told, when you open the door and leave.

These results can be achieved in several training sessions through consistency. The behaviors are easy to teach because most dogs are quick studies and quickly figure out what is to their advantage. They think, "I don't get to eat/go out unless I stay first. This makes my owner so happy and joyful." Yes, joy is the goal for both you and Buddy.

Index

behaviors
  about, 13
  breed-specific, 46–47
  building, 13–14
  deciding what you want, 35–43
  eliminating unwanted, 14
  health issues affecting, 86–97
  hypothyroidism and, 94
  instinctive, 25–31
  reasons for, 387–391
Belgian Malinois, 329
belladonna, 96
biting, 144
Bloodhounds, 49
boarding, vaccinations for, 91
body harness, 112
body language, of dogs, 24–25
bonding, 147–148
Bonham, Margaret H. (author)
  Dog Grooming For Dummies, 138
bordatella vaccine, 88
boredom, chewing from, 278
"The born perfect dog," 41
bowling, 244
breed considerations, 12
breeders, 381–382
breeding, 157–158
breed-specific behaviors, 46–47
Bring It Here command, 284
Brown, Kerry (author)
  Holistic Guide for a Healthy Dog, 2nd Edition, 83
  The Holistic Guide for a Healthy Dog, 2nd Edition, 64
brushing
  puppies, 138–139
  senior dogs, 369
buckle collars
  about, 102
  for walking, 228
building a behavior, 13–14

buildings, exiting/entering, for training, 18
Buster Cubes, 130

C

calorie, 69
Canine Assistants (website), 19
Canine Companions (website), 19
Canine Good Citizen (CGC) test, 18–19
Canine Socialization Period, 146–148
Carbo Veg, 96
carbohydrates, 71–73
carsickness, 352–353
carts, for senior dogs, 374–375
cells, in body, 68
cetyl myristoleate, 368
CGC (Canine Good Citizen) test, 19
chain leash, 101
chamomilla, 96
chasing, 389–390, 397
Cheat Sheet (website), 4
checking teeth in senior dogs, 370–371
checks, leash, 36, 102, 203, 228
chew bones, 130
chewing problems, 277–278
chiropractic veterinarians, 137
chiropractors, 95
choker collars, 107
choosing
  beds, 240–241
  collars, 100–101
  crates, 124–127
  training leashes, 100–101
  training models, 11–15
  treats, 109
chronic conditions, treating with acupuncture, 97

circling, before lying down, 391
citronella collar, 116, 275
cleaning
  accidents, 171
  ears, 141, 370
  ears in senior dogs, 370
  eyes, 142, 371–372
  eyes on senior dogs, 371–372
  teeth, 142
  up after eliminations, 173
clock face training, 230–231
Coffee Table Stretch exercise, for senior dogs, 363
collars
  adding pressure to, 217–218
  bark, 115–116
  choosing, 100–101
  getting puppies used to, 130–132
  GPS, 116
  prong, 105–106, 228–229
  for puppies, 129
  snap-around, 102–105, 228
  touching before rewarding, 202
  for walking, 227–229
colostrum, 368
Come, Jump command, 315–316
Come command, 16, 182, 197–202, 330
commands
  about, 177
  for attention, 178–180
  Automatic Sit, 235
  basic, 16
  Bring It Here, 284
  Come, 16, 182, 197–202, 330
  Come, Jump, 315–316
  consistency with, 60
  Down, 16, 197, 211, 212–218
  Down-Stay, 9, 220–221, 223–225

About the Authors

Wendy Volhard and her late husband Jack have been bestselling authors of many dog-training books, which have been translated into ten languages. They coauthored the first three editions of *Dog Training For Dummies* and also produced a two-set DVD called *Living with Your Dog*, which shows the Volhard method of developing a mutually inspiring relationship with man's best friend. Jack died in 2016, but Wendy carries on the legacy and has joined with her colleague and friend, Mary Ann Zeigenfuse, LVT, to produce the fourth and fifth editions.

Wendy is the recipient of four awards from the Dog Writers Association of America (DWAA). She wrote numerous articles, was a regular columnist for the *American Kennel Gazette*, and coauthored many books, including the *Canine Good Citizen: Every Dog Can Be One*, which was named Best Care and Training Book for 1995 by the DWAA, and *The Holistic Guide for a Healthy Dog*, which is now in its second edition.

Wendy, whose expertise extends to helping owners gain a better understanding of why their pets do what they do, developed the Canine Personality Profile, and her two-part series, "Drives — A New Look at an Old Concept," was named Best Article in a specialty magazine for 1991 by the DWAA. She also developed the most widely used system for evaluating and selecting puppies, and her film, *Puppy Aptitude Testing*, was named Best Film on Dogs for 1980 by the DWAA.

Wendy specializes in behavior, nutrition, and alternative sources of healthcare for dogs, such as acupuncture and homeopathy, and she has formulated a balanced homemade diet for dogs that is now available at www.volharddognutrition.com. The February/March 2010 issue of *Bark Magazine* included Wendy in its list of Best and Brightest 100 for developing the Puppy Aptitude Test and the Drives Profile.

Wendy shares her home with two Labrador Retrievers, two Standard Wirehaired Dachshunds, and two cats. The dogs are more or less well trained, and the cats do their own thing. All are allowed on the furniture, but they do get off when told. Wendy is a true practitioner — she has obtained dozens of conformation and performance titles with her German Shepherds, Labrador Retrievers, Landseer Newfoundlands, Wirehaired Dachshunds, and Yorkshire Terriers.

Through the classes, lectures, seminars, and training camps in the United States, Bermuda, Canada, England, and Puerto Rico, the Volhards and Mary Ann Zeigenfuse have taught countless owners how to communicate more effectively with their pets. Individuals from almost every state and 15 countries have attended their training camps that still continue to this day, run by Theresa Richmond and Mary Ann. Check out www.mahoganyridge.net for more information.

Internationally recognized as "trainers of trainers," Jack and Wendy were inducted into the Hall of Fame of the International Association of Canine Professionals in 2006. Visit their website at www.volharddognutrition.com and look under the Resources tab for information on the Drives profile and Puppy Testing.

Mary Ann Zeigenfuse, LVT, has had her life go completely to the dogs. When she was a child, the one thing she wanted more than anything else was a dog, but she was never allowed to own one. There was one period when the family had a dog, but it was short-lived and it only cemented her desire to acquire her lifelong "best friend" one day. Because of that denial, her life is now filled with dogs. She went to college to be a veterinary technician and practiced veterinary medicine as a licensed technician for more than 40 years. She worked in an emergency practice followed by a humane society and then a 24-hour practice where she ultimately became the head technician in a six-doctor practice. Also, during that time she was on the board of the humane society and started her own dog training business after being the training director of a different dog training school.

In addition to owning her own dogs and showing them in performance sports, she has boarded dogs in her home and helped others train their dogs while giving classes and lessons almost daily.

During her study of dog training, she became involved in the Volhard Motivational Method of dog training where she ultimately met Jack and Wendy Volhard. They became her mentors and eventually they worked together, giving seminars around the country and teaching at their weeklong training camps, where she taught people how to become dog trainers as well as helping them train their own dogs. Her life has been full of dogs, hers and others.

She wrote her first book, *Dog Tricks, Step by Step* (Macmillan Publishing), and tech-edited an earlier version of *Dog Training For Dummies*, so when she was asked to work on the fourth edition as a rewrite, she enthusiastically said yes.

As a dog trainer, she learns something from every dog she teaches. Every dog trainer she meets shows her something even if it's only how they communicate with the dogs with which they work. Communication is the key to all dog training. Without communication, no training can take place. Dogs need to understand what their owners want, they need to know when their owners are pleased, and they need to know when their owners are finished and moving on. Play is a big part of training a dog. After all, training can be viewed as play as well as work — enjoyable either way.

Her goal in writing this book was to show how communication works and how a dog owner must communicate with their dog for both the dog and owner to learn the game of dog training.

Dedication

This book is for people who like their dogs and who have them first and foremost as pets and companions. After reading this book, we want them to love their dogs even more.

Author's Acknowledgments

All of us are the product of our life experiences. While having had dogs all our lives, Wendy's experiences with dogs started in the 1960s, when she and her husband Jack were exposed to many of the famous behaviorists of the day. Being avid readers, they absorbed as much information as they could from individuals such as Konrad Most, Konrad Lorenz, and Eberhard Trummler. They discovered why dogs do what they do and how to apply a behavioral approach to training, one that copies how dogs interact with each other. John Fuller's work in Bar Harbor, Maine, and Clarence Pfaffenberger's work with Guide Dogs for the Blind, as well as the experiments done in Switzerland by Humphrey and Warner to indicate the working abilities of German Shepherds, all went into the mix that eventually became the Motivational Method of training.

Then, Wendy shared all her knowledge with others, including Mary Ann. Mary Ann has often said how Wendy never leaves out any of the secret ingredients in the recipe called "Training a dog," but rather she shares it all with everyone. This is also how Mary Ann has written this book, sharing everything she knows and loves about dogs.

Our sincere thanks to those who have contributed to all five editions of this book and shared their insights.

Finally, we thank our editors at Wiley Publishing: Senior Editor Jennifer Yee and Development and Copy Editor Ted Cains. They have demonstrated the two most important qualities of a good dog trainer — patience and persistence.

Publisher's Acknowledgments

Senior Editor: Jennifer Yee

Development and Copy Editor: Ted Cains

Production Editor: Bharaneedharan Murthy

Cover Image: © Oscar Wong/Getty Images